Developments in French Politics 4

Developments titles available from Palgrave Macmillan

If you have any comments or suggestions regarding the
above or other possible *Developments* titles, please write to
Steven Kennedy, Palgrave Macmillan, Houndmills,
Basingstoke RG21 6XS, UK or e-mail s.kennedy@palgrave.com

---

* Rights World excluding North America

Developments in French Politics 4

edited by
Alistair Cole
Patrick Le Galès
and
Jonah D. Levy

palgrave
macmillan

First published 2008 by
PALGRAVE MACMILLAN
Houndmills, Basingstoke, Hampshire RG21 6XS and
175 Fifth Avenue, New York, N.Y. 10010
Companies and representatives throughout the world

PALGRAVE MACMILLAN is the global academic imprint of the Palgrave
Macmillan division of St. Martin's Press, LLC and of Palgrave Macmillan Ltd.
Macmillan® is a registered trademark in the United States, United Kingdom
and other countries. Palgrave is a registered trademark in the European
Union and other countries.

ISBN-13: 9780230536999   hardback
ISBN-10: 0230536999   hardback
ISBN-13: 9780230537002   paperback
ISBN-10: 0230537006   paperback

This book is printed on paper suitable for recycling and made from fully
managed and sustained forest sources. Logging, pulping and manufacturing
processes are expected to conform to the environmental regulations of the
country of origin.

A catalogue record for this book is available from the British Library.

A catalog record for this book is available from the Library of Congress.

10 9 8 7 6 5 4 3 2
17 16 15 14 13 12 11 10 09

Printed and bound in Great Britain by CPI Antony Rowe

Contents

List of Tables, Figures and Maps

Tables

Figures

Maps

List of Abbreviations

AC!	Agir contre le Chômage (Act against Unemployment)
ANRU	Agence Nationale pour la Rénovation Urbaine (National Agency for Urban Regeneration)
APA	*Allocation personnelle d'autonomie* (personal autonomy benefit)
APP	Annual Performance Plan
APR	Annual Performance Report
ARF	Association des Régions de France (Association of French Regions)
ARH	Agence Régionale de l'Hospitalisation (Regional Hospital Agency)
ATTAC	Association pour la Taxation des Transactions pour l'Aide aux Citoyens (Association for Taxing Transactions for the Benefit of Citizens)
BNP	Banque Nationale de Paris (Paris National Bank)
BOP	*Budget opérationnel du programme* (programme budget)
CAC 40	*Cotation assistée en continu des 40 plus grosses sociétés françaises* (stock market index of the 40 largest firms)
CAP	Common Agricultural Policy
CDC	Caisse des Dépôts et Consignations
CDQ	Children of Don Quixote
CEVIPOF	Centre d'Études sur la Vie Politique Française (Centre for the Study of French Politics)
CFDT	Confédération Française Démocratique du Travail (French Democratic Labour Confederation)
CFSP	Common Foreign and Security Policy
CFTC	Confédération Française des Travailleurs Chrétiens (French Confederation of Christian Workers)
CGC	Confédération Générale des Cadres (General Confederation of Managers)
CGPME	Confédération Générale des Petites et Moyennes Entreprises (General Confederation of Small- and Medium-Sized Businesses)
CGT	Confédération Générale du Travail (General Labour Confederation)
CIR	*Crédit impôt recherche* (research tax credit)
CMU	*Couverture maladie universelle* (universal illness coverage)

CNAM	Caisse Nationale Assurance Maladie (National Fund for Health Insurance)
CNCDH	Consultative National Commission on Human Rights
CNE	*Contrat nouvelle embauche* (new employment contract)
CNIL	Commission Nationale de l'Informatique et des Libertés (National Commission for Information Technology and Liberties)
CNPF	Conseil National du Patronat Français (National Council of French Employers)
CPNT	Chasse, Pêche, Nature, Traditions (Hunting, Fishing, Nature, Tradition)
COR	Comité d'Orientation des Retraites (Pensions Planning Committee)
CP	Confédération Paysanne (Peasant Confederation)
CPE	*Contrat première embauche* (first employment contract)
CRAN	Conseil Representatif des Associations Noires (Representative Council of Black Associations)
CSA	Conseil Supérieur de l'Audiovisuel (High Council for the Audiovisual Media)
CSG	*Contribution sociale généralisée* (general social contribution)
DAL	*Droit au logement* (right to housing)
DATAR	Délégation à l'Aménagement du Territoire et à l'Action Régionale (Delegation for Territorial and Regional Planning))
DD!!	Droits Devant (Right[s] Ahead)
DGAFP	Direction Générale de l'Administration et de la Fonction Publique (Division for the Administration and the Civil Service)
DGME	Direction Générale de la Modernisation de l'État (Division for State Modernization)
DIACTE	Délégation Interministérielle à l'Aménagement et la Compétitivité des Territoires (Interministerial Delegation for Territorial Planning and Competitiveness)
DIRE	Direction Interministérielle de la Réforme de l'État (Interministerial Division for State Reform)
DL	Démocratie Libérale (Liberal Democracy)
DMP	*Dossier médical personnalisé* (personal medical dossier)
EADS	European Aeronautic Defence and Space Company
ECB	European Central Bank
ECHR	European Court of Human Rights
ECJ	European Court of Justice
ECOFIN	Economic and Financial Council
ECT	European Constitutional Treaty

EDF–GDF	Électricité de France – Gaz de France (French Electricity – French Gas)
EFTA	European Free Trade Association
EMU	Economic and Monetary Union
ENA	École Nationale d'Administration (National Administration School)
EPCI	Établissement Public de Coopération Intercommunale (Public Body for Intercommunal Cooperation)
ERM	Exchange Rate Mechanism
ESF	European Social Forum
ETUC	European Trade Union Confederation
EU	European Union
FN	Front National (National Front)
GDP	Gross domestic product
GELD	Groupe d'Étude et de Lutte contre les Discriminations (Anti-Discrimination Study and Struggle Group)
GMOs	Genetically modified organisms
GP	General practitioner
GSP	Growth and Stability Pact
HALDE	Haute Autorité de Lutte contre les Discriminations et pour l'Égalité (High Authority for the Struggle against Discrimination and in Favour of Equality)
HAS	Haute Autorité de Santé (High Authority for Health)
HCI	Haut Conseil à l'Intégration (High Council for Integration)
IFOP	Institut Français d'Opinion Publique (French Public Opinion Institute)
IGC	Intergovernmental Conference
IMF	International Monetary Fund
IRA	Institut Régional d'Administration (Regional Institute for Administration)
JAC	Jeunesse Agricole Chrétienne (Young Christian Farmers)
JOC	Jeunesse Ouvrière Chrétienne (Young Christian Workers)
LCR	Ligue Communiste Révolutionnaire (Revolutionary Communist League)
LO	Lutte Ouvrière (Workers' Struggle)
LOLF	*Loi organique sur les lois de finance* (The Organic Law of 2001 setting out a new budgetary procedure)
MAI	Multilateral Agreement on Investment
MBA	Master of Business Administration
MEDEF	Mouvement des Entreprises de France (Movement of French Business)
MIB	Mouvement de l'Immigration et des Banlieues (Movement of Immigration and the Suburbs)

MIF	Mouvement de Libération des Femmes (Movement for the Liberation of Women)
MODEM	Mouvement Démocrate (Democratic Movement)
MPF	Mouvement pour la France (Movement for France)
MRC	Mouvement Républicain et Citoyen (Citizens' Republican Movement)
MRP	Mouvement Républicain Populaire (Popular Republican Movement)
MTA	Mouvement des Travailleurs Arabes (Movement of Arab Workers)
NATO	North Atlantic Treaty Organization
NPM	New Public Management
NPNS	Ni Putes, Ni Soumises (Neither Whores, nor Submissives)
NYSE	New York Stock Exchange
OECD	Organization for Economic Cooperation and Development
OFCE	Office Français de la Conjoncture Économique (French Bureau for Economic Forecasting)
OMC	Open Method of Coordination
PACS	Pacte Civil de Solidarité (Civil Solidarity Pact)
PAJE	*Prestation d'accueil du jeune enfant* (child benefit)
PARE	*Plan d'aide et de retour à l'emploi* (Assistance Plan for Return to Work)
PCF	Parti Communiste Français (French Communist Party)
PEF	Panel Eléctoral Français (French Electoral Panel)
PERCO	*Plan d'épargne retraite* (retirement savings plan)
PERP	*Plan d'épargne retraite populaire* (popular retirement savings plan)
PLU	*Plan local d'urbanisme* (local town development plan)
PRDF	*Plan régional du développement et de la formation des jeunes* (regional youth training plan)
PS	Parti Socialiste (Socialist Party)
PSD	*Prestation sociale dépendance* (old age incapacity benefit)
PT	Parti des Travailleurs (Workers' Party)
QMV	Qualified majority voting
RATP	Régie Autonome des Transports Parisiens (Paris Public Transportation Office)
RGPP	*Révision générale des politiques publiques* (comprehensive policy review)
RMA	*Revenu minimum d'activité* (minimum activity income)
RMI	*Revenu minimum d'insertion* (minimum insertion income)
RPR	Rassemblement pour la République (Rally for the Republic)
RSA	*Revenu de solidarité active* (active solidarity income)

SCOT	*Schéma de cohérence territoriale* (territorial cohesion plan)
SFPN	Social Forum of Popular Neighbourhoods
SGAE	Secrétariat Général des Affaires Européennes (General Secretariat for European Affairs)
SGCI	Secrétariat Général du Comité Interministériel (General Secretariat of the Interministerial Committee on European Affairs)
SMIC	*Salaire minimum interprofessionnel de croissance* (minimum wage)
SMO	Social Movement Organization
SNCF	Société Nationale des Chemins de Fer Français (National Company for French Railways)
SOFRES	Société Française des Enquêtes par Sondage (French Society for Opinion Poll Surveys)
SRADT	*Schémas régionaux d'aménagement du territoire* (regional planning documents)
SUD	Solidaire, Unitaires et Démocratiques (Solidarity, Unity, Democracy)
TNS	Taylor Nelson Sofres
UDF	Union pour la Démocratie Française (Union for French Democracy)
UMP	Union pour une Majorité Populaire (Union for a Popular Majority)
UNCAM	Union National des Caisses d'Assurance Maladie (National Union of Sickness Funds)
UNIFIL	United Nations Interim Force in Lebanon
UNR	Union pour la Nouvelle République (Union for the New Republic)
VAT	Value added tax
Verts	French Green Party
WMD	Weapons of mass destruction
WSF	World Social Forum
WTO	World Trade Organization
ZEP	*Zone d'éducation prioritaire* (education priority zone)

Notes on the Contributors

Marcos Ancelovici holds a PhD in political science from MIT and is Assistant Professor of Sociology at McGill University, in Montreal, Canada. He works on social movements and the political sociology of globalization. He is currently completing a project on the way French labour organizations have responded to globalization. He has published several articles and book chapters on the anti-globalization movement in France and the transformation of the electronics and apparel industries in Mexico.

Philippe Bezès is Senior Research Fellow in Politics (National Centre of Scientific Research) at CERSA (Paris II University) and he teaches at Sciences Po, Paris, France, where he obtained his PhD in political science. He works on public administration and state reforms in France, on the theory of bureaucracy and public policies. His recent publications include articles in *Governance*, the *Revue française d'administration publique*, *Sociologie du travail* and the *Revue française de science politique*.

Bruno Cautrès is Senior Research Fellow in Politics (National Centre of Scientific Research) at the Centre for Political Research (CEVIPOF/Sciences Po) and he teaches at Sciences Po, Paris, France. He was previously the director of a database research centre in Grenoble. He works on elections and public opinion in European democracies. His recent publications include (co-edited with Nonna Mayer) *Le nouveau désordre électoral. Les leçons du 21 avril 2002* (Paris: Presses de Sciences Po, 2004), as well as articles in the *Revue française de science politique*, *les Cahiers du CEVIPOF*, *Notre Europe* and *Études et recherches*.

Ben Clift is Senior Lecturer in Political Economy in the Department of Politics and International Studies at the University of Warwick. He is author of *French Socialism in a Global Era: the Political Economy of the New Social Democracy in France* (Continuum, 2003), and co-editor of *Where Are National Capitalisms Now?* (Palgrave Macmillan, 2004). His research interests lie in comparative and international political economy, and he has published several articles and book chapters on the French model of capitalism, the political economy of social democracy, global finance and French and British politics.

Alistair Cole holds a DPhil in politics from Oxford University and is currently Professor of European Politics at Cardiff University, Wales, United Kingdom. He has written extensively on French and comparative European politics. His most recent publication is *Governing and Governance in France* (Cambridge: Cambridge University Press, 2008). He has recently published articles in *Governance*, the *Revue française d'administration publique* and *French Politics*. In 2007, he was Vincent Wright professor at Sciences Po, Paris.

Bastien François is Professor of Political Science at the University of Paris I and a researcher at the research centre CRPS (CNRS), Paris, France. He works on the development of constitutional rules and the rule of law in France together with issues of political accountability. His publications include, inter alia, *Naissance d'une Constitution. La Ve République (1958–1962)* (Paris: Presses de Sciences Po, 1996), *Le régime politique de la Ve République* (Paris: La Découverte, 1998) and *Misère de la Vème République* (Paris: Seuil, 2007).

Patrick Hassenteufel is Professor of Politics at the University of St Quentin, France, and he also teaches at Sciences Po, Paris and Rennes. His main research deals with the comparison of public policy and health systems reforms in France, Germany and the UK. He has recently published articles in the *Revue française d'administration publique* and the *Revue française de science politique*. He has published *Les médecins face à l'état, une comparaison européenne* (Paris: Presses de Sciences Po, 1997) and *Sociologie des politiques publiques* (Paris: U Colin, 2008).

Chris Howell is Professor of Politics, Oberlin College, USA. His research interests include European industrial relations, comparative political economy and the dilemmas of centre-left political parties. He is the author of *Regulating Labor: the State and Industrial Relations Reform in Postwar France* (Princeton University Press, 1992), *Trade Unions and the State: the Construction of Industrial Relations Institutions in Britain, 1890–2000* (Princeton University Press, 2005), and numerous articles on industrial relations and labour market policy. He is currently Chair of the Politics Department at Oberlin.

Hussein Kassim is Professor of Politics at the University of East Anglia, UK. His principal research focus investigates the European Commission and the relationship between the EU and the member states, subjects upon which he has published widely. He has recently completed projects on the EU and preference formation and he is currently working on the Europeanization of air transport, and EU coordination in the new member states. Publications include *The National*

Co-ordination of EU Policy: the European level (Oxford: Oxford University Press, 2001, co-edited with G. Peters and V. Wright), *The National Co-ordination of EU Policy: the Domestic Level* (Oxford: Oxford University Press, 2000, co-edited with G. Peters and V. Wright) and several other collective works. He has published recent articles in the *Journal European Public Policy* and *Public Policy and Administration*.

Patrick Le Galès is *Directeur de recherche* (CNRS National Centre for Scientific Research) at the Centre for Political Research (CEVIPOF) and Professor of Public Policy and Sociology at Sciences Po, Paris. His main research interests lie in the field of policy instruments and policy change, the state in France and Britain, urban and regional governance and urban sociology. He was a Stein Rokkan Prize winner for the book *European Cities, Social Conflicts and Governance in 2002* (Oxford: OUP, 2002). In 2007, he was awarded the Research Excellence Prize conferred by the Association Française de Science Politique and the Mattei Dogan Foundation. His recent publications include *The Changing Governance of Local Economies in Europe* (Oxford: OUP, 2004), *Tony Blair, le Bilan des réformes* (Paris: Presses de Sciences Po, 2007, a co-authored book with Florence Faucher) and a special issue (2007) of the journal *Governance* on Policy Instruments and Policy Change.

Eléonore Lépinard obtained her doctorate in sociology from the EHESS in Paris and she is now a lecturer at the University of Montreal in Canada. She works on gender and politics from a comparative angle with an interest in feminist claims in public policy. Notable publications include *L'égalité introuvable. Stratégies de légitimation et mise en œuvre de la parité politique en France* (Paris: Presses de Sciences Po, 2007). She has recently published articles in *Social Politics, International Studies in Gender, State, and Society, Les Cahiers du genre* and the *Revue française de science politique*.

Jonah D. Levy is Associate Professor of Political Science at the University of California, Berkeley, USA. He has published widely in the field of French and comparative economic and welfare policy. Among his numerous works is the monograph *Tocqueville's Revenge: State, Society and Economy in Contemporary France* (Cambridge, Mass.: Harvard University Press). His most recent edited book is *The State after Statism. New State Activities in the Age of Liberalization* (Cambridge, Mass.: Harvard University Press).

Sophie Meunier is research scholar, Woodrow Wilson School of Public and International Affairs, Princeton University, USA. She is the author of *Trading Voices: the European Union in International Commercial Negotiations* (Princeton University Press, 2005) and *The French Challenge: Adapting to Globalization* (Brookings Institution Press, 2001, with Philip Gordon), as well as many articles on France, Europe and globalization. She is also the editor of *Making History: European Integration and Institutional Change at Fifty* (Oxford University Press, 2007).

Nicolas Sauger is research fellow at the Centre for Political Research (CEVIPOF/SciencesPo) and he teaches politics at Sciences Po, Paris, France. In 2006, he was a Vincent Wright fellow at the EUI Florence. He works on political parties, party competition, values and elections in Europe. Recent publications include (with Sylvain Brouard and Emiliano Grossman) *Les Français contre l'Europe? Les sens du référendum du 29 mai 2005* (Paris: Presses de Sciences Po, 2007) and articles in the *Journal of European Public Policy*, the *Revue française de science politique* and the *European Journal of Political Research*.

Frédéric Sawicki is Professor of Political Science at the University of Lille II and is the director of the research centre CERAPS (CNRS), Lille, France. He has undertaken a number of important studies on the sociology of the Socialist Party. He is currently working on the political mobilization of citizens and party activists in France and he is directing a research project on teachers and politics in France. Notable publications include (with Jacques Lagroye and Bastien François), *Sociologie politique* (Paris: Dalloz 2006) and (with Remi Lefebvre) *La société des socialistes. Le PS aujourd'hui* (Bellecombe: Editions du Croquant, 2006).

Cindy Skach is Associate Professor of Government, Harvard University, and Affiliated Professor of International Legal Studies, Harvard Law School, USA. She researches and teaches comparative public law and jurisprudence, and legal ethnography. Notable publications include her monograph *Borrowing Constitutional Designs: Constitutional Law in Weimar Germany and the French Fifth Republic* (Princeton: Princeton University Press, 2005) and articles in the *Journal of Common Market Studies* and several other journals. Her next book investigates the ways legal restrictions on religious liberty shape identity, and is forthcoming as *The Constitution of Peoples* (Harvard University Press). Concurrently, under the auspices of the Film Study Center at Harvard, she is producing 'Cadi Justice', a visual ethnography of Islamic law in transition, and 'Race', a visual ethnography of ethnic politics in a Parisian suburb.

Yves Surel is Professor of Politics at Sciences Po, Grenoble, and is an associate researcher at the CEVIPOF/Sciences Po, Paris. He works on public policy theory and the comparison of institutions and leadership in Europe and in the USA. He has published extensively in the field. Notable publications include *L'Europe en action* (Paris: L'Harmattan, 2007, with Bruno Palier), *Politique comparée* (Paris: Montchrestien, 2004, with Yves Mény) and *Democracies and the Populist Challenge* (London, Palgrave Macmillan, 2002, with Yves Mény), as well as articles in the *Revue française de science politique* and the *Revue internationale de politique comparée*.

Chapter 1

From Chirac to Sarkozy: a New France?

JONAH D. LEVY, ALISTAIR COLE AND
PATRICK LE GALÈS

The election of Nicolas Sarkozy as President in April–May 2007 brought a dramatic shift in the tenor of French politics. Sarkozy's optimistic can-do sentiment contrasted sharply with the ambient pessimism of the *fin-de-règne* Chirac era. After a decade, if not more, of stagnation, immobilism and strife, Sarkozy promised to put France on the move again. Nor was this mere rhetoric. In short order, Sarkozy's administration – often, Sarkozy himself – negotiated a new European Union treaty, slashed taxes, decentralized universities, and scaled back the pensions of powerful public employees. If ever leadership mattered, it would seem to be in France. In changing leaders from Chirac to Sarkozy, France appeared to be shaking off its torpor. 'France is back', as Sarkozy is fond of saying.

The essays in this volume present a more nuanced picture of the transition from Chirac to Sarkozy. For starters, it is not clear that France ever left the reformist trajectory in the first place. Although President Sarkozy has certainly brought a new energy to French politics, adjustment was already taking place under his predecessor. Moreover, France is certainly not all the way back. The economy remains weak, and Sarkozy does not seem to have a coherent strategy for turning the situation around. The President's popularity is dropping, aggravated by irritation over his well-publicized personal escapades, and opposition to his proposals has grown.

This introductory chapter analyses the evolution of French politics from Chirac to Sarkozy. It is divided into three sections. Section 1 presents the evidence of decline, stagnation and policy failure under Chirac. Section 2 suggests that important changes took place during the Chirac years, but that these changes failed to dispel and, in some respects, aggravated concerns about the direction of French policy. Finally, Section 3 considers the extent to which President Sarkozy has set French politics and policy-making on a new, reformist trajectory.

1

A lost decade? Problems of the Chirac presidencies

It does not take a fertile imagination to see how the two Chirac presidencies, running from 1995 to 2007, could be regarded as a 'lost decade' at best and an era of inertia and decline at worst. Three problems stood out during the Chirac years. The first is that France's traditional, statist, Republican model appeared unadapted to contemporary economic, social and geopolitical challenges. The second problem is that the government failed repeatedly, and sometimes spectacularly, in its efforts to reform the system. The third problem is that the mainstream governing parties proved increasingly incapable of enlisting the support of the French electorate.

The limits of the Republican model

French politics has long revolved around a statist Republican model, a set of practices and beliefs that draw their inspiration from a combination of the Jacobin spirit of the French Revolution, the secular, democratizing ethos of the Third Republic, and the nationalist, state-centric ideals of the founder and first President of the Fifth Republic, Charles de Gaulle. The Republican model has four main elements. The first is an unmediated relationship between the citizen and the state. In the Republican conception, all citizens are created equal and are members of a national political community. They owe their allegiance to the nation as a whole, rather than to ethnic or interest groups. The second dimension of the Republican model is secular public education, which serves the dual function of offering opportunities for social mobility and transmitting French values and culture to successive generations. A third element of the Republican model is the belief in a special vocation for France on the international stage. It is the duty of every politician – a duty embraced most enthusiastically by de Gaulle – to spread French culture and uphold French political principles, even if these actions cause conflicts with France's allies, such as the United States. The fourth, related element of the Republican model is a 'strong', activist state. Critical state responsibilities include: modernizing the economy; educating the population, transmitting French norms and culture to successive generations and children of immigrants; providing opportunities for social mobility; transcending class conflict and assuring social cohesion; and projecting French values and influence throughout the world.

If the Republican model has deep roots in French history and culture, over the past 25 years it has seemed increasingly unadapted to contemporary challenges. Two concerns have figured most prominently. The first is economic and geopolitical decline. French economic growth has been sluggish, unemployment has ranged from 9 to 12 per cent (with considerable disguised unemployment and involuntary part-time employment as well), and government public finances have been persistently in the red. As Ben Clift's chapter on economic policy relates, so-called 'declinists' like Nicolas Baverez believe that France's statist model is at cross-purposes with the imperatives of competitiveness in today's globalized economy (Baverez, 2003). State meddling in the economy, along with high wages and taxes, undermines business performance and prices workers out of jobs.

The concern about national decline extends to the international arena. As the chapters by Sophie Meunier and Hussein Kassim relate, there is a pervasive sense that France has lost influence in European and world affairs. The economic, cultural and military weight of the US, as the sole remaining 'hyperpower', has left little space for an alternative French voice. Meunier notes that even Chirac's opposition to the Iraq War, largely validated in retrospect, has not shaken the feeling that France is becoming less relevant, that it no longer offers an attractive, universalist model. Moreover, as the chapter by Yves Surel describes, the increasing salience of the EU and other international organizations means that to the extent that France hopes to be a global player, it will need to work with allies to influence supranational bodies. Such an approach is a long way from the traditional, Gaullist go-it-alone tack and has not come easily to French leaders, although Kassim cautions against excessive pessimism about France's ability to adjust.

Along with anxiety about economic and geopolitical decline, the second source of concern about the Republican model is its manifest inability to integrate minorities and disadvantaged groups. The premise of the Republican approach is that group-specific measures are unnecessary since all citizens are treated equally. Yet as the chapter by Eléonore Lépinard describes, women continue to lag far behind men in economic opportunity and political representation. Lépinard notes that the situation of ethnic minorities, particularly communities of Arab or African descent, is bleaker still. The Republican promise of equality is belied by inferior schools, discrimination in employment and housing, an unemployment rate roughly double the national average, and frequent police harassment. The 2004 legislation banning the wearing of 'ostentatious religious symbols' in public schools, although framed in neutral language, was clearly targeted at Muslim girls who don head-scarves, suggesting that when it comes to religious observance, all French citizens are not treated equally. (Students wearing Catholic crucifixes and Jewish yamulkas had never drawn the ire of state authorities.) Nor was this the only incident in which ethnic minorities felt slighted. The gap between egalitarian rhetoric and discriminatory practice drove what was perhaps the most disturbing event of Chirac's tenure as President, the autumn 2005 riots in the suburbs of France's leading cities.

The 2005 riots were sparked by an abuse of police powers, a recurrent complaint within the immigrant community. Two teenage boys, French citizens of North African descent, were electrocuted when they took refuge in a power station while being chased by the police. Initially, the police denied that they had been chasing the youths. Then, they changed their story to claim that they had indeed been chasing the youths, but because the young men had attempted to steal materials from a construction site. In the end, neither claim proved true, and the youths had no criminal record. The deaths of the two boys, the presumption that if the police were chasing them, they must have done something wrong, and some rather provocative rhetoric by then Minister of the Interior, Nicolas Sarkozy, combined to touch off riots in the Paris suburbs, primarily among boys and young men of African descent. By the time the riots around Paris and other major cities died down three weeks later, the damage had been considerable. The French newspaper *Le Monde* estimated that 10,000 cars that were burned and four deaths could be attributed directly to the 'troubles' (the preferred expression of Prime Minister Dominique de Villepin). There were 217 police wounded, 4770 arrests made, and 763 people imprisoned. A total of 233 public buildings burned down or were damaged (*Le Monde*, 1 December 2005).

The urban riots of November 2005 were highly revealing of the crisis in relations between some young people of immigrant origin and Republican institutions such as the police and fire services, the education system, and public authority in general. The buildings that were burned down were those symbolizing public services: schools and police stations in particular. From the perspective of the rioters, these Republican institutions were sources not of protection or opportunity, but rather of exclusion and discrimination. The 2005 crisis also laid bare the weakness of social capital in the suburbs of France's cities, the absence of networks, parties, voluntary associations, schools or religious organizations that could provide social stability (Cole, 2008).

Failed reform

Taken together, economic stagnation, waning geopolitical influence, and an inability to integrate minority groups have fuelled the sense that the French Republican model is no longer working. Unquestionably, changes are needed. Yet the second problem of the Chirac administration was that it failed repeatedly in its reform efforts. Chirac's tenure as President was bracketed by two spectacular policy failures: the Juppé Plan to overhaul the social security system in 1995, which is analysed in the chapter by Patrick Hassenteufel, and the 2006 first employment contract (*contrat première embauche*, CPE), designed to increase youth hiring, which is analysed in the chapter by Chris Howell. Both initiatives were defeated by protestors.

The Juppé Plan announced in October 1995 by Chirac's Prime Minister, Alain Juppé, sought to curtail France's sky-high levels of social spending through a series of far-reaching reforms. For starters, the social security budget would be voted by Parliament, with the idea of imposing a budget from above, rather than accommodating a series of autonomous spending decisions from below. The Juppé Plan also included a number of controls on hospitals and physicians. In addition, the government sought to raise the retirement age and roll back the pension benefits of civil servants, including eliminating the various *régimes spéciaux* that allowed some civil servants to retire as early as age 50. Finally, the plan included a number of painful tax hikes, most notably an increase in the general value added tax from 18.6 to 20.6 per cent.

Although praised initially by policy experts as a courageous response to France's social security deficits, the Juppé Plan was received much less favourably by the French public. Opposition stemmed from several sources. Some groups were simply defending their particularistic interests: physicians baulked at spending controls; civil servants sought to preserve their pensions; taxpayers despised the hike in VAT; the trade unions feared that the government was evicting them from the management of the social security system. But Chirac and his Prime Minister were also to blame. Chirac had secured election as President by pledging to increase state intervention so as to renew the 'Republican pact' and 'heal the social fracture'. Yet less than six months later, he was proposing to introduce an austerity plan. Moreover, the government had done little to cultivate support for the Juppé Plan. The plan had been prepared in complete secrecy, lest it be contaminated by special pleading. Indeed, the Prime Minister openly bragged that not 10 people had seen his plan prior to its presentation to Parliament. The problem is that few actors felt any need to support a plan in which they had had no say.

The response to Juppé's initiative was a six-week strike by civil servants and public sector workers that paralysed the country. What is more, French public opinion ran resolutely in favour of the strikers and against the government. In order to end the strike, Juppé was forced to abandon his public sector pension reform. Although he maintained a tougher line towards the physicians, ultimately this part of the reform also unravelled, leaving only the unpopular tax hikes intact. The Juppé Plan not only failed on its own terms. More fundamentally, it delegitimized the government. Henceforth, every remotely controversial initiative launched by Juppé, notably in the area of privatizations and fiscal policy, was hotly contested. After 18 months of stalemate, President Chirac opted to dissolve Parliament and hold early elections, in an effort to renew his mandate and press forward with the difficult measures needed to qualify for European Monetary Union (EMU). Instead, in June 1997, the French electorate repudiated Chirac and Juppé, ushering into office a Socialist–Green–Communist coalition headed by Lionel Jospin.

If the Juppé Plan ruined the beginning of Chirac's tenure as President, the CPE reform of 2006 ruined the end. The CPE sought to address the problem of very high rates of unemployment among young people in France – on the order of double the national average. The premise behind the CPE was that restrictions on layoffs discourage employers from hiring less skilled and inexperienced workers, for fear of being unable to shed these workers should they fail to pan out. The CPE proposed to introduce a two-year probationary period for workers under the age of 26, during which time employers would be free to dismiss these employees without providing justification or compensation. The government reasoned that by making it easier to fire young people, the CPE would also make it more attractive to hire young people.

Ironically, young people, the supposed beneficiaries of the CPE, spearheaded the opposition to the reform. Once again, the government had misread public sentiment. French youths saw the CPE as relegating them to substandard employment contracts. Rather than creating jobs, the CPE would simply replace stable, secure jobs with revolving-door, two-year youth hires. Moreover, students in universities and technical institutes felt that the CPE was denying the value of their education because it lumped them in the same employment category as unskilled youths. Not coincidentally, these students formed the core of protestors against the CPE. Prime Minister de Villepin's heavy-handed tactics, reminiscent of Juppé's behaviour, added fuel to the fire. The CPE reform was announced during school holidays in the hope of making it difficult to mobilize student opposition and was rammed through Parliament, using the article 49.3 confidence vote procedure, to avoid prolonged debate. Despite rising student opposition, de Villepin refused to negotiate over the reform. As the protests dragged on and unions threatened to enter the fray, however, the government was forced to retreat. President Chirac announced that the reform was enacted, but its implementation suspended, and in the end, the CPE was withdrawn entirely. The incident sounded the death knell of the Chirac administration's reformist efforts as well as of any talk of a presidential run by Prime Minister de Villepin.

To be fair to President Chirac, he is by no means the only French leader to have been defeated by demonstrators. The student–worker upheaval of May–June 1968 led more or less directly to Charles de Gaulle's exit from power the following year. More recently, the centre–Right government of Édouard Balladur (1993–95) and the leftist coalition of Lionel Jospin (1997–2002) were forced to withdraw planned reforms – from privatizations, to administrative overhauls, to reductions in farm subsidies, to educational changes – on multiple occasions in the face of street protests. But *Schadenfreude* was of small consolation to Chirac. More important, France seemed to be stuck between a rock and a hard place. On the one hand, the old system was increasingly unviable; on the other hand, efforts to move towards a new system were derailed by protestors.

Rejection by the voters

*[handwritten annotation: * French public has power to throw leaders out * Threat of the National Front]*

Aggravating the Chirac administration's difficulties, French voters displayed a growing willingness to vent their dissatisfaction with the ruling parties. As with the case of protests, the problem did not originate with Chirac. Indeed, beginning in 1981, the incumbent Prime Minister, whether Left or Right, was defeated in every national election. Nonetheless, the electoral backlash deepened under Chirac. Two signal events attested to the divorce between the voters and the mainstream governing parties.

The first was the 2002 presidential election. On the initial round of balloting, 21 April 2002, Chirac received less than 20 per cent of the vote, far and away the lowest score of any incumbent President running for re-election. (Valéry Giscard d'Estaing had garnered over 27 per cent in 1981.) Indeed, Chirac's score was lower than in 1995, when there had been another candidate from his own party, Édouard Balladur. What saved Chirac, despite this dismal showing, is that his main rival, the Socialist Prime Minister, Lionel Jospin, fared even worse. Turning against the governing Left as well as the governing Right, the French electorate gave Jospin only 16.2 per cent of the vote. Many French voters opted not to go to the polls at all; the abstention rate approached 30 per cent, the highest figure for a first-round presidential election in the history of the Fifth Republic. Those who did vote flocked to extremist protest parties. Three self-described Trotskyist candidates totalled over 10 per cent of ballots cast, while far-Right candidates captured almost 25 per cent.

The most spectacular development in the 2002 election was the breakthrough of Jean-Marie Le Pen, the leader of the xenophobic, far-Right National Front, who received 16.9 per cent of the vote, edging out Jospin to qualify for the second ballot. A so-called 'Republican reflex' allowed Chirac to crush Le Pen in the run-off election, 82.2 to 17.8 per cent, and to win a solid majority in the ensuing parliamentary elections, but the respite proved temporary (see the chapters by Bruno Cautrès with Alistair Cole and Andrew Knapp and Frederic Sawicki in this volume). The government's popularity quickly plummeted, and the Right was routed in 2004 regional elections, winning only 2 of 22 regions across France.

The second event attesting to the divorce between French voters and the governing parties was the 2005 referendum on a proposed EU Constitution. The 2005 referendum, which is analysed in the chapters by Nicolas Sauger and Sophie Meunier, offered a stunning repudiation of France's mainstream elites. The EU Constitution had been drafted by a committee headed by a former French President, Valéry Giscard d'Estaing. It was officially endorsed by both Chirac's governing UMP and the opposition Socialist Party. Yet the referendum was defeated by a large majority, 54.7 to 45.3 per cent. Part of the reason was concern over the direction of European integration, an issue taken up in Hussein Kassim's chapter. Despite the Socialist Party's formal endorsement of the EU Constitution, many militants rallied to a so-called *non de gauche* position ('no of the Left'), led by Laurent Fabius, and emphasizing the threat posed by 'neo-liberal Europe'. The proposed Bolkestein directive liberalizing services crystallized this concern, which was translated into the apocryphal 'Polish plumber', eager to take jobs away from the French by working for substandard wages. More generally, the 'no' vote reflected frustration over diminishing French influence in Brussels, a sense that European integration was more of an alien imposition than an expression of French interests and identity.

Beyond opposition to the EU Constitution or the direction of EU integration, the 'no' vote was fuelled by dissatisfaction with the French political establishment. Many voted 'no' to send a message to Chirac, to signal their dissatisfaction with a sluggish economy or recent austerity reforms. These voters were determined to punish Chirac and score an electoral victory as much as to decry the Constitution itself. As in 2002, this anti-establishment sentiment affected the mainstream Left as well as the Right. Despite an internal party referendum that had endorsed the Constitution, many Socialists followed Fabius in openly allying with the PCF, the far Left, and anti-globalization groups such as ATTAC to oppose the Constitution.

By the end of Chirac's tenure as President, pundits and observers were drawing comparisons between France and Britain in the late 1970s. Like Britain in an earlier age, France was experiencing economic decline; it was the 'sick man of Europe'; its model was broken. Like Britain, France appeared increasingly ungovernable, with the administration unable to pursue needed reforms in the face of social protest and voter backlash. And like Britain, France could presumably be saved only by a strong leader, who would pursue conviction politics rather than consensus politics, re-establishing the authority of the state and unleashing market forces. Yet this parallel is overdrawn. Although the difficulties in France are real, and reform is a politically parlous undertaking, France is no stalemate society. Indeed, considerable change took place during the Chirac years.

The Chirac years revisited

The chapters in this volume suggest that there was far more movement and reform under the Chirac administration than is commonly acknowledged. France is not an immobilist, stalemate society. Rather, French society is changing, and so too, is government policy.

Movement under Chirac

Sophie Meunier's analysis of French foreign policy suggests that France is moving beyond the Gaullist template. President Chirac's assessment of the situation in Iraq proved largely prescient, certainly more accurate than that of the Bush administration. Chirac's refusal to endorse the Iraq War remains his most popular achievement with the French voters. This opposition reflected more than prickly anti-Americanism. Indeed, France had supported and continues to support the US-led campaign in Afghanistan. It also attested to a fundamental shift in France's approach to international relations. In the place of the Gaullist, go-it-alone tack, Chirac became a leading advocate of multilateralism and the rule of law. Military intervention should be conducted within a multilateral framework, ideally authorized by the UN, as was the case with France's intervention in the Ivory Coast. This move towards multilateralism reflects a more realistic assessment of how France can hope to exert influence in the world today.

Other chapters in the volume describe important changes in the domestic arena. In economic policy, Ben Clift shows that while no one would ever confuse France with post-Thatcher Britain, French officials have steadily moved the country towards the market, even as they pay heed to traditional demands for a more directive state role. Chris Howell describes how French officials have expanded labour market flexibility, in many cases by encouraging the social partners to substitute collective agreements for state regulations. Ironically, the 35-hour working week, which is often portrayed as the antithesis of flexibility, has played a central role in this movement, according to Howell. Finally, Patrick Hassenteufel's chapter on the welfare state demonstrates that notwithstanding the failure of the Juppé Plan, successive governments have enacted a series of important changes. A pension reform in 2003 essentially aligned the pensions of most civil servants with those of workers in the private sector; a health care reform in 2004 reduced the deficit and laid the foundations for computerization of medical records and the introduction of a family doctor-based gatekeeper system; and a series of reforms in the unemployment insurance system have sought to 'activate' the unemployed, that is to bolster both the carrots and sticks favouring employment over the passive receipt of government benefits.

French authorities have also been busily reforming the state itself. Philippe Bezès argues that despite the prevailing image of the French state as frozen, sclerotic and stalemated, there has been continuous administrative reform, what Bezès calls 'silent and low-profile changes'. Over the years, state officials have been experimenting with the ideas associated with the new public management, such as increased accountability, management by objectives, and the decentralization of responsibility. This movement culminated with the passage of a budgetary reform in 2001, the *Loi organique relative aux lois de finances* – LOLF) that is analysed in detail by Philippe Bezès in Chapter 11.

Yves Surel likewise describes important changes to the French state – in this case, in the legal arena. Ironically, although Chirac is widely regarded as the embodiment of machine politics (indeed, once he left the presidency and lost his legal immunity, Chirac was immediately subjected to judicial probes about illegal hires during his tenure as Mayor of Paris), his administration enacted a number of reforms to make the French political system more accountable and less corrupt. Campaign finance reform has restricted private donations to political parties, while providing public funding in proportion to electoral results (see Knapp and Sawicki in this volume). Chirac's government also made the President penally responsible for his actions. In combination with the growing influence of legal bodies, such as France's Constitutional Council and the EU's European Court of Justice, these reforms have contributed to the judicialization of French politics. In other words, politicians and state authorities are increasingly being subjected to the rule of law. Surel notes that they are also being forced to share lawmaking responsibilities with EU and international organizations. Thus, French lawmaking has become more pluralistic and less state-centric.

Patrick Le Galès's analysis of territorial politics echoes this theme of increasingly pluralistic policy-making. During the Chirac years, several key decentralization initiatives were enacted. The Chevènement law of 1999 enhanced the power and resources of intercommunal organizations, while the Raffarin Act of 2003 bolstered the departments. The government also changed the French Constitution to declare that 'the organization of the Republic is decentralized'. The effect of these and other reforms has been to make policy-making in France more decentralized and polycentric, with multiple local authorities launching (sometimes rival or overlapping) initiatives. In addition, while state authorities still aspire to direct local actions and tap local resources, they can no longer issue orders, but rather must rely on subtler means of persuasion, including contracts, partnerships and policy-specific plans (notably in urban renewal and transportation). Taken together, the chapters by Surel and Le Galès suggest that state authorities are learning to work in more pluralistic policy-making environments, negotiating and sharing power with other actors, both above and below.

Le Galès's analysis points to a further line of reform of the French state, an effort to adapt to a more heterogeneous society. Whereas Le Galès emphasizes the territorial dimension, Eléonore Lépinard analyses the state's changing relations with disadvantaged social groups. Traditionally, French authorities have refused to target policies specifically at disadvantaged groups, arguing this would violate the Republican principle of equal treatment of all citizens. To the extent that governments sought to aid disadvantaged groups at all, they did so by crafting ostensibly neutral policies that would have a disproportionate effect on the target group. For example, instead of affirmative action for people of colour, France deployed 'urban renewal' policies (*politique de la ville*) that concentrated resources on geographic areas with high concentrations of minorities. In recent years, however, Lépinard notes that policies designed to promote equality between women and men have gone a step further. French authorities have finally begun to openly break with the Republican model. So-called 'parity' policies have transcended the Republican model in three ways: (1) taking gender into account explicitly for matters of political representation; (2) redefining equality in a substantive way (as opposed to just procedural equality); (3) using gender quotas to achieve the goal of concrete gender equality (in essence, affirmative action for women).

A number of these landmark reforms were not, of course, the work of President Chirac, but occurred during the 'Plural Left' coalition government headed by Socialist Lionel Jospin from 1997 to 2002. The record of the Plural Left government was – and still is – open to plural readings. The reputation of the Jospin government was left in tatters by the humiliation of the Socialist leader in the 2002 presidential contest, when he failed to win through to the second round. A more positive interpretation of the Jospin years is not only possible, but also probably necessary, if only to understand the existence of distinctive pathways of reform in France and the advocacy of competing solutions to the commonly accepted limitations of the Republican model identified above.

The Plural Left government had a significant reformist record. It promoted employment by lowering the working week to 35 hours and creating 300,000 (five-year contract) jobs for young people in the public and associative sector. The Plural Left government adopted bold measures to reduce inequality, such as universal health care and tax credits for the low paid. Even critics – of which there were and are many – had to acknowledge that the Jospin government engaged in original policy experiments in economic, social and employment policy and undertook audacious measures to break down social and cultural blockages within French society and to modernize French politics. The Jospin government engaged in new forms of dialogue with civil society, attempted to give a boost to social partnership (over the 35-hour week), and to promote citizenship rights (as in the civil partnership [PACS], or the parity reforms) as well as promoting an awareness of environmental issues. The Jospin government modified important features of the traditional model of Republican citizenship. It did more than any other to enhance gender equality and to promote diversity awareness. It provided more support and recognition of minority languages than hitherto and launched an ambitious, 'asymmetrical' process of devolution in the case of Corsica. That the French Council of State struck out the more audacious clauses of the Matignon agreements testified to the continuing weight of orthodox traditionalists within the state, but this was not Jospin's fault. The main criticism was not one of a lack of reformist intent, but of a failure to carry through fully on the reformist impetus in the field of justice, civil rights and political modernization.

The Plural Left government was sometimes described in the French press as a 'dual cohabitation'. Alongside tense relationships with President Chirac (see the chapter by Levy and Skach), Jospin had to manage the differing political sensitivities of the five coalition partners (Socialists, Communists, Radicals, Greens and Citizens). Tensions within the Plural Left coalition occurred across a range of policies, such as immigration, the reform of the legal system, the euro, Corsica, decentralization and Europe. In the circumstances, the longevity of the Plural Left was its greatest success, a coalition government held together by the combination of a pre-eminent (but not dominant) party, the ability to deliver political or symbolic side-payments to the main coalition partners (especially the Communists), the lack of an alternative, and a common electoral necessity. The politics of accommodation was time-bound, however, and as time wore on the cohesion of the Plural Left coalition was undermined by its internal contradictions and increasingly intractable policy divisions (over Corsica, the environment, Europe, jobs and many others). Aggravating matters, an initially strong economic performance began to wane. Ultimately, the political failure of the Plural Left proved extremely damaging for all five of the governmental parties, not only for the Socialists. The specific concatenation of circumstances and political alliances that prevailed from 1997 to 2002 is unlikely to occur again. The Plural Left was perhaps the last manifestation of the Union of the Left strategy, upon which the Socialist Party had built its renaissance since the 1970s, but which appears unlikely to be able to support a future majority. The Socialists, on the horns of a strategic dilemma, have had to go back to the drawing board and imagine possible strategic futures, none of which provides much cause for confidence (see the discussion in the Cautrès with Cole chapter). The political defeat of the PS in the two successive presidential elections following 2002 has done little to enhance the reputation of the Socialist-led administration.

The Chirac years were more than a lost decade. Considerable reform took place. Yet for all these changes, the reforms of the Chirac years did little to assuage concern about the direction of French policy. Indeed, in some respects, they aggravated this malaise.

Limits of the Chirac reforms

During the Chirac years, there was an unmistakable and pervasive sense in France that the government was failing to properly address the nation's problems. Two basic features of the Chirac reforms fuelled this malaise. The first was the substance of the reforms; the second was the process.

On a substantive level, a central problem of the Chirac reforms is that they were generally insufficient to fix critical problems. For example, despite the many initiatives described in Patrick Hassenteufel's chapter on welfare reform, French social security deficits have not fallen (health care costs, in particular, are still rising); labour market policies remain overwhelmingly passive in orientation; and the governance of the social security system continues to be problematic, with neither the state nor the social partners able to steer the social security system effectively, that is, to set priorities and enforce them. A similar tale could be told with respect to French economic policy. Notwithstanding the efforts of the Chirac administration to improve growth and competitiveness, as described by Ben Clift, government debt and deficit have continued to undermine the French economy.

It is not just in the economic and social arena that Chirac's efforts seemed to come up short. As Patrick Le Galès relates in his analysis of decentralization, French territorial politics remains messy and uncoordinated. Controversial choices have been avoided – whether between regions and departments or between municipalities and intercommunal organizations. In addition, state authorities have often undermined decentralization by offloading unfunded mandates on French local governments. Finally, none of the actors in the system has confronted the challenge of cost containment. Thus, centre–periphery relations display a lot of activity and reform, but no coherent government strategy, no vision for the ultimate territorial organization of France.

The state's redefinition of its relations with social groups also remains incomplete, a theme that is central to the chapters by Eléonore Lépinard and Marcos Ancelovici. Lépinard shows that while recent parity reforms have improved the opportunities for women, there are plenty of loopholes. Thus, in the 2007 parliamentary elections, only

18.5 per cent of victorious candidates were women (granted an increase over the 12.3 per cent figure in 2002). Moreover, Lépinard notes that gender was defined as 'different from other differences', meaning that parity measures were not extended to other disadvantaged groups, such as racial and ethnic minorities. The suburban riots offered a reminder of the persistence of discontent, despair and marginalization among many members of France's minority communities.

Marcos Ancelovici's chapter on protest politics further attests to the disconnect between the government and civil society. Ancelovici describes the emergence of a series of important social movements seeking to battle social exclusion, poverty and homelessness, to improve the treatment of immigrants and minorities, and to resist or at least regulate globalization. Groups such as ATTAC (Association for the Taxation of Financial Transactions for the Aid of Citizens) and DAL (Right to Housing) staged highly visible protests that generated considerable public sympathy. Yet these groups have remained on the margins of French politics. Governments, especially governments of the Right, have viewed new social movements as more of a threat than an opportunity. At best, governments have engaged in personalistic incorporation, co-opting individual leaders, rather than engaging the movements behind these leaders.

Another factor limiting citizen input is the weakness of the French Parliament, which is analysed in the chapter by Bastien François. Members of Parliament are more accessible to citizens and interest groups than the relatively insular executive branch. However, the Constitution of the Fifth Republic places the French Parliament in a subordinate position. Members of Parliament rarely initiate legislation, and even amendments to government bills are tightly controlled by the executive. Consequently, French citizens and interest groups have little opportunity to shape government policy through conventional lobbying channels. To the extent that they have any influence at all, it tends to be via the kinds of protests described by Ancelovici.

Chirac's reforms were criticized not only for failing to solve fundamental problems, but also for the costs that they imposed. In particular, government policy seemed to speak with an upper-class accent, placing financial burdens on the poor and vulnerable, while sparing the well connected. The welfare reforms analysed by Hassenteufel were emblematic in this regard. Health care reform required patients to shoulder more of the costs of their care, but demanded no sacrifices of physicians; indeed, the government boosted physician fees. Pension reform lengthened the number of years that employees must work to qualify for a full pension without imposing any costs on employers, whose contribution levels were frozen. Finally, labour market reform tightened supervision of benefit claimants in the name of activation, but did little to reward those moving from welfare to work by boosting their take-home pay. The CPE initiative offered an almost perfect illustration of this skewed distributional logic. French youths were asked to accept a two-year probationary period, during which they could be fired without justification or compensation, in return for a vague hope that this diminished protection would increase hiring. Vulnerable young people would have less job security, while employers would gain additional flexibility in hiring and firing.

The class bias of many Chirac reforms reinforced anxiety about the direction of policy. Instead of protecting the French population against the effects of globalization and combating social exclusion, government reforms seemed to be aggravating the hardship and vulnerability of those at the bottom. Yet at the same time, as noted earlier, the Chirac administration's reforms were not solving France's economic and fiscal problems. There was a lot of pain, but not much gain. In a kind of perverse Goldilocks formula, the Chirac administration seemed to introduce just enough painful, regressive change to alienate large swathes of the French electorate, but not enough to resolve the economic and social problems that had motivated reform in the first place.

The process of reform under Chirac, like the substance, was a source of considerable malaise. The government failed to provide a coherent legitimating discourse for the changes that it was pursuing. Again, Chirac was not the first to engage in such behaviour. Observers have noted a 'stealth reform' approach, dating back at least to Mitterrand's U-turn in 1983, characterized by governments pursuing change, often economic liberalization, under the radar, without publicly acknowledging it (Gordon and Meunier, 2001). Governments on both sides of the political spectrum have regularly blamed the EU for changes that they knew were necessary, instead of defending these changes on their own terms. Refusals to bail out uncompetitive, loss-making companies were blamed on EU competition policy; deficit reduction was portrayed as a necessary evil under EMU. Actions such as these undermined the legitimacy of European integration (no small factor in the French rejection of the EU Constitution in 2005), since the EU was associated with unpopular domestic reforms. Equally important, the European blame game meant that French leaders were not educating the public and building support for necessary changes.

If 'stealth reform' has been a persistent feature of French politics over the years, the gap between discourse and practice arguably reached new heights under Chirac. Chirac secured election as President in 1995 by promising to increase state intervention to 'heal the social fracture', yet sought to introduce an austerity plan less than six months later. He also engaged in the traditional blame-shifting exercise by attributing the need for austerity to the EMU. Even for a French population accustomed to unfulfilled campaign promises, this immediate and cynical shift was too much to swallow and played a significant part in the resistance to the Juppé Plan.

The contrast between rhetoric and reality, repeated recourse to 'stealth reform', and the unwillingness of the government to assume responsibility for its actions left the French public disoriented and dismayed. Adding to the sense of malaise in Chirac's France was a second feature of the reform process, the top-down, authoritarian manner in which the administration often proceeded. The Juppé Plan, as noted earlier, was devised in complete secrecy, without any input from the social partners. Juppé also refused to make any concessions to the strikers. Much the same could be said of the CPE. De Villepin rammed the reform through Parliament using article 49.3, then dismissed student protestors as spoilt children. While the Juppé Plan and the CPE reform were extreme cases, they were hardly isolated incidents. Indeed, it seemed as if the government's modus operandi was to formulate reforms in secret and without consultation, present them to the public, then wait for the reaction in the streets. If the demonstrators came out in force, the reforms were retracted; if not, they were implemented, whether popular or not.

In the end, the Chirac reforms provoked anxiety on two counts. From a substantive perspective, the reforms were painful and, to many, unfair, while failing to fix France's problems. From a governance perspective, the reform process combined authoritarianism with duplicity. The government's reforms lacked both a legitimating discourse and a political process that could produce buy-in from the key stakeholders.

Renewing reformism? Sarkozy in action

Nicolas Sarkozy assumed office under far more favourable political circumstances than Chirac in 1995, as the chapter by Jonah Levy and Cindy Skach relates. Whereas Chirac won the presidency on a campaign of improved social protection, then sought to implement an austerity programme, Sarkozy openly criticized the French social model, which he blamed for many of the country's economic difficulties. Sarkozy made it clear that, if elected, he would pursue an agenda of far-reaching change, a 'rupture' with the traditional French way of doing things – from foreign policy, to the economy, to social protection, to law and order, to immigration. Thus, unlike Chirac in 1995, Sarkozy earned a mandate for the kinds of reforms that his government is now seeking to implement.

Another advantage enjoyed by Sarkozy is a clear electoral horizon. When Chirac took office in 1995, he was facing parliamentary elections by 1998 at the latest. Part of the reason for Chirac's ill-fated decision to call early elections in 1997 was the desire to secure a majority before moving forward with controversial austerity reforms. Sarkozy confronts no such strategic dilemmas. In the wake of the 2000 constitutional reform that reduced the President's term in office from seven years (*septennat*) to five years (*quinquennat*), the presidential and parliamentary mandates are essentially coterminous. Sarkozy won the presidency in May 2007, followed by a parliamentary majority in June 2007, and therefore faces no meaningful national elections for the next five years. Consequently, Sarkozy is free to pursue controversial or painful reforms that he believes will pay off down the road, whether economically or politically.

Movement under Sarkozy

The movement from Chirac to Sarkozy produced an upswing in the French political climate. The turnaround started with the election itself, which is analysed in the chapters by Bruno Cautrès with Alistair Cole and by François Sawicki and Andrew Knapp. The 2007 presidential election marked a striking reversal of the main electoral trends of the previous 25 years that had culminated in the debacle of 21 April 2002. Voter participation, which fell to an all-time low of 71.6 per cent in 2002, increased by over 12 per cent in 2007, reaching its highest level in more than three decades. Part of the reason was the desire to avoid a repetition of 2002, when Le Pen had been able to qualify for the second ballot because many left-leaning voters had not bothered to vote. This same, 'useful-vote' calculation benefited mainstream candidates, especially on the Left. The mainstream governing parties made a dramatic recovery, with Sarkozy and the Socialist, Ségolène Royal, winning a combined 57.1 per cent of the vote on the first ballot, as opposed to 36.1 per cent for Chirac and Jospin in 2002. Conversely, the seemingly inexorable march of far-Right and far-Left parties was put into reverse. The self-styled 'anti-liberal' Left (Communists, Trotyskists and opponents of globalization) dropped from 13.8 per cent in 2002 to 9.0 per cent in 2007, while Le Pen received only 10.4 per cent, far below his 16.9 per cent share in 2002.

The recovery of the mainstream governing parties was due to more than luck and strategic voting. In the years since 2002, both the UMP and the PS had rebuilt their party organizations, increasing their ranks by scaling back membership requirements and expanding opportunities for participation via the Internet. More important, both parties put forward a new generation of candidates, fresh faces promising a departure from the tired ideas and practices of the Chirac years. Sarkozy's campaign was especially skilful. Despite being the head of the governing UMP and having held several of the most senior cabinet positions under Chirac (including Minister of the Interior and Minister of

Finance), Sarkozy managed to position himself as an outsider, a rebel, who would break with the status quo. Equally important, through tough law-and-order and anti-immigration pledges, Sarkozy was able win back conservative voters who had defected to Le Pen over the years, while still retaining centre-Right and centrist swing voters. Thus, whereas Chirac had stood by helplessly as the National Front grew from election to election, Sarkozy cut Le Pen down to size. If Chirac was a *machine à perdre* (losing machine), Sarkozy was an electoral steamroller.

The sense of hope and optimism surrounding the 2007 election carried over into the initial period of the Sarkozy presidency. Just as Sarkozy reversed many of the electoral trends under Chirac, so he has reversed or corrected many of his predecessor's political debacles. In foreign policy, whereas Chirac precipitated the worst crisis in transatlantic relations since de Gaulle's withdrawal from the NATO integrated command in the 1960s, Sarkozy quickly patched things up with the United States, picnicking with the Bush family in Kennebunkport, Maine. Sarkozy is seen as the most pro-American French President in history and received repeated standing ovations in a speech to the US Congress, yet he has also insisted on the right, as a good friend, to criticize US policy when appropriate.

The European front presents a similar contrast between Sarkozy and Chirac. On the one hand, Chirac almost single-handedly sank the European Constitution by submitting it to a referendum, rather than parliamentary ratification. Given an opportunity to vent their frustration with Chirac's administration, French voters showed no hesitation in vetoing the EU Constitution at the same time. On the other hand, despite their rejection of the EU Constitution, within a few months in office, Sarkozy had personally negotiated a new 'mini-treaty' for European integration with essentially the same provisions (minus some symbolic trappings). Unlike Chirac, Sarkozy has no intention of submitting this mini-treaty to the French voters.

Sarkozy has also registered a number of accomplishments at home – once again, in areas that frustrated his predecessor. For example, Sarkozy rather skilfully navigated the treacherous climate of university reform. French universities have long been a hotbed of student protest, most notably in 1968, and student unrest has triumphed over reform-minded governments on numerous occasions. Sarkozy's proposals to give French universities more autonomy over personnel and educational matters also prompted protest. However, Sarkozy was able to overcome this opposition and get most of his reform through by sitting down with student and university leaders, making a few concessions, and hammering out a deal.

The same holds true of social security reform. Whereas the Chirac presidency was more or less destroyed by the Juppé Plan six months into its term, six months into the Sarkozy presidency, the administration successfully implemented a reform of the so-called 'special regimes' (*régimes spéciaux*) that had enabled certain categories of public employees (mainly transportation and energy workers) to retire as early as age 50. Like the Juppé Plan, the reform of the *régimes spéciaux* prompted strikes and protests in the public sector, but unlike his predecessor, Sarkozy could claim a democratic mandate for the changes that he was proposing. He also displayed greater political skill. Sarkozy made a point of meeting repeatedly with the unions, stating that he was open to negotiating the terms of the reform, and holding out the prospect of some compensation to workers who lost their early retirement benefits. Perhaps for these reasons, unlike in 1995, public opinion polls in 2007 leaned towards the government over the strikers.

Thus, optimism about the direction of French politics has several sources. First, the President was solidly elected on promise of 'rupture' and renewal. Second, in the wake of the 2000 *quinquennat* reform, he enjoys a five-year, national-election-free opportunity to implement his agenda. Third, President Sarkozy has displayed undeniable energy and political skill. He has assumed an almost larger-than-life status. As the chapter by Levy and Skach relates, Sarkozy is omnipresent on the political scene, making all decisions, big and small. To his supporters, Sarkozy is finally tackling the issues that had befuddled Chirac for 12 years. Even Sarkozy's opponents on the Left initially seemed overwhelmed by the frenetic, activist pace of France's 'hyper-President'.

Uncertainties ahead

If the Sarkozy presidency got off to an active start, problems have begun to accumulate, and there is considerable uncertainty as to where France is going. Two questions loom large. The first concerns the character of Sarkozy's reformist agenda; the second concerns its sustainability.

Sarkozy's ideological position defies easy categorization. At first glance, as suggested earlier, he displays much in common with Margaret Thatcher. Both came to power against a backdrop of economic decline and concerns about ungovernability; both are strong, charismatic leaders; and both combine economic liberalism with an authoritarian approach to law-and-order and interest groups. That said, Sarkozy is clearly less committed to neo-liberal principles than Thatcher. He was an interventionist Finance Minister, using his resources to create national champions and scare off foreign bidders. Such interventionism has continued since Sarkozy became President, notably when his office helped put together the merger between Gaz de France and Suez to create a 'national champion' in the energy sector.

Although Sarkozy is clearly drawn to liberal ideas, he seems to be a friend of French business more than of free markets. He relishes the glamour and wealth of the business world, counts a number of business leaders among his friends, and has not hesitated to take lavish vacations (a yacht in the Mediterranean, a mansion on a New Hampshire lake, a jet trip to the Egyptian pyramids) at their expense. In addition, Sarkozy is a political animal, and electoral calculations have figured prominently in his decisions on economic issues. For example, Sarkozy's inaugural budget included some 15 billion euros annually in tax cuts. While tax cuts are certainly part of the neo-liberal agenda, many of the specific components of this 'fiscal shock' (partial deductibility of interest payments on home mortgages, diminished inheritance tax, etc.) were motivated by electoral considerations, whether past campaign promises or efforts to woo electoral constituencies, rather than economic theory. Of course, every politician, including Mrs Thatcher, must make allowances for political reality, but Sarkozy seems to do so with alacrity. Thus, a first uncertainty surrounding Sarkozy is whether he will pursue a reasonably coherent, liberal modernizing strategy or a more opportunistic and politically driven approach, rewarding (business and middle-class) friends, while punishing (labour) enemies.

The second uncertainty surrounding Sarkozy's reformist strategy concerns its sustainability. Part of this uncertainty stems from Sarkozy's mercurial personality. Already divorced and remarried (to Italian supermodel and singer, Carla Bruni) since assuming office, prone to public demonstrations of anger and tremendous mood swings, the President is anything but predictable. In addition, Sarkozy is drawn to the dramatic gesture, the policy coup, so it is unclear that he will remain committed to a single strategy over time. Finally, Sarkozy has been working at a blistering pace, and commentators openly speculate whether a President often compared to the 'energizer bunny' may some day run out of batteries.

Beyond the psyche and stamina of the man in the Élysée, Sarkozy's reformism confronts more conventional challenges. Like all new leaders, Sarkozy enjoyed a honeymoon period, and there are signs that this respite is drawing to a close. After a brief hiatus, the French are taking to the streets again. University and pension reform, even if implemented in the end, stirred up considerable public protest. Moreover, in November 2007, the *banlieues* erupted in arson and violence again following the death of two youths of North African descent. Indeed, the intensity of violence escalated as compared to the 2005 riots, with rioters repeatedly using live ammunition against the police.

Not coincidentally, protests have revived as Sarkozy has begun to take up some of the more difficult and controversial reforms. Whereas during his initial months in office, Sarkozy reaped popularity from foreign policy successes and tax cuts, he now confronts the politically treacherous challenges of reducing the budget deficit, controlling social spending, reforming labour markets, turning around an anaemic economy, and addressing violent crime. Aggravating matters, the 2007 tax cuts have left Sarkozy with almost no fiscal room to manoeuvre. An important ingredient of successful reforms in France is the ability to offer at least some compensation to those who are harmed, yet a cash-strapped state has no money to finance such side-payments. Once again, French policy seems to be speaking with an upper-class accent, delivering tax cuts for the affluent and luxurious holidays and a 170 per cent pay increase to the President, while cutting benefits and pro-tections to low-income and disadvantaged groups. With the French economy remaining weak, Sarkozy is likely to confront growing demands for relief from needy workers and businesses, but he lacks the resources to respond to these demands. Thus, as he moves from deliv-ering tax cuts and rescuing hostages to cutting pensions and loosening job protections, Sarkozy enters a more dangerous political universe, where his popularity and political capital could quickly dissipate. Already Sarkozy's approval rating has dropped below 50 per cent, fuelled by a combination of unhappiness over the economy and stag-nant purchasing power, resentment of painful austerity reforms, and distaste for Sarkozy's tendency to personalize politics and popularize his personal life. The Left capitalized on Sarkozy's unpopularity to score a decisive victory in the March 2008 municipal elections, picking up a number of large cities including Caen, Metz, Reims, Saint-Étienne, Strasbourg and Toulouse.

Certainly, the election of Nicolas Sarkozy as President has been a very important 'development in French politics'. But there is more continuity between Sarkozy and his predecessor than Sarkozy's sup-porters acknowledge. Sarkozy may have jump-started the reform process, but significant changes had been taking place under Chirac. Moreover, like Chirac, Sarkozy remains befuddled by the French economy, and his reforms display the same upper-redistributional bias. Perhaps for these reasons, along with irritation over his conspic-uous consumption and flamboyant personal life, Sarkozy's popularity has fallen to roughly the same level as Chirac's at this point in his presidency. Thus, if Sarkozy has introduced a new sense that France may indeed be reformable, it remains to be seen whether he is the man for the job – whether Sarkozy possesses the vision, discipline and com-mitment to provide meaningful solutions to the serious challenges still facing France.

Chapter 2

The 2007 French Elections and Beyond

BRUNO CAUTRÈS WITH ALISTAIR COLE

One word describes better than any other the 2007 French presidential election: this is that of *rupture* (loosely translated as 'break' in English), at the heart of the campaign rhetoric of the winner. The first understanding of *rupture* is in terms of the sharp contrast between the 2007 and 2002 presidential elections. The two elections were a story of some simple contrasts: between the high level of turnout in 2007 and a high level of abstention in 2002; between the concentration of votes on the main candidates in 2007 against the dispersion of votes on 'small' candidates in 2002; or, perhaps most fundamentally, between the decline of the extreme Right in 2007 against the qualification of Jean-Marie Le Pen for the second round in 2002. This chapter will provide the main explanations as to why the 2007 election was such a contrast with that of 2002. It will also provide some discussion about the new characteristics of French politics that came to the fore in 2007, notably the role of the leading candidates, their belonging to a new generation (at the time of the election Sarkozy was 52 and Royal 53) and the role of gender (with a woman winning through to the second round for the first time). It will concentrate mainly on the presidential election, the legislative one being largely a consequence of the presidential election since only five weeks separated the two.

The campaign

The process of candidate selection is referred to by Knapp and Sawicki in their chapter, so commentary here will be brief. If Royal obtained the Socialist Party nomination, this was in part because she was seen as a likely winner against Sarkozy. For the duration of the internal PS campaign in 2006, Royal performed consistently better than her two rivals (former Premier Laurent Fabius and former Finance Minister Dominique Strauss-Kahn) in terms of voting intentions against Nicolas Sarkozy. The prospect of her possible victory had a very clear impact on the internal campaign, even if we must not reduce the selection of Ségolène Royal only to her popularity in the polls.

Though Royal led briefly at the beginning of 2007, she did not enjoy the status of front-runner for long. Sarkozy's nomination as UMP candidate on 14 January 2007 marked a step change in the campaign. By February 2007, Royal's lead had all but evaporated. While UMP candidate Sarkozy occupied the political limelight in January and February 2007, Royal lost the political initiative through focusing upon the slow development of her 'participative' campaign. Though the promise of new forms of participatory democracy had initially sustained her campaign, it proved a disadvantage once the campaign proper started, as it equated with hesitation and slowness to react.

Previous presidential election campaigns have suggested that a negative effect often accompanies a declaration of candidacy on behalf of an incumbent politician. This was certainly the case in 1995, when incumbent Premier Édouard Balladur announced he would be standing for President. Ahead on the Right in all the polls in February, by April 1995 Balladur trailed in third position and was eliminated from the run-off by Chirac. In 2002, Premier Jospin announced his intention to stand for the presidency in a fax to the media. Rather like Balladur seven years previously, Jospin also failed to win through to the second round and was eliminated from the run-off by Le Pen. These two examples highlight the difficulty of non-presidential incumbents from escaping from deeper governmental unpopularity.

Unlike Balladur in 1995, or Jospin in 2002, Sarkozy was not affected by any such negative effect. The Villepin government was one of the most unpopular since records began, brought low by the atmosphere of the *fin de règne* discussed in Chapter 1. But Sarkozy's carefully cultivated image – as a man of governmental responsibility with a good record over five years, while not being fully of the government – allowed the UMP leader to escape the opprobrium of government unpopularity. This point is worth noting. Sarkozy managed to be perceived not as an incumbent, though his governmental experience allowed him to retain the rewarding part of the incumbent effect. He positioned himself ostensibly as an outsider, a challenger to the largely discredited Chirac regime and a victim of the machinations of Premier Villepin over the Clearstream affair. Sarkozy was able to position himself, in a very skilful manner, not as an opponent but as a rebel within his own camp. The rebellion was against Chirac and the old neo-Gaullist guard (men such as Jean Louis Debré or former Premier Dominique de Villepin). The metaphor of the rupture portrayed Sarkozy as a man of action, the embodiment of a personal dynamic style of leadership that would settle with the declining and rather discredited Chirac era. Opposition to Chirac, on grounds of policy and personality, allowed Sarkozy to develop his own political persona and style of political leadership.

Operating skilfully as a political newcomer with a new vision, but also a politician with a record of achievement, the Sarkozy campaign was not damaged by the record of the incumbent government.

The official entry into the electoral arena of Sarkozy was accompanied by a lasting opinion poll lead over Royal, from which the Socialist candidate never recovered. According to a very detailed analysis conducted by Jean Chiche and Daniel Boy of all voting intention surveys published after 3 January 2007, the declaration by Sarkozy that he would be a candidate was a key campaign moment (Boy and Chiche, 2007). Chiche and Boy identify a first phase in the evolution of voting intentions that lasted from 3 January to 12 February, the day after the presentation by Royal of her programme. There was a brief period in the first fortnight of January when the two main candidates (Royal and Sarkozy) were very close to each other, both obtaining high voting intentions (approximately 30 per cent each). From the second half of January onwards, however, the voting intentions in favour of Sarkozy far exceeded those of all other candidates. There would be no significant change in the next three months.

Sarkozy's decisive entrance into the campaign was in contrast with the apparent hesitations of Royal over her presidential platform. The first few months revealed the inexperience of the Socialist candidate, in foreign policy notably. In January 2007, Royal's trip to China received bad press both at home and abroad. Mme Royal made several remarks that were open to criticism (such as her praising of Chinese tribunals for their rapidity compared with their French counterparts), or ridicule (such as her invention of the word 'bravitude' [signifying a quality of courage] to talk about herself). To Royal's own comments were added the (deliberately calculated?) remarks of her then partner, the Socialist Party leader François Hollande, who raised the prospect of increasing taxes for those earning more than €4000 per month. Then, there was the resignation from the Royal campaign team of Eric Besson, a Socialist MP who was also an important member of the PS executive and the politician in charge of the PS economic programme. All of this was extremely damaging for the Socialist candidate and spoiled her image of presidential stature and credibility.

The period from mid-January onwards was highly significant for another reason: namely the rising voting intentions in favour of the Centre candidate François Bayrou. By mid-January, voting intentions for Bayrou had almost doubled from their November start point (from 6 per cent to 10 per cent) and exceeded those in favour of Jean-Marie Le Pen. The emergence of Bayrou as the 'third man', and the prospect that he might even be the second one, completely changed the campaign. In a different register from Sarkozy, Bayrou also constructed his image as that of an opponent to the incumbent government. The Bayrou campaign was organized on the basis of a very strong adversarial discourse against both the main parties (UMP and PS), accused of confiscating the political system for their own purposes. Bayrou staked out a powerful claim for a new and reformed institutional system, one in which the domination of the two big parties would be broken. The centre candidate saw himself as voicing the frustrations of all those who were disillusioned by the performance of Left and Right governments for the past 25 years. Bayrou also very cleverly used an anti-media discourse, complaining of the links between Sarkozy and the bosses of the press and media. He pointed to specific incidents to back his claims, such as the firing of Alain Genestar, the boss of *Paris Match*, a weekly magazine that had published a photo of Cecilia Sarkozy with her lover on its front page.

In summary: Sarkozy succeeded with his entry into the 2007 campaign, while Royal squandered her initial advance and was soon being challenged by Bayrou for the position of number two. This first phase of the 2007 campaign ended with a good deal of confusion on the extreme Left of French politics. Buoyed by the success of the No campaign in the 2005 referendum on the draft constitutional treaty, the Communists and the extreme Left (the Trotskyites in particular) attempted to agree on a common candidate, a position the PCF obviously wanted for itself. The PCF argued in favour of its superior grassroots membership and its stock of local elected councillors to stake out a claim to lead an eventual anti-liberal coalition. But PCF attempts to dominate the anti-liberal coalition backfired badly, leading to three separate Trotskyite candidates (the veteran Arlette Laguiller for the Lutte Ouvrière [LO], Olivier Besancenot for the Ligue Communiste Révolutionnaire [LCR] and Gérard Schivardi for the Parti des Travailleurs [PT]) and the anti-liberal candidacy of Jose Bové, as well as the inevitable PCF candidate (Marie George Buffet). All in all, five candidates disputed the limited political space of the extreme Left. Bové was the last to announce his candidacy on 31 January, in reaction to what he called the 'divisive' candidacies of Buffet (PCF) and Besancenot (LCR).

A second period of the campaign opened in mid-February and lasted until early March, when Chirac (on 11 March 2007) officially announced that he would not be a candidate for the 2007 elections and that he would be supporting Sarkozy. This period was characterized by the growing domination of Sarkozy in voting intentions. With only two exceptions (on the 20 and 28 February) all surveys predicted that Sarkozy would lead the first round (with around 30 per cent) and win the second one. During this second period, voting intentions in favour of Bayrou also increased sharply, reaching 19 per cent according to IFOP on 26 February. Bayrou achieved his best score (24 per cent) in a CSA poll in February, with the centre candidate obtaining almost the same level of predicted support as Royal.

By the end of this second period the leading candidates had all developed the main lines and themes of their programmes and campaigns. Sarkozy articulated a quite traditional right-wing programme: economically liberal, but culturally conservative and adopting a hard line on issues of law and order and immigration. Sarkozy's presidential campaign was successful because he managed to appeal for support from centre to extreme Right. The core message of the presidential platform, however, was addressed to right-wing voters frustrated with the inability of the previous regime to challenge a number of policies held to have contributed to France's decline. Sarkozy was vociferous about the need to reform the labour market and to abandon (or at least empty of its substance) the 35-hour week introduced by the Left in 1997–98. A further play to the traditional Right was the commitment to introduce the principle of a minimum service in public transport and to introduce strike ballots. Candidate Sarkozy also made specific pledges over pensions, promising to reform the special pension regimes that gave particularly favourable terms and conditions to public sector workers. Sarkozy made a pitch for support from Le Pen voters, with the help of blunt phrases such as 'you either love France or you leave it' ('la France on l'aime ou on la quitte'). Sarkozy also made a clever appeal to working people, especially those on low incomes, with the promise 'work harder to earn more' and the prospect of allowing more overtime to be worked.

Faced with Sarkozy's strategic falling to the right (in an attempt to attract FN voters from the first round), Royal defended her priorities on social issues and education, combining these traditional leftist positions with some non-orthodox views about social issues. For instance, Royal appealed to family values but also made declarations in favour of homosexual marriage and adoption of children by homosexual couples (contrary to Sarkozy). Throughout her campaign, Royal was torn between her own preferences and the priorities contained in the Socialist project, upon which her 2007 platform was in part drawn. This tension produced an uncomfortable relationship between the candidate and her party and an unconvincing espousal of her core campaign themes. The case of the 35-hour week was a good one to illustrate these tensions. During the early phases of the campaign, Royal emphasized the need to create more flexibility in the workforce and to move away from the 35-hour week. Once a candidate, however, Royal repeated the classic 1970s-style promise to create 500,000 public sector jobs, to penalize companies that delocalize production out of Europe and to create new contracts for disadvantaged young people, a marked change of tempo from 2006. While she had criticized the 35-hour week in the PS primary election contest, she was forced to defend it in the campaign itself. Her protestations that she had not believed in this policy after the election did little to enhance her prestige either within or beyond the ranks of the Socialist Party.

Rather like Bayrou, Royal called for more institutional innovation and democracy, going so far as to advocate a Sixth Republic shortly before the first round. Together with the call for more participatory and democratic forms – such as citizens' juries – Royal also voiced a number of themes that were in rupture with the traditional discourse of the Left. Thus, the candidate stressed the need to fight delinquency and to impose tougher sentences on young offenders, proposing that they be sent to military camps. She called for a restoration of authority, a strengthening of national identity, more choice in education and a reform of the teaching profession – all themes more usually associated with the Right. But this original mix ended up dissatisfying traditional constituencies on the Left, while not attracting sufficient support elsewhere on the political spectrum.

For his part, Bayrou focused most of his campaign attention on the need to overhaul the political system of the Fifth Republic. The various reforms he proposed were intended to drive home his core message that the Left–Right divisions encouraged by the Fifth Republic are outdated. Bayrou called for the formation of a government of national union, the introduction of proportional representation for all elections and the creation of a new party (MoDem) as a replacement of the old UDF. On the economy, Bayrou's main propositions were economically liberal, even more than those of the UMP and Sarkozy. Bayrou insisted upon the need to reduce the size of the budget deficit, trim back the public sector and exercise a much tighter control over public expenditure. His call to speak the truth about the economy was directed against the two leading candidates, both of whom he accused of making economically irresponsible promises.

Far more so than in 2002, the 2007 campaign was dominated by these three leading candidates. Of the others, Jean-Marie Le Pen offered few surprises in concentrating his campaign message and main programmatic issues on immigration, the need for a more protectionist economy and defending the nation through adopting more vigorous anti-EU and anti-globalization positions. It is worth noting that, like five years earlier, Le Pen tried to make a subtle and tactical use of his real difficulties in getting the 500 signatures for 'sponsorship' of its candidature. Unlike in 2002, his difficulties did not garner much sympathy. Of the other candidates, only the far-Left Besançenot made a real impact, eclipsing the more seasoned Laguiller, the media-focused Bové, Buffet for the Communist Party and the hapless Voynet for the Greens. Also-rans included the colourful Schivardi, the lacklustre Nihous and the ultra-conservative de Villiers.

The first round of the 2007 presidential election

The results of the first round (Table 2.1) were marked by the very high level of turnout. Fully 83.77 per cent of registered electors (82.56 per cent of valid votes) voted on the first round on 22 April. Turnout progressed by almost 12 percentage points compared to the first round of the 2002 presidential election and by 5 percentage points as compared to the 1995 first round. With an abstention of 16.4 per cent of the total registered voters, the 2007 first round was comparable to the 1974 (15.77 per cent) or 1965 (15.25 per cent) first rounds of the presidential election.

Turnout and participation

Turnout progression could be observed in all sociological or political segments of the electorate. Several explanations can be forwarded for this very high increase in turnout, especially compared with five years earlier. First, pre-election surveys registered a high level of interest in the presidential election, widely perceived as being the decisive one. Shortly before the election, the city councils announced that they had registered many new voters. Before every presidential election electoral registration goes up, but the 2007 figures were higher than usual: 4.2 per cent of new registered voters, compared with 2.3 per cent in 2002 and 3.7 per cent in 1981. This increase in electoral registration followed an active campaign led by associations, especially in the poor city suburbs, calling for a civic mobilization to avoid a 'new 21 April'.

Second, the 2007 election was marked by a strong attention to the more personal dimension of the main candidates, their personality and their fitness to govern. Some commentators linked this interest in the personality of the candidates with an increase in electoral participation. The main candidates succeeded in giving a picture of renewal of themselves, not only in their campaigns and personal styles but more importantly in the appreciation of the presidential function. Sarkozy, Royal and Bayrou each defended themselves first and above all as outsider personalities within their own camp. These three candidates did a great deal to increase interest in the election campaign. Each came under close scrutiny as to their ability to exercise the presidential function, a battle won comfortably by Sarkozy in the series of surveys undertaken by the CEVIPOF (2007, Baromètre politique français).

The third explanation for increased turnout lay in the '21 April' effect, in reference to Le Pen's progression to the second round in 2002 and the awareness by 'Left abstentionists' that they had contributed to this calamity. Both Sarkozy and Royal benefited from a double '21 April effect'. There was a much higher degree of electoral turnout and there was less dispersion of votes to minor candidates, the only excep-

Table 2.1 *The French presidential election, 22 April 2007, first ballot*

Candidate	Party	% valid votes
Schivardi	Parti des Travailleurs (Trotskyist)	0.34
Laguiller	Lutte Ouvrière (Trotskyist)	1.33
Besancenot	Ligue Communiste Révolutionnaire (Trotskyist)	4.08
Buffet	Parti Communiste Français	1.93
Bové	Anti-Globalization Left	1.32
Voynet	Les Verts (Greens)	1.57
Royal	Parti Socialiste	25.87
Bayrou	Union pour la Démocratie Française (UDF–Centre)	18.57
Sarkozy	UMP (Conservative)	31.18
de Villiers	Eurosceptic Conservative	1.19
Nihous	Chasse, Pêche, Nature, Traditions (Hunters' Rights)	1.15
Le Pen	Front National (Far Right)	10.44

Note: Valid votes cast 36.7 million (= 82.56% of registered electorate).
Source: French Interior ministry figures

tion being Olivier Besancenot, the high-profile leader of the LCR who obtained just over 4 per cent of valid votes. On the Right, voters moved en masse from Le Pen (who lost over one-third of his electorate) to Sarkozy. In 2007, the three leading candidates were successful in recovering for the mainstream a significant part of the protest politics that had characterized France for many years. The geography of turnout on the first round showed that the increase was shared in most regions. Everywhere, abstention declined significantly as compared to 2002 and in particular in western and eastern France (Muxel, 2007). In terms of the sociology of abstention, turnout increased in most segments of the electorate, even if abstention is still sociologically defined: the unemployed, the working class, young voters, and those with low levels of education are the most likely to abstain. As compared to 2002, turnout increased very significantly in that segment of the electorate in which the memory or the reference to '21 April' was important: the fraction of educated voters, in particular leftists, who had abstained as a protest in 2002.

Interest in the 2007 campaign was much higher than for that of 2002. However, the importance of context can be considerable in explaining levels of turnout, as Bréchon (2007) observes. A well-defined campaign and a sense of the importance of the 2007 presidential election as the key contest does not mean that there will be a return to lower abstention levels in forthcoming elections. It must not be taken for granted that politics is back in the mind of French citizens.

The results

While the 2002 election had witnessed a dispersion of first-round votes to minor or unelectable candidates, in 2007 there was a concentration of votes from the first round on the three candidates who stood a realistic chance of being elected President. In marked contrast to the previous three presidential elections, the two qualifying second-round candidates polled a majority of valid voters (57 per cent) from the first round, something that had not occurred since the 1988 presidential election (54 per cent). By way of contrast, in 2002, the two leading candidates polled only 36.7 per cent in 2002 and 44.1 per cent in 1995.

Sarkozy . . . by a margin

Nicolas Sarkozy was the uncontested winner of the first round. With 31.2 per cent of the valid votes in the first ballot, Sarkozy came well ahead of the PS candidate (25.9 per cent) even though Royal's score was much better than some feared. In absolute numbers, the victory of Sarkozy was even more clear and net. He led Royal on the first round by 1,950,000 votes. Sarkozy's score was far and away superior to any obtained by Jacques Chirac in any of the last four presidential elections in which he was candidate. Chirac reached a high point of about 21 per cent of the share of the vote in his first candidacy in 1981. Sarkozy's 2007 score came somewhere in between Chirac's 21 per cent in 1981 and the strong performance of the first two Presidents of the Republic: De Gaulle (44.6 per cent in 1965) and Pompidou (44.5 per cent in 1969). A more accurate comparison is with Mitterrand. Sarkozy's score was quasi-equivalent to that of François Mitterrand in 1988 (33.90 per cent of valid votes). In other words, the Sarkozy score can be compared to some of the strongest scores ever obtained by candidates to the presidential elections. The key mechanism explaining such a victory was the capacity of the UMP candidate to capture a significant and numerous segment of the Le Pen electorate. The electoral success of Sarkozy at the expense of Le Pen has been qualified in France by several different expressions, each of which is significant for understanding what happened. Some talk of Sarkozy 'siphoning off' the Le Pen electors, others, such as Nonna Mayer (2007), of the 'shrinkage' of the Le Pen electorate. Le Pen himself complained of a 'hold up' by Sarkozy and called in vain on his electors not to support the UMP candidate on the second round. These metaphors all point fundamentally to the same thing: the belief that Sarkozy's strategy since first becoming Interior Minister in 2002 was aimed at breaking the hold of the FN over a substantial part of the electorate that he would need to win a presidential election.

Sarkozy's first-round electorate was clearly a right-wing electorate first and foremost, even if he managed to attract some voters coming from elsewhere in the political spectrum. Sarkozy did appeal to some left-wing voters, the so-called 'dissonant' voters analysed by Perrineau (2007b). But the core of the electorate was a traditional right-wing one, strongly mobilized by the context and the candidate. Some figures illustrate this. Thus, Sarkozy obtained 64 per cent of first-round votes in the 16ème *arrondissement* of Paris, a traditional right-wing bastion. Sarkozy also performed especially well among the over 60s, and among regular churchgoers, two core right-wing constituencies. Sarkozy comfortably won the support of a very large part of the 2002 right-wing candidates (Jacques Chirac, Alain Madelin, Christine Boutin). He also took advantage of the high electoral mobilization and captured about 6–7 points of the 2002 Le Pen votes. In other words, Sarkozy was able to federate the different segments of the right-wing vote, and increase the total vote as a result of a much higher electoral mobilization.

At the same time, Sarkozy appealed beyond the traditional right-wing vote. One way of measuring this is by observing the modified geography of the right-wing vote compared to Chirac. Sarkozy did well in the traditional strongholds of the moderate *and* the extreme Right. Sarkozy demonstrated the ability to attract votes from Le Pen voters and territories. The map of Sarkozy voting in 2007 is a unique mix between the Chirac and Le Pen maps of 2002. In 2002, Chirac's vote was strong in regions that were the traditional territories on the Right: the west of France for instance (Mayenne, Manche, Maine et Loire, Finistère), areas where Chirac did much better than in the south-east or Alsace, strongholds in 2002 of Le Pen. In 2007, the exact opposite occurred for Sarkozy, who performed very well in the south-east (the Provence–Alpes–Cotes d'Azur region, with a very high score in Alpes-Maritimes and in Var with 43.6 per cent and 39.7 per cent respectively) and in Alsace (over 36 per cent). In the west of France, Sarkozy obtained his national average, or – in the case of Brittany – slightly below. It is also noteworthy that Sarkozy attracted a proportion of UDF voters, the most right-leaning part of that electorate which suspected Bayrou of harbouring a hidden Left strategy.

Royal: heading for a victorious defeat

The first-round gap between Sarkozy and Royal left the latter in a difficult position. Royal's first-round total – 25.9 per cent – was almost identical to that of Mitterrand in the 1981 presidential election. Royal's strong first-round performance was above all a result of the changing distribution of the votes within the Left, rather than a powerful basis to challenge Sarkozy for the second round. As Dupoirier (2007) remarks, the main electoral problem that Royal faced at the end of the first round and in the perspective of the second, was the poor performance of the other candidates of the Left. The two other candidates of the 'governing Left' (Buffet for the PCF and Voynet for Les Verts) polled 1.93 and 1.57 per cent of the valid votes respectively, historically low results for their respective political parties. The Communist Party obtained its worst score in any national election in France under the Fifth Republic. The Green candidate Voynet polled a score which was just superior to that of René Dumont, the historical figure of the Greens in France, in the 1974 presidential election (then 1.32 per cent of the valid votes). Voynet's 2007 score was far from that of her own total in 1995 (3.32 per cent of the valid votes), still further from the 5.25 per cent of her rival Noël Mamère in 2002. In other words, the first round of the 2007 presidential election swept aside the non-PS component of the governing Left, a key element of the explanation of Royal's final defeat.

The core political lesson drawn from the humiliation of 2002 was that it was essential to vote 'usefully' for the PS, even in second-order elections such as the regional (2004) and European elections (2004). Paradoxically, however, the concentration of support around the PS has its downside; it reduces the 'pool' of electors that are likely to transfer their votes to the Socialist on the second round. The overall total of the Left (excluding extreme Left) in 2007 was 29.37 per cent, only marginally ahead of 2002 (27.12 per cent). The French Left could not be unduly optimistic about Ségolène Royal's first-round score. Rather than conquering new voters and attracting voters coming from other political families, there was only a redistribution of Left voters between the components of the Left. This movement favoured the PS candidate in 2007, but there were few reserves. The total progression of the Left candidates, when we compare the 2002 and 2007 first rounds, was only 1.8 percentage points.

Royal benefited from the pressure to vote 'usefully' in 2007 and prevent a rerun of 2002. A significant part of the difference between Jospin's 2002 score and her score in 2007 (11.2 percentage points) came from Left voters giving priority in 2007 to tactical voting. Electors on the 'Left of the Left', having voted for extreme Left candidates in 2002, voted tactically for Royal in 2007, not because she was their favourite candidate but because she could defeat Sarkozy. According to the CEVIPOF post-election study, Royal obtained the votes of 54 per cent of the Left non-PS supporters (voters declaring themselves as close to a Left party, but not the PS), whereas Jospin in 2002 had polled only one-third of their votes. She also was supported by 71 per cent of Socialist Party supporters, as compared to only 51 per cent for Jospin in 2002. Nevertheless, this return of support among core supporters should be interpreted in the context of a long-term trend which is the weakening of party proximity (the main measure of party identification in France) for the PS. According to the CEVIPOF post-election studies, in 1998 40 per cent of the electorate declared themselves to be 'close to' the PS, but only 23 per cent in 2007. In addition, we note the weakening of the links between party proximity and vote, a process which can be observed in countries beyond France. The counterpart to this decline of PS identifiers has been a rise of those feeling close to other Left parties.

From a sociological point of view, Royal performed well among traditional segments of the Left electorate in which Jospin lost significant support: employees and routine manual workers, high-grade professionals, young voters and the unemployed in particular. But this revival of the core Left constituency was relative; if she comfortably outpolled Jospin in these groups, she was far behind Mitterrand in 1981 or 1988. And, as we saw above, Sarkozy did well in all sections of the electorate, including among workers and employees that had once been regarded as the kernel of the Left electorate. Those groups among whom Royal actually scored more than Sarkozy were few and far between: the teachers (+26 points), 18–24 years old (+9 points), the unemployed (+8 points). But the lead over Sarkozy was not very large among traditional Left voters, such as the intermediate professions (+3 points), public servants (+4 points) and workers (+0 points). In all other segments of the electorate Sarkozy led Royal: for example, among higher-grade professionals (–15 points), employees (–8 points) et even women (–7 points). Rather surprisingly, Royal did not obtain more votes from women than from men, though she was the first woman to be qualified for the second round of the presidential election and she made gender a key campaign argument. The most striking sociological difference between the Royal and Sarkozy voters was generational. One may talk about an emerging generational gap in the French electorate. According to the CEVIPOF post-election study, 23 per cent of voters aged 65 and over voted for Royal, but 45 per cent for Sarkozy.

From a political point of view, the Royal electorate was a very traditional leftist one: 70 per cent of her first-round voters declared themselves to be on the 'Left' according to the post-election study of the CEVIPOF. The geography of the Royal vote was also the traditional geography of the Socialist vote in France with strongholds in the southeast (departments such as Ariège where she obtained 35 per cent of the votes), Haute Vienne (31.5 per cent), Brittany (30 per cent in the Côtes d'Armor) and Paris (31.8 per cent). More generally, the Royal vote was quite strong in the big cities and in urban areas, a phenomenon that has been apparent in every recent election and that was repeated in the municipal elections of 2008, at which the PS made important gains in France's largest cities. The geography of the Royal vote confirmed the poor results of the PS in rural areas, as well as in traditionally industrial working-class regions in the north and east.

The useless 'victory' of François Bayrou

One of the core questions in debates about French political space in the Fifth Republic has been: is there any room for a 'third way' between the right-wing and the left-wing coalitions? The 2002 presidential election had provided one response to this question with the qualification of Le Pen for the second round of the election. The 2007 election once again forced attention on the question, this time because of the Bayrou score (18.5 per cent of the valid votes, 6.75 million votes) (Sauger, 2007). Bayrou largely contributed to the impression of renewal given to the 2007 presidential election.

There were several reasons for this 'success', a very relative one given that Bayrou did not qualify for the second round. First, Bayrou's stance against the Left–Right 'system' found an echo and attracted new voters, non-UDF ones, in the context of large mistrust of the French towards politics and politicians. His criticisms about the collusion between Sarkozy, the media and the business world rang true with many voters worried by the personality of Sarkozy. Bayrou also benefited from the weaknesses of the Royal campaign, in particular in terms of her image and credibility. These two explanations have their limits, as Sauger (2007) has suggested. In ideological and sociological terms, Bayrou voters formed a composite block, though all Bayrou voters shared liberal economic values and liberal cultural values. If the core Bayrou voters were the educated, centre-Right voters who had already supported him in 2002, the Bayrou 2007 electorate comprised much more than this core vote. Bayrou's electorate contained recognizable centre-Left, centre and centre-Right components, fragments of the electorate not looking for exactly the same things. Sauger (2007) has proposed a typology of these different Bayrou voters. The Left Bayrou voters – 39 per cent of the total – came from the Socialist electorate and were ideologically very close to the Royal electorate. The Right Bayrou voters – 28 per cent of the total – were much closer to Sarkozy voters on economic and cultural issues. The remainder were the core 2002 centrist voters alluded to above.

The paradox of the Bayrou vote is in the uselessness of this 'victory'. Only a few days after the first round, the great majority of the UDF deputies announced their decision to leave the UDF, to create the 'Nouveau Centre' as a component of the UMP majority. An isolated Bayrou eventually created his own party – the MODEM – in December 2007. Because of the voting system (the two-ballot system), a small party like the UDF needs an electoral coalition to have any chance of having elected deputies, a condition that explains the choice of the UDF incumbent deputies.

Le Pen: the end of a French exception?

The very strong decline of the Le Pen vote (10.44 per cent of the valid votes) arguably signalled the end of a French exception. Compared to 2002, Le Pen declined by −6.5 points or even by −8.8 points if we add the Le Pen and Megret votes on 21 April 2002. This result represented a clear failure for the historic leader of the National Front. Le Pen had seemed somewhat less in control in 2007 than in previous elections, the FN diffusing the image of division and post-succession rivalry between Bruno Gollnish and Marine Le Pen, his daughter. During the election campaign, Le Pen was a shadow of his former self. Indeed, if we set to one side the 1974 election (when he polled 0.76 per cent of valid votes), 2007 was Le Pen's worst score in a presidential election, well below the 14.4 per cent in 1988, 15 per cent in 1995 and 17.2 per cent in 2002. The Le Pen electorate was reduced to the alliance of workers and small business electors that had formed the core of the far Right since the 1988 presidential election.

The Le Pen electorate remains a very rightist one, with its own authoritarian and xenophobic values. But the evidence from the 2007 election suggests that significant changes have occurred in its sociological underpinnings. The Le Pen vote is in sharp decline among traditional groups such as shopkeepers and non-manual employees. On the other hand, the Le Pen vote held up well among artisans, the more popular fraction of the self-employed (16 per cent), and among the working class (16 per cent). These changes in the Le Pen vote are increasing in 2007 the 'working-class character' of the extreme Right voting.

According to the calculations made by Nonna Mayer, only 54 per cent of the 2002 extreme Right voters (Le Pen and Mégret) voted for Jean-Marie Le Pen on 22 April 2007. It is possible to look at the profile of the defectors thanks to the big sample sizes of the CEVIPOF studies. In 2007, the 'lepeno-sarkozistes' shared the same ideological motivations and values as the Le Pen voters but they considered a vote for Sarkozy to be a more effective way of defending their ideas. The combination of strong statements and positions by Sarkozy about immigration, law and order and the value of work, along with his enhanced presidential credibility (by comparison to Le Pen), seduced the less popular part of the extreme Right electorate. The dominant reference of the Sarkozy campaign on issues related to work played a key role in attracting social groups who consider that the public sector and the salaried workers have become overprotected and privileged members of French society.

The victory of Nicolas Sarkozy

At the end of the first round, it was clear that Sarkozy had the advantage and that to win Royal had to capture a high proportion of Bayrou votes. The 2007 election revealed that the logic of the Fifth Republic and of the presidential election is more than ever in operation. In order to win on the second round, the successful candidate must recover the full electorate of his or her camp plus a small but significant part of the other one. The problem for Royal was that victory would require attracting a large part of Bayrou voters, as well as holding onto her own and ensuring the near perfect transfer of the far-Left voters. The structural weaknesses of the Left made this a near-impossible feat, even though Royal attracted the support of the leaders of the other Left parties, even the extreme Left, including Laguiller who had refused to call for a Chirac vote in 2002 against Le Pen.

Her slim chances of victory depended upon attracting most first-round Bayrou voters, and Royal certainly made a sustained attempt to achieve this. On 28 April, a debate with Bayrou was organized in Paris and broadcast on cable TV. Weeks after, it transpired that Royal had offered in private the job of Prime Minister to Bayrou if she was elected. At a press conference on 25 April, Bayrou was very critical of Sarkozy personally (and made it clear that he would not be voting for him), but also declared himself opposed to the 'statist' programme of Royal. Bayrou's 'maximalist' strategy was a very risky gamble: most UDF deputies immediately switched their support to Sarkozy in exchange for the UMP support in the legislative elections. Le Pen exercised even less influence on his followers than Bayrou: he called upon his voters to abstain, but most voted Sarkozy anyway.

The televised debate between Sarkozy and Royal on 1 May 2007, Royal's last chance, turned to Sarkozy's advantage, revealing an aggressive Royal and a Sarkozy remaining calm under pressure. The results of the second round (Table 2.2) confirmed what could be expected from the first. Sarkozy was elected by a large majority (with 53.06 per cent of valid votes) in the context of a very high turnout (83.97 per cent of participation, with 3.53 per cent of blanks and nil votes).

How did Sarkozy win on the second round? The clear victory of Sarkozy could be explained first by the strength of the support he obtained on the first round, fully five percentage points ahead of Royal. The specific dynamics of the second round were also important, especially transfers between first- and second-round candidates. According to the TNS-SOFRES polls (on the day of voting), 60 per cent of Le Pen voters supported Sarkozy on the second, along with about 40 per cent of the Bayrou supporters and the quasi-total of de Villiers and Nihous voters. The electoral geography of the second

Table 2.2 *The French presidential election, 6 May 2007, second ballot*

Candidate	% of valid votes cast
Sarkozy, Nicolas	53.06
Royal, Ségolène	46.94

Note: Valid votes cast 35.8 million (= 80.44% of registered electorate).
Source: Interior Ministry figures.

round was also a consequence of the first ballot. As in the first round, Sarkozy obtained his best scores in Alsace and on the Mediterranean coast as shown in Map 2.1. This map clearly shows that Sarkozy performed particularly well in areas of traditional support for Le Pen, even if this variable is only one among many. Map 2.1 illustrates big sociological differences between the victory of Sarkozy in 2007 and that of Chirac in 1995 (any comparison with 2002 being meaningless given the context of that election). The increase in the total number of the second-round right-wing votes is mainly due to the progression in former Le Pen strongholds.

For her part, Royal benefited from a strong transfer of votes from Left voters, including those on the extreme Left, and of about 40 per cent of the Bayrou electorate, a proportion not sufficient to win the election. From post-election surveys it became clear that first-round Bayrou voters voting for Royal on 6 May, came mainly from the Left. They were Left voters who had been seduced during the campaign by the 'neither Left nor Right' slogan of Bayrou and who were not convinced by the style of Royal during the campaign. Royal obtained her best scores in the south-west and in urban areas, in particular big cities. The generational gap between the two electorates was confirmed: Royal won a majority among voters less than 50 years old, while Sarkozy was very dominant in older segments, in particular the oldest ones (see Map 2.2).

Epilogue: the parliamentary elections of 10 and 17 June 2007 and beyond

In the parliamentary elections of 10 and 17 June, the widespread expectation was that the UMP of Sarkozy would obtain a crushing majority, a blue horizon to rival that of 1993. In that year, the PS had declined to under 20 per cent of the vote, and only 57 PS and 22 PCF deputies had been returned. The announced landslide appeared even more

Map 2.1   *Sarkozy's second-round support in the presidential election, 2007*

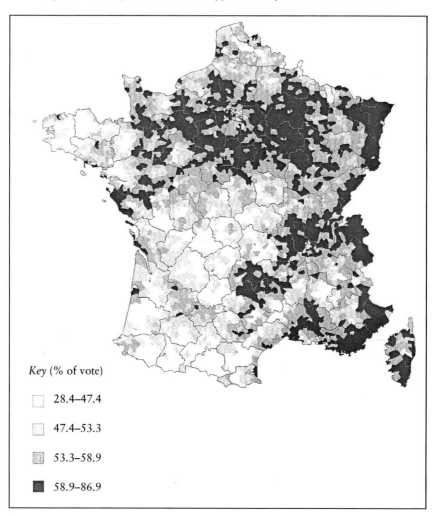

Key (% of vote)

☐   28.4–47.4

☐   47.4–53.3

▒   53.3–58.9

■   58.9–86.9

likely in the light of the 'inversion' of the order of the presidential and parliamentary elections that has pertained since 2002. Coming shortly after the decisive presidential election, it is now expected that a parliamentary election will confirm the results of the presidential contest. The 2007 parliamentary contest duly produced a UMP majority and gave Sarkozy the means to govern. After the second round on 17 June, the UMP by itself had an absolute majority, with 313 deputies out of 577. With its allies, the UMP obtained 45.58 per cent of valid votes, one of the highest of any party in the Fifth Republic. The UMP could count as allies the 22 deputies representing the New Centre (who were

Map 2.2 *Royal's second-round support in the presidential election, 2007*

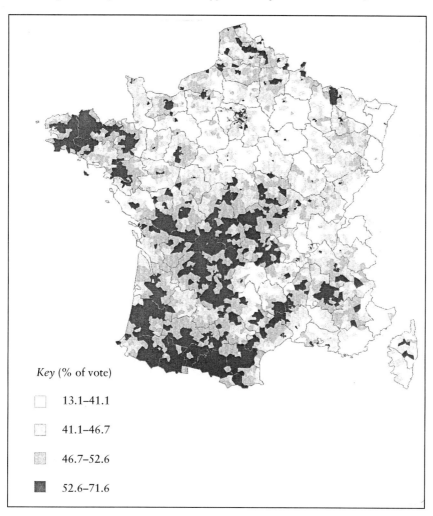

Key (% of vote)

☐ 13.1–41.1

☐ 41.1–46.7

▨ 46.7–52.6

■ 52.6–71.6

all sitting deputies of the UDF who deserted Bayrou to join Sarkozy in between the two rounds of the presidential election), as well as 10 other deputies (MPF, independent right). The presidential effect (the requirement of a majority to govern for Sarkozy) and the electoral system effect (the magnifying effects of the second ballot system) combined to give the UMP and allies a comfortable overall majority of seats on 45.58 per cent of the votes. The only consolidation for the Left was that it could have been much worse. Far from being eradicated, the PS (with allies) increased its deputies from 149 in 2002 to 208 (212 including the Greens) in 2007, avoiding the worse scenarios. Indeed, even the PCF held onto most of its sitting deputies (15 of 21) and produced some fine local performances. The real losers were the FN (with 4.68 per cent of the votes and no seats, the FN lost over half of Le Pen's 22 April electorate), Bayrou's MoDem (7.61 per cent, and three deputies) and the Greens, reduced to four deputies after refusing a nationwide alliance with the PS.

In the four ballots of the electoral series of 2007, if the first most likely secured Sarkozy's presidential victory, the fourth and final one (the second round of the parliamentary election) reminded the new President that the electorate wanted some safeguards to remain in place. The PS performed much better than expected. In a highly symbolic defeat for the Sarkozy government, Alain Juppé, Sarkozy's ephemeral Minister of the Environment, was defeated in his fief of Bordeaux. But this semi-victory was, above all, a victory, the fourth successive one in a row, providing the political foundations for the exercise of uncontested presidential authority for at least five years.

Conclusions

The victory of Sarkozy can be explained in the terms of the two main dimensions that have organized French political life for more than two decades: the economic and social dimension, and the immigration/insecurity dimension (Schweisguth, 2007). In relation to economic and social divisions, Royal (partially) mobilized a Left electorate which is still unsure about how to understand the transformations that France has been undergoing. This electorate remains attached to the traditional economic arguments of the Left, but is aware that globalization and the open economy make it more difficult to implement such orientations. Royal's campaign difficulties were due in part to the contradictions of the PS and the French Left on economic and social topics. She tried to invent new ways to cope with these contradictions by developing propositions about citizenship (participative democracy for instance), but these were largely inaudible.

It was on Schweisguth's second dimension – the nexus of issues around immigration and insecurity – that Sarkozy was perceived by large segments of the electorate as coherent and convincing, in particular among a significant segment of the Le Pen electorate. Sarkozy's strategy and campaign will probably remain as one of the most successful ever during the presidential race in France. Three fundamental points of its victory must be underlined. First, he developed his strategy over a long period of time (at least from the time of his nomination as President of the UMP in 2003). Second, he successfully combined a party political role with exercising the highest ministerial portfolios (the key position of Ministery for the Interior, twice, with a short break as Minister for Economy). Third, he was able to combine ministerial office with criticism of Chirac's record since 1995. Last but not least, he developed a very clear, coherent and successful strategy to recover a significant part of the Le Pen voters. Perrineau (2007) cautions against concluding about the end of protest politics in France. He prefers to talk about the 'end of a political cycle', but cautions that this cycle could be revived in the not too distant future if Sarkozy is seen not to be delivering major promises, in particular on unemployment, salaries and security. We will see in the coming months and years whether there has really been a sea change in attitudes among French voters.

Chapter 3

Political Parties and the Party System

ANDREW KNAPP AND FRÉDÉRIC SAWICKI

France's party system under the Fifth Republic has been precariously balanced between fragmentation and bipolarity. On the one hand, as Table 3.1 shows, the French voter has an impressive array of parties to choose from. Each of these parties has been capable of fielding both a presidential candidate and parliamentary candidates in many or even all of France's 577 parliamentary constituencies. Despite this fragmentation, every French government since 1962 has been supported by a stable parliamentary coalition of Right or Left.

The French party system is best characterized as one of bipolar multipartism. There are several parties that operate, in the main, within two broad coalitions, one of the Left and one of the Right. Bipolar multipartism is rather loose-fitting: it can accommodate a number of precise configurations of parties. It was unsurprising that the dominant party for the first 15 years of the Fifth Republic was created to support the Republic's founder, de Gaulle; unsurprising too, that with de Gaulle's departure and the left-wing opposition's gradual accommodation to the new rules of the political game, that dominance ended. The configuration of the late 1970s was known as the 'bipolar quadrille' because it comprised two opposed coalitions, each consisting of two parties of roughly equal size – the PCF and PS on the Left, the UDF and the Gaullists on the Right. A seemingly 'natural' outcome of the two-ballot electoral system, the bipolar quadrille in its purest form was only present in the elections of 1978 and 1981, and fell victim to fierce rivalries within each camp and to the Europe-wide decline of Communism. That left the PS as the dominant partner on the Left, and the Gaullists, to a lesser extent, on the Right.

Altogether more dramatic developments, however, were the new regularity of alternation in power and the multiplication of new players, especially protest parties. From 1981, the French electorate took to replacing the parliamentary majority, and the government that depended on it, at *every* parliamentary election, with the Left winning in 1981, 1988 and 1997, and the Right in 1986, 1993 and 2002. They

Table 3.1 *The main political forces in France, 2007*

Party	Typical share of vote (%)	Remarks
Trotskyists (three parties)	5	Vote shared by three fiercely competing small parties: Ligue Communiste Révolutionnaire (LCR); Lutte Ouvrière (LO); and Parti de Travailleurs (PT). LCR currently the strongest with the best presidential candidate
Parti Communiste Français (PCF)	<5	Vote >20% before 1980s, in decline since then. Strong municipal implantation and alliance with Socialists secure 15–20 National Assembly seats
Parti Socialiste (PS)	25	France's main left-wing party. Best results (35–36%, and absolute National Assembly majority) in 1980s; worst at 16% (presidential election, 2002)
Les Verts (Greens)	5	Depend on alliances with Socialists to win a handful of seats. Best results (± 10%) at second-order (European or regional) elections (1989, 1992, 1999, 2004), often divided between two or three lists
Union pour la Démocratie Française (UDF)	10–18	Remnants of Giscard d'Estaing's Centre–Right federation of the 1970s. Split since 2007 between an independent centrist wing, the Mouvement Démocrate (MoDem) with 3 seats, and the Nouveau Centre, part of the ruling Centre-Right coalition with 30 seats
Union pour un Mouvement Populaire (UMP)	30–45	France's major conservative party, formed in 2002 out of the former Gaullist party with elements of the old UDF
Front National	<10	Major electoral breakthrough in early 1980s brought party score to 10–17% between 1986 and 2002; but 2007 results showed sharp decline, with <5% at parliamentary elections
Chasse, Pêche, Nature, Traditions (CPNT)	<5	Single-issue party of shooting lobby: some surges at second-order elections, and 2002 presidential election

also spread their votes well beyond the confines of the bipolar quadrille, allowing the FN's breakthrough in 1983–84, those of the Greens and CPNT (both on a smaller scale) in 1989–93, and a slow rise of the far Left in the early 1990s. In part, these developments had institutional origins. The opening of the European Parliament (from 1979) and French regional councils (from 1986) to election by direct universal suffrage diluted the impact of the two-ballot system, because these two types of election were held on proportional representation, allowing smaller parties, without allies, to gain a foothold in the system.

Moreover, the progressive institution of public finance for parties in laws of 1988, 1990 and 1995 lowered the entry costs for new players; even if the big parties took the lion's share of the new money, many smaller competitors received just enough to survive (see further discussion in Chapter 9). In part, however, the rise of smaller and protest parties reflected a wider trend in the major democracies towards disenchantment with politics (Webb, 2002). This was especially marked in France, where it was fuelled by the inability of successive governments to deal with persistently high unemployment, by concerns over crime, immigration and the integration of ethnic minorities, and France's place in Europe and the world, and by a series of high-profile corruption scandals involving all of the governing parties through the 1990s. The 2002 presidential elections were remarkable not only because Le Pen reached the second ballot but because they marked a record low level of support for France's mainstream governing parties. On a generous definition (including the PCF and the Greens, as well as the PS, UDF, Gaullists and other centre-Right candidates) the mainstream won two-thirds of valid votes, equivalent to a mere 45.7 per cent of registered voters. On one interpretation, this resulted from deep-seated alienation from mainstream politics, which would surface again in the referendum of 2005 on the European Constitution (see Chapter 4).

Even before the results of 2007, Grunberg and Haegel (2007) noted an increasing 'rebipolarization' of French politics, amounting to something approaching an imperfect two-party system and appearing to have sent this fissiparous tendency sharply into reverse (see Table 2.3). They pointed to the Socialists' steadily increasing dominance of the Left, and the success, since 2002, of the UMP in achieving a similar hegemony within the Right. In 2007, the presidential candidates of the PS (Ségolène Royal) and the UMP (Nicolas Sarkozy), won 57 per cent of the first-ballot votes between them – more than their counterparts in any election since 1974. At the ensuing parliamentary elections (Table 2.3), following Sarkozy's presidential victory, the PS and the UMP achieved a combined total of over 73 per cent (as well as 90 per cent of the National Assembly seats); the FN was marginalized, with under 5 per cent of the vote; and an incumbent coalition retained its parliamentary majority for the first time since 1978. Other tendencies of earlier years were also reversed, as both party membership and turnout rose for the first time in a generation.

If, as we have argued elsewhere (Knapp, 2004a), a major cause of fragmentation in the French party system was the strategic failure of the big mainstream parties, the converse is also true; rebipolarization was in part due to their strategic success. The rest of this chapter aims to evaluate both the extent of the rehabilitation of mainstream politics in France and the degree to which it is now dominated by just two parties. In doing so, however, it will also aim to assess how success-fully the mainstream parties and their leaders have responded, organi-zationally and strategically, to the challenges of the early twenty-first century.

The parties of the Right

The single most important outcome of 2007, and one which con-tributed most powerfully to rebipolarization, was the drop in the FN vote, both at the presidential and at parliamentary elections. This can be explained partly in the light of the FN's own strategic difficulties; but the efforts of Sarkozy and the UMP also helped. A secondary outcome, testifying to the continuing institutional underpinning of bipolarization in France, was the failure of François Bayrou's attempt to reposition the UDF at the perfect centre of the political spectrum.

The Front National: strategic impasse

The FN remained, for the quarter-century between its breakthrough and 2007, a 'force solitaire' (Perrineau, 1993). It could win 10–15 per cent of the vote, set a part of the political agenda, win seats at regional and European level (under PR) and office in a handful of municipalities, and (especially in 1997) damage the mainstream Right's chances at three-cornered second ballots in parliamentary elections. But it could not win parliamentary seats for itself under the two-ballot system, and so had no leverage in the National Assembly. It lacked, despite its regional council-lors and its sprinkling of mayors, the local 'bastions' characteristic of successful French parties; and from 1988 it was frozen out of any alliances, national or local, with the mainstream Right – a policy on the part of the UDF and the Gaullists that remained intact despite some local breaches.

Le Pen's record score of 2002 would have no significant effects on the FN's longer-term positions. Without a reservoir of competent can-didates (thanks in part to a damaging party split in 1998–99), the FN saw its score at that year's parliamentary elections sink to 11.1 per cent. At the (second-order) 2004 elections, the FN failed to capitalize on the government's unpopularity, remaining close to the 10 per cent mark at both regional and European level. The following year it was largely absent from the referendum campaign on the European Constitution. Meanwhile the FN continued to suffer from organizational weakness. Its leading mayor, Jacques Bompard of Orange, withdrew from the party after appearing to aspire to the leadership. The main contenders for the succession, Bruno Gollnisch and Le Pen's youngest daughter Marine, divided the party into rival camps. Marine Le Pen, who was given the task of running Le Pen's 2007 campaign, had sought to 'dediabolize' the FN by giving it a proper economic programme, toning down some of its more obviously racist rhetoric, and liberalizing its positions on issues such as abortion and homosexuality. This provoked the departure of the party's traditionalist Catholic wing led by Bernard Antony, without drawing in new activists to compensate.

The FN's setbacks of 2007 should be read in this context: an ageing leader (who remained his party's chief asset), a damaged organization (which contributed to the poor parliamentary result), and a lack of any effective strategy beyond protest. These are the main reasons to doubt the party's ability to recover. The detail of Le Pen's losses is also explicable in these terms: he lost most heavily among the FN's middle-class electorate, ideologically right-wing without being committed to protest, and maintained his positions among workers in the post-industrial regions of north-eastern France (Fourquet, 2007). Indeed, according to the SOFRES post-election poll, fully 49 per cent of Le Pen's voters came from blue-collar working-class households (see Chapter 2). But the FN's defeat was also, of course, caused by a determined competitor in the shape of Nicolas Sarkozy and the UMP.

Nicolas Sarkozy and the transformation of the UMP

France's parties of the mainstream Right have also had difficulties developing a stable institutional structure. The three major traits of the Gaullist model were a strong party leader, whether informal (Presidents de Gaulle and Pompidou, till 1974, and Chirac from 1995) or formal (Chirac, from 1974 till 1995); a dearth of active members; and a dependency, for the party's material needs, on the perquisites of national and local office. No institutional mechanism existed for choosing the party's presidential candidate because, in the Gaullist mythology, a presidential election was supposed to be a meeting between an individual, not a party, and the nation. The UDF model, on the other hand, resembled the 'cadre party' of Maurice Duverger (Duverger, 1951): a federation of local notables, each well installed in his town or region, but with even fewer members than the Gaullists and little central direction – at least after the UDF's de facto creator, Valéry Giscard d'Estaing, had lost the presidency in 1981 (Hanley, 1999). The UDF's local centre of gravity had made it vulnerable to the temptations of local alliances with the FN, and the party had split in 1998, with its right wing reforming as Démocratie Libérale (DL). The years before 2002 saw a partial convergence between the two models, as the Gaullists won more local positions and became partly 'notabilized' while the reformed UDF's leader François Bayrou attempted to structure the party around his own presidential ambitions. But no party of the moderate Right in 2000–1 could boast even 100,000 members, and none had a stable, competitive and well-used procedure for choosing either its leader or its presidential candidate. It was in this context that Chirac, directly after his re-election in 2002, was able to merge the Gaullists, DL and most of the UDF, and to require – through his trusted lieutenant, former Prime Minister Alain Juppé – all parliamentary candidates who supported the President to run under a new label – the UMP. Only Bayrou and a minority of the UDF chose to stay out.

But although it won a huge National Assembly majority in 2002, the UMP initially failed to produce the modernized, institutionalized, conservative party that its creators had sought. Most UMP parliamentarians had joined from a resigned acceptance that the UMP's endorsement was the safest way to keep their seats. At the inaugural congress in November 2002, only 47,621 members voted in the election of the party president, suggesting that real membership was well below the 164,000 officially claimed. Juppé, the party's first president, had been irredeemably unpopular with the public – and most of the Right's élites – since his disastrous two years as Prime Minister from 1995 to 1997; and in January 2004 he was convicted for political corruption offences, effectively taking the punishment for Chirac's stewardship of the Paris Town Hall from 1977 to 1995. Banned from elective office, Juppé left the UMP leadership shortly afterwards, leaving the party to a run of poor election results; all but two of the UMP-controlled regions were lost in March 2004, while the party's lists won a mere 16.6 per cent of the vote at that June's European elections.

Juppé's successor was Nicolas Sarkozy, elected (after an interregnum of several months) on 28 November 2004 by 85 per cent of those 70,830 members (out of a registered total of 132,922) who chose to vote. Once elected leader, he set about transforming the UMP. Within two years, it was claiming 285,000 members, a level often claimed, but very rarely achieved, in the history of French right-wing parties. The notion of membership, it is true, had changed. You could join the UMP via the Internet and a fairly nominal subscription. 'Activism' could consist, not in going to draughty meetings, canvassing or leafleting, but in sending 'contributions' to the party programme, or voting for the leader or the presidential candidate, from the comfort of one's home computer. These 150,000 or so new members were to prove Sarkozy's most precious asset in 2004–6. Most had joined precisely in order to help him win the presidency. As party president, Sarkozy could see off competing conservative candidacies – especially after the UMP's *bureau politique* agreed in December 2005 that the presidential candidate would be nominated by the full membership vote. Neither Chirac (still, at 74, hankering after a third term), nor his protégé de Villepin, nor yet the Defence Minister Michèle Alliot-Marie – credible candidates all, in principle – was prepared to face this humiliation; and so Sarkozy's nomination, in January 2007, was unopposed.

To attract this kind of loyalty, however, Sarkozy had first had to establish himself as the Right's most popular politician. This was far from automatic. He had entered the SOFRES/*Le Figaro* popularity polls in May 1993, shortly after his appointment as Budget Minister and government spokesman in the government of Édouard Balladur. His closeness to Balladur had led him to hope for the post of Prime Minister to Balladur's President, a dream ended by Balladur's defeat in 1995. And his (fairly modest) positive poll rating of 37 per cent, achieved in June 1993, was not regained for another *nine* years (Perrineau, 2007c). Nor did he hold office from 1995 (when his energetic support for Balladur ensured his exclusion from Chirac's governing team) until 2002. What is remarkable, then, is that when he returned to government in 2002, as Interior Minister under Raffarin, he had the rank of *Ministre d'État,* second only to the Prime Minister, and was already viewed as an obvious potential President. The combination of a firm anchorage on the right of the Gaullist party, a more direct and modernist discourse than most of his competitors (he is distinguished among the French political élite by *not* having attended the élite civil service college, the École Nationale d'Administration), excellent contacts in the business world, often gained via his legal practice, a willingness to break taboos and (occasionally) to borrow an idea from the Left, plus a rock-solid political base in Neuilly and no political debts to Chirac or anyone else, positioned him as a political heavyweight who could aspire again to the premiership in 2002. In retrospect, the fact that Chirac finally preferred Raffarin can be counted as Sarkozy's good fortune.

For Sarkozy, who accepted the consolation prize of the Interior Ministry and the number two rank in government, contrived to prosper as a minister in (but never quite *of*) two deeply unpopular governments. By May 2003, with the government's honeymoon period over, Sarkozy had broken away from the pack to become the Right's most popular politician: his positive ratings were running at 59 per cent, over 20 points higher than any right-wing rival, and they remained at an average level of 51.5 per cent from then until the presidential elections (SOFRES, accessed 12 September 2007). He owed this achievement to his performance both as Interior Minister over two periods (from May 2002 to April 2004, and from June 2005 to March 2007), and as party leader from November 2004 (by contrast, his eight months as Finance Minister, from April to November 2004, made little impact). Sarkozy's hyperactive style as Interior Minister, after an election in which Chirac and the press had made a central issue of law and order, was welcome both to the Right's voters and to some of the Left's. Five months after taking office, his performance was approved not only by a massive majority on his own side (85 per cent, according to Ipsos, in October 2002) but also by a sizeable minority (36 per cent) on the Left.

What sort of party did Sarkozy leave behind when he exchanged the UMP presidency for that of France? On the face of it, the UMP was extremely powerful. It was indisputably France's biggest party; indeed, it was the *only* party in the history of the Fifth Republic to have won National Assembly majorities in two successive elections. Its membership had been more than doubled under Sarkozy; and its high vote in June would give it the lion's share of public finance for parties, entrenching it as France's wealthiest party for five years. In practice, however, the picture was more complex. French parties of government have always been pulled between a natural tendency to factionalism and the requirement for strong personal leadership dictated by the centrality of direct presidential elections under the Fifth Republic (Cole, 1993). Within the UMP after its creation in 2002, this tension was enhanced by the fact that the party inherited the Gaullist tradition of charismatic leadership and opposition to factions, while at the same time incorporating, in whole or in part, several different parties, each more or less inclined to perpetuate some form of distinct identity. As Haegel (2007b) remarks, the UMP's original statutes of November 2002 therefore included quite generous provisions for 'movements' (effectively, factions) within the party – but their implementation was put on ice the following year and never revived. What was allowed instead was, on the one hand, 'associated organizations', typically former micro-parties like the Parti Radical or the Centre National des Indépendants anxious to preserve an identity, however symbolic, and on the other, a variety of clubs representing the main ideological tendencies within the UMP: neo-liberal, Eurosceptic 'sovereignist', and centrist or 'social'. While capable of lobbying to influence the party's policy platform, none was in a statutory position to compete openly for power within the UMP on its own ideological platform. Nor was Sarkozy as UMP leader ever keen to offer opportunities to his opponents within party and government by giving factions free rein.

Nor indeed, once installed in the Élysée, did he wish to see a strong

UMP leader in his stead. There would be no new party president; Sarkozy was replaced (pending a party congress in autumn 2007) by an interim leadership consisting of Pierre Méhaignerie and Jean-Claude Gaudin (each too old to pose a significant challenge) and his personal henchman Brice Hortefeux. When Hortefeux was appointed to government days later, he was replaced by Patrick Devedjian, the Gaullist party's eternal also-ran, who was given the demeaning title of 'secretary-general delegate'. With no clear leader and no structured and active internal currents, the UMP showed every sign of suffering the characteristic fate of newly elected presidents' parties under the Fifth Republic – being put on ice until needed again. Moreover, Sarkozy had compounded this well-worn habit by his policy of 'opening' to the Left, denying his own party a part of the fruits of victory. The danger of this practice lies chiefly in the party demobilization it engenders. Every President since 1974 has suffered acute unpopularity within two years of being elected; and in each case his partly decommissioned party has been unable to mobilize effectively in his support.

Bayrou and the chimera of the centre

If the UMP represents one component of the bipolarization argument – the consolidated, broad-based, conservative party, dominating one pole of the party system – the case of Bayrou and the UDF represents another: the failed attempt to break free from bipolarity altogether. Bayrou has attempted to transform the UDF in two ways, both of which do violence to its established identity. In the first place, he has tried to change a party of notables, not primarily interested in presidential politics, into the instrument of his own presidential ambitions. Secondly, he has sought to end the UDF's traditional alignment on the Right and make of it a party of the 'true' centre. The political capital with which he embarked on this enterprise consisted in his success in maintaining an independent UDF group of 30 deputies in the 2002 Assembly, and the UDF's score of 11.9 per cent – less than 5 points behind the UMP – at the 2004 European elections. The 'founding act' of the Bayrou presidential bid (Robert, 2007: 13) was his decision to vote a censure motion against the de Villepin government in May 2006, and thus to break his party's conservative alignment of 30 years' standing.

Bayrou's presidential campaign was directed against a 'duopoly' of Right and Left held responsible for France's difficulties. The campaign was so successful that it propelled Bayrou from the rank of a minor contender with 7 per cent of voting intentions in December 2006 to that of a 'third man' with 17 per cent of voting intentions, and some prospect of reaching the top two, in February 2007. This was partly due to the behaviour of the two front-runners, as Bayrou attracted centre-Right voters worried by Sarkozy and Socialists disappointed in

Royal. But Bayrou also projected attractive personal qualities, being viewed as the least worrying, most honest and most understanding of the major candidates. Polls run in February for the second round of voting showed that Bayrou would beat either Royal or Sarkozy if only he could reach the second round. But the main characteristic of the Bayrou electorate was that it was not big enough: with 18.6 per cent of the vote, Bayrou was eliminated (see Chapter 2 for more discussion).

At this point, presidential and party strategies diverged. For Bayrou, to endorse either Sarkozy or Royal would be to overturn the central theme of his campaign, and to compromise his future bid for the presidency in 2012. He therefore backed neither, and relaunched the UDF as the Mouvement Démocrate (MoDem). But the deputies and local elected officials of the UDF could not afford to maintain this degree of independence. All 30 UDF deputies had been elected with UMP support at the second, or more frequently the first, ballot in 2002; not all had followed Bayrou in supporting the motion of censure; and over 20 of them decided, in the week after the first ballot, to endorse Sarkozy and enter the 'Nouveau Centre' structure created for those prepared to ally themselves with the UMP but not to join it.

In the votes that followed, the Bayrou electorate split into its constituent parts. The second round saw both Royal and Sarkozy backed by (roughly) 40 per cent of Bayrou voters, while 20 per cent abstained or spoilt their ballots. At the first round of the June parliamentary elections, the MoDem ran candidates in about half of France's 577 constituencies, and achieved a total score of 7.6 per cent. Only 29 per cent of Bayrou voters supported a MoDem candidate, against 45 per cent who voted for the UMP or another right-wing candidate. At the run-off, finally, among those MoDem voters (the vast majority) whose candidate had already been eliminated, a majority (55 per cent) supported a left-wing candidate, against only 28 per cent who voted for the UMP – a distribution which contributed significantly to the Left's partial second-round recovery (CSA, 2007). But by this time Bayrou's 18.6 per cent had been scattered to the four winds, and only three MoDem deputies were elected.

Bayrou was one of them, but his task in 2007 – to maintain a visible and independent political presence to support a credible run at the next presidential elections – appeared even more daunting than in 2002. The question of loyalties would again be posed to the UDF's notables in the 2008 municipal and cantonal elections: 60 per cent of the Right's larger town halls in 2007 were run by a UMP–UDF alliance, as were 30 out of the councils for the *départements* with a right-wing majority (Robert, 2007: 27). Breaking these ties was a hazardous project indeed for anyone concerned to be re-elected. The obvious danger for Bayrou was that the MoDem would end as the worst of all possible worlds – a 'party of notables' without any notables.

The parties of the Left

Sarkozy's victory was also the Left's defeat. This outcome had seemed far from inevitable a year before polling day; the deep unpopularity of President, Prime Minister and government alike in 2006, had made the Left's prospects appear most promising. If the defeat of 2007 resulted in part from proximate causes – the main left-wing candidate and her campaign – it also had deeper roots, which can be traced at least as far back as the previous double defeat of 2002.

The Socialists in disarray

For the Socialists, Lionel Jospin's weak score (16.18 per cent) at the first round of the 2002 presidential election, and above all his failure even to reach the run-off ballot, had been a profound shock. He was widely credited with a strong record as Prime Minister; he had held together a coalition including Communists, Greens and smaller left-wing parties for five years; his chief opponent was ageing and weakened by the failed dissolution of 1997. Between 1997 and 2002, the Jospin government had carried out a programme that ostentatiously placed itself to the left of both Tony Blair in the UK and Gerhard Schröder in Germany. The Jospin government carried out an ambitious, active employment policy, lowering the legal working week to 35 hours and creating 300,000 (five-year contract) jobs for young people in the public and associative sector. The Plural Left government adopted bold measures to reduce inequality, such as universal health care and tax credits for the low paid. The Socialists and their allies in office could boast a higher growth rate than most of their EU partners (3 per cent per annum) and a spectacular increase in the number of jobs created. In these circumstances, Jospin's failure provoked disbelief and disorientation among leaders and party activists.

In the inevitable post-mortem, a classic debate developed between left-wingers such as Henri Emmanuelli and modernizers like Jospin's two former Finance Ministers Dominique Strauss-Kahn and Laurent Fabius. For the former group, Jospin's weakness (with just 13 per cent of the vote among white- and blue-collar workers) showed that the PS had lost touch with these popular classes (*classes populaires*) and their concerns, even as it undertook reforms supposedly in their interests, and that their 'reconquest' should be the party's top priority. The modernizers, on the other hand, argued that even if the *classes populaires* were important, the party should not revert to the vocabulary of class struggle; that it should present itself as unashamedly reformist; and even that it should revise its whole sociological analysis of French society. Meanwhile the rank-and-file activists were showing, via debates and a questionnaire, a deep disenchantment with the party's leaders. First Secretary François Hollande concluded that the PS needed to be 'more representative', with more consultation of the membership via British-style annual conferences, internal party referendums on key topical issues, or forums open to other left-wing groups (Mandraud, 2002).

But this post-2002 ferment closed rapidly and inclusively. The Dijon congress of March 2003 did nothing to settle the key strategic issues. Organizational reform stopped halfway and the leadership was barely renewed. One reason for this failure was that strategic debate was too readily muddied by the competition for the 2007 presidential nomination opened by Jospin's withdrawal (in principle) from politics after his 2002 defeat. Laurent Fabius and Dominique Strauss-Kahn, for example, though on broadly the same side in the modernization debate, were fierce rivals as *présidentiables*. A second reason was that the Socialists were busy fighting intermediate elections – and, thanks to the government's plummeting popularity, winning them. In March 2004 the Socialists, with their left-wing allies, won control of 20 regions out of 22 in metropolitan France (a gain of 12), and of 51 *départements* out of 96 (a gain of 10); at the European elections three months later the PS lists achieved 28.9 per cent to the UMP's 16.6. The temptation, in this context, was to put off any organizational changes or strategic definitions that might compromise what appeared to be the party's excellent prospects for 2007. Thus the line of 'left-wing reformism' fixed at Dijon was reinterpreted in the light of outside events – particularly the right-wing government's reform bills.

Meanwhile the Left's apparently radiant outlook for 2007 was suddenly darkened by the referendum on the European Constitutional Treaty, announced by Chirac in July 2004 and held in May 2005 (see Chapter 4). Hollande's decision to allow an internal party referendum on the treaty backfired badly when Fabius, in a shift away from his long-standing orientation, took the head of the No camp, mobilizing a continuing anti-capitalist, anti-free-market culture within the PS, and expressing disappointment among activists both with the EU's recent evolution and with the treaty's supporters in the PS leadership. The Yes vote won among PS members, but at 59 per cent, it proved less massive than expected, and did not prevent Socialists opposed to the treaty from continuing to campaign against it. Above all, the No vote at the nationwide referendum in May 2005, particularly marked among the *classes populaires*, dealt a fatal blow to Hollande's calculations. He had failed to persuade left-wing voters to vote Yes; the internal party referendum had merely legitimated the arguments of the treaty's opponents. It was a party that had just torn itself apart that Hollande attempted, at the Le Mans congress later in 2005, to stick back together. He and the other Socialist leaders now found themselves divided on the crucial question of Europe but nevertheless resolved to agree on a single conference motion. They did so, but the resulting document, like the programme for the 2007 elections on which it was based, suffered from its overriding aim of not offending any of the party's factions.

Le Mans did, though, introduce one organizational novelty. A 20-euro PS membership was created, limited to a year, available on the Internet, and carrying the right to vote at the presidential nomination. Inspired by the UMP, this arrangement was unexpectedly successful. Total PS membership rose from 120,000 to 200,000. With Hollande out of the running, and Fabius's credibility damaged by his surprising switch from Right to the Left, this sudden arrival of new members facilitated the nomination of an outsider, Ségolène Royal. Popular in the opinion polls, untarnished by factional struggles, she appeared to offer a providential life raft for all those who sought an end to the party's internal crisis. It was a 'miracle solution' that proved illusory.

Ségolène Royal was a typical product of the Mitterrand years. Coming from a provincial, bourgeois Catholic family, she was admitted in 1978 into the Voltaire promotion of the National Administration School (ENA), the same as future partner François Hollande. Thanks to Hollande's influence, after leaving ENA Royal was introduced to President François Mitterrand. Royal served in Mitterrand's office (*cabinet*) in the Elysée palace from 1981 to 1988, and was then parachuted into a constituency in the Deux-Sèvres department, where she would be elected without interruption from 1988 to 2007. Her local political base was strengthened further in 2004, when she became president of the Poitou-Charentes region, symbolizing PS success in the regional elections. Royal first entered government in 1992 as Environment Minister. In Jospin's 1997–2002 government, Royal was a junior minister for education, then the family. Though her functions were relatively modest, she established a reputation for efficiency by addressing everyday concerns, such as extending parental leave to fathers and fighting against violence in schools.

Royal's power base was in Poitou-Charentes and in the Association des Régions de France (ARF). But she held no major office within the PS. In 2004, no one imagined that she could be the Socialists' presidential candidate for 2007; she was not even mentioned as a possible runner in a book on presidential contenders by journalist Alain Duhamel in 2004. But her victory in the 2004 regional elections in the regional fiefdom of then Premier Jean-Pierre Raffarin pushed her into the public limelight. Strategically astute, at least insofar as her own career was concerned, Royal undertook a highly personal strategy of political communication, directed notably at the feminine press, aimed at presenting herself as a modern woman, who had combined a brilliant professional life with a strong sense of family (she is the mother of four children), while remaining young-looking and seductive.

Very popular in the opinion polls, seemingly outside of manoeuvres within the party organization, Royal appeared as the ideal candidate to overcome the crisis occasioned by the defeat in the constitutional referendum of 2005, a defeat that cast doubt upon the credibility of party leader Hollande. Royal was attractive to the 40-something generation, awaiting their turn to exercise leading positions in the party. Moreover, she was a natural magnet for the other 19 Socialist regional presidents, who rallied to her support. Above all, Royal was supported by most of the new party members that joined the PS in part to support her presidential bid. She was unassimilated by the press and public opinion with the 'elephants' – Fabius, Jospin, Strauss-Kahn – who had long dominated the party.

In order to reinforce the image that she would be autonomous vis-à-vis the Socialist Party, Mme Royal and her advisers launched an interactive website – Désirs d'avenir – and an association with the same name. The website invited everybody, whether party members or not, to contribute to drawing up the candidate's presidential platform. Next, local committees of the Désirs d'avenir association were created throughout France and set about organizing 'participative debates' in support of Royal's candidacy. Though often led by Socialist activists, these committees provided a flexible structure to attract new members of the party to Royal's cause, as well as to engage with those who had left the PS. Royal was able to convince a majority within the party that she was carried by a genuine popular movement, and was not a mere product of the media and the polls.

But the miraculous solution soon proved illusory. Royal's campaign was fought on the margins of the Socialist Party, and was deeply ambivalent about the Socialist programme upon which she, as party candidate, agreed to stand. She focused upon 'values' (a just order, participatory democracy, gender equality, the value of work) that were not really those of the traditional Left. At the same time, the candidate refused to distance herself fully from the party programme or organization, giving the impression of imprecision, drift and being unprepared (see Chapter 2 for further discussion). True, Royal did make a number of genuinely innovative proposals, such as those relating to citizens' juries and the parental freedom to choose schools for their children. But the overall impression was that she had not worked out her position on the great issues of the day, such as the financing of social protection and pensions, tax, the working week and education. It was highly significant that the promised personal manifesto, based on the work of her association Désirs d'avenir, never saw the light of day. Press commentaries on her campaign focused on the difficult relationship with the PS organization, rather than with the substance of her presidential platform. Initially determined to keep the PS leaders at a distance (especially the two rivals she defeated in the PS primaries,

Fabius and Strauss-Kahn), she was forced to call upon them to engage themselves more fully in support of her candidacy. But by early February it seemed likely that she would not win the presidency and it was now the turn of those she had formerly derided to keep their distance.

The far Left and the Greens

The Socialists' defeat of 2002 was caused in part by the strong performance of the non-government Left. The two leading Trotskyite candidates – Arlette Laguiller of LO (Lutte Ouvrière) and Olivier Besancenot of the LCR (Ligue Communiste Révolutionnaire) together polled just under 10 per cent of valid votes, that is 3 million voters. The Socialists' allies in the Plural Left coalition experienced contrasting fortunes. The PCF (with 3.37 per cent, then their lowest score) were comfortably outpolled by the Greens, represented in the 2002 presidential contest by former journalist Noël Mamère (5.2 per cent). Jean-Pierre Chevènement, standing on a Eurosceptic and law and order platform, convinced 5.3 per cent of French voters. Christine Taubira, for the Left-Radicals, performed creditably with 2.3 per cent of votes. But the overall picture was one of extreme fragmentation, rendering implausible from the outset any prospect of a renewed governmental Left coalition.

  The parties of the governmental Left were in a rather similar posture in 2002 to that of the UDF and RPR in the 1980s and 1990s faced with the FN. The strength of the far Left deprived the PS, PCF, Greens, Citizens and Radicals of the prospect of resurrecting the Plural Left majority in the immediate future. The decline of the PCF provoked a hardening anti-Socialist position; to a lesser extent the same was true for the Greens. The PCF, facing stiff competition from the Trotskyites, modified its Popular Front strategy. The leader associated most closely with the Socialist alliance, Robert Hue, was forced to give way to Marie-George Buffet. Though she had been a popular Youth and Sports Minister in the Jospin government, Buffet moved the PCF a bit further away from the Union of the Left position. The PCF refused to join in two regional executives alongside the Socialists after the 2004 elections, in Nord/Pas-de-Calais and Auvergne. The Greens, also, moved closer to an autonomist position. Former Environment Minister Dominique Voynet was criticized for her failure to obtain satisfaction over nuclear energy during her period in the Jospin government, and was forced out from her position as general secretary, opening a renewed period of factional infighting and instability. Torn between multiple factions, the Greens exhausted themselves from 2002 to 2007, good results in the European and regional elections of 2004 notwithstanding. Environmental concerns were more convincingly articulated by individuals, such as Nicolas Hulot (the presenter of *Ushuaïa*, a popular television programme), than by the leadership of the Green Party itself. The autonomist strategy of the Greens was repeated even after the poor performance of Voynet in the 2007 presidential election (1.3 per cent), when the Greens rejected the PS offer to stand down in their favour in 12–14 winnable constituencies.

The referendum on the EU Constitutional Treaty strongly divided the Greens. But for the Communists, the extreme Left and the anti-globalization militants, the referendum was an unforeseen opportunity to federate the 'Left of the Left'. Throughout the campaign, past rivalries were buried as the forces of the Left of the Left converged in opposition to the EU treaty and the neo-liberal Europe they considered it represented. The campaign brought new organizations into the limelight, such as the Copernic Foundation or ATTAC, the anti-globalization movement (see Chapter 5 for further discussion). These groups were able to influence some within the PS and the Greens. Taken together, the good score of the Left of the Left in the 2002 presidential election and the 2005 referendum opened the prospect that a new radical coalition might emerge in French politics, somewhat like the Linkspartei in Germany. In the event, the various parties and movements of the 'anti-liberal' Left were unable to agree on a joint candidate and went into the 2007 presidential election as disunited as ever. The performances of the far Left and the Greens are discussed in more detail in Chapter 2.

Ségolène Royal's defeat in the second round of the 2007 presidential election was not only a personal defeat. It was a setback for the PS as a whole, a party that has proved incapable of drawing lessons from three successive defeats in the key presidential election. It was also a testament to the lasting disunity of the extreme Left and their inability to federate the forces of the Left of the Left around a single candidate or political organization. The June 2007 parliamentary election, which followed the presidential contest, proved that the PS maintained strong local roots. The PS not only improved its vote share against 2002, but also increased the number of its deputies by over 50. The 2007 legislative elections supported the hypothesis of the rebipolarization of French politics discussed above. The vast bulk of deputies now belong to the UMP or the PS, with only the PCF offering enough resistance to form a parliamentary group. For all of his 18.7 per cent in the parliamentary election, François Bayrou's MODEM returned only three deputies who were forced to sit as *non-inscrits* (independents) in the new Assembly.

It is still far too early fully to accredit the bipolarization hypothesis enunciated by Grunberg and Haegel. Bayrou's high score (18.7 per cent), the enthusiasm created among many for his new MODEM party, combined with the discredit, divisions and disorientation of the PS faced with Sarkozy's clever political tactics, leave open several possible scenarios. But the old Union of the Left is dead; it can no longer mathematically produce a majority. The 2008 municipal elections represent a key step in assessing the future evolution of the party system. At the time of writing, a number of leading Socialist mayors had declared their support for an alliance with MODEM. The PS is too weak to hope to return to power by itself. It needs new allies.

Conclusion

At the core of Grunberg and Haegel's (cautious) claim that France is heading for a two-party system is the observation that only two parties in France, the PS and the UMP, are in a position to win the presidency; to command an overall parliamentary majority, or at least a dominant position in such a majority; and to hold the post of Prime Minister (Grunberg and Haegel, 2007). This is not a 'perfect' two-party system (but such purity is rare, and certainly does not exist, for example, in the UK). Smaller parties still exist. But they are constrained, like the Radicals of Left or Right, and, increasingly, the Greens and Communists on the Left, to exist in a quasi-feudal relationship of fealty to larger partners, to mount a frontal attack on the bipolar system, or to accept marginalization in the hope of better days. Grunberg and Haegel stress, moreover, that this is a tendency rather than an accomplished state of affairs, and even that it is reversable.

There is much in the 2007 results to support this view. The level of first-ballot support of Royal and Sarkozy in April, and of the PS and the UMP in June, all testify to a bipolarity that is not merely the constrained product of the electoral system. The (possibly terminal) decline of the FN reflects, not only the deliberate strategy of its major competitor on the Right, but also the systemic strains placed on a party that chooses to remain at the margins. The failure of Bayrou's frontal assault indicates the resilience of the two-party stranglehold even against an attractive, moderate and popular candidate. At the same time Grunberg and Haegel's caution is amply justified. While Sarkozy has argued that the French will accept reforms that are clearly explained, fair and backed by an electoral mandate, his reform programme will provoke resistance and unpopularity. It is far from certain, however, that the Socialist opposition, suffering both from the short-term impact of its third consecutive presidential defeat and the longer-term difficulties of adjusting to a liberal world economic order, will be able to reap the benefits. From the perspective of 2007, indeed, France's party system appeared asymmetrical, with a weak and divided Socialist Party confronting a (provisionally) dominant

UMP. The UMP's likely future unpopularity, if not exploited by a credible mainstream opposition party, will find other forms of expression. It would be imprudent to argue that the centrifugal tendencies within France's party system, so manifest in 2002, have been permanently banished.

Chapter 4

Attitudes towards Europe in France

NICOLAS SAUGER

In voting against the European Constitutional Treaty (ECT) in May 2005, France was directly responsible for the collapse of a major European project, for the second time in European history. There was a ring of déjà-vu; the French Parliament had voted against the European Defence Community in 1954, thereby burying the project to create a single European defence force. Of course, the failure of the ECT was not only France's fault. The Dutch followed the French in a negative vote three days later against the same treaty. There have been other occasions in recent history when a European treaty has been rejected by voters, in referenda in Ireland (Treaty of Nice) and Denmark (Treaty of Maastricht) notably. In the case of Ireland and Denmark, No votes in referenda were followed by these countries renegotiating limited opt-out clauses and resubmitting the treaties to a referendum, in both cases successfully (Garry et al., 2005; Svensson, 2002). The French referendum of 29 May 2005 might now be considered as history. The 2007 presidential campaign rapidly overshadowed the failed referendum. After only a few months, the event had lost most of its salience. The rejection of the ECT had more consequences on the European scene than on the French political landscape. With Sarkozy's claimed leadership of the new 'simplified' version of the treaty, France can be regarded as having returned to the forefront of Europe and even being at the heart of European initiatives. To some extent, the rejection of the ECT is now interpreted as an accident, the result of Chirac's mediocre performances at all levels.

The 'no' to the European Constitution was not an accident, however (Sauger et al., 2007). Even if this failure was not inevitable, evidence about scepticism over European integration has been provided several times in the past two decades. The Maastricht Treaty was approved in France by a majority of only 51 per cent of the votes in the referendum of 20 September 1992. In 1999, the openly Eurosceptic list led by Charles Pasqua and Philippe de Villiers finished second at the European election (Grunberg et al., 2002). This chapter explores the

60

extent and the meaning of this Euroscepticism *à la française*. It is structured into three parts. The first part describes the basic attitudes of the
French towards Europe. Though sceptical, the majority of French do
not seem to reject Europe. Hence a first puzzle: why did France vote
against the ECT in 2005? This puzzle is solved in the second part but
leads to another puzzle: why is Europe not more important in national
politics? The third part tackles this issue.

Euroscepticism in France

Attitudes towards Europe have been widely studied (see Bréchon et al.,
1995; Eichenberg, 1998; Niedermayer and Sinnott, 1994). Thanks to
the European Commission's own tools for public opinion analysis, the
Eurobarometer surveys, we have a quite clear idea about the relationships that people have with the European Union. Eurobarometers regularly ask whether people support European integration as well as
questions about their cognitive, evaluative and affective attitudes
towards Europe and its institutions (Niedermayer and Westle, 1994).
On most of these indicators, France stands globally very close to the
European average. In 2007 (Eurobarometer 67, spring 2007), the 50
per cent of the French declaring they had a positive image of Europe
are very comparable to the average within the EU (52 per cent, from a
low 29 per cent in Finland to a high 68 per cent in Ireland). The feeling
that France's adhesion to the EU is a good thing is a bit lower than
elsewhere in Europe (52 versus 57 per cent on average) but remains
clearly ahead of the most Eurosceptical countries such as Austria (36
per cent) or Latvia (37 per cent). France has, however, a more positive
evaluation of the euro (72 per cent in favour of the euro in France, 63
per cent on average) and shows good knowledge about the number of
member states (74 per cent of the respondents in France know that
there are more than 15 member states in Europe, only 57 per cent in
the rest of Europe). In other terms, a majority supports European integration whereas a strong minority is divided into opponents of Europe
and scepticism or indifference (but not formal opposition).

France has, however, considered itself and been viewed as an exception in Europe. Whether such perceptions are rooted in reality can be
elucidated by considering the meaning of Euroscepticism and the evolution of French public opinion in relation to Europe.

Euroscepticism and 'souverainisme'

Euroscepticism is a widespread but also ambiguous concept to
describe attitudes towards Europe. Two different components of
Euroscepticism should be identified. One the one hand, Euroscepticism

refs to opposition to the logic of European integration, in the sense of the delegation of national competencies to the supranational level of the EU institutions. This is the classical definition of Euroscepticism (see for instance Gaffney, 1996; Taggart, 1998). On the other hand, European integration can also be challenged as a result of the belief that the values upon which the EU has been built are contestable. The most contentious issues at this level are the ideas of market liberalization through the restriction of state intervention in national economies (Gabel, 1998). In other words, there are two sides of Euroscepticism, one based on defence of the national community and the other on opposition to market integration (Hooghe and Marks, 2007). In France, emphasis has above all been put on the question the defence of the national community, through the notion of *souverainisme.*

Souverainisme is probably not a coherent doctrine. Nevertheless, it is the common label of a network of organizations in France, asserting together their opposition to a 'federal Europe', preferring rather a 'Europe of nations'. Forged in the 1980s, this label has been claimed mainly by organizations from the Right end of the political spectrum with leaders such as Charles Pasqua, Philippe Séguin (until the mid-1990s), Philippe de Villiers and Jean-Marie Le Pen from the National Front. There have also been some left-wing opponents of a federal Europe, notably Jean-Pierre Chevènement, a Socialist dissident and former minister in the Rocard and Jospin governments (for a general panorama of Eurosceptic organizations in France, see Rozenberg, 2007). *Souverainisme* is in fact based on the perpetuation of General de Gaulle's attitude towards Europe, and, more generally, on the ambivalent relationships between France and Europe since its foundation (for a general review, see Balme and Woll, 2005).

Right from the beginning, France has had a special relationship with Europe (Drake, 2005c; Parsons, 2003). Membership of the EU has derived from a strong sense of a lack of an alternative. European integration has been viewed as the only available means of reaching France's primary foreign policy objective, i.e. *grandeur* on the international scene and national security through the reconciliation with Germany. Both aim and means soon became rather consensual. The path of European integration was chosen because it had the fewest opponents within the Fourth Republic and appeared best designed to preserve French prestige (Parsons, 2002). With the beginning of the Fifth Republic, General de Gaulle took over this definition of Europe, adding a subtle balance between integration, under French leadership, and the sovereignty of states, themes developed in more detail in Chapter 16. In other terms, market integration has been perceived as a relatively minor issue compared to the question of delegation of national sovereignty to a supranational level. This defence of national sovereignty was illustrated by the 'empty chair' episode from 1965 to

1966, when General de Gaulle refused to allow the French government to take part in meetings of the Council of Ministers because the veto power of France was challenged by the other member states.

In 1978, Jacques Chirac, leader of the newly created RPR (Rassemblement pour la République, a right-wing party claiming de Gaulle's legacy) was probably the first leader to put Europe as a major issue for the first European elections of 1979, already framed in the terms of the sovereignty of the nation. In the famous declaration from Cochin (Chirac was in hospital after a car accident), he vehemently denounced the appropriation of France by 'the foreign party' (i.e. the second significant right-wing party, the UDF), which had sacrificed the national interest and the independence of the country in order to build a federal Europe. From that period onwards, Europe began to be regularly mobilized in elections by the major parties and also by minor ones sometimes created specifically for this purpose (Sauger, 2005). In the 1990s, France was described as one of the few party systems where European integration had a direct impact (Mair, 2000).

Souverainisme is not the only component of Euroscepticism in France, however. *Souverainisme* has been balanced by a less explicit but at least as important current of scepticism based on the rejection of capitalism and the market economy. Already in 1954, the European Defence Community was rejected by an alliance of Gaullists and Communists. Of course, Communists were opposed to Europe not only because of their opposition to a market economy but also because of the hostility of the USSR towards the unification of Europe. Throughout the Fifth Republic, the different currents of the extreme Left have opposed European integration. The 'anti-globalization' movements have now renewed the old rhetoric of anti-capitalism. This rhetoric remains rooted in a frontal opposition to the idea of economic liberalism. The ECT referendum campaign, in 2005, illustrated this by the focus put on the third part of the treaty (which mainly consolidated former treaties in a single text), on the issue of public service and more generally the social dimension of Europe. If nobody would deny that this dimension of Euroscepticism was central in 2005, the point is this is not new.

This point notwithstanding, Europe did not form part of core policy competition among and within left-wing parties until the 2000s. Isolated politicians, such as Jean-Pierre Chevènement, were the exception that proved the rule. Chevènement, several times minister under François Mitterrand's presidency, rejected the idea of supporting the ratification of the Maastricht Treaty in 1992. He finally split from the Socialist Party to build his own party (the Mouvement Républicain which has changed its name a few times since then). But Chevènement did not emphasize the market dimension of his opposition to the EU so much as the threat to national sovereignty. He preferred to import the *souverainisme* from the right to build, according his own terms, a new Republican discourse (in the French sense of the expression) going beyond the Left–Right cleavage.

There were several reasons for the internal divisions of the Socialist Party in 2005. In part, rivalries stemmed from the values of the different actors, but divisions were also related to issues of strategy and opportunity. There were genuine doubts about the substance of the ECT, though there were also doubts about the sincerity of the leaders of the 'no' side such as Fabius. In 2005, Laurent Fabius (former Prime Minister of Mitterrand) seized the opportunity offered by the debate on the ECT to transform Europe as an issue within the moderate Left. More interestingly, on both Left and Right positions on the European issue were adopted for reasons of political strategy and opportunity. The divisions of the Left in 2005 were very similar to those of the Right during the 1990s. Splitting over Europe tends to be a feature of governmental parties in opposition without strong leadership to keep divisions in check. The European dimension can be latched on to by ambitious leaders to promote their standing within the party. Thus, in 2005 the PS politician Fabius tried to exploit the gap over Europe between the party elite and the grass roots (either rank and file members or voters) to challenge the leadership of the party. Gaullist politicians Charles Pasqua and Philippe Séguin had attempted the same strategy on the Right in the 1990s.

In other words, political circumstances and opportunism could explain the importance of *souverainisme* in the 1990s at least as much as the appeal of market-led criticisms. A more systematic study of party programmes by Hans-Peter Kriesi demonstrates that France shows no exceptional pattern of Euroscepticism in Europe from the 1970s to the 1990s, either in terms of the prominence of the European issue or as regards the evaluation of Europe (Kriesi, 2007). From this point of view, only Switzerland and United Kingdom stand out.

The evolution of attitudes towards Europe

The second particularity of France within Europe deals with the evolution of attitudes of voters this time towards Europe. For a long time, the dominant thesis was that of the absence of mass attitudes towards European integration: the mass public had very little awareness of the issues at stake and no settled opinions. The European issue was regarded as lying in the domain of foreign affairs. This lack of popular interest contrasted with the elites' strong and continuous support. This period of opposition between the indifference of citizens and the commitment of the elites was called the 'permissive consensus' (Lindberg and Scheingold, 1970). Things began to change in the 1980s, following the progress of European integration (from the Single European Act of 1986 onwards) and the accompanying public debates about integration. European MPs were directly elected from the first European elections in 1979. Furthermore, the activism of the European institutions in attempting to build a European polity with European citizens fostered communication around the issue. Europe became more contentious (Franklin and Van der Eijck, 2004).

France differs from this general picture not only because the consensus among its elite has not been as solid as elsewhere (see above). Figure 4.1 depicts the evolution of one of the classical measures of support for Europe among the population from 1979 to 2007. The question asks people whether they think that France's adhesion to the EU is a good thing, a bad thing or neither good nor bad. Though basic, this question has been chosen since it has remained untouched for more than 30 years and has moreover been asked biannually. If the beginning and the end of the period are compared, what is striking is the overall impression of stability. A bit more than 50 per cent of respondents say that adhesion to Europe is a good thing in 1979, as in 2007; slightly fewer less than 30 per cent think that Europe is neither good nor bad, a remarkable stability after an interval of 30 years. The only significant evolution has been the rise by 10 percentage points of the answer 'a bad thing', from 10 to 20 per cent. If the evolution is followed more precisely, it is worth noting the rise of positive evaluations of Europe in the 1980s and then their steady decline throughout the 1990s. If data are summarized this way, an important gap exists between the general evolution in Europe and the evolution in France. Up to a certain extent, the French trends support the general pattern. Consensus about Europe developed in the 1980s and the issue became more contentious in the 1990s.

This conclusion is nuanced by a closer look at the data. The answers 'neither good nor bad' and 'don't know' (the two best indicators of loosely defined or non-attitudes) both declined during the 1980s. This decline boosted the positive evaluations of Europe, not the negative ones. This movement towards a more positive appreciation of Europe is explained by the context of the late 1980s, and is in part explicable by the experience of 'cohabitation' (the first experience of cohabitation between Mitterrand and Chirac being between 1986 and 1988). The presence of all the governing parties within the core institutions increased the general consensus about Europe, all the more since European policy was jointly led by Mitterrand and Chirac. In other terms, the initial formation of opinion about Europe crystallized in a particularly favourable context.

On the other hand, the politicization of the European issue, especially during the referendum campaign for the Maastricht Treaty in 1991–92, left a durable imprint on public opinion in a less positive

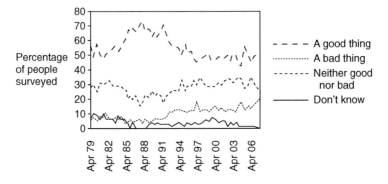

Percentage of people surveyed

- - - - A good thing
············· A bad thing
------ Neither good nor bad
——— Don't know

Source: Compilation of Eurobarometer data (EB11 (April 1979) to EB 67 (April 2007)). The Eurobarometer uses a random sampling technique with country populations of around 1000. The surveys can be found on: http://ec.europa.eu/public_opinion/archives/eb/

Figure 4.1　*Public support for France's membership in the EU (1979–2007)*

sense. The Maastricht episode divided French public opinion over Europe, rather than rallying support for European integration as in other countries (Christin and Hug, 2002). The 2005 referendum campaign, in contrast, does not seem to have had any long-standing effect on attitudes towards Europe.

In summary, Euroscepticism represents an important strand among political parties and within public opinion in France. However, Eurosceptics are not in the majority (an absolute majority supports European integration) and they are deeply divided. Changing circumstances have pushed either the *souverainiste*, or the anti-liberal dimensions of Euroscepticism to the fore. But the rejection of the ECT in 2005 by a majority of 55 per cent of the French still remains a puzzle.

The puzzle of the European Constitutional Treaty

The rejection of the ECT in France was a shock. Early polls, in 2004, had indicated that up to 75 per cent of the people were in favour of a European constitution and likely to vote for such a text (Sauger et al., 2007). If doubts existed about the possibility of victory in referendums in Denmark or the United Kingdom, the victory of the Yes was taken for granted in France (Hug and Schulz, 2005). The forecast of such an outcome can, however, be regarded as unrealistic since, on most of the indicators, the core of the Eurosceptics represents around 25 per cent of the French population. More generally, analysis of behaviour in referendums about European integration has showed the limited role of preferences over Europe in individual decisions. Three other types of variables are generally proposed to explain individual decisions and aggregate outcome in such a context. These variables are those of party identification, the general socio-economic context and evaluation of the government in office.

Because attitudes towards Europe have been considered as loosely structured, many studies have supposed that party identification represents a heuristic largely used by individual voters to make up their mind about the issue of a referendum (Franklin et al., 1994; Franklin, 2002). From this perspective, changes in support for European integration can reflect either electoral volatility or an alteration of party positions. People follow their parties' recommendations. This rule can be tested both in relation to the ECT referendum of 2005 and the referendum on the Maastricht Treaty of 1992. At the presidential election of 1988 or the European election of 1989, those who claimed they would explicitly support the ratification of the Maastricht Treaty represented not much more than 50 per cent of the votes. The extreme Left and the extreme Right performed quite well in these elections and a large sector of the electorate was 'unguided' since neither the RPR nor the ecologists took clear stances toward Maastricht. If Chirac finally said he would personally vote in favour, he also explicitly stated that this was not a public call for support. The narrow support for the Yes vote in the Maastricht referendum thus did not allow a conclusive judgement on the party identification thesis. The party variable was blurred in 1992, insofar as Chirac chose to downplay the internal importance of the issue by allowing freedom of choice within the RPR.

Party identification was also only a partial guide to explain the negative vote in the 2005 referendum. Certainly, there were a number of warning signs that might have been taken as a precursor for the eventual rejection of the ECT in 2005. The 2002 presidential elections demonstrated the importance of the protest vote on the extreme Left and the extreme Right. If, in 2002, candidates who would endorse the ECT gathered about two-thirds of the vote, this was only because a number of parties and their candidates did not officially take sides for or against Europe. But parties remained internally deeply divided. For the Socialist Party (now the principal component of the opposition) in 2005, the party's internal rules and the strategy of the leadership triggered an internal referendum on the issue. On 1 December 2004, 59 per cent of the PS members who took part in the vote (on a turnout of over 83 per cent) cast a ballot supporting the ECT. This internal referendum was organized for democratic reasons, to make the party more cohesive over this issue (one hotly debated since 2003) and to strengthen the first secretary of the PS (François Hollande) in his position. The second aim obviously failed. The party remained split after the referendum, the No supporters refusing to come back to support the party line. Despite the official party position supporting the Yes vote, the PS was perceived by a majority of the public (54 per cent in

one poll) as too internally divided to know whether the party was supporting the Yes or the No.

Beyond the case of the Socialist Party, there was much greater coherence between party identification and the EU referendum vote. More
than two-thirds of UMP supporters voted in favour of the ECT
(whereas a majority of the former RPR had voted against Maastricht).
In other terms, the importance of party identification is dependent on
the cohesion of the party. But major parties of the opposition in bipolarized systems as France are generally uncohesive when they have to
cope with such questions since they face divergent incentives. On the
one hand, their beliefs encourage them to support the progress of
European integration but, on the other, their role as opposition parties
prompts them not to act in favour of a government which has initiated
the process and will be rewarded in case of success.

The second explanation of voting decisions in referendums about
European integration refers to the general socio-economic context.
Unemployment and economic crises have been proved to be a cause of
distrust towards Europe (De Vreese, 2005). Context matters for 'objective' reasons. Weakening the social status of those exposed to market
fluctuations and economic crises raises the number of the 'net losers' of
European integration (Kriesi, 2006). Crises can also be associated with
waves of nationalism, with a sense of belonging to a national community representing a kind of compensation for difficulties in personal
economic situations. In 2005 (as in 1992 by the way), there was no
economic crisis in France. Unemployment was about 10 per cent
(which is quite high but it was over 12 per cent in 1996–97) and economic growth was steady, but at a rather low level of 2 per cent per
year. The idea of crisis in France is in fact more widespread and
anchored in the long term. Pessimism about the future is the norm, a
clear majority of people thinking that their children will have worse
living conditions than them. In this context, Europe is perceived as a
threat. Interviewed about the consequences of European integration,
78 per cent of the respondents answered in 2005 that it means more
unemployment and 69 per cent less social protection. A majority of 56
per cent also added that Europe was responsible for the rise of the
number of migrants in France and 48 per cent agreed that Europe
results in a loss of French identity and culture. In other words, the
overall level of perceived threats to living conditions reached an aston-
ishingly high level in 2005. Among these threats, social issues were the
more salient, with questions linked to the defence of the national community being more divisive. Europe was feared for its perceived consequences for social advantages and the standard of living, rather than as
a threat to the national community.

Naturally, perceiving Europe as a threat increased the likelihood of
voting no to the ECT in 2005. Yet, the evidence suggested that the fear

of enhanced market integration was more closely linked to voting no in the referendum than sovereignty-based threats to the national community. If 87 per cent of the people in the first quartile of those perceiving Europe as a social threat voted no, only 74 per cent of those in the first quartile of those perceiving Europe as a threat to national sovereignty voted no. In other words, the rejection of the ECT was the result of the conjunction of the two sides of Euroscepticism even if, once again, the balance and the salience of each of these sides can change depending on the context.

Evaluation of the government in office may also play an important role. Referendums about European elections can indeed be analysed as a certain type of 'second-order elections' (Reif and Schmitt, 1980). Without any serious consequences, these elections can be used as a means to express protest against an unpopular government. In the case of the ECT in 2005, there was no compulsion to call a referendum; the executive could have avoided being implicated in the whole process (Hug, 2002). President Chirac had a discretionary power over the decision whether to trigger a referendum or not. His stance was for many long months one of indecision. Waiting for more information on the state of public opinion, he had finally no choice in July 2004. Competition with the Left and within his own camp (both Sarkozy and Bayrou having begun to explicitly challenge him) made any other decision too costly. And the lack of popularity of the government can be viewed as a central reason for the failure of the referendum. Figures 4.2 and 4.3 chart the evolution of the popularity of the President and

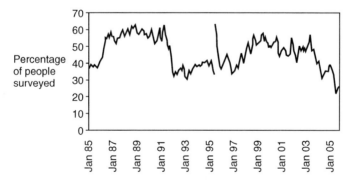

Source: Compilation of data from SOFRES-TNS surveys (http://www.tns-sofres.com). The SOFRES-TNS surveys are telephone surveys (using the CATI technique) of a nationally representative sample of 1000 individuals aged over 18, selected according to the quota method. The surveys are carried out monthly. Figure 4.2 measures the popularity of the President by asking whether people have confidence in the President or not. Figure 4.3 adapts the same question for the Prime Minister

Figure 4.2 *Popularity of the President (1985–2005)*

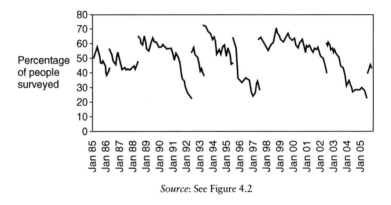

Source: See Figure 4.2

Figure 4.3   *Popularity of the Prime Minister (1985–2005)*

Prime Minister from 1985 to 2005, so that comparison between 1992 (referendum on Maastricht Treaty) and 2005 is possible. In 2005, the two heads of the executive experienced a historically high level of unpopularity. After three years of reforms, Prime Minister Jean-Pierre Raffarin's reputation was ruined (partly because of the internal rivalries within his government between Dominique de Villepin and Nicolas Sarkozy). Chirac's own popularity collapsed during spring 2005. In June, only 24 per cent of the people said they trusted Chirac as President and 22 per cent Raffarin as Prime Minister. In 1992, Mitterrand chose probably more wisely to replace the highly unpopular Edith Cresson with Pierre Bérégovoy.

These three variables – party identification, the socio-economic context and views on the incumbent government – thus each informed the referendum vote of 2005. The failed ratification of the EU Constitutional Treaty also suggested that Europe may matter for political competition. The European dimension depends upon the way in which Europe is framed, enabling people to forge their opinion. General and principled preferences over Europe can be overshadowed by more immediate issues dealing with everyday life. In 2005, the most salient frames were thus centred on the consequences of European integration for France's organization of its economic and social life. Debates about the so-called 'Bolkestein' directive are very illustrative at this level. The image of the Polish plumber (used by Fabius) was especially significant because it managed to combine the two faces of Euroscepticism: fear of unemployment because of market liberalization and, more implicitly, fear for the national community because of immigration. If this is right, the question is now why Europe disappeared as an issue very few months after the referendum.

The isolation of national politics from the European issue

Until now, Europe has never been a salient electoral issue except during European elections and referendums. If fierce debates on such issues have regularly emerged since the 1950s, no direct spillover effect has been observed on national politics. There are different general explanations for this general observation.

The first explanation of the difficult emergence of Europe as an issue in national electoral competition is the resilience of party systems. The hypothesis of cleavage freezing in Europe since the 1920s has been challenged but remains generally accepted (Lipset and Rokkan, 1967; Bartolini and Mair, 1990). The logics sustaining the argument are institutional: firstly, because party systems are bounded, no actor within the system has interest in changing the structures of the system; secondly, change is costly, at least in cognitive terms because of the need to learn the new organization of the system. Hence, party systems resist and are only likely to be challenged by fundamental crises. Europe has not achieved the status of a cleavage that can disrupt and override existing patterns of party support. This argument is generally solid, but does not explain why the environment or immigration became issues of electoral competition in the 1980s and not Europe.

The lack of salience of Europe on the national political scene can also be explained by the relationship between European issues and other dimensions of political competition. There is a strong ambivalence in the general positioning about Europe. Europe is a largely consensual issue within governing parties. This is demonstrated by the fact that treaties are often ratified by sizeable parliamentary majorities, with up to 90 per cent of MPs. Most Eurosceptic parties are de facto excluded from any parliamentary representation; the only exception has been the Communist Party since 1993. Ambivalence comes from the contradiction for governing parties between their actual proximity on the European issue and the institutional need for opposition, especially in the majoritarian context of the Fifth Republic. This helps to explain the 'neutralization' of Europe as a source of party division, because governing parties of Right or Left normally have no interest in framing Europe as a political issue.

In a similar perspective, Europe does not stand alone as a cross-cutting cleavage in national politics. It forms part of a broader change that Inglehart calls post-modernization (Inglehart, 1997). In this context, attitudes towards Europe reflect deeper attitudes about authority or libertarianism. Grunberg and Schweisguth (1997) have thus shown that Europe is part of their second dimension of French political space, that ranges from universalism to anti-universalism. In this sense, Europe contributes to the transformation of the political space in France, even if it is not particularly salient. Going further, Belot and Cautrès (2004) claim that despite the fact that Europe remains 'invisible', it contributes to redefining the whole meaning of political cleavages in France, transforming rather than replacing them. With finally quite similar conclusions, Evans (2007) shows that the limited impact of Europe on French electoral competition is explained because views about Europe simply replicate traditional delineations in social structures and mass ideological views. In other terms, the European issue is interpreted from the traditional frames of national politics.

The final explanation of the low salience of Europe is the lack of interest by most people, in a perspective very close to the 'permissive consensus' thesis. Most politicians in France do not believe Europe to be an important electoral issue. Part of the 'world of negligence' (Falkner et al., 2005), the analysis of how Europe is tackled within the French Parliament is sufficient to demonstrate the little attention paid to the issue (Grossman and Sauger, 2007). Data on public opinion largely comfort the views of French politicians. In 1995, Europe was ranked as the least important issue in a set of 13 different issues. Only 13.5 per cent of the respondents considered it as a very important issue (CEVIPOF, 1995); 57.3 per cent considered employment as an important issue. In 2002, 1.9 per cent of the voters considered Europe as the most important issue (and 8 per cent as the second or third most important issue), thus showing the stability at a very low level of salience of the issue for people at the moment of voting (source CEVIPOF, 2002). More qualitative work shows that most people would not mention the EU spontaneously and that they still do not feel Europe plays an important role in their life (Favell, 2005).

Conclusion

If France has had a special relationship with Europe, the attitudes of the French towards Europe largely conform to a European model. If their salience varies over time, the two overlying faces of Euroscepticism are present in France with a frequency comparable to the European average. As elsewhere, the European issue is both contentious at specific moments of time, when opportunities are clearly favourable, but not very salient on the whole, in terms of consequences on the national structures of electoral competition. And there is no sign, for the near future, that things will change. This is largely confirmed by the reform of electoral system for the European election (which makes it more difficult for new parties to emerge) and the recent declarations of President Sarkozy clearly in favour of avoiding any referenda on European issues (especially for future enlargements).

To conform to the European norm does not, however, feel particularly European. Only 14 per cent of the French declare themselves very attached to the EU whereas 59 per cent are very attached to their nation (Eurobarometer 67). [Even if national and European identity are not systematically in conflict or in competition (Duchesne and Frognier, 2002), the emergence of a European identity is still a long way off.] ✳

Chapter 5

Social Movements and Protest Politics

MARCOS ANCELOVICI

France is often depicted as the land of contention par excellence (Tilly, 1986). The presence of a strong centralized state and the weakness of secondary associations and other intermediate bodies between the state and society arguably push the French to take the streets to assert their rights and press their claims. This picture is only partly true. First, although it remains strong, the French state is no longer as centralized as it was during most of the twentieth century. Second, the number of secondary associations has increased significantly over the last 25 years (Barthélémy, 2000). Third, the French are prone to engage in protest and other unconventional events but primarily to address socio-economic issues. In contrast to many other West European countries, there have not been strong environmentalist and peace movements in France. Fourth, when it takes place protest is organized not only by social movements but also by traditional organizations like political parties and trade unions. It follows that grasping protest politics in France requires that we look at the role of parties and unions in public life and at the persistence of the class cleavage underlying them.

This chapter first lays out the state of protest politics in France. Second, it presents the influence of societal cleavages and the state on this politics, and discusses the relationship between social movements, on the one hand, and traditional organizations like parties and unions, on the other. Third, it traces the evolution of three social movements that have engaged in protests and marked French politics since the early 2000s: the movement against social exclusion, the anti-globalization movement and the immigrant movement. Finally, it concludes with some considerations on the impact of Sarkozy's presidency on social movements and protests in France.

The state of protest

The French regularly engage in extra-institutional or 'unconventional events' of a demonstrative, confrontational or violent nature. But do they do so more often than other West Europeans? At first glance, not really. Although some authors have questioned its methodology (for example Fillieule, 1997: 71–85), a comprehensive survey of protest events in France, Germany, the Netherlands and Switzerland between 1975 and 1989 found that Germany was the most contentious of the four, with 211,000 participants in unconventional events per million inhabitants; the Netherlands followed with 198,000, then France with 178,000 and Switzerland with 156,000 (Kriesi, 1995: 22). Similarly, membership of social movement organizations (SMOs) is particularly low: during the 1980s, 19,000 persons per million inhabitants were members of an SMO in so-called 'new' social movements like the environmentalist movement, the anti-racist movement, the gay movement, and the women's movement, compared to 49,000 in Germany and 88,000 in the Netherlands (Kriesi, 1995: 45).

However, if one takes into account the strikes that took place in this same period, then France stands out as by far the most contentious country of the four. It is relevant to include strikes because, particularly in France, they often centre on political issues, rather than immediate industrial relations issues (Kriesi, 1995: 23). Between 1975 and 1989, there were 225,000 participants in strikes per million inhabitants in France, compared to 37,000 in Germany, 23,000 in the Netherlands and 2000 in Switzerland. Thus, overall there were 403,000 participants in unconventional events per million inhabitants in France, compared to 248,000 in Germany, 221,000 in the Netherlands and 158,000 in Switzerland (Kriesi, 1995: 23).

The fact that strikes make up more than half of the total participation in unconventional events in France speaks to the nature of protest politics in this country. In France, participation in so-called 'old' social movements – the labour movement, student movement, regionalist movement or farmers' movement – represents two-thirds of the total participation in social movements, as opposed to one-third in so-called 'new' social movements. In the Netherlands and Switzerland, the proportion is exactly inverted, whereas in Germany participation in 'new' social movements makes up to three-quarters of the total participation in social movements (Kriesi, 1995: 20).

What do the French do when they protest? Among the range of possible ways of engaging in protest – petitions, demonstrations, sit-ins, occupations of buildings, festivals – the French engage overwhelmingly in street demonstrations (in 41.7 per cent of cases) and 'heavy violence', that is, 'bomb or fire attacks and other severe property damage, sabotage, physical violence against persons' (25.4 per cent of cases) (Kriesi, 1995: 50 and 268). Some authors have criticized Kriesi's coding of 'heavy violence' and pointed out that it leaves a wide gap between threats and limited property damage (what Kriesi calls 'light violence'), on the one hand, and terrorism, on the other (Fillieule, 1997: 107). Furthermore, drawing on police records in two French cities – Marseilles and Nantes – Fillieule (1997: 107) estimated that only 5 per cent of French demonstrations involved violent events. The fact, underscored by Kriesi (1995: 51), that between 1975 and 1989 74 persons died in protest events in France, compared to 59 in Germany and almost none in the Netherlands and Switzerland, could actually indicate levels of police repression rather than protesters' violence. Although there are no recent studies of the death toll of political violence in France in the 2000s, in light of the disappearance of the far-Left terrorist groups of the 1970s and early 1980s, such as Action Directe, one can contend that the use of heavy violence is less important today.

Protests and society

The morphology of French protest politics is closely intertwined with national societal cleavages. The more old cleavages are salient, the more they will absorb and frame new issues, and the more mobilization will take place along their lines. Conversely, a decline or pacification of old cleavages opens a space for new types of mobilizations that cut across traditional lines of division. Among the four old cleavages commonly identified as the most distinctive of modern Europe – centre–periphery, state–church, urban–rural and labour–capital – the labour–capital or class cleavage stands out. This is particularly the case in France, where the salience of the class cleavage leaves little room for new political identities and organizations (Kriesi, 1995).

The centre–periphery was salient in the 1970s and early 1980s, when regionalist movements demanded more autonomy from the central state. However, today these movements have almost disappeared. The state–church cleavage remains important in French politics and has not been pacified, as recurrent conflicts around the status of private Catholic schools and the importance of the issue of *laïcité* in French public debates indicate. Nonetheless, today there no longer are major national organizations built along this cleavage. Except for the Popular Republican Movement (MRP) in the Fourth Republic, there has never been a strong French Christian Democratic Party, like in Italy or Germany, and organizations like the Christian Labour Youth (Jeunesse Ouvrière Chrétienne, JOC), that trained union leaders of the French

Confederation of Christian Workers (CFTC) and the French Democratic Labour Confederation (CFDT) in the past no longer enjoy a strong public presence. The state–church cleavage retains the capacity to provoke lay–religious divisions, as underlined by the massive demonstration to defend Catholic schools against the Savary Law in 1984, but such events are exceptional. Although some religious organizations, like Emmaüs and Secours Catholique, actively support the movement against social exclusion that I will present below, this movement transcends the religious subculture and the state–church cleavage.

At first glace, the alleged predominance of the class cleavage may seem exaggerated, for there has been a boom of secondary associations in France. The number of associations created annually is an indicator of people's involvement in structures that offer an alternative to parties and unions. This number went from 12,000 in 1960 to 40,000 in 1982 and 62,000 in 1992. The highest increase took place between 1982 and 1987, when the number of secondary associations created annually grew by 30 per cent compared to 20 per cent between 1977 and 1982 and 21 per cent between 1987 and 1992 (Barthélemy, 2000: 60–1). In contrast, trade unions have declined dramatically. Today, with about 8 per cent, France has the lowest union density rate – percentage of unionized workers as a share of the total workforce – among OECD countries. Similarly, the French Communist Party (PCF), which used to be the most contentious party in French politics, has lost more than half of its members since the late 1970s and obtained less than 2 per cent in the 2007 presidential election. These numbers challenge the assumption that class remains one of the core organizing principles of collective action and protest politics in France.

Despite the changes in the associational landscape, however, trade unions still play a central – perhaps the leading role – in organizing protests. For example, in the early 1990s, trade unions organized 43 per cent of all street demonstrations taking place in Paris; in contrast, other secondary associations organized only 14 per cent of these demonstrations (Fillieule, 1997: 184). Outside Paris, the gap appears even wider. In the 1980s, at the peak of the wave of secondary associations' creation outlined by Barthélemy (2000), the proportion of street demonstrations organized by trade unions in the provinces exceeded 70 per cent (Fillieule, 1997: 182–3). In spite of the rise of secondary associations and new social movements, protest politics in France is still closely intertwined with labour politics.

Nonetheless, two qualifications are in order. First, the nature of labour involvement in protest politics has changed since the late 1970s. Although trade unions still organize an overwhelming proportion of street demonstrations, the number of strikes has declined significantly (Figure 5.1). In spite of strong waves of mobilization during the 1995

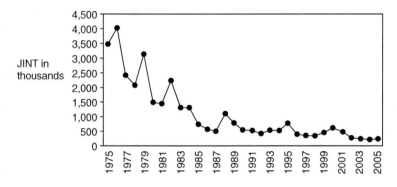

Source: DARES, French government
Note: For the 1975–95 period, the available data reflect strikes in all sectors, including public transport (i.e. SNCF, RATP, Air France). After 1995, the data no longer include public transport, a change that has deep implications for the calculation of days not worked because many strikes take place in public transport, as the autumn 2007 strikes at the SNCF and the RATP, for example, have shown

Figure 5.1   *Strikes, 1975–2005 (number of individual days not worked [JINT] because of a strike in a firm)*

strikes, the 2003 protests against pension reform, and the 2006 protests against the reform of the labour code (with the introduction of the *contrat de première embauche*, CPE), industrial conflict has to some extent been pacified in the private sector. Insofar as strikes made up more than half of the total participation in unconventional events in the 1970s and 1980s, this trend is likely to have an impact on the magnitude of protests. The nature of strikes is also changing, as they have declined steadily in the private sector while remaining relatively stable, or even increasing, in the public sector, particularly in transportation (see also Chapter 13 in this volume).

Second, even though the PCF has become politically marginal and traditional trade unions lost large segments of their membership in the 1980s, small radical parties and unions play an increasing role in protest politics. These organizations have taken advantage of the crisis of traditional parties and filled a void stemming from the shift to the centre of the largest trade unions. As mainstream organizations have become less confrontational, they have been outflanked on their left. Two organizations that embody this radical challenge are particularly active: the Revolutionary Communist League (Ligue Communiste Révolutionnaire – LCR), and the SUD (Solidarité, Unité, Démocratie) trade union. The LCR candidate, Olivier Besancenot, obtained around 4 per cent of the vote in the 2002 and 2007 presidential elections, outpolling the candidate of the PCF. SUD has also been growing.

Although in 1998, it had only 11,000 members, which was insignificant compared to the 600,000 members of the CGT and 700,000 of the CFDT at the time, in 2000 it represented about a quarter of all postal and telecommunications workers in the public sector, where it was originally founded in 1988. The LCR and SUD have actively supported small social movement organizations related to the defence of the unemployed and immigrants without official documents (the *sanspapiers*) as well as the promotion of housing rights. In so doing, they have contributed to the consolidation of mobilization networks that underpin many protest events. They have also been instrumental in the emergence of the anti-globalization movement. Competition between these new actors and old left-wing and labour organizations contributes to the enduring salience of the class cleavage in France.

Protests and the state

While the persistence of the class cleavage in France may explain the weight of trade unions in protest politics, it does not explain why the French protest in the first place. A major factor relates to the structure of incentives and constraints – what is commonly called the 'political opportunity structure' in social movement studies – that shapes and channels collective action. Simply put, the more open a state is, the more social and political actors can access the policy-making process through conventional channels, hence the less likely they are to adopt confrontational strategies and protest. Conversely, a closed state like the French one lacks institutional receptivity and fosters confrontation and protest (Tarrow, 1996).

The French state tends to operate in a closed and exclusive manner. Rather than fostering cooperation among social actors, it plays them off against one another and favours polarization and repression. This is not a political–institutional environment favourable to social movements (Kriesi, 1995). Thus, France has a lower rate of movement membership than several other West European countries but, as mentioned above, a higher rate of strikes and heavy violence. The use of radical and violent tactics is directly related to the level of state closure.

The political opportunity structure is not completely stable, however; it also has a dynamic dimension. As the access to the decision-making process opens, existing alignments crumble, elites become divided and allies obtain influential positions (Tarrow, 1996). The presence of the Left – a potential influential ally – in government thus makes a difference for the tactics of social movements, for the latter assume that left-wing parties will advance reforms that they have been advocating, while simultaneously open the policy-making process. The need to engage in protest politics decreases and activists often turn instead to lobbying.

In the 1980s, when Mitterrand was President, participation in protest politics declined. The Socialist government carried out a strategy of selective opening, abandoning the environmentalist movement that was heavily invested in anti-nuclear mobilizations while supporting the anti-racist movement to thwart the rising far-Right National Front (Kriesi, 1995: 62–3). However, the main SMO of the anti-racist movement, SOS Racisme, and particularly its leaders, Harlem Désir, Fodé Syll and Malek Boutih, were co-opted by the Socialist Party. The structure of the French polity contributed to this dynamic, insofar as it implies that social actors such as trade unions and SMOs must pressure political parties to shape public policy. The structural bias in favour of politicization puts them in a situation of relative dependence vis-à-vis parties. The recent opening strategy implemented by President Sarkozy suggests that a different dynamic might be emerging. I will return to this point in the last section of this chapter.

Social movements in the 2000s

There are many social movements, and this chapter does not claim to draw an all-inclusive picture of French protest politics. For example, it leaves out the environmentalist movement for several reasons. First, whereas in the 1970s, the French environmentalist movement mobilized large numbers of people (some protest events ranged from 60,000 to 100,000 participants), today it is primarily a localized movement driven by civic associations organized at the municipal level to stop infrastructural projects like the extension of TGV lines or the construction of tunnels (Hayes, 2002). Second, even though it emerged out the mobilizations of the 1970s, the small Green Party grants only symbolic support to these mobilizations and is essentially invested in institutional politics. Third, the most vocal leaders of the environmentalist movement, like José Bové of the Peasant Confederation (CP), have tended to focus their energies on the anti-globalization campaign, which this chapter does analyse.

The remainder of this chapter focuses on three social movements that have managed to capture the public's attention and shape political debates in the 2000s: the movement against social exclusion, the anti-globalization movement and the immigrant movement.

The movement against social exclusion

The movement against social exclusion first emerged in the early 1990s as several civic associations were created by activists and unemployed workers. Three of them stood out: Right to Housing (Droit au

Logement – DAL), Right Ahead (Droit Devant – DD!!) and Acting Together against Unemployment (Agir contre le Chômage – AC!).

DAL was created in 1990 and organized highly publicized occupations of vacant buildings with homeless families and the support of public figures (Péchu, 2002). DD!! was created in December 1994, during an occupation organized by DAL. It brought together sympathizers of anarchism and social Catholics. DD!! aims at widening the scope of the mobilization beyond housing rights to include all types of social rights. However, its main concern has been immigrants without official papers (*sans-papiers*). AC! was founded in 1993. It does not so much mobilize the unemployed as gather activists and intellectuals against unemployment. It defined itself from the beginning as a toolbox or think tank against social exclusion (Mouchard, 2002: 325–7). Its main demand has been the reduction of working time (such as the 35-hour week) as a solution to unemployment and then, after the Socialist government of Lionel Jospin introduced this reform in the late 1990s, the promotion of a minimum universal income (Mouchard, 2002: 327). These three SMOs participated in mobilizations against economic liberalization and the privatization of public services and managed to politicize conditions of precariousness and poverty. They brought the sense of urgency of humanitarian interventions into domestic politics.

These organizations remain active today. Their actions throughout the 1990s and 2000s prepared the field for the last episode of mobilizations against social exclusion that focused on housing. In summer 2006, after the police expelled homeless people camping on the temporary beaches that the Socialist mayor of Paris, Bertrand Delanoë, had installed along the Seine, a small group of people began to follow the Parisian homeless. Augustin Legrand, a 31-year-old actor, and his companions began to meet with some of Paris's 2000–5000 estimated homeless and recorded interviews on camera. Then, in October 2006 they founded an association called the Children of Don Quixote (CDQ) and posted the video interviews they had collected on the web. In early December, CDQ called the homeless to camp on the Place de la Concorde, one of Paris's busiest intersections and the main site of guillotining during the French Revolution. A couple of weeks later, it decided to move the camp to the Canal Saint-Martin, in the 10th district of Paris, where they stayed, with more than 100 tents, until April 2007. CDQ demands include: the opening of homeless shelters 24/7; a ban on expelling the homeless from these shelters unless they are offered alternative housing; the construction of temporary as well as subsidized, low-cost housing; the development of alternative forms of housing, such as boarding houses; and a legally enforceable right to housing (*droit au logement opposable*).

CDQ's campaign was a partial success. Although it did not obtain everything it demanded, it had a deep impact on public debates and politics. First, it innovated by using not only the traditional media but also the Internet to diffuse video interviews with the homeless and convince non-homeless Parisians to come and spend a couple of nights with them in the tents. Several well-known artists joined them and increased their visibility, while public opinion supported the entire initiative. Second, the 2007 presidential election brought strong media coverage and pressured candidates to express their concern over housing issues and make promises that their electoral programme did not originally include. Third, in early March 2007, right before the presidential election, the government of Dominique de Villepin passed a law increasing the possibility of making legal complaints in the name of the right to housing, as CDQ had demanded. Finally, CDQ's tactic of installing tent camps in the middle of Paris inspired other social movement organizations and is becoming an integral part of the French repertoire of collective action. For example, in early October 2007, DAL tried to install a tent camp along the Canal de l'Ourq, in northern Paris, and in front of the Ministry of Housing. In both cases, the attempt failed because of police intervention. DAL repeated the attempt on the rue de la Banque and this time the strategy paid off. On 14 December 2007, after more than a month of street camping, the government signed an agreement with three civic associations – DAL, the Comité des Sans-logis and the Comité Actions Logement – pledging to find housing for 1500 persons within a year.

The evolution of the homeless issue is symptomatic of the effects of the exclusive nature of French state that I discussed above. The homeless, a completely resource-deprived social group, had to engage in protests with the help of more well-connected individuals in order to pressure a policy-making process that was otherwise closed. The presidential election provided an opportunity to draw the attention of the French elite and advance an agenda. Now that Sarkozy has been elected and has a comfortable majority in the National Assembly, this opportunity is gone. As a result, social movement organizations are even more likely to engage in unconventional rather than conventional events. For example, in December 2007 the CDQ's spokesperson Augustin Legrand announced that his association would install homeless camps in downtown Paris anew so as to denounce the government's failure to fulfil the promises that Sarkozy made during the presidential election campaign. A first camp of 250 tents in front of the cathedral of Notre-Dame of Paris was dismantled by the police on 15 December 2007. However, in contrast to CDQ's campaign in winter 2007, this new campaign is unlikely to get massive media coverage insofar as no presidential and legislative elections are scheduled in

2008 (municipal elections, which took place in March 2008, generally do not get as much media coverage).

The anti-globalization movement

The anti-globalization movement (AGM) emerged in the late 1990s, in the wake of the mobilization against the Multilateral Agreement on Investment (MAI) that was being negotiated at the OECD and the protests against the World Trade Organization (WTO) in Seattle. However, the emergence of the anti-globalization movement was foreshadowed by earlier events. For instance, in 1989, following the example of the 1988 Berlin protests against the International Monetary Fund (IMF) and the World Bank and taking advantage of the meeting of the G7 hosted by President Mitterrand in Versailles, a counter-summit celebrated the bicentennial of the French Revolution and denounced the debt of Third World countries and global inequalities. Similarly, in 1992, the debate over the Maastricht Treaty put at the centre of public affairs the same issues that would subsequently be the basis of the globalization debate. But the real turning point that laid the ground for the rise of the AGM in France was the series of strikes of December 1995 against RPR Prime Minister Alain Juppé's plan to reform social security (Ancelovici, 2002). Led primarily by public employees and students, the strikes paralysed the country for over three weeks. The strikes enjoyed the support of wide sectors of French society, including workers in the private sector, and eventually forced the government to withdraw most of its planned reforms.

The 1995 strikes thus extended on a global scale the themes that the movement against social exclusion had introduced previously. Afterwards an increasing number of actors began to engage in 'global framing', that is, 'the use of external symbols to orient local or national claims' (Tarrow, 2005: 60). The 1995 strikes also played the role of a 'brokering' event by bringing together and consolidating the ties between a wide range of organizations critical of the liberal turn of the Socialist Party who had not really cooperated in the past. This informal ad hoc alliance came to be called the 'Left of the Left' or the 'leftist Left' (*Gauche de la gauche* or *Gauche de gauche*) by the media and activists. Most of these organizations later participated in the emergence of the anti-globalization movement in France and also the creation of its leading social movement organization, the Association for the Taxation of Financial Transactions for the Aid of Citizens (ATTAC).

Founded in 1998 by an informal alliance of civic associations (including DAL, DD!! and AC!), trade unions (minor workers' federations of big labour confederations like the CGT and CFDT but also small radical unions like SUD), and newspapers (*Le Monde diplomatique*,

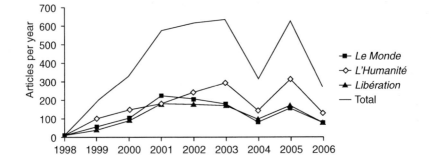

Source: *Le Monde* and *L'Humanité*, electronic archives; *Libération* data based on Biblio Branchée

Figure 5.2   *Coverage of ATTAC in leading left-wing newspapers*

Politis), ATTAC managed to get incredible media coverage until the mid 2000s (Figure 5.2). At the international level, it also played a key role in the creation of the World Social Forum (WSF) in 2001 in Porto Alegre, Brazil, and was also a central actor behind the 2003 European Social Forum (ESF) in Paris in November 2003. The WSF was founded to denounce the World Economic Forum, which meets annually in Davos, Switzerland, and is seen as one of the institutions of neo-liberal globalization, and to foster the cooperation of activists and social movements on a global scale. The success of the WSF subsequently led to the multiplication of regional and local social forums throughout the world.

Several distinctive features of ATTAC's individual and organizational membership should be underscored. First, intellectuals play a central role as active rather than just symbolic members. This is reflected in the willingness to popularize abstract and complex economic issues and in ATTAC's self-definition as 'a movement of popular education oriented towards action'. Second, there is a strong predominance of trade unions of the public sector, in particular teachers' and postal workers' unions. In contrast, workers in sectors directly challenged by globalization, such as the textile–apparel and the electronics industries, are completely absent. In this sense, there does not seem to be a relationship between joining ATTAC and defending specific economic interests. This social profile fits studies of participation in ESFs, the main annual meeting of opponents of globalization in Europe since 2002. During the 2002 ESF in Florence, Italy, 39.4 per cent of participants were white-collar employees while 22.1 per cent were professionals and 14.6 per cent teachers; 48.2 per cent worked in public services and 39.2 in private services. Finally, 34.9 per cent had at least a few years of college education. This trend is even more accentuated for the French participants: 47.6 per cent were white-collar employees and 19 per cent teachers, 53 per cent worked in public services, and 71.9 per cent had at least a few years of college education (della Porta, 2005: 13). Similarly, during the 2003 ESF in Paris, which was attended by 51,000 people, 46.1 per cent of participants worked in the public sector, as opposed to 21.6 in the private sector. Low-skilled workers (*ouvriers*) represented only 2.2 per cent of participants. Even more than in the 2002 ESF, the proportion of highly educated participants is striking: 69.2 per cent had at least a few years of college education, two-thirds of whom had a college degree (Gobille and Aysen, 2005: 107–8).

If intellectuals and trade unions are prominent within ATTAC, the political establishment is not. When ATTAC was created, not a single political party officially played a role, although some founder members were also members of political parties. Likewise, representatives of the entertainment sector and environmentalist organizations did not join ATTAC. The absence of environmentalist organizations clearly distinguishes the French anti-globalization movement from its counterparts in other Western countries and indicates once more the persistence of the class cleavage in France.

ATTAC is emblematic of the anti-globalization movement not only because of its emergence and social composition, but also because of its discourse. It defines globalization as the convergence of two trends: first, the restructuring of the mode of state intervention in the economy, the liberalization and opening of national markets, and the emergence of global – primarily financial – markets; second, the incorporation of an increasing share of human activities in the market. This perspective led ATTAC to frame a whole series of domestic issues as consequences of globalization and its agents. For instance, during the June 2003 protests against the reform of French pensions, it claimed that the World Bank and the European Commission were at the origin of this reform. Similarly, during the autumn 2005 riots in depressed French suburbs, it claimed that the living conditions of the rioters and thereby the riots themselves were a direct product of neo-liberalism and globalization. Finally, social classes are surprisingly absent from ATTAC's discourse. There is no reference to the labour movement and even old-fashioned 'capitalism' is barely mentioned. The new privileged actors are 'the' social movement and an active citizenry. Instead of presenting globalization as the result of a macro-structural process bringing about the hegemony of a transnational bourgeoisie or insisting on the class background of the alleged victims of globalization, the issues are framed in terms of citizenship, democracy, solidarity, global markets, financial institutions, and corporations. ATTAC praises civic engagement and claims to be defending not sector or class interests, but rather the common good and society as a whole against market colonization understood as a process of com-modification.

Although ATTAC experienced a crisis from 2005 to 2007, as com-peting factions struggled to control the organization (the crisis eventu-ally ended with the departure of several leading members who created a new organization called Avenir d'ATTAC), and the level of mobi-lization has apparently declined, the anti-globalization movement has had a huge impact on public debates in France. The case of the Tobin Tax is emblematic of this influence. Named after the late Nobel lau-reate and Yale economics professor James Tobin, the Tobin Tax would create a 0.05 per cent tax on foreign exchange transactions. The idea is to discourage rapid, short-term capital flows from one country to another, which can be extremely destabilizing to govern-ments and place them at the mercy of global investors. In addition, the Tobin Tax would generate about US$100 billion a year in revenue that could be given to international organizations fighting against inequality and supporting public health, education and sustainable development in developing countries. The Tobin Tax remained an arcane proposition for many years and was completely absent from the French public debate until the 1995 presidential election, when the Socialist Party included it in its programme. The PS lost the election and the Tobin Tax remained in the shadows. It was only in 1998, with the creation of ATTAC (whose name first meant Association for a Tobin Tax for the Aid of Citizens), that this issue gained some public visibility and began to be widely debated (see Figure 5.3). In September 2001, 71 per cent of the French were in favour of the implementation of the Tobin Tax.

The immigrant movement

Talking about 'an' immigrant movement is a simplification. The several immigrant social movement organizations (SMOs) that have risen and fallen over the last 30 years in France do not share a coherent set of demands or agenda. Nonetheless, they all formulate their claims in the name of the immigrant population – particularly of North African descent – and focus on issues of discrimination and citi-zenship.

The most well-known SMO of the immigrant movement is SOS-Racisme, founded in 1984 by young leaders who quickly climbed the hierarchy of the Socialist Party. SOS-Racisme emerged out of the momentum generated by the 1983 *Marche des Beurs*, the first national mass protest organized by second-generation North African immigrants. Thanks to strong public-relations tactics and close links with the Socialist Party, SOS-Racisme became the central SMO of the immigrant movement throughout the 1980s and 1990s. All other

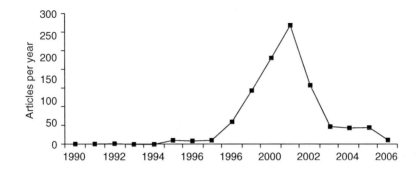

Source: *Le Monde* and *L'Humanité*, electronic archives; *Libération* data based on Biblio Branchée

Figure 5.3 *The rise of the Tobin Tax in leading left-wing newspapers*

SMOs evolving in this movement either built on SOS-Racisme or opposed it.

The Immigration and Suburbs Movement (Mouvement de l'immigration et des banlieues, MIB) is among the opponents. It was founded in 1995 by several civic associations based in poor suburbs in the wake of instances of police abuse and riots. Insofar as the main goal of the MIB is to fight against the 'double sanction' (*double peine*) that threatens criminal immigrants (i.e. prison plus deportation), its targets are the French legal system and the police. In 1999, it followed about 2000 cases of potential deportation (Siméant, 1998: 481). The MIB has a strong social base in disenfranchised suburbs and cooperates with French rap and hip-hop icons like IAM, Assassin and Stomy Budsy. This cooperative relation led to a CD against the Debré Law in 1997 – that asked French citizens hosting foreigners to report them to public authorities – and another one after the strong performance of National Front candidate Jean-Marie Le Pen in the 2002 presidential election. The MIB also favours disruptive direct action, like disturbing public meetings and TV shows as well as occupying public administration offices and political parties' headquarters. The collective identity of the MIB involves a class dimension – it stresses its social anchoring in poor suburbs – and an ethnic dimension – it presents itself as the inheritor of the Arab Workers' Movement (MTA) of the 1970s (Siméant, 1998: 482). In contrast to SOS-Racisme, whose links to the PS eventually undermined its credibility, the MIB targets both right-wing and left-wing politicians and consistently denounces the emphasis on security and repression advocated by most mainstream parties – both Left and Right – in today's French politics.

In a similar vein, the Indigenous of the Republic (Indigènes de la République) established, more than all other actors in the immigrant movement, a direct link between the postcolonial condition and the domination experienced by immigrants in France. Founded in 2005, the organization claims that today, as during the colonial era, post-colonial immigrants are depicted, seen and treated as 'indigenous', that is, as neither French nor foreign. While presenting itself as the heir to past anti-racist, anti-colonialist and anti-imperialist mobilizations, the Indigenous of the Republic blame all political parties and trade unions for neglecting this indigenous status that afflicts immigrants. Like the MIB, it is thus suspicious of institutional politics and favours alternative venues (see Chapter 6 for a fuller discussion).

In June 2007, together with organizations active in other social movements, such as, among others, SUD, DAL, Act Up and the Motivés, the MIB and the Indigenous of the Republic organized a Social Forum of Popular Neighbourhoods (SFPN). Like the World and European Social Forums, the SFPN offered a great diversity of workshops and conferences over a several-day period. A year and a half after the autumn 2005 riots that took place in the depressed French suburbs, the SFPN claimed a direct lineage with past immigrant protests and riots and tried to draw parallels between the immigrant or postcolonial question and other larger sociopolitical issues related to education, the environment and globalization.

Another organization that has recently come to play a leading role in the immigrant movement is Neither Whores Nor Submissives (Ni Putes, ni Soumises, NPNS). NPNS was founded in 2002 by Fadela Amara after the murder of a young girl of immigrant descent. Soon after, in February and March 2003, NPNS organized a successful mobilization that involved a nationwide march of women against sexism in disenfranchised suburbs (the *Marche des femmes contre les ghettos et pour l'égalité*), receiving extensive media coverage. The march finished in Paris on 8 March for Women's Day, with 30,000 protesters. NPNS's petition obtained 65,000 signatures and in 2007, NPNS had more than 40 local committees throughout France.

NPNS focuses on the condition of immigrant women in impover-ished suburbs. It denounces both the racism that immigrants face and the oppression that immigrant women experience as a result of the imposition of Muslim traditions. It demands gender equality and *laïcité* in the name of Republican ideals. Although such a message receives positive coverage in the French media and fits the Republican tradi-tion, some critics (e.g. Marteau and Tournier, 2006) have argued that NPNS is putting forward a simplistic and dangerous picture that associates Muslims with violence and other practices that threaten the Republican order.

In contrast to the MIB, which originated in the poor suburbs, it claims to represent and favours unconventional or extra-institutional tactics, NPNS is, like SOS-Racisme, close to the PS and institutional politics. Amara began her militant career in SOS-Racisme in the late 1980s and later joined the PS. Other leading members of NPNS, such as its Secretary General Mohamed Abdi and a spokesperson Loubna Méliane, also sit on top committees of the PS. That said, Fadela Amara personally participated in several institutional committees and boards: she cooperated with the Observatory on Parity and the Consultative National Commission on Human Rights (CNCDH); in December 2003, she testified before the Stasi Commission to denounce the growing influence of Islamist groups in poor suburbs; in 2005, she sat on the evaluation committee of the National Agency for Urban Regeneration (ANRU) and was appointed by the government to the High Authority of the Fight against Discrimination and for Equality (HALDE) (see Chapter 6 for fuller discussion of the HALDE). Most recently, in June 2007, Amara was appointed Secretary of State for Urban Policies in the government of François Fillon.

Future prospects

Historically, French social movements have been dependent on institutional actors like political parties to pressure the state and influence the policy-making process. The decline of the Communist Party and the crisis that the Socialist Party has been experiencing since the defeat of Jospin in 2002 have thus deprived social movements of resources and had a negative impact on their ability to shape public policy. The increasing mobilization capacity of the Communist Revolutionary League (LCR) will not replace these two parties, insofar as the LCR is very unlikely to ever have deputies elected to the National Assembly.

In such a context, some social movements have tried to access additional resources by building transnational coalitions. For example, since the mid-1990s the number of trans-European protest events, like the 1997 Euro marches, has increased. Similarly, the European Trade Union Confederation (ETUC), which represents most West European trade unions, has become more vocal and participated in several counter-summits organized with social movements. Nonetheless, as Imig and Tarrow (2001) have shown, most protest events remain subordinated to, and contained by, domestic politics. The nation state continues to be one of the crucial factors shaping and channelling collective action.

In this respect, the 'opening' strategy implemented by President Sarkozy since June 2007 could potentially be fostering a new dynamic. By appointing several well-known and symbolic figures of the Left like Fadela Amara and Martin Hirsch, the former president of Emmaüs (appointed High Commissioner to Active Solidarity), Sarkozy has implicitly suggested that social movements could access the state directly, by virtue of the status of their leaders, rather than through parties. This strategy has several consequences. First, it accentuates the personalization of protest politics and makes grass-roots and party linkages less significant. One of the symbols of this bypassing of traditional relays is Fadela Amara's decision to open a blog supposed to foster a direct debate with disenfranchised youths. Second, Sarkozy's opening strategy destabilizes the institutional Left and divides social movements. The PS has not managed to prevent some of its leaders and allies from joining the Fillon government, thereby projecting the image of a sinking ship being abandoned by its officers. Similarly, NPNS is in crisis since Amara joined the Fillon government to work under the supervision of an ultra-conservative minister, Christine Boutin, who is known for her pro-life position. In November 2007, more than 20 local committees of NPNS closed down and most of them founded a new organization called Les Insoumis-es on grounds that Amara implicitly supported Sarkozy's policies and that NPNS was controlled by Amara's special adviser and NPNS's Secretary General Mohamed Abdi. Third, Sarkozy's strategy also divides the Right, thereby perhaps opening a space for new ad hoc alliances between the most centrist elements of the ruling coalition and moderate social movement organizations.

Still, it remains to be seen whether Sarkozy's opening will go beyond symbols and rhetoric. Will Amara and Hirsch really have autonomy and leverage to advance their agenda? Will they get the necessary votes at the National Assembly to introduce new laws? Will the parliamentary majority stand by them when the moment to make a decision comes?

Although it is impossible to reach a conclusion at this stage, two broad themes are likely to change the nature of Sarkozy's opening: immigration and the reform of the French 'social model'. Sarkozy's tough positions on immigration and delinquency are well known. They did not prevent Amara and Hirsch from joining the Fillon government. Nonetheless, the new law introduced in October 2007 by the Minister of Immigration and National Identity, Brice Hortefeux, according to which certain potential immigrants should be submitted to DNA testing, triggered an intense debate. Amara firmly criticized this point on the grounds that it partook in political calculations, thereby implicitly suggesting that it aimed at attracting far-Right votes. Hirsch also criticized the law, not only with respect to the use of DNA testing but also because it prevented immigrants without official papers from having access to homeless shelters. Eventually, Hirsch prevailed, as Sarkozy declared that access to homeless shelters should be unconditional, whereas Amara was not able to convince the government to abandon DNA testing. Amara's position in the government was also weakened by her silence during the riots that shook Villiers-le-Bel in late November 2007. Several leading members of the Union for a Popular Movement (UMP), Sarkozy's party, criticized her reluctance to condemn the riots and support the police.

Thus, these two left-wing appointees, who embody Sarkozy's reaching hand not only to the Left but also to civil society, will be facing increasingly tough dilemmas. The choices they make and the results they obtain will be major signals to social movements. If they back down, they are likely to become the focus for social movement discontent. This could be Amara's fate. If they do not manage to advance their agenda, they will appear as potential allies for social movements that will pressure them to advance their cause. This scenario seems to emerge in Hirsch's case. In both cases, they will channel protests and shape the issues upon which social movement organizations will focus.

The second broad theme that will change the nature of Sarkozy's opening strategy is the reform of the French 'social model'. Although Sarkozy and Prime Minister Fillon stated that they would include social partners in the elaboration of reforms, trade unions are unlikely to easily support wide-ranging reforms. This will be a real test for Sarkozy. If he abides by his declared intention to open up the policy-making process and makes compromises, substantial reforms could perhaps be implemented. The way the reform of pensions was handled in early December 2007 suggests that a real opening and compromises will not come about without large mobilizations. If Sarkozy sticks with the media-oriented and Bonapartist style he developed when he was Minister of the Interior in Raffarin's government, he will probably reinforce the exclusive nature of the French state and thereby foster polarization and the use of unconventional and disruptive tactics. France will then resume its contentious pattern. Most protest will be carried out by divided trade unions through unconventional – and yet, paradoxically, traditional – protest events, while weak social movements will look for new institutional allies.

Chapter 6

Gender and Multiculturalism: the Politics of Difference at a Crossroads

ELÉONORE LÉPINARD

Since the end of the 1990s, the politics of difference, be it gender difference or ethnic/racial/religious difference, has witnessed dramatic changes in France. These changes are both the result of social actors' mobilization around new identities – such as blackness asserted by the Conseil Représentatif des Associations Noires (CRAN, Representative Council of Black Associations) – and of the institutional responses designed by the state to address old and new dilemmas of social inclusion. Indeed, in both policy domains of gender and multiculturalism, the crisis of the French Republican model has been increasingly obvious. As early as the mid-1990s, the parity movement asking for gender balance in political representation, called into question the doctrine of abstract universalism enshrined in the Constitution. Simultaneously, the failures of the integration model that used to define public policies towards migrants and visible minorities have become more and more patent. Although affirmative action measures still trigger heated public controversies, and although public institutions still use territory as a proxy for ethnicity in order to avoid collecting ethnic statistics, the dominant terms of the debate have shifted.

The 2005 uprisings in the *banlieues* have certainly contributed to that shift. The outburst of violence in the outskirts of Paris reminded the rest of French society that the integration model favoured by the elites and state institutions was not meeting its goals. Many observers linked the unrest in the suburbs with an ongoing crisis of political representation in France. Because the protesters belonged to groups marginalized in the political process and with no access to representational politics, the riots appeared as an expression of their permanent exclusion from the public and political space. During and after the violent uprisings, many raised the question of the representation of the sons and daughters of immigrants in the media, of how the riots could be a way to claim their share of public discourse and media attention.

From this perspective, the riots were only one in a chain of events that consistently posed the question of the representation of French populations of migrant descent. In 2003 and 2004 the last episode in the headscarf affair in public schools addressed the representation of Muslim girls in the public space and in the Republic's core institution. Then the Natives of the Republic's manifesto (*Manifeste des Indigènes de la République*), a petition launched in January 2005 to denounce public policies towards ethnic groups as an extension of French colonial politics, also asked that the sons and daughters of migrants be recognized and represented within the nation's political body. They reclaimed the identity of their fathers and mothers, former native subjects of the Republic, and confronted the ideal of Republican citizenship with its continuous discriminatory practices towards those defined as 'different'. During each of these episodes, issues of race, gender and representation were played out, drawing the contours of the crisis of the Republican politics of representation. This chapter explores to what extent these new social and political mobilizations have transformed the French Republican model based on colour blindness and abstract universalism. By looking simultaneously at gender and ethnic/racial identities, this chapter follows a twofold aim: it compares institutional and political responses that these claims have triggered, and it examines how they intersect in contemporary French politics.

First, the chapter looks at the renewal of gender politics since the parity debate, showing how the parity reform has both revealed a crisis of the French Republican model and contributed to legitimize this model. Second, it investigates the development of race relations and minority politics in France. In each case, the chapter examines the depth of the crisis of the French model, underlining how political actors and social movements are organizing to frame and address these new demands, and it scrutinizes the similarities and tensions between gender and race politics in various contexts.

From equality to parity: successful politics of (gender) difference?

Historically, the French Republic has been both officially gender blind – since women won suffrage in 1944 – and factually gender biased as it consistently promoted family values through family and work public policies (Jenson and Sineau, 1995; Mazur, 1995). Familialism and paternalism have shaped numerous public policies and promoted and legitimized the idea of different roles for women and men (Mazur, 2005). However, as early as the 1960s, the slow institutionalization of women's rights institutions promoting equality, especially equal pay, within the state bureaucracy shattered this model (Revillard, 2006). The emergence of state feminism, in conjunction with the second wave of the feminist movement, radically transformed the landscape of French public policies targeting women, and partially debunked the traditional familialist bias to promote gender equality policies. A momentum was reached at the beginning of the 1980s when Yvette Roudy became in charge of the first full Ministry for Women's Rights. After more than a decade of stagnation, the end of the 1990s witnessed a major change in many policy domains. Amy Mazur has identified the year 2000 as a turning point for gender politics in numerous domains such as abortion politics, equal pay, violence against women, harassment and gender mainstreaming (Mazur, 2005). In all these domains, Mazur shows that gender equality and feminist values have been incorporated in the official political discourse and have thus contributed to the gendering of the Republican motto.

The reform that has probably contributed the most to this recent shift is the parity reform, which entailed a revision of the Constitution adopted in 1999 and an ordinary law passed on 6 June 2000. Indeed, the parity claim, voiced by women's rights activists along with the female political elite, implied a 50 per cent gender quota for political representation and therefore directly targeted the Republican refusal of identity politics: by demanding that women be elected qua women, parity advocates thus clearly challenged the gender blindness of the Republican model, and, quite unexpectedly, won (Scott, 2005a; Lépinard, 2007a). The parity reform can therefore be scrutinized as an emblematic example of a shift in the politics of difference in France, and one must ask: to what extent has parity challenged the Republican doctrine?

The parity challenge to Republicanism

The parity claim emerged in France at the beginning of the 1990s. Several fractions of the second wave women's lib (Mouvement de Libération des Femmes, MLF) as well as female politicians and reformist women's organizations, mobilized for a constitutional reform that would guarantee, thanks to a 50 per cent quota, women's presence in political assemblies. Parity, as a concept, as a political claim and as a legal tool, has been an attempt to change previous conceptions of gender equality in order to ensure concrete equality and not just formal equality (or equal treatment). After having gained equal formal rights in almost every domain of social, economic and political life, French feminists incredulously contemplated the persistence of gender inequalities and discriminations. They sought a concept, a word and idea that could reconcile the right to equality with the facts. The concept of parity answered this necessity to go beyond equal treatment by equating gender equality with the equal co-presence of men and women in an assembly, therefore asking for a form of affirmative action in favour of women.

Hence, the parity claim's challenge to the Republican doctrine was threefold: parity entailed (1) taking into account gender identity for matters of political representation, (2) redefining equality in a substantive way, and (3) logically using gender quotas to achieve the new goal of concrete gender equality.

At the heart of the parity project lies an attempt to challenge and redefine the Republic's motto, as the subtitle of the book that launched the debate in the public sphere, *Au pouvoir citoyennes*, suggests: the authors replaced 'liberty, equality, fraternity' with 'liberty, equality, parity' (Gaspard et al., 1992). Indeed, parity contravenes both the fiction of the abstract individual and the norm of equality as equal treatment. As historian Joan Scott has indeed noted – and as the Constitutional Council has stated as early as 1982 – by definition, the Republican interpretation of citizenship 'refuses any link between belonging to a group or having an identity, and political representation. Only individuals are represented, not as social agents but as abstract figures of the universal human subject' (Scott, 1997). Beyond the domain of political representation, the abstract nature of the citizen is a fiction that sustains a formal definition of equality, and guarantees its uniform application to all citizens, without discrimination on the ground of gender, race or religious belief. It also sustains a vision of the nation as homogeneous, undivided by private or group interests.

Parity campaigners argued that the doctrine of abstract citizenship was in reality gender biased, that universal meant masculine, and that it contributed to exclude women from the political realm. Their demand in favour of women's inclusion as women, rather than as abstract individuals, thus went against the grain of the dominant Republican doctrine and asked the Republic to take into account gender difference.

The second challenge that parity posed to the Republic's doctrine regards the definition of equality. Indeed, formal equality is one of the pillars of the Republican doctrine. It is enshrined in the Constitution, especially in article 6 of the Declaration of Human and Citizen's Rights and article 1 of the Constitution of 1958. The Constitutional Council established further legal restrictions on the definition of equality in 1982 when it banned gender quotas for township elections. To become effective though, parity presupposed some form of affirmative action, some compulsory mechanisms enabling women to enter massively into the political realm to ensure equality of outcomes, that is an assembly composed of 50 per cent elected men and 50 per cent elected women. Parity activists thus devised parity as a compulsory gender quota of 50 per cent. For parity opponents, this specific legal tool embodied exactly what was wrong with the parity claim: it created categories among the citizenry and it introduced a preferential treatment for women that contravened the principle of formal equality between all citizens.

The ambivalent legitimization of the Republican doctrine

Although the parity claim challenged the Republican doctrine, the parity reform did not achieve the intended breach with the Republican model. To understand the reasons why the parity reform did not provoke the expected changes, one must go back to the complex legal and political processes that led to the 1999 revision of the Constitution 'encouraging women and men's equal access to political functions'. In its 1982 decision (Decision 82-146 DC) the Constitutional Council, in charge of reviewing laws' constitutionality, banned gender quotas for local elections. In its public statement, the council reminded the deputies who had proposed the bill that the French conception of sovereignty, as well as the Republican conception of equality, could not allow such type of positive discrimination in favour of women (although the quota was only of 25 per cent). Because this jurisprudence linked the use of affirmative action measures with principles central to the Republican regime, the debate on affirmative action measures was silenced until the parity claim emerged in the 1990s. The 1982 jurisprudence had two other direct effects on the parity campaign. First, it forced parity campaigners to ask for a revision of the Constitution that would enshrine parity in the Constitution in order to trump the Constitutional Council's rejection of affirmative action measures. Secondly, the 1982 decision opened the door for parity opponents to argue that such a principle was 'anti-Republican', anti-French or an 'American importation' (Scott, 1997). Despite the inaccuracy of the latter statement, this accusation underlined that what was at stake was also national identity. Parity campaigners were therefore facing the clear risk of being labelled un-Republican, and to subsequently see their reform buried before it was even discussed in the Parliament. This opposition to parity in the name of the Republic prompted parity campaigners to reframe their claim to make it compatible with the Republican doctrine.

Parity opponents argued that parity followed a communitarian logic, giving specific rights to specific groups and that this logic was dangerous and contradicted the Republican model, which recognizes only abstract individuals, not group members. Along this difference-blind line of reasoning, equality can be achieved only through the suppression of difference and the negation of group boundaries. Pursuing gender equality by other means, such as the implementation of positive action measures that imply the recognition of gender difference, is not only illusory but also dangerous.

In response to these arguments, and in order to convince the members of the Parliament of the necessity to revise the Constitution, parity advocates argued that parity was not contradictory with Republican principles but on the contrary was a means to truly enact them and therefore achieve a genuine democracy. This move helped them define parity as a way to achieve a common good rather than as preferential treatment for women. However, although parity could be justified as a way to perform concretely the democratic promise of equality for all, or at least for women, it still used a mechanism of positive action targeting a specific group, and therefore still considered individuals as gendered, as members of a specific group rather than abstract individuals.

To legitimize this gender-conscious approach, parity advocates argued that an exception had to be made for gender difference. They tried to convince public opinion as well as the legislator that although the distinction between men and women had been prohibited by the constitutional judges, it was not incompatible with the Republican doctrine. For many parity advocates parity meant symbolically taking into account the division of humanity between two sexes. In other words, these activists imbued gender difference with a specific status, that of being a universal difference, which could therefore be mirrored in political representation. Whereas other socially constructed differences such as race or religion would indeed, in some parity activists' opinion, divide the nation into groups, gender difference was not fraught with such a risk. Parity would not undermine national cohesion; it would rather symbolically mirror a universal and almost 'natural' difference in political representation. Parity was hence less about achieving concrete gender equality and more about perfecting democracy or perfecting the Republican ideal. In a way parity was republicanized through the public and legal debate launched in the second half of the 1990s.

However, the 1999 revision of the Constitution reveals three main flaws of the reform: first, it did not meet the expectations of parity advocates in terms of efficiency and degree of coercion over political parties to promote female candidates. Indeed, the term used in the revised article 3 of the Constitution is 'equal access', which is more akin to equality of opportunity than to equality of outcomes. Moreover, men and women's equal access to political mandates and functions is only 'encouraged' by the Constitution, rather than 'imposed', a term that activists and left-wing MPs failed to enshrine during the parliamentary discussions of the reform. The implementation of the parity laws, with poor results for the parliamentary level, has proved parity activists right. With only 12.3 per cent of women elected at the National Assembly in 2002, and 18.5 per cent in 2005, the financial mechanisms to encourage political parties to ensure gender balance within their pool of candidates are a failure – especially on the right of the political spectrum. Second, the reform restricted the use of gender quotas to the political domain so that affirmative action measures for women in hiring, promotion, etc. were not included (contrary to what the Conseil d'État had suggested when reviewing the proposed bill). Nevertheless, following the parity reform, some progressive pieces of legislation were voted, either to amend and strengthen the parity provisions in the political realm (the 31 January 2007 law extending parity provisions to city council executive boards), or to deepen equal pay legislation and increase women's representation in labour relations institutions (the 23 March 2006 law on equal pay).

Third, the parity reform restricted the use of affirmative action devices in politics to gender. Indeed, arguing that gender was a difference 'different from other differences' was clearly a move to distinguish gender equality issues from racial/ethnic equality ones. This move was necessitated by the social, legal, political and ideological context parity advocates faced at that time, but the majority of parity campaigners also considered it as an acceptable concession to make. Women were therefore granted advantages from affirmative action measures that other politically excluded categories could not claim because their difference was not 'different', i.e. 'universal'.

Thus, the parity reform led to both a break with the traditional legal understanding of equality and therefore with the Republican model, and, paradoxically enough, to its relegitimization. Indeed, parity activists insisted upon the fact that parity was neither a quota nor a type of affirmative action policy, because gender difference was universal and unique. This argument, while it presented parity as compatible with the Republican doctrine, also legitimized the Republican stance against quotas for racial/ethnic groups. Parity advocates challenged the Republican legal doctrine, but their claim was finally incorporated in the Republican hegemony, as an exception that shall not be extended further to other groups (Lépinard, 2007b). With respect to the politics of difference, parity could be compared to a half-open door with a sign saying 'women only'.

Times are changing? Conflicting developments in multiculturalist politics

Women won a partial recognition of gender difference, and some new tools to combat gender discrimination in the political realm. But what about other minority groups? Before examining the recent evolution of the politics of ethnic, racial and religious difference, it is critical to assess the relevance of the term 'multiculturalism' to ethnic, racial or religious group-based policies in the French context. Indeed, French political elites have long refused the multiculturalist model, and officially contrasted the ideal of integration to the British/American model of multiculturalism](on the French assimilationist model see Brubaker, 1992 and Favell, 1998).[In their view, multiculturalism is based on communities rather than individuals, and emphasizes religious and cultural differences instead of fostering the acculturation of migrants and their descendants] In its 1991 report, the Haut Conseil à l'Intégration (HCI, High Council for Integration) – an institution in charge of defining policy guidelines for the integration of immigrants and their descendants – stated that the French model was based on the idea that the Republic cannot be divided into communities. It contrasted this philosophy with the recognition of ethnic communities that underpins British and Dutch integration policies (Hargreaves, 2004). However, as a multicultural and postcolonial nation, France has had no choice but to develop policies targeting ethnic minority groups.

[handwritten margin note: Ironic as they treaty Roma by group/community]

It is useful here to distinguish between two definitions of multiculturalism. According to the first one, multiculturalism is a philosophical and political doctrine that delineates the conditions for social inclusion of minorities. The second definition designates multicultural policies, that is to say political responses to the reality of ethnocultural and religious diversity that characterizes postcolonial states and former immigration states such as France. If France still does not embrace multiculturalism as its model for race relations and minority politics (Bleich, 2003), it nevertheless implements policies addressing the multicultural and multi-denominational character of its society. There is therefore a politics of multiculturalism in France insofar as the state implements policies aimed at the social inclusion of racial and ethnocultural minorities. The question this section examines is to what extent the French politics of multiculturalism is at odds with multiculturalism as a model for race relations.

Recent multiculturalist policies have targeted four main domains: the politics of memory vis-à-vis France's colonial past and slavery, the visibility and public acknowledgement of a 'race issue', affirmative action policies based on race/ethnicity and the politics of the French government towards Islam. For each domain, both governmental policies and social mobilization have evolved in new directions since the end of the 1990s. In the light of these developments is the French state still pursuing a colour-blind policy that poses assimilation as the only legitimate goal and multiculturalism as alien to the French model?

Slavery and colonialism: reluctantly revisiting an uneasy past

The French state has slowly agreed to put under scrutiny its colonial past through various declarations, laws and symbolic political decisions. On 21 May 2001, the National Assembly passed a law, called the Taubira Law after the deputy from French Guiana who proposed it, to recognize that the slave trade that France took part in was a crime against humanity. A few years later, responding to increasing pressure from associations, President Chirac encouraged the Parliament to inaugurate a national day celebrating the abolition of the slave trade and slavery, commemorated for the first time on 10 May 2006. This emerging official politics of memory was completed by the 5 January 2004 law creating the Comité pour la Mémoire de l'Esclavage (Committee for the Memory of Slavery). The committee is in charge of writing an annual report for the government considering the creation of possible *lieux de mémoire* of the slave trade. It can also propose initiatives to increase public awareness on this issue, as well as possible amendments to history textbooks used for high-school education. The title of the committee itself is a sign that times are changing in France. Indeed, the focus on slavery and the slave trade as events to be commemorated and etched on national memory shifts the attention away from the more traditional celebration of the abolition of slavery, that Republican institutions used to stress as a sign that the Republic did fulfil its promise of equality for all, and rather promotes a plural memory of these historical events.

However, signals sent by the government and the President remained ambivalent, as illustrated by the controversy over the French presence in the colonies. Indeed, on 23 February 2005 the right-wing majority at the National Assembly proposed and passed a bill mentioning the 'positive role' played by the French presence in the colonies overseas. A heated debate followed that forced a reluctant President to ask his Prime Minister to abrogate the contested article of the law with a governmental order executed on 16 February 2006. This shift in the presidency's attitude is only one of many recent examples of ambivalent policy-making in the domain of multiculturalist politics.

Another landmark that involves history, national memory and the colonial past is the creation of a Cité Nationale de l'Histoire de l'Immigration (National Museum of the History of Immigration) which opened its doors to the public on 10 October 2007. In 2001, Jospin's government launched this ambitious project of a site that would retrace the history of immigration waves and immigrant lives in France, as well as offer a perspective on the contemporary evolution of immigrants' presence. The project's development illustrates the ambiguities and paradoxes of the French government's attitudes towards immigrants' integration and the ways in which it has changed national identity. Indeed, the Cité, as defined by Prime Minister Jean-Pierre Raffarin, aimed at recapturing the place of immigration in the nation-building process, by showing that 'their history' is also 'our history'. This framing, however, operates a double 'movement of inclusion/exclusion' (Jelen, 2005). Whereas this sentence attempts to show the inclusion of previously marginalized individual and collective histories and memories in the national mainstream culture and history, it paradoxically emphasizes the divide between 'them' and 'us' rather than illuminating how both are interrelated (Jelen, 2005). Moreover, the many complications and criticisms that the project faced, as well as the delay in the opening of the Cité, indicate the difficulties that arise when official policies began to go against the grain of the traditional assimilationist model, without ever truly and publicly acknowledging their departure from it. Indeed, the site chosen for the Cité raised several criticisms. The Palais de la Porte Dorée is an edifice that remained from the 1931 International Colonial Exhibition in Paris which was subsequently transformed into the Museum of Overseas Territories; then, after decolonization, into the Museum of African and Oceanic Arts. How will visitors interpret the frescoes and sculptures that decorate the walls of the edifice and represent 'natives' in orientalist and colonialist ways (Jelen, 2005)? How will the focus on various waves of immigration deal with colonialism, populations from the Caribbean who are not immigrants but most of the time are treated as such? How will the focus on immigration challenge the dichotomy between 'them' and 'us'? These questions will remain until the Cité opens its doors to the public.

Another episode in the Cité's history also reveals current ambivalent attitudes. When President Nicolas Sarkozy announced the creation of a Ministry in charge of Immigration and National Identity, eight eminent scholars who were members of the scientific committee of the Cité resigned on 18 May 2007 from their position to protest and condemn the representation of immigration as alien to national identity implied by the naming of this new ministry. They underlined the fact that the purpose of the Cité was precisely to counter such a narrow and chauvinistic vision of France's nation-building process.

In each case examined here, the government or the President has reacted under the pressure of newly organized constituencies. Indeed, if times are changing with respect to multiculturalist policies, the new orientations taken are often responses to pressures from social movements. The commemoration of slavery followed the active and unprecedented mobilization of French citizens from the overseas *départements* (DOM), that is the French Caribbean islands, Guiana and Réunion island. On 23 May 1998, to commemorate the 150th anniversary of the abolition of slavery, more than 40,000 of them demonstrated in Paris (Vergès, 2006). The creation of the Cité is also the by-product of grass-roots mobilizations in former slave-trade cities such as Nantes and Bordeaux, as well as of the long-lasting mobilization of scholars to legitimize the history of immigration and colonialism within French academia and vis-à-vis governmental institutions.

Finally, two other mobilizations have dramatically boosted the visibility of the colonial past and its significance in contemporary politics.

The first is the Mouvement des Indigènes de la République (the Republic's Natives Movement), launched with a manifesto and a petition on 16 January 2005 by several organizations of left-leaning French Arabs and French Africans. They denounced the lack of official commemoration and condemnation of France's colonial past, and argued that this oblivious national memory has paved the way for postcolonial policies that treat individuals from migrant descent as second-class citizens, permanent aliens never fully recognized as Frenchmen and consistently discriminated against, especially on the job market. The other event that put the issue of France's colonial past at the forefront of the news was the uprisings in the *banlieues*, the suburbs on the outskirts of Paris, and to some extent Lyon, in November 2005. The unrest was triggered by a chain of events including then Minister of Interior Affairs Nicolas Sarkozy's declaration in Argenteuil on 26 October 2005 calling the youth living in the suburbs 'racailles' (scum), and a police chase that ended up with the death of two young men of migrant descent in Clichy-sous-Bois on 27 October 2005. The violent insurgency lasted for a month with hundreds of cars being burnt each night as signs of protest. Both events, although one took the more traditional form of a contentious social movement while the uprisings did not lead to formal political organization, have largely contributed to shift the terms of the debate on postcolonialism, ethnicity and multiculturalism in France.

Integration and citizenship: making race visible

The new Movement of the Natives of the Republic is clearly organizing around the issue of colonialism and postcoloniality to point out the continuity between the Republic's action under colonial rule and in contemporary France, especially in the suburbs. However, woven into this new political fabric is also the issue of race relations. Indeed, in colonial times, the Republic's laws and actions followed a racial logic and contributed to racialize Arab populations in the colonies. Hence, reclaiming the status of a native from the colonies is part of an effort to combine analyses of colonialism and racism to understand the political exclusion as well as the social and economic marginalization suffered by large segments of the French population. This new analytical lens attempts to break away from explanations focusing only on class or urban problems. The Natives of the Republic therefore recast in a new way the issue of racism towards French Arabs, after two decades of silence on this issue. Indeed, only in 1983 did French Arabs organize against racism following racial lines, rather than a universal rhetoric, during the *Marche des Beurs*.

At the same time, another new social movement has organized around blackness. This first attempt to promote the visibility of black

French people broke with traditional patterns of mobilization. Indeed, ethnic group associations, for example the association of French citizens from the Caribbean living in metropolitan France, traditionally view themselves as bounded by culture rather than race or ethnicity (Beriss, 2004), and therefore organize along lines of nationality or geography (various DOM) rather than colour. Hence, the founding of the Conseil Représentatif des Associations Noires (Representative Council of Black Associations – CRAN) on 23 November 2005 clearly shows a sea change. CRAN openly promotes blackness as a common denominator and a platform for political action demanding visibility, representation and policies to put an end to systemic racial discrimination. Several books, such as *Nous les Noirs de France* written by CRAN's president, were published, giving visibility to the specific experience of being a black French citizen. When the first government of Nicolas Sarkozy's presidency was formed in May 2007, CRAN lobbied its members on the grounds that no there was not a single member who was black. When François Fillon reshuffled his team after the legislative elections, it answered CRAN's request by nominating Rama Yade as secretary of state for foreign affairs in charge of human rights. CRAN also sponsored a study on black candidates for the 2007 legislative elections in order to demonstrate their under-representation in the political sphere. Finally, CRAN also supports the idea of ethnic statistics, a contested one so far in France, in order to count black French and to measure the discrimination they face, for example in employment.

Hence, the idea of organizing along colour lines has emerged and taken root in the social landscape. Are these new mobilizations the sign that the French model of citizenship based on assimilation and integration is finally giving way to another, more multicultural one in which race can finally be made visible?

During the 1990s, the assimilationist model of citizenship was successively challenged and reinforced (Guiraudon, 2005). Whereas integration into French society demanded that migrants and their offspring assimilate into the mainstream and progressively erase their differences – be they cultural, social or religious – so as to become truly French, the failures of this model became more and more patent by the mid-1990s. Research on migrants and their descendants showed that the official rhetoric of colour blindness was hiding the reality of pervasive racial and ethnic discrimination. As Virginie Guiraudon has suggested, the outcome of the process of integration officially promoted by the state institutions was the acquisition of French citizenship (Guiraudon, 2005). Quite symbolically, the institution in charge of immigration politics founded in 1991, the HCI, had the word *intégration* in its name. Once made a French citizen, the foreigner could assimilate into the dominant mould, and therefore become invisible. However, commitment to equal treatment on the part of the state contradicts to some extent the initial idea that it is each individual's responsibility to integrate within the wider society.

In the second half of the 1990s, the model for immigration policies began to evolve and to depart from the discourse on integration. Several studies by demographer Michèle Tribalat launched the debate on 'integration' as they offered a first estimate of the population in question, that is immigrant residents and French citizens with a parent or grandparent who was an immigrant, of 13.5 million individuals, that is between one-quarter and one-third of the overall population. In 1997, the drafting of European Union's Amsterdam Treaty, which includes antidiscrimination provisions in several areas including race and ethnicity, created a political awareness among the Jospin government that another model for immigration policies and race relations existed. Moreover, since the treaty came into force in 1999, antidiscrimination, immigration and asylum policies are competences of the EU. This new impetus at the European level had some consequences in the French context. In 1998, for the first time the HCI focused its annual report on the issue of discrimination towards immigrants and their descendants rather than integration. Martine Aubry, then Minister for Social Affairs, turned the immigration policy upside down by focusing on antidiscrimination. During the negotiations on EU directives on antidiscrimination in 2000 (2000/43 and 2000/78), France was unexpectedly at the forefront of the battle for stronger provisions (Geddes and Guiraudon, 2004). At the national level, these new reflections on antidiscrimination led to the creation of the Groupe d'Étude et de Lutte contre les Discriminations (GELD) and the implementation of a hotline for victims of discrimination 'Dial 114'.

However, the new headway made was only partial (Hargreaves, 2004). GELD's first meeting was postponed for a long time because of internal resistance in the bureaucracy, and as soon as the right-wing party UMP won the elections in 2002, the whole dynamic was called into question. The assimilationist model resurfaced in the HCI's 2004 report, through the *contrat d'intégration*, an integration contract that every immigrant should sign upon entering the territory. Nevertheless, GELD's activities led to several studies demonstrating the pervasiveness of discrimination, for example in the domain of access to housing, and paved the way for the creation, under EU pressure, of the Haute Autorité de Lutte contre les Discriminations et pour l'Égalité (HALDE) in 2004. HALDE replaced GELD, and it enjoys extended judicial powers to combat discrimination. It can fine firms that do not comply with various new pieces of French antidiscrimination legislation – passed on 16 November 2001 in order to make national law conform with the EU's 2000 directives. Anybody can appeal to HALDE and this openness offers a new route for plaintiffs to contest discrimination based on the six criteria covered by the 2000 directives: handicap, age, religion, beliefs, sexual orientation and race or ethnic origin. HALDE also gives recommendations, especially to governmental agencies or bureaucracies that might inadvertently issue rules or decisions that do not comply with antidiscrimination provisions. Finally, HALDE works with firms to encourage fair processes in recruitment and advancement, and publicly promotes antidiscrimination and equality through advertising campaigns to inform and encourage victims of discrimination to press charges. In 2006, almost 31,000 people called HALDE to ask for information or to complain of discriminatory treatment. HALDE registered 4058 claims, of which 338 led to formal complaint procedures – processed by HALDE itself or by the courts. On 31 March 2006, the law on equal opportunities enlarged HALDE's judicial powers and legalized testing procedures to prove discriminatory practices, for example in hiring.

Diversity, affirmative action measures and ethnic monitoring: partial headway

How have these changes in policy orientation and social mobilization been translated into concrete public policies? Here too, headway has been only partial: initiatives by higher education institutions or firms are dismantling some parts of the old model, while resistances and taboos limit these changes. Two sites of contention and change can illuminate this complex evolution: the issue of diversity in firms and education, and the debate over ethnic statistics.

Both major firms' human resources teams and higher education elite institutions have embraced the notion of diversity as a way to promote the inclusion of members from ethnic groups and antidiscrimination practices. Following governmental incentives and propositions from think tanks such as the Institut Montaigne and Capdiv (an association promoting diversity and closely linked to CRAN), firms have become more and more aware of the burning issue of employment discrimination. The *Charte de la diversité*, a charter for diversity signed by more than 1500 firms in March 2007, exemplifies this shift in business practices. The charter is not only a way to comply with new antidiscrimination legislation but also a tool to increase awareness on the issue. In higher education, the Institut d'Études Politiques de Paris (Sciences-Po Paris), a prominent private – but also state-funded – elite school, has engaged in a programme to increase the diversity of its student body. This rapidly growing enthusiasm for the notion of diversity, and the way it is changing recruitment practices in firms and schools, shows that the issue of antidiscrimination is finally shaping social practices. However, the path taken to reach this goal illuminates the resistance that affirmative action policies still face in France.

For example, rather than using race or ethnicity as criteria to be taken into account in order to increase diversity among students, Sciences-Po used a territorial criterion (Sabbagh, 2004). Sciences-Po built partnerships with high schools in deprived suburbs and located in *zones d'éducation prioritaires* – the 'priority education zones' first created in 1981 to allocate more funding to schools situated in deprived neighbourhoods. These partnerships enable students from these high schools to apply to Sciences-Po through a separate channel with specific exams. These exams were designed to evaluate skills rather than value the elitist knowledge, possessed mostly by children from upper classes, which is still at the core of the regular competition to enter this school. Why did Sciences-Po use territory over ethnicity or colour? The ban on the use of racial/ethnic categories for statistical monitoring or policy purposes is one of the cornerstones of the colour-blind model that remains in the new landscape of the French politics of difference.

Indeed, one of the main domains that has not been challenged by the recent policy changes is the restriction on ethnic monitoring and racial/ethnic census of the population. This restriction was first enshrined in a 1978 law on freedom and computing technologies, declaring that ethnicity and race are 'sensitive' data categories and should therefore be submitted to the highest scrutiny from the Commission Nationale de l'Informatique et des Libertés (CNIL – the National Commission on Freedom and Computing Technologies). The debate on the usefulness of these restrictions on data gathering was revived during the 1999 national census. The controversy opposed demographers who wanted to maintain nationality as a proxy for race and ethnicity in the census, in order to respect the CNIL's ban on racial and ethnic categories, and those who wanted to introduce new questions in the survey to better measure ethnic groups' presence in France. The former accused the latter of racializing groups, fostering ethnic communities and dividing the nation, whereas the latter remarked that the ban on ethnic statistics made it impossible to actually measure, and therefore combat, racial and ethnic discrimination. The debate continues today among demographers and policy-makers, while the CNIL's policy remains the same. Despite the fact that EU legislation authorizes ethnic monitoring, the 2007 decision of the Constitutional Council reaffirmed the very strict limits within which ethnic data can be collected and monitored.

The ban on racial and ethnic data gathering has had two interrelated consequences. First, it prevents the implementation of affirmative action policies based on ethnicity or race. Indeed, the French political elite has consistently refused to design and implement affirmative action policies based on colour and erroneously called 'positive discrimination' measures. Following a colour-blind logic, they argue that the Republic cannot use a prohibited criterion such as ethnicity or race to discriminate between individuals, even when the aim is to reach a fairer representation of members from minorities or to ensure equality of outcomes. The use of a proxy is therefore the only remaining possibility for organizations and institutions wanting to implement affirmative action policies.

However, in spite of its use of a proxy, Sciences-Po's programme was still scrutinized by the Constitutional Council in 2001. The council imposed restrictions on affirmative action practices, stating that the evaluation of candidates should remain individualized. This restriction aimed at banning the use of quotas or quantitative targets to be reached during the selection process. The programme was also challenged before the Paris Administrative Appeal Court of Justice by the right-wing student union, UNI, in 2003. The support of then Minister of Education Jack Lang helped Sciences-Po win its case before the court and its diversity programme is still in place. However, the court also limited what Sciences-Po was allowed to do. Since then, several elite schools in engineering and business, such as Polytechnique and ESSEC, have developed their own outreach programmes to increase social and ethnic diversity among their students. However, despite the multiplication of private initiatives among higher education schools, the official ban on affirmative action or ethnic monitoring remains. Twice, in May 2003 and June 2005, while Minister for Domestic Affairs, Nicolas Sarkozy called for affirmative action policies terming them an 'urgent necessity'. His position was widely criticized in his own political party, as being at odds with the Republican tradition of colour-blindness. Legal restrictions and institutional resistance from the state apparatus and the political elite have not given way yet, and what Sarkozy's take will be on this issue as President of the Republic is a matter of conjecture.

In terms of policy-making, the second consequence of the ban on ethnic monitoring is to prevent the elaboration of consistent and effective policies to fight against discrimination. Indeed, whereas the transposition of the 2000 EU directives introduced the notion of indirect discrimination into French law, the absence of ethnic monitoring makes it very hard to actually track and measure indirect discrimination. Indeed, indirect discrimination happens when the use of apparently neutral criteria (such as size or language proficiency) by an employer leads to systemic discrimination against one group (such as women or foreigners). To prove indirect discrimination based on race or ethnicity, one must therefore show a systemic bias in numbers between ethnic groups. The ban on ethnic monitoring makes such proof unavailable in the French context, and therefore weakens the new legal tools designed to combat ethnic discrimination (Simon and Stavo-Debauge, 2004).

There are no religious or race statistics in France — only estimated

French policies vis-à-vis affirmative action and diversity are charac-terized by inconsistent stances and half-measures (Hargreaves, 2004). Changes in one direction often meet resistance leading to inconsistent policy-making. A typical example is the nomination of Louis Schweitzer, former CEO of the automobile company Renault and a strong opponent of ethnic monitoring, as the president of HALDE by President Chirac in 2004. Similarly, Chirac named Bladine Kriegel, a philosopher committed to the traditional vision of Republican integra-tion, as head of the HCI. Thus, political willingness to respond to the claims of new social movements is often counterbalanced by bureau-cratic blockage or resistance from key institutions such as the Constitutional Council.

Religion: the survival of a French exception?

If multicultural politics has changed in France since the mid-1990s, one policy domain remains untouched by these evolutions. Despite the recent developments in antidiscrimination law from European institu-tions, one area of discrimination remains a site of contention, where the state maintains its prerogatives vis-à-vis European incentives and directives. That site is religion. Indeed, religion, and in particular Islam, has been treated along different lines than immigration, integration and discrimination on racial or ethnic grounds. Through the 1990s, the French state recast its official relations with Islamic authorities. The political will to organize and formalize the relationships between the state and the Islamic religious hierarchies was first expressed in 1998 by Jean-Pierre Chevènement, Minister of Domestic Affairs in Lionel Jospin's government. It led to the creation of the Conseil Français du Culte Musulman (French Council for the Muslim Cult) in April 2003 while Sarkozy was in charge of the Ministry of Domestic Affairs and Cults. Despite the difficulties that the creation of the CFCM faced, the initiative was saluted as a mark of the highest political authorities' recognition of Islam as France's second religion, as well as the need to treat Islam fairly with respect to other religions. Indeed, before the offi-cializing of state–Islam relations, demands from Muslim communities to build mosques or ensure the production of halal meat were primarily dealt with by local authorities, and thus received diverse and sometimes arbitrary responses. With a new institution, aiming to represent the diversity of Islam in France (in terms of religious practice and nation-ality), the relationships with political authority are therefore being normalized.

However, while the government promoted the normalization of state–Islam relations, it proposed a law banning the wearing of Muslim headscarves in public schools (for an analysis of the chain of events that led to the headscarf affair, see Scott, 2005b). The 2003–4 affair was the third public headscarf affair to emerge in France. In 1989, the Conseil d'État ruled against the expulsion from their high school of two Muslim girls for wearing headscarves. In 1995, when the then Minister of Education François Bayrou issued a governmental directive trying to support and even promote the expulsion of Muslim girls from high schools if they wore their headscarves, the Conseil d'État again reversed his decision. When the affair resurfaced in 2003, the political situation had changed and, under the joint pressure of Minister of the Interior Sarkozy and President Chirac, a commission presided by Bernard Stasi – then Ombudsman of the Republic – was entrusted with proposing recommendations for the drafting of a law that would preserve the Republican principle of *laïcité* in schools. As Sophie Duchesne has noted, schools in France have always been the main battlefield for state/church politics (Duchesne, 2005). During this new episode, secularism was reinterpreted and enshrined in the 15 March 2004 law as the banning of religious signs from schools, a definition quite at odds with previous historical understanding of *laïcité*, or with contemporary commitments to 'diversity'.

Nevertheless, it is important to underline that some recent European jurisprudence has backed up the French legal decision. Indeed, the European Court of Human Rights has substantiated the idea that in matters of religion state sovereignty must prevail and therefore human rights claims made in the name of the European Convention on Human Rights article 14 are not receivable. In its decision *Leyla Sahin* v. *Turkey* the ECHR ruled that the Turkish state had the right to forbid the wearing of Muslim headscarves in public universities. The Stasi Commission was aware of inclination of the ECHR and knew that the ban on religious signs in public schools in France would not meet with any resistance from the European judges. In matters of religion, European institutions appear much more timid than with gender equality or racial discrimination issues. This retreat gives more latitude to national governments to design their public policies, and reveals the lack of articulation between antidiscrimination/affirmative action policies and multiculturalist policies, at least in the French context. In the report the Stasi Commission submitted to President Chirac, the members of the commission explored legal issues that could make the ban on headscarves illegal or unconstitutional. However, they never suggested that the ban could constitute discrimination based on religion.

The transposition of EU directives 2000/43 and 2000/78 has nevertheless introduced new contradictions in the Republican model, and therefore maybe offers some new sites of action and contention. For example, following the headscarf affair, some school authorities barred Muslim mothers from accompanying children during school activities on the grounds that they were wearing headscarves. Several mothers lodged complaints with HALDE alleging discrimination on the grounds of religious belief and HALDE took their side in its 2007 ruling. Here the antidiscrimination provisions adopted by the EU could have a direct impact on what type of claims French residents and citizens can make and on how they can try to seek remedies.

Conclusion: similarities and tensions

To conclude, recent developments in the politics of difference in France reveal two similarities between gender and race politics. First, in both cases the crisis of the old Republican model is obvious and deep. However, its reconstruction with new principles and norms is proving more difficult (Cole et al., 2005). In no other area has the search for political answers to new challenges been more ambivalent. Resistance within institutions, half-measures and symbolic politics (in the case of parity or ethnic monitoring, for example) have produced inconsistent multiculturalist policies. This reluctant policy-making leads to internal contradictions within the state apparatus and recurrent public debates that often do not provide optimal political solutions. Second, in both areas the influence of the EU on national policy-making has been crucial. EU legislation and incentives in the domain of gender equality and antidiscrimination have forced French legislators to amend the legal framework in order to address these issues. For both policy fields, the multi-level polity is a key dimension in explaining recent political developments.

However, tensions are also palpable between gender and race politics in France today. Instead of reflecting upon the commonalities between the processes that exclude women from the realm of politics, and those excluding other minorities, the parity reform has given preferential treatment only to women, and has broken up potential solidarities with other groups discriminated against on the basis of their ethnicity or race. The most recent headscarf affair also illuminates the tension between women's rights and minority rights that the policy framing of this new issue has caused. Indeed, some major feminist organizations have mobilized in favour of the law banning headscarves in high schools. Their stance against the headscarf, interpreted as a sign of masculine domination imposed on young girls, has created a rift between feminist associations and groups mobilized on the base of ethnic and religious affiliations. The Natives of the Republic have been very vocal against French white feminists and the 'Native feminists', a group of young feminists, members of the Natives of the Republic, have decided to organize apart from traditional feminist organizations. How this tension will develop, how bridges between groups might be built, and how these alliances might challenge the remnants of the old Republican model are still open questions.

Chapter 7

The Return to a Strong Presidency

JONAH D. LEVY AND CINDY SKACH

For centuries, France was plagued by oscillations between ineffective parliamentary democracy and tyrannical rule by a strongman. In the 1960s and 1970s, the Fifth Republic, founded in 1958, was widely seen as having finally provided a democratic solution, a synthesis of the competing principles of representation, according to which the people decide who shall rule and speak for their interests, and governability, according to which the rulers are able to take decisive, effective action. Yet, in spite of this unique structural synthesis and its successful practice for the first few decades of the Fifth Republic, by the 1980s, the performance of the Fifth Republic was faltering, with leaders appearing weak, embattled, short-sighted and unable to impose necessary socio-economic reforms (Levy, 1999). More recently, the performance of the Fifth Republic appears to have changed yet again. The new President, Nicolas Sarkozy, seems to be acting with a vigour and decisiveness not seen since the Gaullist heyday in the 1960s. Further complicating matters, in July 2007, just after his inauguration, Sarkozy appointed 13 'sages' to a committee headed by former Prime Minister Édouard Balladur and entrusted with undertaking the task of reflecting on the modernization of the Fifth Republic.

This chapter analyses the shifting performance of the French executive, paying particular attention to the dynamics of constitutional design. It is organized into three sections. Section 1 presents the key institutional features of strong presidential leadership put into place by the founders of the Fifth Republic. Section 2 describes the limits of the French semi-presidential model and the role that political parties and leadership styles have played in conditioning institutional performance. Section 3 brings the institutions, actors and ideas together to assess the apparent return to a strong presidency under Nicolas Sarkozy.

The construction of a strong presidency

The central objective of the framing fathers of the Fifth Republic was to enable the executive to govern effectively, but within a democratic context. Toward this end, three main techniques were deployed. The first and most important was semi-presidentialism. The second technique was rationalized parliamentarism and the third was a two-round majoritarian electoral law.

Any effort to analyse the development of French politics over the course of the Fifth Republic begins with the semi-presidential or dual executive system (Skach, 2005). Semi-presidentialism is defined by two structural characteristics: (1) the head of state is a popularly elected President with a fixed term of office; (2) the head of government is a Prime Minister who is responsible to the legislature. Under semi-presidentialism, the executive is divided into two parts: an indirectly chosen head of government, and a popularly elected head of state. Executive power, including the power to preside over cabinet meetings and direct national policy, is shared between these two executives, and power sharing by definition excludes a neat division or separation of powers, often leading to constitutional ambiguity. For example, the President in the Constitution of the French Fifth Republic is commander in chief of the armed forces (article 15), and, as such, presides over 'higher national defence councils and committees'. Yet the Constitution *also* states that the *Prime Minister* is 'responsible for national defence' (article 21).

Despite the constitutional ambiguity, semi-presidentialism was conceived of as a system for assuring presidential leadership. The President under the Fifth Republic enjoys an array of political powers. Unlike the President in a parliamentary regime, s/he is directly elected by the people (since 1965), a process that confers considerable popular legitimacy. Prior to a constitutional amendment in 2000, the President served for seven years and, as we shall discuss below, the shortening of the presidential term to five years in 2000 was actually designed to bolster the President's power in this complex institutional configuration. In a crisis, under article 16 of the Constitution, the President may declare a state of emergency and rule by decree. The President also possesses considerable leverage in his or her dealings with Parliament. S/he can dissolve Parliament and organize new elections as often as once per year. Moreover, the President can appeal over the heads of Parliament directly to the people by calling referenda, a strategy used on several occasions by Charles de Gaulle, the first President and one of the founders of the Fifth Republic. Most important, the President appoints the Prime Minister and, for a variety of reasons, has generally been able to name (and dismiss) prime ministers who are willing to accept a subordinate role.

A second constitutional device for bolstering the executive, whether the President or the Prime Minister, is the system of 'rationalized parliamentarism'. Michel Debré, a de Gaulle loyalist and the first Prime Minister of the Fifth Republic, crafted the system of rationalized parliamentarism with the idea of allowing the executive to govern effectively, even in the absence of a reliable majority in Parliament. Toward this end, Debré drafted a series of provisions to curb parliamentary autonomy and influence, of which three stand out. First, under article 34 of the Constitution, Parliament can only legislate in specifically designated areas. The executive controls the parliamentary agenda and, via article 44.3 (the *vote bloquée* or package vote), it can force Parliament to vote for or against a bill, without the possibility of introducing changes. Second, under article 38, the executive can gain authorization from Parliament to issue ordinances having the force of law in a designated area, thereby avoiding the need to obtain a vote from Parliament for each piece of legislation. Third and perhaps of greatest importance, under article 49.3, the 'confidence' vote can be used as a technique for enacting laws without recourse to a parliamentary vote (the operation of this rationalized parliamentarianism is considered in more detail in Chapter 8).

Although the techniques of rationalized parliamentarism have facilitated the passage of legislation in the absence of a solid parliamentary majority, the founders of the Fifth Republic attempted to make this situation less likely by reforming the electoral law so as to bolster the majority party or coalition. The Fourth Republic (1946–58) used a system of proportional representation, which allowed for a proliferation of small parties (Bogdanor, 1984). The resulting governments tended to be shaky coalitions of four or five parties that were unable to take decisive action for fear of defection and that rarely lasted more than one year. The framers of the Fifth Republic sought to remedy the problem by adopting a two-round majoritarian system. On the first ballot, many candidates compete, but if no single candidate wins an absolute majority, a run-off is held, in which only candidates receiving at least 12.5 per cent of the registered vote (what is called an electoral threshold) are eligible. In practice, the vast majority of run-offs pit a candidate of the Right against a candidate of the Left. Moreover, much like the single-round majoritarian systems of the US and UK, the French electoral law tends to amplify small shifts in voter support and even manufacture comfortable majorities for the winning coalition.

Taken together, the combination of strong presidential powers and popular electoral legitimacy, rationalized parliamentarism and a majoritarian electoral law would seem to give French presidents the best of both the presidential and parliamentary constitutional worlds. The French President can dominate Parliament in the manner of a British-style parliamentary system – perhaps even more effectively, thanks to the techniques of rationalized parliamentarism and the recourse to referenda. Yet unlike a British Prime Minister, the French President is not obliged to resign if the government loses a parliamentary election or a confidence vote (which is tilted in favour of the government anyway). Rather, this dubious honour falls to the Prime Minister, who has generally served as a buffer or 'fuse' for the President – loyally administering the President's agenda, taking the political heat from day-to-day battles and unpopular measures, before being cast aside after two or three years in favour of a fresh, new face (Suleiman, 1994).

By the 1970s, the Fifth Republic had come to be associated with strong, stable, presidential leadership. Indeed, when the countries of Eastern Europe and the former Soviet Union threw off the yoke of communism and drafted new democratic constitutions, many took their inspiration from the French Fifth Republic (as did Taiwan and Niger) (Elgie, 1999). Semi-presidentialism seemed to offer a way of bringing effective, yet democratic leadership to countries suffering from political instability and ineffective executives. In point of fact, however, presidential leadership under the Fifth Republic was far more tenuous than admirers and emulators believed.

The limits of semi-presidentialism

In the mid-1970s, France's semi-presidential system first started to falter. French presidents seemed increasingly weak and indecisive, unable to pursue modernization, contested and defeated by protestors, and regularly repudiated by the voters. Three developments underpinned this erosion of semi-presidentialism.

The first development was a more constrained policy-making environment. In a sense, French leaders found themselves squeezed from both above and below. Above, as European integration and globalization advanced, the French executive, whether the President or the Prime Minister, had less room to manoeuvre. Policy-making increasingly involved negotiations with the EU (see the chapter by Yves Surel in this volume for more detail), and some policies, notably economic initiatives, were constrained by international competition and capital mobility.

French leaders were also challenged from below. The May 1968 upheaval marked the beginning of an almost uninterrupted wave of protests and street mobilization by dissatisfied groups, from students frustrated over the underfunded schools and poor job prospects, to workers threatened with lay-offs, to farmers unable to compete in global agricultural markets, to shopkeepers threatened by the spread of supermarkets. In this context, French leaders discovered that the concentration of power in the executive branch was something of a double-edged sword (Levy, 1999). Along with high capacity for action came high responsibility for dissatisfaction. Whereas discontented groups in the US or UK might blame the market for their plight and those in much of continental Europe might blame the social partners, in France, it was the central state in general and the President in particular who was called to account. Groups took to the streets to demand either support and relief from the effects of competition or the repeal of government austerity or liberalization measures designed to meet that competition. More often than not, street protests brought results, as governments acceded to large parts of the protesters' demands.

The second important factor behind the erosion of the semi-presidential model occurred in the electoral arena. The strong, presidential leadership of the 1960s and early 1970s was as much a product of conservative electoral hegemony as the institutional logic of semi-presidentialism. We now understand that the performance of semi-presidential systems can vary tremendously with the character of the party system (Skach, 2005). In fact, there are three subtypes within the semi-presidential model, each corresponding to a different party system. The subtype of 'consolidated majority government', which occurs when the President is backed by a majority in Parliament, most closely approximates the Fifth Republic ideal of strong presidential leadership. This situation prevailed during the Gaullist heyday as well as when the Left swept to power under François Mitterrand in 1981. There are two other subtypes within semi-presidentialism, however: 'divided majority government', when the majority in Parliament is opposed to the President (what the French call 'cohabitation'), and 'divided minority government', when there is no clear majority in Parliament. As the French electoral context veered toward these scenarios, the performance of semi-presidentialism became much more problematic.

Divided minority government is the most conflict-prone subtype. In this subtype, neither the President, the Prime Minister, nor any party or coalition, enjoys a substantive party majority in the legislature. The legislature in this subtype is filled with multiple, competing party factions. The absence of any stable legislative majority can generate political instability, characterized by shifting party coalitions, as leaders attempt to form governments and survive confidence votes. If no viable government can be formed because the legislature is so fragmented, or if governments are so short-lived because they are unable to count on majority support for confidence votes, presidents may resort to legislating without government, through emergency or decree powers. The outcome can be a vicious circle: the greater the instability in the legislature, the more pressured (or justified) the President may feel using emergency and decree powers as a substitute for a legislative majority.

A number of countries that have also employed variations of the

French semi-presidential model have experienced this same movement toward authoritarian rule. Germany's Weimar regime (1919–33), the predecessor in Europe to the Fifth Republic's model, combined a President possessing considerable powers with a Chancellor or Prime Minister representing the majority in Parliament. However, a fragmented party system in Parliament made it all but impossible for the Chancellor to govern effectively. In the early 1930s, an increasingly authoritarian President Hindenburg issued decrees in the place of legislation from (an increasingly ineffective) Parliament, so that the appointment of Adolf Hitler as Chancellor in 1933 seemed less of a break with democracy than the culmination of an ongoing authoritarian evolution under Hindenburg. The plight of another semi-presidential regime, that of Russia since 1991, displays a similar trajectory. In Russia, a divided and ineffective Parliament, unable to tackle the problems of the nation, gradually ceded power to an authoritarian President – in this case, Vladimir Putin (Colton and Skach, 2005). While the cases of Weimar Germany and contemporary Russia may seem far removed from the French context, it is important to note that France suffered some of the same problems during the early years of the Fifth Republic.

When the French Fifth Republic was established in 1958, the party system was in a state of flux. The majoritarian electoral system we discussed above, which eventually did help bolster majorities, was used for the first time in 1958, but the threshold for the second round was still relatively permissive, and political actors were still adjusting to its rather complicated incentives well into the early 1960s. The first President of the Republic, Charles de Gaulle, for his part, was committed to building a democratic Fifth Republic. He was less committed, in the first years, of doing so via political parties, as he refused to join any party in existence (Charlot, 1967). As a consequence of these combined factors, coherent and stable legislative majorities did not exist in the first years of the Republic. The pro-de Gaulle party, Union pour la Nouvelle République (UNR), governed with support from the Algérie Française legislative faction for the first few years under the new institutions. But this alliance soon dissolved, leaving President de Gaulle, and his Prime Minister, Michel Debré, in divided minority government in 1959.

Relations between the government and the legislature during this period were turbulent. At least three important anti-democratic developments bordering on constitutional dictatorship occurred. First, de Gaulle and Debré relied heavily on restrictive legislative procedures, the aspects of rationalized parliamentarism that we discussed above, including articles 44.3 and 49.3 of the Fifth Republic Constitution (Avril, 1965; Chagnollaud and Quermonne, 1996). These procedures were used deliberately to limit parliamentary debate and pass legislation without inter-party compromise. In response to the use of article

49.3 to constrain the legislature, deputies would often walk out of Parliament in protest at their exclusion. Second, in 1961, following the 'Crisis of the Generals' in Algeria, de Gaulle instituted a period of presidential rule under the auspices of article 16. Although the crisis in Algeria lasted only four days, de Gaulle extended his use of emergency powers under article 16 for five months, during which he issued 16 substantive decrees. Third, in 1962, de Gaulle used referenda power in what was seen as a controversial, unconstitutional way of bypassing the divided legislature to change the Constitution. De Gaulle, who was originally selected by the legislature as President in 1958, proposed a constitutional amendment for the direct election of the President, an amendment that made de Gaulle and successive presidents accountable to the electorate, rather than the National Assembly. In response to de Gaulle's attempt to alter the Constitution via a popular referendum, the National Assembly voted a motion of censure against the government, noting that 'the President of the Republic is violating the Constitution of which he is guardian' (Keesings Contemporary Archives 19159: 1963). De Gaulle, utilizing his constitutional power to respond to this motion of censure, then dissolved the Assembly and called new elections. During this conflict-ridden period of divided minority government from 1959 to 1962, which often bordered on constitutional dictatorship, public opinion regarding the new institutions was often negative. When asked in 1962 about the statement that 'in France, democracy is in danger', a substantial 35 per cent agreed (*Revue française de l'opinion publique*, 85: 1963).

Fortunately, under the influence of the majoritarian electoral law, with its progressively prohibitive thresholds, France began to develop a party system that became institutionalized and depolarized over time, evidenced in part by a steady decline in electoral volatility (Parodi, 1991). The threshold for remaining on the second ballot was set initially at 5 per cent of votes cast. Beginning with the 1967 legislative elections, however, the threshold was raised to 10 per cent of *eligible voters*, then to 12.5 per cent of eligible voters as of the 1978 legislative elections. Moreover, the election of 1962 gave President de Gaulle and his Prime Minister, Georges Pompidou, a 60 per cent majority in the National Assembly, and France spent the crucial years of 1962–69 in consolidated majority government. President de Gaulle gradually became more integrated into the party system, progressively relying on support from the UNR party, and appointing an ever-increasing number of UNR members to his cabinets. The successive presidents of the Fifth Republic followed suit with their respective political parties. These developments encouraged the coincidental presidential and legislative majorities that kept France operating in the least conflictual subtype of semi-presidentialism, consolidated majority government.

The lesson of the early Fifth Republic is that semi-presidentialism is no guarantee of effective, yet democratic presidential leadership. When the President lacks a stable majority in Parliament, the executive is tempted to fill the legislative void in less than fully democratic ways. For a time, the emergence of a hegemonic Gaullist party made possible a return to democratic practices. That said, as the electoral context became more contested, divided minority government reoccurred on several occasions. Moreover, from 1976 to 1981, the President and Prime Minister issued from the centre-Right UDF party, and although the Right held a majority in Parliament, President Giscard d'Estaing was at odds with the head of the Gaullist party, Jacques Chirac, who was hoping to unseat Giscard d'Estaing as President in 1981. Chirac's RPR was a prickly ally, often criticizing and seeking to create distance from the government. Lacking a reliable and loyally cohesive majority in Parliament, the Giscard d'Estaing regime resorted increasingly to restrictive legislative procedures, such as article 49.3, with consequences for democratic practice.

Although the Giscard d'Estaing presidency was not formally a case of divided minority government, it was plagued by some characteristics of this type because of tensions within the governing coalition. The divided minority situation did formally arise from 1988 to 1993. In 1988, François Mitterrand was re-elected as President and called new parliamentary elections that boosted his Socialist Party's share of the vote, but left it just short of a majority. As a result, the Socialists would govern without a parliamentary majority for five years. Not coincidentally, recourse to article 49.3 peaked during this period. Nearly half of all uses of article 49.3 in the 50-year history of the Fifth Republic occurred between 1988 and 1993, under the divided minority government of the Left.

Another constitutional subtype in semi-presidentialism that is problematic for strong executive rule is divided majority government. In this subtype, there is a stable and coherent party majority in the legislature, made up of either a single party or a coalition, but the President is from a party that *opposes* the majority, or is from no political party at all. The divided majority is often referred to in the French literature as 'cohabitation', conveying the idea that two non-compatible individuals are forced to govern together. During the first quarter-century of the Fifth Republic, cohabitation never occurred. By contrast, since 1986, there have been three instances of cohabitation. Socialist President Mitterrand was forced to cohabit twice with the Right, from 1986 to 1988 and again, from 1993 to 1995. Mitterrand's successor as President, Jacques Chirac, was forced to spend most of his first term cohabiting with a Parliament controlled by the Left, from 1997 to 2002.

Generally speaking, cohabitation has entailed a shift in power from the President to the Prime Minister. Backed by a majority in

Parliament, the Prime Minister holds the reins of power, while the President, who does not have this party backing in Parliament, is pushed largely to the sidelines. That said, the Prime Minister is by no means omnipotent. Indeed, the Prime Minister's ability to steer the ship of state falls short of that of the President under conditions of consolidated majority government for two reasons. The first is that the Constitution of the Fifth Republic is often unclear about the division of power and responsibility between the two executives, so the Prime Minister's leadership does not always go unchallenged. Presidents have been particularly assertive in the areas of defence and foreign policy, which have tended to remain primarily under presidential control during periods of cohabitation.

The second limitation is that with the President possessing the right to dissolve the Parliament and call new elections, cohabiting prime ministers operate under a perpetual sword of Damocles. Any Prime Minister who pursues painful or unpopular reforms intended to yield benefits in the medium or long term runs the risk that the President will exploit the initial backlash, call early elections, and oust the Prime Minister from office before the reforms have a chance to bear fruit. This concern seems to have weighed heavily on Socialist Prime Minister, Lionel Jospin, during the 1997–2002 cohabitation. Jospin repeatedly convened expert committees to devise much-needed reforms, notably of France's health care and pension systems, only to decline to move forward with these reforms out of fear of popular and electoral backlash.

Along with contestation from above and below and frequent hostile or minority cabinets emanating from Parliament, the third development compromising presidential leadership is a feature of the semi-presidential system itself – a potentially short electoral cycle. The semi-presidential regime offers two ways of changing the course of government policy. Under the classic alternation scenario, if the opposition wins a presidential election, the new President can immediately dissolve Parliament and appeal to the voters for a sympathetic majority to implement his/her programme; under the cohabitation scenario, if the opposition wins a parliamentary election, the President is more or less compelled to submit to the will of the new legislative majority. Thus, in a semi-presidential or dual executive regime, the government confronts twice as many elections that could potentially unseat it (presidential and parliamentary) as in a typical parliamentary system (parliamentary elections only). Aggravating matters in the French case, because the presidential term originally established by the Constitution of the Fifth Republic ran for seven years and the parliamentary term for five years, presidential and parliamentary elections often took place in different years. In practice, this meant that in many instances, French presidents had only a short respite before the next election that could potentially strip them of power.

The challenge posed by the different presidential and parliamentary electoral cycles played a central part in Jacques Chirac's ill-fated decision to call early parliamentary elections in 1997, despite possessing the largest parliamentary majority since 1815. Chirac planned to implement an austerity programme to qualify France for EMU, but feared that French voters would punish him for trying in the 1998 legislative elections. Chirac's strategy was to win an early parliamentary election in 1997 before implementing the austerity programme and hope that all would be forgiven by the next election in 2002. Instead, the Right went down to defeat, and Chirac was forced into a five-year cohabitation. Had Chirac's election as President in 1995 coincided with parliamentary elections, there would have been no need to gamble on early parliamentary elections in 1997. Chirac would have enjoyed a clear horizon for five years before confronting the voters, instead of three years, which would have given him enough time to implement an austerity programme and recover politically.

The possible frequency of meaningful elections may not have posed significant problems during the era of triumphant Gaullism, but as elections became more closely contested, the dual executive structure evolved into a dual threat to government. Indeed, beginning in 1981, incumbent governments were ousted at every national election. In this context governmental time horizons shortened dramatically. Confronted with the prospect of losing power, whether via presidential or parliamentary elections, successive governments tended to shy away from or withdraw controversial proposals in an effort to preserve their fragile popularity. Thus, French governments not only lost power with frequency, but even when they were in power, they were often unable to make hard choices in the face of social protest and looming electoral challenges.

The return to a strong presidency?

After several decades of torpor, the French executive has suddenly displayed renewed vigour under President Nicolas Sarkozy. Three developments underpin this dramatic shift. The first is a 2000 constitutional reform that bolstered the President vis-à-vis the Parliament. The second development is the nature of Sarkozy's campaign for President. The third is Sarkozy's style of governance.

As we noted above, one of the factors sapping the vitality of presidential leadership was the frequency of elections that could potentially change the government. In 2000, leaders of the Left and the Right agreed to modify the Constitution by shortening the presidential mandate from seven years (*septennat*) to five years (*quinquennat*). President Chirac put the idea of moving to a *quinquennat* to popular vote, through a referendum that was held on 24 September 2000. This was the first major reform of the French executive since the introduction of the direct election for the President in 1962 and the first elections under this rule in 1965. The question on the ballot asked French voters, 'do you approve of the proposed constitutional law that would fix the presidential term at five years?' Although the referendum was approved by 73.2 per cent of the voters, it was seen as something of a setback for Chirac, since barely 30 per cent of the population bothered to vote.

Part of the rationale behind the *quinquennat* reform was the goal of democratic control. Seven years is a long time for citizens to be expected to wait before voicing judgement on the performance of the President, and the *septennat*, which had first been enshrined in 1873, was seen as a relic from a monarchic age. Another motive for the reform came from Chirac himself, who thought that it would enhance his own chances for re-election in 2002. At the time this reform was being discussed, some critics had expressed concern about Chirac's age, so by shortening his second term in office to five years, he would be scheduled to step down at age 75, rather than 77. The shorter term would also respond to the argument floating around for some time that no individual should be at the helm of a country for as many as 14 years. Still, the most important reason for the *quinquennat* reform was not to enhance democratic control or Chirac's re-election prospects, but rather to bolster the power of the President by aligning the cycles of presidential and parliamentary elections, thereby increasing the chances that the presidential and parliamentary majorities would coincide.

With the move to a five-year presidency, the mandates of the President and the legislature have become essentially coterminous. Both the President and the National Assembly are elected for five years. Further aiding the President's coat-tail effect on parliamentary elections, the presidential election is scheduled just before the parliamentary elections. In practice, the French choose their President, then go back to the polls around one month later to choose their Parliament. Although there is no rule preventing voters from splitting their ticket, that is, electing a President from one party and a Parliament from another, in practice, French voters have always persuaded by the argument that a newly elected President should be given the means to implement his or her agenda in Parliament. In both 2002 and 2007, the victorious presidential candidate won a sizable majority in the ensuing parliamentary elections. Ironically, then, a shorter term in office has bolstered the President by eliminating the need to confront the voters in a parliamentary election during his or her *quinquennat*. Of course, the President could opt at any time to dissolve Parliament and call new elections, but it is hard to see why a President would ever do so.

The return to a strong presidency under Nicolas Sarkozy has been fuelled to a degree by the *quinquennat* reform. The electoral sword of Damocles stemming from the dual executive has been lifted. President Sarkozy knows that he has a free hand for five years. Backed by a sizable parliamentary majority, Sarkozy can make hard or controversial choices now, even if the benefits are not for several years, without risking being turned out of office by the voters. The new President's time horizon is 2012, not 2009 or even 2010.

If the *quinquennat* has bolstered Sarkozy, it is not the only explanation of the return to a vigorous presidency. After all, Jacques Chirac also benefited from the *quinquennat* reform, receiving a large parliamentary majority following his re-election as President in 2002. Yet few would describe the second Chirac presidency as 'vigorous'. The return to a vigorous presidency has also stemmed from the character of Sarkozy's electoral campaign.

Sarkozy's election in 2007 differed fundamentally from that of Chirac in 1995. Chirac secured election as President on a pledge to restore the 'Republican pact', to increase state intervention to 'heal the social fracture'. When his government subsequently sought to implement austerity reforms, Chirac was widely seen as having betrayed his mandate. French voters elected Chirac to preserve or enhance the Republican, statist model, not to curtail it. Thus, Chirac lacked a democratic mandate for the kinds of liberalizing, austerity measures that his government generally pursued. The President had been elected to do one thing, but then attempted to do another, and this contradiction was a regular source of social conflict and electoral backlash.

Nicolas Sarkozy, by contrast, campaigned on an agenda of radical reform or 'rupture' as he often put it. The French model was broken; it needed to be changed, not fine-tuned. Sarkozy made it clear that he intended to fundamentally overhaul the French system, from foreign policy, to the economy, to relations with the social partners, to immigration, to law and order (see discussion in Chapter 2). Unlike Chirac, Sarkozy secured a democratic mandate for change, although the details of that change were not always well specified. Still, the French chose Sarkozy with the expectation that he would shake things up and put France on a new path. They expect their President to act decisively, to unblock the reform process, and Sarkozy has been more than happy to oblige. This points to the third factor behind a return to a kind of presidentialism, or what we might call a presidentialization of the semi-presidential model – the governing style of Nicolas Sarkozy.

Three aspects of Sarkozy's governing style have contributed to the presidentialization of French politics. The first is tremendous government activism. Sarkozy's government has been inordinately busy. Hardly a day goes by without the announcement of some new reform or initiative. In its first six months in office, to focus on just the most important changes, the government negotiated a new European 'mini-treaty' to replace the Constitution rejected by French voters in 2005, patched up relations with the United States, legislated substantial tax cuts, tightened the restrictions on immigration, enacted (and more important, implemented) a reform of the pension system, and greatly expanded the autonomy of the university system. Nor is this activism confined to major policy issues. When a father and his child were killed on a carnival ride in August, Sarkozy – while vacationing in the United States – publicly ordered his Minister of the Interior to draft new safety rules and ensure that 'the security of rides and attractions in service throughout French territory is immediately verified and enhanced'. This activism has led observers to compare Sarkozy to the Energizer bunny, and the new President has earned such nicknames as 'the Omni-President', the 'Hyper-President' and 'Super-Sarko'.

The second aspect of Sarkozy's leadership that has enhanced the role of the President has been a blurring of political boundaries between Left and Right. Following his election, Sarkozy appointed a number of leaders from the other side of the political spectrum and left-leaning associational groups to positions within his government. These figures included: Bernard Kouchner, a co-founder of Doctors without Borders and a leader in the Socialist Party, who became Minister of Foreign and European Affairs; Jean-Marie Boeckel, a Socialist senator and mayor of Mulhouse, selected to be State Secretary for Cooperation and Francophone Relations; Jean-Pierre Jouyet, a former Jospin cabinet director, who was chosen to serve as State Secretary for European Affairs; Eric Besson, who had been Ségolène Royal's economic adviser until breaking with her just prior to the presidential election, named State Secretary in Charge of Forecasting and the Evaluation of Public Policy; Martin Hirsch, the head of the Emmaüs France organization that works to help the homeless and poor, who was named High Commissioner of Solidarity; and Fadela Amara, founder of the feminist group, Ni Putes ni Soumises, who became State Secretary for Urban Policy. In addition, the committee presided over by Édouard Balladur that was charged with presenting suggestions for modernizing the Constitution of the Fifth Republic included a number of opposition figures. Among them were: Jack Lang, perhaps the most popular leader within the Socialist Party, who has held multiple cabinet positions and who advised Royal during her presidential campaign; Olivier Schrameck, Lionel Jospin's cabinet director for then Prime Minister, Lionel Jospin; Guy Carcassonne, a former adviser to Michel Rocard; and Olivier Duhamel, a former Socialist member of the European Parliament.

Sarkozy's opening up to the opposition, arguably without precedent under the Fifth Republic, at least in its scope, has multiple motivations. Sarkozy maintains that he is simply trying to get the best people for the job, that there is no reason to deny his government people of talent for petty political reasons. In addition, figures like Hirsch and Amara give the administration contacts with a world where the Right is not well represented along with valuable feedback to improve and humanize policy. For example, at Hirsch's insistence, the government removed a provision from its immigration bill that would have barred homeless shelters from accepting illegal immigrants. Including the opposition also offers clear political benefits to Sarkozy. Sarkozy's raid on leftist leaders has disoriented and demoralized the Socialist Party, which gives the appearance of a sinking ship abandoned by its crew. The Socialist Party has divided over the issue of participation in the Sarkozy administration, with some factions calling for punishment or even for the exclusion of figures who 'collaborate' with Sarkozy. In response, several Socialists, including Lang and Boeckel, have either been temporarily estranged from the Socialist Party and its governing body or left the party altogether. Another important political benefit is to accentuate the role and power of the President. With the blurring of political and ideological boundaries, politics takes on an even more personalistic hue. French politics no longer revolves around Left and Right, around parties or ideologies. Rather, it revolves around relations with Nicolas Sarkozy.

The third feature suggesting a return to strong presidential rule is that Sarkozy and his staff at the Élysée Palace have been at the forefront of almost all French policy, big and small. It was Sarkozy who went to Brussels to win support for a 'mini-treaty'; it was Sarkozy's wife at the time (they have since divorced) who secured the release of the Bulgarian nurses held in Libya; and it was Sarkozy who met with student and personnel representatives to hammer out a deal on university reform.

Conversely, the power of the other side of the French executive, the Prime Minister and his cabinet, has arguably never been so low. The Minister of Foreign Affairs played almost no part in the negotiation of the European mini-treaty or the liberation of the Bulgarian nurses in Libya. The Minister of Education was sidelined in the negotiations over university reform. Cabinet members have also been kept on a very short leash. When Jean-Louis Borloo, the Minister of Ecology, Development and Sustainable Planning, the ostensible number two figure in the cabinet, floated the possibility that France might freeze new plantings of genetically modified crops (GMOs), he was immediately contradicted by an Élysée spokesman, who insisted that 'nothing is decided'. Borloo responded that he was only describing what he thought to be a general, long-term tendency in French politics. The next day, a close adviser to Sarkozy gave an interview in the French press, declaring that the GMO question should not be treated 'cavalierly' and that the ultimate decision would be made by 'the President of the Republic and the Prime Minister' – that is, not by Borloo (*Libération*, 24 September 2007). The Prime Minister, François Fillon, likewise appears devalued, even by the low standards of Fifth Republic prime ministers. Fillon has bravely sought to assert that he is Sarkozy's partner, but it is clear that the President is calling all the shots. Fillon's main role seems to be to serve as the voice of conservative UMP deputies, demanding more far-reaching market and law-and-order reform – in short, to serve as a lobbyist, rather than a decision-maker. Indeed, unkind critics have compared Fillon to a US Vice President.

The de facto return to presidentialism, even as the Fifth Republic remains *de jure* semi-presidential, stems from a combination of institutional changes that preference presidential leadership, notably the *quinquennat* reform, and the character of Nicolas Sarkozy's electoral campaign and governing style. Looking forward, the extreme concentration of power in the hands of Sarkozy and his advisers may well continue, but if the history of the Fifth Republic teaches us anything, it is that presidential power can ebb as well as rise. The current presidentialization of power faces three potential challenges.

The first is constitutional reform. The Balladur Commission submitted its recommendations in October 2007. Some of its proposals are seen as bolstering the President, such as allowing the President to speak directly to the Parliament. Others affirm in theory what already exists in practice. For example, the Balladur Commission is recommending changing the wording of article 21 to state that the President, rather than the Prime Minister, 'defines' government policy, while the Prime Minister 'conducts' (i.e. implements) this policy. Going in the opposite direction, the Balladur Commission put forward a number of proposals to either bolster the Parliament or curtail some of the perceived excesses of presidential power. Proposals that might weaken or constrain the President include: (1) restrictions on the use of article 49.3 (probably confined to votes on the budget and social security); (2) controls on certain nominations (by the Parliament) and on recourse to article 16 (by the Constitutional Council); (3) enhanced guarantees of judicial autonomy; (4) a dose of proportional representation for parliamentary elections (initially only 20–30 seats out of 577, but one could imagine the scope being extended subsequently). Although it is too early to tell which reforms will be enacted, most of them point toward slightly diminishing or controlling presidential power.

A second, more immediate threat to presidential power is the end of the honeymoon period enjoyed by President Sarkozy. The French political graveyard is littered with presidents and prime ministers who began with sky-high approval ratings, only to see those ratings plummet when they began to tackle difficult or controversial reforms. Sarkozy's obvious talents as a rather seductive, populist leader may allow him to prolong the honeymoon period and even improve his standing as a result of successful reforms. That said, he faces a difficult agenda. Whereas during his initial months in office, Sarkozy reaped popularity from foreign policy successes and tax cuts, he now confronts the more politically treacherous challenges of reducing the budget deficit, controlling social spending, reforming labour markets, turning around an anaemic economy and addressing violent crime. As recent strikes and protests over pension reform reveal, reforming France is a politically parlous exercise. In the past, such efforts have quickly consumed the political capital and popularity of once promising politicians.

The final, related threat to presidential leadership is the downside of Sarkozy's hyperactivism and the personalization of power. As French leaders discovered beginning in the 1970s, being on the front lines of reform is not always an advantage. When times are good, when the results are positive, an activist President can engage in credit claiming. But when the situation turns sour or the reforms are unpopular, the President incurs the blame. Moreover, with the concentration of power comes the concentration of accountability. France's new President runs the risk of becoming the target of every aggrieved party in society, the scapegoat for anything that goes wrong. Given that the French economy and budget remain weak, Sarkozy is likely to confront far more blame for pain and demands for relief than opportunities for credit claiming. Such political circumstances do not bode well for strong presidential leadership.

Conclusion

This chapter has shown that under France's semi-presidential system, the President is neither inherently strong nor inherently weak. Rather, the French semi-presidential system is a living, dynamic, politically mediated arrangement. Presidential power is shaped not only by the logic of the dual executive, but also by the electoral context, the mobilization of French society, and the mandate and governing style of the President. For this reason, the French President's authority has shifted rather dramatically over time – from the prototypical strong presidency of the 1960s, to embattled, contested governance beginning in the 1970s, to the more robust reformism of the early Sarkozy presidency. If history is any guide, we have not seen the last of the twists and turns, the ebbs and flows, of executive authority in France.

Chapter 8

Parliament and Political Representation

BASTIEN FRANÇOIS

The French Parliament is without a doubt one of the least powerful contemporary parliamentary systems especially in comparison to those of the European Union. This is the case to such a point that French political commentators regularly and repeatedly question 'what the Parliament does' and why legislative elections, in spite of widespread media coverage and a significant investment on the part of the political parties (whose public financing depends on the result of these elections), are those that register the highest rate of abstention, a trend which has been increasing during the past 30 years. Thus, the rate of abstention on the first ballot of the legislative elections was 16.8 per cent in 1978, but 39.5 per cent in 2007.

The French Parliament's power is undermined principally because executive power is not exercised, for the most part, by the Prime Minister, as provided in the Constitution, but rather by the President of the Republic who is not accountable to the Parliament (see Chapter 7). This situation is increasingly the subject of criticism, to the point that in the eyes of many political commentators this imbalance is treated as an indicator of a crisis affecting French democracy as a whole.

After reviewing the constitutional and political reasons behind the subordination of the Parliament in the French political system (Section 1) and more contemporary factors of the French parliamentary crisis (Section 2), this chapter will examine various plans for constitutional reform that are currently under discussion, laying special emphasis on their parliamentary aspects (Section 3).

The French Parliament: a subordinate (yet paradoxically central) position

The main purpose of the 1958 Constitution was to ensure government stability against a politically divided and undisciplined Parliament. In

127

the 1950s, nobody in France could have imagined that a coherent and disciplined parliamentary majority could support a government on a long-term basis. Consequently, the Constitution which established the Fifth Republic took pains strongly to restrict the powers granted to the Parliament.

The Constitution strictly limits the areas in which the Parliament has the power to enact laws and drastically reduces its budgetary competence (the Parliament can neither lower taxes nor authorize new expenditures), while the executive branch can, if it is deemed necessary, circumvent Parliament altogether by enacting laws by referendum. In the already restricted field of its legislative competence, the Parliament shares legislative initiative with the Prime Minister, yet even here it has an inferior record as regards legislative achievement: about 90 per cent of the laws passed since 1959 are of governmental origin versus slightly less than 30 per cent under the Fourth Republic (1946–58). Moreover, the government, which determines the agenda and timetable of parliamentary activities, has many tools to control both the legislative process and the relations between the upper and lower houses of Parliament. In particular, the government can limit or restrain recourse to amendments by members of Parliament. According to article 44, the 1958 Constitution states that the government can refuse amendments presented by MPs. Article 44.3, sometimes termed the blocked vote (*vote bloqué*) procedure, allows the government to insist upon one chamber (the National Assembly or the Senate) voting upon a bill which only takes the government's final amendments into account. The government can thereby legitimately refuse to consider amendments from the floor of either chamber or its committees. To this must be added that, since 1958, laws enacted by the Parliament are subject to review by the Constitutional Council which is charged with verifying the constitutionality of new legislation before its promulgation. This constitutional review has considerably increased since the 1970s to the point that, at present, most major legislative initiatives are subjected to this scrutiny (see Chapter 9 for full discussion of the Constitutional Council).

In addition to being deprived of many key elements necessary to exercise legislative power, the Fifth Republic Parliament has a correspondingly limited power of oversight. If the Constitution of the Fifth Republic recognizes the principle of governmental accountability to the Parliament, it does so in an extremely restrictive way. Thus, the 'interpellations' used in the Fourth Republic, those formal demands addressed to the government requiring it to provide explanations of its policies, are forbidden, as are parliamentary votes on general political resolutions. Parliamentary boards of inquiry are authorized, but the conditions imposed on their activity deprive them of any meaningful effectiveness: convening an oversight hearing is contingent upon majority consent, the hearing cannot last beyond six months and does not have the power to order judicial proceedings. A total of eight parliamentary boards of inquiry were convened at the National Assembly during the XIIth legislature (2002–7), but deputies, in the majority as well as in the opposition, asked for the creation of 174 boards of inquiry during that same period. The only board of inquiry that has had any measurable media following was a hearing in 2005 about judicial dysfunctions concerning a paedophile scandal (referred to as the Outreau affair) because, for the first time in France, the hearings were open to the public and televised.

The 1958 Constitution explicitly affirms that 'the government is accountable to the Parliament'. In common with most parliamentary systems, the Senate, the upper chamber, has no power to vote a government out of office. The house of Parliament that can overturn the government – the National Assembly – is, in its turn, itself subject to dissolution by the executive. On this point, the creators of the Constitution relied on the principle of 'dissuasion' inherent to parliamentary systems of government. The process whereby the National Assembly exercises its primary check on the power of the government – the 'motion of censure' – is extraordinarily difficult to implement. This process is so constrained that in only one instance, in 1962, did such a motion actually pass. The conditions for a successful motion of censure are quite draconian. A motion of censure must be sponsored by at least 10 per cent of the deputies (which prevents smaller parliamentary groups from taking the initiative) and each deputy can sign only three such motions during the same parliamentary session (which lasts nine months). Above all, only explicit 'yes' votes count (which means that abstaining members are deemed to have voted 'no') and, finally, the motion of censure can prevail only if it is supported by the absolute majority of the National Assembly members. As a result of this, in practice opposition parties do not use the motion of censure to attempt to turn a government out of office, but rather, as a part of a communication strategy, the purpose of which is to highlight symbolically their disagreements with the government. In this spirit, the opposition parties on the Left presented five motions of censure between 2002 and 2007. The last motion of censure, presented by the Socialist deputies in May 2006, resulted in only 190 votes (the total of the left-wing votes and a part of the centre-Right votes) out of 577 deputy votes.

The overarching philosophy lying behind the structure of relations between the government and the Parliament is summarized in the infamous and much debated article 49.3 of the Constitution. Article 49.3 has been criticized by the political parties on the Left as well as the Right. Combining governmental domination of the legislative process with the material limitations on the right of parliamentary oversight, the principle consists of the following: the Prime Minister can at any moment of the legislative process commit the responsibility of the government on the vote of a bill (or a part of it). If during the following 24 hours no motion of censure is brought forward by the Parliament, the bill is then considered adopted, without a vote. If, on the other hand, a motion of censure is presented, it must be adopted by the absolute majority of the members of the National Assembly, with abstentions again counting as votes against the motion. If these conditions are not fulfilled, the motion is rejected and the law is then considered as adopted. No successful motion of censure has been carried under this procedure since 1958. By this means, the government can pass a bill which under the normal conditions would not get the majority of the deputies' votes. Moreover, using other constitutional provisions, the government can also overcome the nuisance of delaying tactics in the Senate and force the adoption of a law, without the need for a formal vote of a single deputy or senator.

All parliamentary democracies have some kind of 'confidence' procedure used by the government to mobilize its supporters in Parliament by committing itself to resign if it loses the vote, but the French system is tilted strongly in favour of the government. A confidence vote is not held automatically just because the government engages its responsibility. In most cases, the government can invoke article 49.3 on behalf of a bill, and the bill becomes law without any parliamentary vote. Article 49.3 is generally deployed in two situations. The first is when the government has a plurality or slim majority in Parliament and fears that its legislation will not pass. This situation occurred in 1967–68, when the Right barely outnumbered the Left in Parliament, from 1976 to 1981, when the Right held a majority but was divided and the Gaullists could not be counted upon to support the Giscard–Barre UDF government, and from 1988 to 1993, when the Socialists were just short of a majority. The second situation in which article 49.3 has proven attractive is when the government wants to move fast on controversial reforms, such as the Left's nationalizations in the early 1980s, and the Right's neo-liberal reforms from 1986 to 1988.

To this constitutional background we must add the political effects of the presidential election by direct universal suffrage in use since 1965. Direct election gives the President of the Republic – who is not held accountable before the members of Parliament – a higher legitimacy than any other political figure. The introduction of the direct election of the President in 1965 further strengthened the governing role that the first President of the Fifth Republic – de Gaulle – had arrogated for himself. In time the direct presidential election has contributed to producing a complete reconstruction of the political system (B. François, 2006). Vested with popular legitimacy, the use made by successive presidents of constitutional weapons at their disposal has gradually evolved. To take one example, the President's right to dissolve the National Assembly is no longer used to solve a conflict between the legislative and executive power (as in 1962) or a political crisis (as in 1968) but to allow the President to have at his disposal a parliamentary majority that supports him (1981, 1988, 1997).

French political life at the beginning of the 1960s was marked by the birth of the de facto majority, the existence of a politically coherent majority in the National Assembly which supported in a disciplined manner the government throughout the legislative term. De facto parliamentary majorities were strengthened by the development of the Left–Right 'bipolarization' of the party system which gathered pace throughout the 1970s (see Chapter 3 for fuller discussion). This structural transformation produced the conditions for regular political alternation in power after 1981, as well as allowing for several periods of 'cohabitation' between the President and parliamentary majorities of a different political complexion (1986–88, 1993–95 and 1997–2002). Cohabitation refers to the coexistence of a President of the Republic elected by universal suffrage with a Prime Minister deriving his power from a parliamentary majority holding different political views.

The directly elected President, the strengthening of executive government in the 1958 Constitution and the development of a more rationalized party system have combined to increase the subordination of Parliament. Henceforth Parliament is no longer a structural factor of political instability, as it was during the Third and Fourth Republics. The executive power, on the other hand, jealously preserves the battery of weapons that the 1958 Constitution provides for it. Despite the general trend of maintaining comfortable majorities, governments have not hesitated to override the Parliament. For example, successive governments in the period from 2002 and 2007, although relying on the support of a hegemonic majority derived from the 2002 legislative elections (the President's political party, the Union for a Popular Movement [UMP] had during this period an absolute majority of the seats in the National Assembly), repeatedly used article 49.3 of the Constitution to adopt a number of important and controversial reforms. Such was the case in 2003, when new electoral rules were approved for the regional and European elections, or in 2005, when Premier Villepin pushed through the extremely controversial 'first employment contract' by using article 49.3. Such haste did not prevent the defeat of the first employment contract in the streets several weeks later.

This situation of a subordinate Parliament and overbearing executive also results in a paradox: the Parliament, which is wholly politically subordinated to the executive power, also becomes the central locus of authority that grants the President of the Republic the power to govern. Due to the particularity of the French institutional system – the existence of a double electoral circuit for conferring governing power: the legislative elections and the presidential elections – and the 'bipolarization' of resulting political forces, alternating periods of presidential power may derive their legitimacy from either the presidential or the legislative elections. But the consequences are not the same. When the change in government comes from a presidential election it can only be 'complete' – that is, fully transfer governing power to a new political coalition – if the newly elected President wins the ensuing legislative elections. On the other hand, the victory of an opposing political camp at the legislative elections can, in and of itself, confer the main weight of governing power to the new parliamentary majority, and thereby to the Prime Minister representing this new majority (in which case there is a 'cohabitation'). In other words, in France the determining elections which bestow the power of governing to the President of the Republic, are the legislative elections; but once the members of Parliament have been elected, their remaining duties amount mostly to faithfully following the presidential agenda. The constitutional reform of 2000 which aligned the length of the presidential mandate with that of the deputies (five years), along with the fact that the presidential elections (since 2002) occur one month before the election of the deputies, strongly emphasize the presidential-centric character of the French Fifth Republic.

The current criticism of the institutional structure of the Fifth Republic owes much to this observation: the Parliament serves little real purpose other than to determine who will govern, the President of the Republic or the Prime Minister. In other words, in the French Parliament resides much of the ambiguity of a political system that does not provide a clear answer to the question of who holds final executive authority.

Parliament and the crisis of political representation

The current heightened interest in the role of Parliament, as well as in various proposals for its reform (see Section 3 below), are not only due to its subordination and to the imbalance between the legislative and executive powers. This interest is equally the result of a crisis of confidence in the representatives themselves, specifically whether or not they meaningfully represent the interests of their constituents and whether they are committed to their parliamentary work.

Does the Parliament represent the French people?

It is of course very difficult to define what constitutes good political 'representation' or what the criteria for correct representation entail, but the idea has gained prominence in France, if still somewhat vaguely defined, that the Parliament is no longer representative of the interests of society. Different factors illustrate this phenomenon, the first being the system for electing deputies. Since 1958, deputies have been elected by a two-round uninominal majority ballot for the 577 electoral districts. Proportional representation has only been used once, for the 1986 legislative elections, with the principal consequence the arrival of 35 extreme Right deputies in the National Assembly. Under the system in use at all other elections, in order to be elected on the first ballot a candidate must poll an absolute majority of valid votes, usually corresponding to at least a quarter of the registered electors. If no candidate reaches this threshold, another ballot is organized in which only the candidates who have achieved a number of votes at least equal to 12.5 per cent of the registered electors can participate. In order to be elected at the second ballot, a candidate only needs a plurality: the candidate who has obtained the highest number of votes is declared elected.

This two-ballot system has important effects on the transformation of votes into seats. Table 8.1 shows the effects of this distortion. In the 1997 and 2002 legislative elections, the winner gained, proportionally speaking, nearly twice as many seats as the number of votes received on the first ballot. Thus the Socialist Party (PS) which had 23.5 per cent of the votes on the first ballot obtained 43.3 per cent of the seats after the second ballot of the legislative elections in 1997. More

Table 8.1   *Results in votes and seats of the main French parties at the legislative elections of 1997, 2002 and 2007 (% of the valid votes and seats won at the National Assembly)*

	Votes at first ballot of the legislative elections, 1997	Seats, 1997	Votes at first ballot of the legislative elections, 2002	Seats, 2002	Votes at first ballot of the legislative elections, 2007	Seats, 2007
PS	23.5	43.3	24.1	24.4	24.7	32.2
PCF	9.9	6.2	4.8	3.6	4.3	2.6
Verts	3.6	1.2	4.5	0.5	3.2	0.7
RPR/UMP	15.7	24.3	33.3	63.25	46.3	56.3[a]
UDF	14.2	19.6	4.9	5	7.6	0.5
FN	14.9	0.17[b]	11.34	0	4.3	0

[a] This figure includes those former UDF deputies who created the New Centre (Nouveau Centre) and who rallied to Sarkozy in-between the two rounds of the 2007 presidential election.

[b] This number reflects the nomination of one deputy whose election was then invalidated by the Constitutional Council.

emphatically, the UMP with 33.3 per cent of the votes on the first ballot of the legislative elections in 2002 took 63.25 per cent of the seats in the National Assembly.

In 2007 the situation was somewhat more balanced even if the winner's bonus remained very important (ensuring the winner an absolute majority of the seats). In part due to the strong local roots of their outgoing deputies, but also owing to pre-electoral agreements within each coalition, the 'second rank' political parties – such as the Communist Party (PC) – were able to win seats in 2007 in near equal proportion to their percentage of votes. In contrast, when a political party finds itself outside the traditional political bipolarized system, as was the case for the Union for the French Democracy (UDF) in 2002, the sanction is very heavy. Under the two-ballot system, political parties that have weak local roots – and this is the case for the Greens – have limited power to directly attract voters and can thus only obtain seats by participating in a partisan coalition. It is practically impossible for candidates representing isolated parties, such as the National Front (FN), or the parties of the extreme Left, to be elected to the National Assembly. Except in very rare circumstances, only parties that belong to potential majority partisan coalitions can elect deputies.

Distortion effects in legislative elections

The distortion in the political representation of different political parties has been accentuated by the fact that the principal governing parties have had for the past 20 or so years a weakening electoral base, due to both a higher abstention rate and an increasing number of protest votes in favour of the extreme Left or Right. Whereas at the end of the 1960s the Left and Right coalitions gained in the aggregate nearly 80 per cent of the registered voters, the same groups have obtained less than 50 per cent in the 2000s. The figures presented here are those of registered voters (rather than electors actually turning up to vote), as this gives a better picture of the overall penetration of the main parties.

If the overall penetration of the governmental parties has been in decline, the gender balance between elected deputies has shifted somewhat as a result of the 2000 parity reform (see Chapter 6 for fuller discussion). The parity reform of 2000 gave full legislative and constitutional force to a reform 'aiming to favour equality in the access of men and women to electoral mandates'. This reform has had some impact: 18.5 per cent of the deputies elected in 2007 were women, as were fully 41.6 per cent of the candidates (against only 10.9 per cent in 1997). But the two-ballot system continues to provide an obstacle to the feminization of deputies because it favours local 'notables' (who are usually male) who have established long-standing grass-roots connections and can profit from the leverage derived from holding several elected offices. The same occurs, but in an even more pronounced way, in relation to what are called in France the 'visible minorities', in particular citizens of African and Arab origin. On this point, there are no official numbers, but the Black Associations Representative Council (CRAN) estimates that only 0.5 per cent of the candidates presented by the main political parties at the 2007 legislative elections in metropolitan France were black (see Chapter 6 for further discussion of CRAN and HALDE).

There is also a generational dimension to these inequalities in representation. Members of Parliament are getting older, substantially more so than the 'natural' effects of an ageing baby-boom generation. In 1981, 38.1 per cent of the deputies were less than 45 years old; only 13.2 per cent were that age in 2007. In 2007, the absolute majority of the deputies (59 per cent) were more than 55 years old, while 48 per cent were that age in 2002. This trend stalls the turnover in the French political class, which is also increasingly professionalized and strongly implanted locally as a result of the popular practice of holding, simultaneously, local and national elected positions.

One might add to the above the socio-professional characteristics of the deputies. There is, in particular, a very strong over-representation of deputies from the civil service sectors, for example teachers and senior officers, and an under-representation of employees and factory workers: merely 6 per cent of the deputies come from the popular social categories which represent more than half of the working population. This socio-professional imbalance adds to the feeling that the French Parliament does not adequately reflect the diversity of society. One can understand why the issues of quality, as well as the representative claims of France's political representatives, have been receiving so much attention.

While the present debate focuses mainly on the National Assembly, many of the same observations could apply to the Senate; since the beginning of the Fifth Republic, the Senate has been under the control of a right-leaning majority, much to the dismay of the Left. In 1998 Prime Minister Lionel Jospin called this a 'democratic anomaly'. In 2003, the Senate, well aware of the strategic advantages in appearing to initiate reform, proposed, with the agreement of the National Assembly, a reduction in the members' term (which decreased from 9 to 6 years) and a marginal modification of their mode of election (the senators are elected by indirect universal suffrage by an electoral college essentially comprised of town councillors). This reform, however, has not had much of an impact. As very aptly observed by Professor Guy Carcassonne: 'When the left wing loses everything, they lose everything; when the right wing loses everything, they keep the Senate.'

Members of Parliament: a low commitment to their legislative duties

In spite of its subordinate position in the political system, according to the official statistics the French Parliament has a relatively high level of activity. It holds public sessions for 120 days per year, spends roughly 70 per cent of its time in legislative activity, 15 per cent on the budgetary debate and 15 per cent in oversight of the government. Between 2002 and 2007, the members of Parliament passed 466 laws, presented 243,259 legislative amendments, compiled 1863 reports and asked 117,971 'written questions' of the government. The public is regularly informed of marathon debates, like the one dedicated to pension reform in 2003 during which the members of Parliament met for a total of 156 hours.

There is a srong sense, however, that the members of Parliament do not legislate effectively. They overlegislate, often in an incoherent way, without following up or evaluating the laws they have adopted. Some recent reforms have attempted to address these issues, in particular the creation, in 1999, within the Finance Committee of a public spending audit office (the Mission d'Évaluation et de Contrôle) inspired by the National Audit Office in the British Parliament. But the impact of the audit office has been limited.

If the average number of laws passed over the course of a year (88 a year from 1988 to 2007, not including the ratification of international treaties) is lower than during the Fourth Republic (241 a year), their individual size has undergone a marked increase. The yearly compendium of laws enacted has risen from 380 pages in 1964 to 1600 pages in 2002. This inflation has led to an attempt to limit 'legislative bulimia', for which the government bears primary responsibility as the controlling force behind the parliamentary agenda.

But most of all, there is a weak commitment by the members of Parliament to their official functions. The reasons behind this are numerous. The main reason – or at least the most emphasized by commentators – is the fact that members of Parliament combine a national elected office with a local office (which can be very important such as president of a region or of a large city). As a result, two-thirds of parliamentary assistants work in their members' constituency and the Parliamentarian him/herself seldom comes to the National Assembly or the Senate more than twice a week. To some degree an explanation for this state of affairs can be found in the fact that the ballot system for the election of members of Parliament requires them to maintain a visible presence in their constituencies in order to ensure their re-election.

The chronic lack of job commitment and absenteeism of members of Parliament are also to a great extent the result of the stranglehold of the party in power and overly rigid party platforms. The strong voting discipline in most of the parliamentary groups, the weak autonomy of the individual members and the opposition's near total absence of room to manoeuvre all discourage initiative from deputies. As discussed in Chapter 11, however, cross-party alliances of like-minded deputies can occasionally crystallize to call the executive to account and demand more responsibility for the elected Parliament. The passage of the LOLF, narrated in detail by Bezès, presents the best recent example of this more general trend.

The context of globalization and Europeanization is leading to a widespread sentiment that members of Parliament are losing their remaining capacity for taking initiatives. Between 2002 and 2007 the Parliament passed 436 laws, but a closer look at the distribution of these laws shows a different picture: 160 were of governmental origin, 55 of parliamentary origin and 222 aimed at authorizing the ratification of a treaty or an international agreement. In other words, at the present time, more than half of the laws ratify international agreements that have been negotiated by the executive power without the advice and consent of Parliament. The same is true of the translation of European law into French law. Between 2002 and 2007, less than 20 per cent of the European directives required the intervention of legislators to be transposed into French law, and even when called on to act, the members of Parliament have most of the time delegated their (limited) power to the government or have adopted the European legislation by 'package' with no real discussion. Even if the role of the members of Parliament increased with regards to European matters (following two constitutional revisions [1992, 1999], adopted at the time of the ratification of the treaties of Maastricht and Amsterdam, which provided for a greater up-front level of information and documentation on EU legal projects on which Parliament henceforth could adopt resolutions), the French Parliament remains very largely sidelined with respect to European policy.

This general situation has a doubly undermining and negative effect on both the Parliament's procedures and work product. On the one hand, it encourages delaying tactics (e.g. the 'filibuster') from the opposition (and sometimes even on the part of the majority), especially by the disproportionate use of the right to propose amendments. One of the most spectacular demonstrations of this type of obstruction was the filing of more than 100,000 amendments on the bill organizing the privatization of Gaz de France in September 2006. This is not a new phenomenon, but it recently took on new proportions in spite of a very firm intervention by the Constitutional Council. Since 1981, there has been a massive inflation of amendments. Under the XIth legislative term (1997–2002) 50,851 amendments were put forward at the National Assembly of which 3141 were at the government's initiative

(85.7 per cent of which were adopted), 12,405 by legislative committees (86.9 per cent were adopted) and 35,305 by the deputies themselves (9.4 per cent adopted). Under the XIIth legislative term
(2002–7), this figure was nearly multiplied by five (243,259 amendments were put forward and 16,878 adopted).

On the other hand, and this is to a great extent the product of their
increased irrelevance, the weakness of the parliamentary members'
roles motivates them to fall back on their roles as mediators for special
interests. The best example of this is the increase in the number of
'written questions' sent to the government (more than 30,000 in 2006
at the National Assembly, more than double the number in 2002).
These 'questions', which are addressed to ministers in order to solicit
an explanation on a particular law or to clarify an aspect of government policy, are in fact increasingly used by the members of Parliament
to answer constituents' requests.

The prospects for reforming the French Parliament

Following Jacques Chirac's first election as President of the Republic
(1995), repeated politico-financial investigations directly concerning
the President of the Republic, the political failure associated with the
dissolution of the National Assembly in 1997 and the long 'cohabitation' which followed (1997–2002), all favoured a renewal in the criticism of the Fifth Republic's institutions. Jacques Chirac's re-election in
2002, against a candidate of the extreme Right, resulted in a real political trauma, even if the President of the Republic from that time
forward enjoyed hegemonic parliamentary control of the National
Assembly. For the first time in French history, one political party alone
had the absolute majority in both houses, and could even obtain, on its
own, the necessary congressional majority of three-fifths to adopt a
constitutional revision. This presidential superpower status, which
came as a result of having a parliamentary majority at its disposal
(even if it was deeply divided between Nicolas Sarkozy and Dominique
de Villepin, both of whom had their sights on running in the upcoming
presidential election), coupled with the President's numerous failures
(in particular the May 2005 defeat concerning the referendum on the
European Constitution), fuelled a mounting criticism of the political
status quo. An increasing number of politicians from the Left, but also
from the centre of the political spectrum, began to speak of the necessity of a transition towards a so-called Sixth Republic.

The presidential election of 2007 gave a real impetus to this rising
criticism. On the Left, as well as on the Right, the same conclusion was
drawn: as it stands, the Fifth Republic is out of date. The feeling
behind this was so strong that 7 out of the 12 candidates for the presi-

dency of the Republic proposed changes designed to move France towards a Sixth Republic. In all political factions, the broad diagnosis was the same: the absolute concentration of the state's power in the person of the President, answerable to neither the judiciary nor the Parliament, is no longer acceptable. Curiously, however, with some exceptions (the Communist Party, the Greens and the extreme Left), the institutional structure of the Fifth Republic is not fundamentally under challenge. Ségolène Royal, François Bayrou and Nicolas Sarkozy all have a very similar view of the institutional reform required: on the one hand they want the text of the Constitution to square with actual practice – in other words, to admit that the President of the Republic, since he is elected directly by the nation, is the real head of government; on the other hand, they want to balance the political system by giving new powers to the Parliament.

The institutional reform platforms espoused by the main presidential candidates did not stray far from the 'presidential system' *à la française* or *présidentialisme* in French political language. This approach to governing is neither that of a European parliamentary system in which the head of government is the leader of a coalition which has won the legislative elections, nor a real presidential system in which the President is the chief of the executive power facing a powerful and self-governing Parliament. It remains a sort of hybrid regime in which the *effective* chief of government – the President of the Republic – is not answerable for his actions before Parliament, and preserves the right to dissolve the National Assembly where necessary (see also the discussion by Levy and Skach).

It is in this context that the new President of the Republic, Nicolas Sarkozy, instigated a wide-ranging constitutional reform project, the outlines of which should become visible in 2008. The main part of this reform deals with the Parliament.

The forthcoming institutional reforms will almost certainly formally recognize the President as leader of the government. While Nicolas Sarkozy does not wish to abolish the function of the Prime Minister (which could be useful in the case of a 'cohabitation' or as a 'circuit-breaker' in the case of a political crisis), a way of reaffirming the pre-eminence of the President would consist in authorizing an annual address delivered directly to both houses (at present, the President is the only French citizen who does not have the right to enter into the Parliament) providing a summary of his actions and a presentation of future plans, a sort of 'state of the union' speech. This reform, which has been presented, wrongly, as the imposition of a duty on the President to come before Congress, remains at best symbolic.

A second facet of the ongoing constitutional reform should lead to a loosening of governmental ascendancy over Parliament, for example by giving more autonomy to the Parliament in setting its own agenda, or by limiting the government's power to commit its responsibility on a proposed bill (which is then adopted without any vote). A third facet deals with Parliament's oversight role vis-à-vis the executive power. The aim is to empower Parliament to offer its advice and consent in the appointment of senior civil servants or managers of public organizations (hitherto decided solely by the President). Further, the idea is to grant more discretion to the opposition members of Parliament, allowing them to chair legislative commissions, for example, or to call for the establishment of boards of inquiry. Echoing the Socialist leader Ségolène Royal's idea, Nicolas Sarkozy has already insisted that the president of the Finance Committee of the National Assembly be a Socialist deputy of the opposition.

Finally, the proposed changes, as currently envisaged, include a reform of the ballot system for parliamentary elections. This reform, which, in its present form, would lead to the election of some number (between one-tenth and a half) of deputies by proportional representation, is the subject of broad disagreement among the President's supporters. Notwithstanding such dissent, this proposal has become a key condition for the political Left and centre for their support of Sarkozy's reform plans for the Fifth Republic. Whatever the result of this dialogue, a redrawing of parliamentary districts is under way, something which has not been done since 1986, in spite of the Constitutional Council's criticism of the disparities of parliamentary representation.

Conclusion

The main contenders in the 2007 presidential election each recognized the shortcomings of France's hybrid political model that separates power and responsibility. In their own way, each of the leading candidates called for the development of more accountable and transparent political arrangements. While Royal and Bayrou supported moving to a Sixth Republic, based on strengthened parliamentary institutions, the eventual victor Sarkozy, in his first six months in office, initiated a more overt presidentialization of the regime than any of his predecessors, a development charted in Chapters 1 and 7. The presidential turn of the Sarkozy regime has placed those calling for a Sixth Republic on the defensive – for the moment at least. But it is not excluded that the one consequence of the move to a more presidential-centred regime under Sarkozy will be the discovery of a more affirmative role for the French Parliament.

Chapter 9

Checks, Balances and the New Rules of the Political Game

YVES SUREL

If we consider democracy as a political regime characterized by an essential tension between populism (legitimacy belongs to the people) and constitutionalism (respect for individual rights and the rule of law), we have to recognize that the French political system has long been considered as an 'imperfect' democracy. This traditional image is linked to the classical analyses of the American and the French political systems made by Tocqueville during the nineteenth century. In *La démocratie en Amérique*, Tocqueville identified the rule of law and the respect for moral and political principles as characteristic elements of the American democratic regime and as one of the main reasons for its legitimacy and durability. Contrasting with these institutional characteristics, Tocqueville, when he analysed the evolutions of the French political system in *L'ancien régime et la Révolution*, underlined a different tension between a rigid judicial system and political traditions based on the sovereignty of an abstract people, which was closer to an uncontrollable crowd than to a free association of citizens.

On the basis of these (sometimes oversimplified) conceptions, analyses of the French political system and its judicial characteristics have more often than not been constructed on this fundamental contrast to the American democratic regime. In this perspective, the French political system has never really been based on an equilibrium between populism and constitutionalism but on the institutionalization of a conflict between these fundamental traits. As a consequence, French political life is often characterized by a 'genetic' instability, precisely because of the absence, or at least the weak presence, of institutional mechanisms based on the respect of a Bill of Rights and guaranteed by a supreme court. Whereas American civic culture is attached to the pacification of private and social relations by law, French civic culture is often depicted as dominated by 'passions' (Zeldin, 1979) and regulated by the state. And this conclusion seemed to be true for macropolitical processes as well as for micropolitical dynamics. If the number of electoral mandates was strictly restricted in the American political system, one of the main

141

reasons for the 'corruption' of the French Republic, according to some authors (Mény, 1992), was the opportunity left to some politicians to accumulate power resources and to concentrate mandates at different levels of government. These institutional configurations allowed then some kind of arrangements based on obscure compromises between politicians and civil servants (the famous cross-regulation [*régulation croisée*] identified by French sociologists such as Crozier, 1987 or Dupuy and Thoenig, 1985).

Another feature of this disequilibrium was sometimes attached to the limitation of accountability procedures in the French political system. The traditional principle ('le Roi ne peut mal faire') inherited from the monarchy had been transferred to the Republican regime: no real judicial mechanisms had been adopted and implemented to allow control of the executive. Until recent constitutional reforms (see below), the President of the French Republic was therefore submitted to no real political or penal responsibility. Political power was not held in check by effective 'checks and balances' mechanisms, which gave the impression that politicians were protected from any *recall* or *impeachment* procedures.

This common perception of the French political system is present in some 'large-*n*' comparative studies. One example is provided by Lijphart's classical analyses of democracy, where he considered France as a political regime characterized by two features related to constitutional dynamics: a relatively flexible Constitution, with rules for constitutional amendments that give some real room for manoeuvre to political actors; but a weak practice of judicial review. More precisely, Lijphart states that 'France was long considered the prime example of a country in which the principle of popular sovereignty was said to prevent any application of judicial review' (Lijphart, 1999: 225). And despite some institutional reforms, notably the constitutional amendment adopted in 1974, which gave to 60 MPs the ability to appeal to the Constitutional Council, the result of his comparative analysis is that France is still characterized by a 'medium-strength' index of judicial review.

But times are changing. This traditional image of French political life has been transformed by recent developments. During the 1980s and the 1990s, a new equilibrium emerged between populism and constitutionalism in the Fifth Republic. The causes of this evolution are diverse and sometimes difficult to identify or to analyse. In this introduction, it is nevertheless possible to develop some basic arguments. Some authors and political actors claimed that this new situation was partly due to the coming of age of the Fifth Republic that followed the election of a Socialist to the presidency in 1981. With this election, and the success of the Left at the legislative elections in June 1981, the Republic experienced for the first time a political shift without an institutional shift. In one account, this continuity of institutions produced 'pacification' of French political life and a broad acceptance of France's semi-presidential system (Favier and Martin-Roland, 1990; Winock, 1995, 2003).

Parallel to this evolution, and maybe even related to it, French politics was then characterized by a growing dissatisfaction of public opinion towards politicians. In the 1980s and 1990s, a number of affairs and scandals broke out that revealed a high degree of corruption and cast a different light on political practices in France. It was as if the tacit acceptance of institutional rules was replaced by a growing mistrust of politicians. To follow Heidenheimer's typology, we could say that what was sometimes accepted as a 'white' or a 'grey' corruption in the past was now perceived as 'black' (Heidenheimer, 1978). These political scandals were linked to the revelation of occult forms of political financing. They demonstrated that there were complex relations between private firms and the political sphere (Pujas and Rhodes, 1999; Lascoumes, 1999).

A last set of elements could be seen as explanatory variables for the changes that occurred in the constitutional form of the French political system and are related in the growing importance of legal norms defined at supranational levels of government. European integration and the impact of international norms or standards have become, over the past few years, a core feature of French political life. This development has transformed the legal hierarchy and has obliged political actors to take into account different sets of legal norms and institutions in the definition of their strategies and interactions.

All these elements, be they endogenous or exogenous to the French political system, have produced adaptive pressures. Two core dimensions of these changes are addressed in this chapter. First, there has been an opening up of the law, and the emergence of a more pluralistic, less state-centric production of new laws, norms and standards. This evolution is certainly not specific to the French political system. The argument is made here that these changes have had deeper consequences in France than elsewhere, given that the process of producing new legal norms was previously so tightly controlled by politicians in the executive branch. Second, the chapter will insist upon the linkage between the succession of political scandals in the 1980s and 1990s, the growing distrust of the Fifth Republic that this produced, and the recognition by political actors that there needed to be root and branch reforms of some important aspects of the Republic. By introducing constitutional amendments or by implementing new measures, the rules of the political game in France have progressively been changed. The announcement of a new constitutional reform initiated by President Sarkozy is only the latest manifestation of a deeper trend.

Defining and controlling the law

The process of defining and controlling the law has become less of an executive-centric affair. Arend Lijphart was one of the first to stress this point in his comparative research. Analysing the consequences of the 1974 constitutional reform, he remarked that the opportunity given to MPs to appeal to the constitutional court was a key factor in promoting more pluralism in French political life. Following Stone's analysis of the strengthening of the Constitutional Council (Stone, 1992), he considered that 'parliament is no longer the ultimate interpreter of the constitutionality of its own laws' (Lijphart, 1999: 225). Since the executive power was the real master in the legislative procedure, this reform was mainly seen as a way to institutionalize some counterweights to the overall centrality of the President in the political regime.

More generally, classical analyses of democracy in France have always identified a high degree of centralization and a strong concentration of political power in a limited number of institutions. The definition of the law and the control of judicial procedures were just one of many different aspects of this statist tradition, which sometimes led some authors to depict France as the paragon of a 'strong state' (Birnbaum and Badie, 1982). The centralization of decision-making was justified in terms of the political legitimacy of the main institution (the Parliament in the Third and in the Fourth Republic, the President in the Fifth Republic), a centralization coupled to an absence of judicial autonomy and the weakness of other institutions.

The Fifth Republic, in this regard, was characterized by a certain degree of continuity. The institutions designed by General de Gaulle and his collaborators were conceived as a means of making political power more efficient and more legitimate (Quermonne, 1991; Favoreu, 2007; Duhamel, 1999). One of the main aspects of this rationalization of political power was the concentration of the power to define legal norms in the hands of the executive branch. According to article 39 of the Constitution, the initiative for laws is shared by the Prime Minister and MPs. But in practice, the regime has seen the development of an increasing asymmetry between the government and the Parliament, a theme explored more fully by François in Chapter 8. The new equilibrium between populism and constitutionalism in the French political system is thus not correlated to a new equilibrium in the balance of institutional powers. Even if there have been some minor adjustments, Parliament remains a weak institutional actor and this weakness is mainly due to its structural incapacity to influence the lawmaking process. Changes have therefore to be identified and analysed in other parts of the political system and/or in factors exterior to it.

The Constitutional Council

The first decisive change is linked to the growing influence of the Constitutional Council in France, which has nurtured a progressive 'judicialization' of the lawmaking process. We make use here of the definition proposed by Alec Stone of judicialization. In his comparative study of constitutional courts in Europe, Stone identified the judicialization of lawmaking as one of the main transformations of European political systems. More precisely,

> by judicialization, (he) mean(s) (a) the production, by constitutional judges, of a formal normative discourse that serves to clarify, on an ongoing basis, the constitutional rules governing the exercise of legislative power, and (b) the reception of these rules, and of the terms of this discourse, by legislators. (Stone, 2000: 195)

The creation of the Constitutional Council by the 1958 Constitution remains a considerable event in this respect. As many authors have shown, this was in fact the first time that constitutionalism was clearly institutionalized in the French political system by the creation of a supreme court, which was then able to warrant the principle and the norms attached to the Republican regime (Favoreu and Philip, 2005; Avril and Gicquel, 2005; Stone, 1992). This function was not so clear at the beginning, since the new Constitutional Council was more often than not perceived by General de Gaulle as a way to protect the presidency and the government against encroachments from the Parliament. But, from the early 1970s onwards, the Constitutional Council demonstrated its independence from the executive branch and became more like a 'classical' supreme court.

The first step in this more autonomous development is usually related to the already cited 1974 constitutional reform. Following his election to the presidency, Valéry Giscard d'Estaing initiated a number of political reforms in order to modernize the French political regime (Sirinelli, 2007). The 1974 amendment authorized 60 parliamentarians to petition the Constitutional Council, which made possible a constitutional control over the lawmaking process that had until then been largely dominated by the executive branch. After 1974, the number of referrals grew rapidly: whereas only 51 texts had been referred to the constitutional court from 1959 to 1974, there were 76 referrals under the Giscard presidency (1974–81) and 92 under the first term of Mitterrand from 1981 to 1988. Even if Parliament as an institution was not revamped in terms of lawmaking influence, parliamentarians were then the mediators of popular or partisan discontent and could activate the French constitutional supreme court and therefore 'judicialize' political decisions.

This institutional and political shift was reinforced by the strategy developed by the Constitutional Council, which had begun to assert its independence even before this constitutional amendment. By a decision taken in 1971, the constitutional judges had decided to extend the 'constitutional block' (*bloc de constitutionnalité*), the set of principles and norms on the basis of which they could exert their judicial control. 'In that year, for the first time, the Council declared a government-sponsored law unconstitutional on the grounds that the law violated constitutional rights' (Stone, 2000: 41). This first decision was followed by others by which the constitutional judges developed an extensive interpretation of their role and of the Bill of Rights, incorporating some classical texts or references, notably the French declaration of the rights of man adopted in 1789 during the French Revolution. This new independence was implemented in several famous decisions, in particular after the election of François Mitterrand in 1981, when the Constitutional Council obliged the new government to modify some important aspects of its political programme, especially with regard to its proposed nationalizations. On the basis of this enhancement of the Constitutional Council, some authors considered that the judicialization of lawmaking had given birth to a so-called 'government of judges' or that this evolution could be termed as the 'law without the state' (Favoreu, 1988; Cohen-Tanugi, 1992).

These analyses have to be nuanced. If we look back at the two criteria defined by Stone to identify the judicialization of politics, we could consider that the first one (the diffusion of a formal normative discourse) has effectively characterized the evolution of the Constitutional Council in France since 1971. With the 1974 reform and the growing influence of the judges on the definition of their own judicial and institutional resources, it seems quite clear that the Constitutional Council has succeeded in formalizing a normative discourse, which serves as a clarification for the hierarchy and legitimacy of laws, as well as an instrument of counter-power against the executive. Nevertheless, the achievement of the second criterion (the reception of this formal normative discourse by legislators) remains unclear and contestable. It does not appear that the decisions of the Constitutional Council are systematically incorporated by the legislators into the decision-making process. Quite the contrary, since the government has sometimes tried to subvert council decisions by elaborating new texts. The recruiting authorities being political actors (three judges are nominated by the President, three by the President of the National Assembly, and three by the President of the Senate), the composition of the Constitutional Council is sometimes 'very' political, which tends to qualify the 'independent' stance of the supreme court. For example, if we look at the current composition of the council, we have to underline the fact that only one of them, Pierre Joxe, was nominated by a political actor from the Left. Political nominations do not mean that the institution will be less independent, but they tend to make this independence less probable and less systematic, as the 2007 decision on DNA controls for immigrants recently proved.

More generally, the French political system is still far from the separation of powers, which Montesquieu saw as the main institutional requirement for democracy. The French Constitutional Council is still not the equal of the American Supreme Court. It has to share its judicial power with two other institutions: the Court of Cassation (Cour de Cassation) for private law and the Council of State (Conseil d'État) for administrative norms. The judicial review which the court operates is only abstract (before laws are enacted). It has no power of *auto-saisine*. Those that can refer a bill to the council for judicial review are limited: the President, the presidents of legislative chambers, 60 deputies and 60 senators. The idea of opening up the initiative of judicial review to individual citizens has often been discussed but never adopted (Jan, 1999). Lastly, there is no process of ongoing judicial review in the French political system. Once adopted as laws, there is no further recourse on grounds of constitutionality.

In fact, the judicialization of lawmaking is not only a consequence of changes within the French political system. As many analyses have shown, this shift can also be connected to the growing influence of European law and to the rising influence of international norms and standards. It has become commonplace to stress the role and the impact of European legislation in the political systems of the member states of the European Union. Joseph Weiler was probably one of the first authors who underlined that the EU was more often than not a lawmaking institution and that political integration was driven by the common definition of norms and the judicialization of political processes (Weiler, 1999). Central to this process has always been the European Court of Justice (ECJ) with its jurisprudence, which has defined the main features of European law and ensured the enforcement of treaties and directives (Dehousse, 1998). This 'constitutionalization' of Europe and the prominence of European law can thus be analysed as a path-dependent process with ever more important consequences for lawmaking and decision-making processes at the domestic level (Stone et al., 2001; Pierson, 1996). Over the past few years, the notion of 'Europeanization' has been largely discussed in several comparative studies (Caporaso et al., 2001; Featherstone and Radaelli, 2003) with the idea that it might be more interesting to assess the dynamic impact of the European integration process on the domestic political systems than to try to identify the form of the process and its possible outcomes.

The French political system is no exception in this regard. As recent analyses have shown, a large set of policies and institutions have been transformed by the direct or indirect impact of European norms. For example, the welfare state in France, which has often been presented as a case for inertia, is now submitted to different types of adaptive pressures, some of them attached to the evolution of European law (Palier, 2000). The same argument could be developed in other sectors, such as education (Mégie and Ravinet, 2007), immigration (Guiraudon, 2000) or telecommunications (Thatcher, 1999), even if the relative impact of European law differs from one policy to another. This Europeanization of the French political system could also be identified in the analysis of interest groups, which have often made use of legal expertise in the definition of their strategies (Woll, 2006). As a result, the evolution of public policies or domestic institutions is now often depicted as a process of compliance, with a convergence of political systems as a logical consequence.

Even if these analyses are validated in empirical case studies, the French political system is still characterized by a certain degree of inertia or even rejection of this European-driven legal process. If we look for example at the transposition rates of European directives, France has always been ranked at very low levels. This poor performance has often been related to the weakness of the Parliament, which has not been able to develop a real expertise in European affairs and to act as a 'positive' veto player in the interpretation and the integration of European law (see Chapter 8). This result has also been connected to the inertia of jurisprudence, notably for administrative law. Until 1989 and a famous decision taken by the Council of State (the Nicolo ruling), the French administrative court considered domestic legislation as superior to European law if the domestic lawmaking process had taken place after the relevant European treaty. This particular attitude was seen as a way of maintaining the statist tradition in France and was sometimes correlated with a protective administrative culture. But with the deepening of the European integration process, especially after the Maastricht Treaty, this strategy was no longer sustainable and Europeanization has indeed become one of the main explanatory variables for recent changes in the French political system.

Lastly, we can add to these transformations the emergence of new forms of regulation, which have changed the lawmaking process. These new processes are sometimes linked to the globalization or the internationalization of standards and norms. Some recent analyses have contended that there has been a transnationalization or internationalization of politics over the past few years. Even if international institutions or standards had already emerged in the past, the last decade has seen the generalization of international norms and the growing influence of institutional dynamics at the international level, which challenge domestic political systems (Dudouet et al., 2006).

The concept of the international regime has been proposed to explain this reallocation of political resources and the emergence of new forms of governance (Rosenau and Czempiel, 1992). This trend can be illustrated by emphasizing the growing importance of the World Trade Organization (WTO) as an international political forum as well as a complex set of institutions and rules. National political systems have also had to adapt to this new international institutional framework by developing new types of expertise and by integrating some of the norms or instruments defined and implemented by these institutions.

France is sometimes depicted as a country which faces specific problems related to this globalization process and this institutionalization of norms at the international level. But there is no doubt that international norms have contributed to the judicialization of domestic politics. The influence of internationalization can take the form of soft law or the emulation of 'best practice' identified in international circles. Thus, Palier (2003) links the 2003 pension reform in France to the influence of reports published by the IMF or the OECD from the 1980s onwards, calling upon national governments to liberalize their pension regimes. A rather harder example is provided by the generalization of regulation agencies in France, which can be seen as a kind of institutional isomorphism by which the political sphere has progressively transferred some of its competences to independent actors and to quasi-judicial procedures (Chevallier, 1995; Stone and Thatcher, 2003). These elements then put further pressure on the French political system, sometimes challenging or colluding with European dynamics, in the redefinition of the lawmaking process and the repositioning of politics.

To conclude on these points, since the beginning of the Fifth Republic, we have seen a progressive shift from a political system characterized by a high degree of centralization and politicization to a more pluralist and more 'judicialized' institutional framework. The growing influence of the Constitutional Council was probably a decisive factor here until the 1980s, but the effects of the European integration process or even the impact of international norms have replaced this dynamic since then. Such pluralism is, however, not really correlated with a shift in political power at the domestic level. Even if the executive power has now to coordinate its actions with, or at least to take into account, the Constitutional Council, the European Court of Justice and international organizations, this has not meant an upgrading of Parliament's power. As we have seen, MPs are still weak actors, especially in lawmaking. This leads us to our second main area of enquiry: to what extent have these changes in the definition of norms been complemented by transformations in the rules of the political game?

The new rules of the political game

This adaptation of lawmaking is but one aspect of the changes that have occurred in the French political system. A number of institutional reforms have progressively altered the characteristics and the dynamics of the traditional semi-presidential political system. Two aspects are important here: first, the examination of successive constitutional reforms, which have changed the Fifth Republic in a way which is more than incremental; second, the analysis of new 'rules' of the political game, which have reinforced the cartelization of the French party system.

French political life was rocked by a series of scandals in the 1980s and 1990s. True enough, political scandals are neither new nor specific to the French political system. But history suggests that new critical junctures in France can be opened by the revelation of scandals. Such was the case during the Third Republic, when the parliamentary regime was threatened by corruption scandals, which gave rise to the growth of extremist parties that mobilized popular resentment against the political elites (Winock, 2003). Under Valéry Giscard d'Estaing's presidency, a number of damaging affairs contributed to Giscard's failure to win the presidential election in 1981. Moreover, comparative studies have clearly identified similar phenomena in other countries (Pujas and Rhodes, 1999; Pelizzo, 2004). But the political corruption revealed in the 1980s was different in intensity and with regard to its impact on the institutions. Two points are particularly important here: the fact that these scandals affected all the political parties, especially the governmental parties, the Socialist Party and the UMP (Union pour un Mouvement Populaire – UMP, the former Gaullist Rassemblement pour la République – RPR); the growing dissatisfaction towards political elites and the political system as a whole. These developments put enormous pressure on the main parties and were at the root of some important reforms.

It would take too long to expose in detail these scandals and this topic is far beyond the main purpose of this chapter. It is nevertheless important to stress the fact that the corruption revealed in the 1980s surprised and shocked public opinion in its intensity and its extent. All the parties were forced to confront the fallout from political scandals related to party finance and to the revelation of occult exchanges between private firms and public organizations. The PS, the most important party in the 1980s, was the first to confront these scandals. The media revealed in 1989 that a fictive consulting group (Urba) had been created in order to channel financial resources to the Socialist Party and Mitterrand's presidential campaign of 1988 (Favier and Martin-Roland, 1996: 351–82). The result of these affairs was all the more critical in that Mitterrand and his entourage had sometimes presented the 1981 political shift as an opportunity to 'moralize' French political life and to put an end to corruption practices. But the left-wing parties were not isolated cases in this period. The Gaullist Party and its allies (notably Démocratie Libérale, which has now disappeared) were also affected by the revelation of these political 'routines'. The start of legal proceedings against former President Jacques Chirac in an affair related to financial transfers operated from the City of Paris is the latest event of an ongoing judicial process.

As a result of these scandals, public opinion polls registered a growing dissatisfaction with political elites and democracy as a whole (Perrineau, 2003). There was a widespread perception that a huge gap had developed between politicians and their constituents, and that financial corruption was just one aspect of a more general corruption of moral principles and institutional dynamics (Mény, 1992). One object of criticism was the practice of accumulating offices (*cumul des mandats*). As André Blais puts it, 'French politics has many peculiarities. Perhaps the most striking and intriguing, from a comparative perspective, is the long-standing practice of the accumulation of mandates. Almost 90 percent of present French MPs hold a local office' (Blais, 2006: 266). The causes of this phenomenon are diverse and sometimes related to the centralization of the political system, to the strategic calculus operated by politicians who try to maximize political resources, or even to organizational dynamics and the weakness of political parties (Knapp, 1991; François, A., 2006; Foucault, 2006, Dewoghélaëre et al., 2006). But the fact is that this peculiarity has become less sustainable, embedding the idea that the political elite is a social group characterized by corruption and conspiracy.

These growing criticisms put under pressure the input-oriented legitimacy of political actors. They were coupled with another kind of scandal related to the dramatic failure of public policies which, in turn, undermined the output-oriented legitimacy of political parties and leaders (Scharpf, 1999). The main example of this is probably the so-called contaminated blood scandal, which occurred in the 1980s, when a number of patients were contaminated by the AIDS virus as a result of blood transfusions they received in public hospitals. A number of associations, in particular interest groups which represented people affected by haemophilia, took the former Prime Minister, Laurent Fabius, and several ministers (Edmond Hervé and Georgina Dufoix, who shared the Health departments) to court over this matter. In fact, expert analysis has shown that causality is difficult to identify in these policies and responsibility quite impossible to assess (Setbon, 1993). But the fact that governments appeared complicit in the transmission of AIDS yet no one was held to account became the illustration of the lack of responsiveness and the failure of accountability of traditional mechanisms.

On the basis of these various elements the idea grew that the French political system had to be reformed in order to resolve its democratic deficit and to re-establish accountability procedures. We can make a distinction here between constitutional amendments and legal innovations, which have together changed the Fifth Republic over the past few years.

It is indeed striking to see how far the French political system has recently been reformed by amendments to the Constitution over the past few years, challenging the widespread depiction of the regime created by de Gaulle in 1958 as the first real stable political system in French history. Since 1992, the French Constitution has been amended (at the time of writing) by 17 constitutional laws, which contrasts deeply with the period 1958–92, when only five constitutional amendments were adopted. A number of these recent amendments have been directly related to the European integration process and constitute another proof of the adaptive pressures identified in the first part of this chapter. For example, the revision enacted in March 2003 was linked to the definition and the implementation of the European arrest warrant, which followed the building of 'a space of liberty, justice and security' at the European level. Another constitutional law in March 2005 was explicitly conceived as a means of anticipating the adoption of the Constitutional Treaty. The March 2005 amendment integrated new provisions within the French Constitution, such as article 88.5 which states that 'any bill authorizing the ratification of a treaty relating to the adhesion of one State to the European Union and the European Communities is subjected to the referendum by the President of the Republic'.

But other amendments were clearly formulated and adopted to try to resolve the political crisis. One of the most important reforms of the Constitution is probably the reduction of the duration of the presidential mandate. Since the Third Republic and the installation of a seven-year mandate, the successive republics had always confirmed this initial choice. But the length of this mandate, coupled with the absence of any limitation on re-elections, was increasingly criticized as one of the mechanisms that nurture a gap between political actors and the people. The five-year term was thus rapidly discussed as one desirable adjustment to the Constitution of the Fifth Republic. President Pompidou had even launched the revision process in 1972, but political uncertainties and his health (Pompidou died in office in 1974) hindered the final adoption of this measure. After this episode, though many political actors and academics supported the change, no president had taken the initiative until Jacques Chirac in 2000. Elected in 1995 and facing cohabitation after the success of the Socialist Party at the legislative elections in 1997, Chirac viewed this reform as a way of reaffirming his own power as President and of potentially making easier his re-election in 2002 for a shorter term. The Constitutional Law no. 2000-964 (*Journal officiel*, 3 October 2000) was thus adopted and brought the presidential mandate into line with the terms of the deputies. Two presidential elections have taken place since this reform, and most commentators analysed this constitutional amendment as a further reinforcement of the presidency. In 2002, as well as in 2007, the organization of the presidential election just before the legislative elections tends to imbue the latter with less importance. The real choice is made in the presidential elections and parliamentary elections are now considered by many as a simple confirmation of the first vote.

The year 2007 also saw the adoption of a constitutional law which now makes the President penally responsible for his acts. As we saw in the introduction, the absence of any sort of accountability for the President was sometimes depicted as an inheritance from the past, especially from the monarchy and the empire. In practice, it meant that the elected President was politically responsible (via his possible re-election) but protected from any lawsuit attached to his penal or civil responsibility. With the emergence of corruption scandals, this traditional principle was considered as archaic, and the President's legal responsibility became a recurrent debate in the political sphere. An expert committee, which was chaired by a famous professor of law, Georges Vedel, discussed for example the possibility of implementing in France an impeachment procedure inspired by the American system.

The situation became really problematic under Jacques Chirac's second term, when the Constitutional Council decided that a president in office could not be subjected to any legal proceedings, although revelations of corruption affairs were increasingly frequent. Before the end of his second term, Jacques Chirac and his Prime Minister Dominique de Villepin thus initiated a new constitutional law, enacted in February 2007, which has reformed presidential accountability. Article 68 of the Constitution now states that 'the President of the Republic can only be relieved of office in the case of exercising his duties in a manner obviously incompatible with the presidential office. The dismissal is pronounced by Parliament sitting as the High Court.' This reform, without explicitly anticipating penal responsibility, has nevertheless contributed to a relative redefinition of the presidency and could be seen as a means to give to the legislative power a more explicit instrument of control over the executive power.

The rules of the political game have also been transformed by a raft of new laws. First of all, as we have seen before, the problem of party finance has been very sensitive. The multiplication of lawsuits related to the above-cited scandals affected public opinion and made new laws necessary. Until 1988, indeed, there was no law fixing the rules of party finance. Successive governments thus took the initiative of defining new rules for party finance by passing four main laws (11 March 1988; 15 January 1990; 19 January 1995; and 11 April 2003). The new rules still authorize private financing, but with severe limitations: for example, donations made by individuals are limited to €7500 per person per year; private funds from firms are prohibited. But the main innovation brought about by these successive laws is the public financing of political parties. France now has a system of partial state funding of political parties. This system is governed by two criteria: public finance is available for parties whose candidates obtain at least 1 per cent in at least 50 constituencies at the legislative elections; and the amount of public funds is proportional to the number of MPs obtained by each party. Thus, in 2004, the total amount of public funds rose to €73 million (33 million for the UMP, 19 million for the Socialist Party, 4 million for the National Front, etc.). This device is further guaranteed by a strict control of spending during election campaigns, which is policed by a special committee, the National Committee for Campaign Accounts and Political Finance (Commission Nationale des Comptes de Campagne et des Financements Politiques). Elected deputies whose campaign expenses are above the authorized maximum can be subjected to a recall procedure.

Another shift in the 'rules of the game' has been linked to the reform of the practice of accumulation of elected offices (*cumul des mandats*). The Constitution of 1958 initially prohibited combining membership in Parliament and in the government. When deputies were named to serve in the government, their assistants (*adjoints*) would take up their seats in the National Assembly. In recent years, the accumulation of elected offices has come under attack. Successive governments have limited the practice of accumulating two or more political offices, with laws passed in 1985 and 2000 providing the key benchmarks. In addition to the prohibition of accumulation of the offices of deputy and senator, a French deputy can no longer be a member of the European Parliament (a member of Parliament elected in Strasbourg loses his or her domestic mandate). Moreover, combining national and local mandates is now strictly limited. An individual has the right to combine being a deputy with only one of the following offices: regional councillor, department councillor, member of the Parliament of Corsica, municipal councillor of Paris, or municipal councillor of a commune of more than 3500 inhabitants. The effects of this reform seem to be quite limited, at least for the time being (Dewoghélaëre et al., 2006). The practice of *cumul des mandats* is still a systemic attribute of French political life. But, in addition to the constitutional amendments and the new laws analysed above, these measures might help to make democracy in France more pluralist, less centralized and (a little more) moral.

Conclusion

When analysed from a legal or institutional perspective, the French political system has undergone a number of transformations over the past 20 years. The first process of change, driven by Europeanization and the internationalization of norms, is that there has been the emergence of a more pluralistic, less state-centric production of new laws, norms and standards which was traditionally concentrated in the hands of the executive branch. By making the hierarchy of norms more uncertain and complex, these forces have produced a partial 'judicialization' of politics in France. If we use once more the categorization proposed by Alec Stone (see above), this judicialization is limited to the growing influence of constitutional judges (be they domestic with the Constitutional Council, European with the ECJ, international with the role of international organizations) on the interpretation and the implementation of rules. But Stone's second criterion (the internalization of new legal norms by legislators) appears less relevant. The legislator in France (mainly the executive branch) is still quite independent of this 'judicialization', at least when it comes to the substantial definition of laws.

Parallel to this evolution, the French political system has also been affected by other reforms, which have progressively altered the classical rules of the political game. With the help of constitutional amendments or more limited laws, political actors have tried to answer the 'crisis of representation' by modifying some basic rules relating to the responsibility of the executive branch or to party finance. The Fifth Republic is therefore now an institutional configuration which is dramatically different from the regime that General de Gaulle had in mind. Institutional changes are ongoing. The current constitutional reform initiated by President Sarkozy is a case in point here and might serve to draw a quite different picture of the French political system in a future volume.

Chapter 10

Territorial Politics in France: le Calme avant la Tempête?

PATRICK LE GALÈS

Politics in France was and remains profoundly territorially rooted within regions, rural communes, small towns and cities. This deep territorialization continues to have an impact on the way in which society and the economy operate. As in most continental European countries, conflicts about redistribution, norms of political behaviour or public policy implementation remain rooted in contrasting regions and localities. Governing Marseilles is a different experience and reality than that of governing Nantes or Strasbourg. The electoral geography of Toulon or Nice is at odds with that of Bordeaux or Toulouse. Raising taxes in Paris, Corsica or Brittany can lead to surprising results. As the great historian Fernand Braudel put it, governing diversity was always the engine of the centralization of the state in France. However, the rootedness of politics in different regions and localities does not suggest immobility. Slow, incremental, but over time radical, changes are transforming territorial politics in France and French politics altogether (Le Galès, 2005). The French polity, as most European polities, is being eroded, restructured uneasily under the combined pressures of transnational forces, population flux, firms, immigrants, the upper middle classes and the European Union, on the one hand, and identity-conscious and politically ambitious regions and cities on the other. France has become a much more open polity transformed by external influences including the globalizing economy and culture, but it remains deeply rooted in this territorial tradition. Recent debates about the globalization of wine and the reaction of local and professional interests in Bordeaux, for instance, clearly show this profound territorialization of politics. Territorial understandings, more especially when rooted in the defence of specific economic sectors, can provide a powerful obstacle to the changes provoked by globalization or at least can mediate these changes (Smith et al., 2007).

Understanding decentralization in France would require a relatively long-term perspective. Since the 1960s, and the late urbanization and the major modernization drive of the Gaullist regime, France has followed the road of a slow, incremental, chaotic but unstoppable march towards decentralization, more local autonomy and more fragmentation of politics and policies. Nowadays subnational territories, be they localities, cities or regions, are becoming more central to understanding the dynamics of French society and the conflicts around redistribution and economic development.

The chapter aims firstly to underline the dynamics of decentralization in France before presenting the system as it currently stands and finally discussing the pressures that are mounting within the current system. The chapter argues that a long cycle of decentralization, which has radically changed the French polity, may now be reaching the end.

The dynamics of decentralization: competition between levels, overlapping powers and resources

Over the last 30 years, French local authorities have more or less lived the good life. They have enjoyed a cascade of never-ending decentralization reforms that have produced increasing legal powers, increasing legitimacy, increasing budgets and increasing numbers of staff. Taking advantage of a contested state (contested by social movements, local groups or large firms), local and regional authorities seemed for a long time to be virtuous, effective, responsive and much more democratic than the remote state.

The dynamic of decentralization gradually began in the late 1960s (Mény, 1974). After the failed referendum of 1969 (about the reform of the Senate and the creation of regions), informal and sometimes illegal forms of decentralization took place in the 1970s, leading to the decentralization reforms of 1982 and 1984, which legalized many practices and ways of making policy which were already taking place. A new wave of important reforms was adopted in the early 1990s. In 1992, the Territorial Administration of the Republic law strengthened the prefectures while devolving more power to the field services in the *départements* and (for some ministries) regions. Between 1997 and 1999, the Jospin government embarked on a number of important reforms that embedded intercommunal authorities and enhanced the role of (mainly public sector) contracts as means of coordinating public policies. In 2004, a new Decentralization Act implemented under Premier Raffarin transferred more resources, powers and staff to the 96 *départements* and the 22 regions. Of great symbolic importance, the Constitution was changed and now officially states that 'the organization of the Republic is decentralized'. All looked rosy from the point of view of local elites.

Three points of particular importance should be emphasized in the form of a summary. First, there have been sustained pressures between the pre-decentralization territorialization system and the new one produced by decentralization reforms. Second, there has been a progressive marginalization of the territorial apparatus of the state. Third, there has been a large-scale transfer of powers and resources to local and regional authorities.

During the Revolution, the organization of the French state was a major constituent of the new regime: old provinces with their parliaments were dismantled, 36,000 communes were created based on medieval parishes (thus undermining powerful regional capitals) and the effort of rationalization led to the creation of less than 100 *départements.* The *département* became the pivotal level of the rural politics and policies that characterized governing in France. Public policy was, in the main, run by a state-appointed important civil servant, the prefect, who operated in tight collusion with the departmental services of a number of central ministries, the most important of which was the Highways and Bridges Ministry (Ponts et Chaussées) which became the Ministry of Infrastructure, Transport [or Transporation] and Housing. During the late ninteenth century and the making of the Third Republic, the democratization of the regime led to the recognition and political autonomy of *communes* and their elected mayors representing the diversity of the little villages and small towns in France. This system still constitutes the backbone of the French political system and was consolidated under the Fifth Republic. After 1958, the role of the *département* was strengthened. The prefect began to negotiate with elected notables (mayors) who combined political offices (typically those of mayor, councillor on the departmental assembly and member of Parliament). This 'tamed Jacobin' system (to use the phrase of Pierre Grémion whose *Le pouvoir périphérique* was the major book about the French system in the 1970s) was in fact very flexible. Mayors and representatives of territories had a widespread access to resources in the centre even if, within a centralized system, the expertise, the resources and the legitimacy for public policy remained in the hands of civil servants and ministers. In Parliament, most of the *députés* were also mayors. Most importantly, the second chamber, the Senate, is the conservatory of local rural interests and it has the power to block reforms of local authorities. This system was based on those five elements: 36,700 communes, 100 *départements*, the Senate, the prefect as the head of the territorial state in each *département* for the vertical integration, and the *cumul des mandats* (holding multiple mandates) for politicians to ensure the integration of the system.

All those elements are still in place today, though the prefect's role has been eroded. However, on top of this, a second system has developed over the past four decades based upon the regions, the cities, the 'intercommunal' organizations of local government and the marginal-

[handwritten marginalia, left margin:] very incredibly decentralized w/ more municipalities than communes, all of EU combined, but still tied to center as usually politicians hold more than one position

[handwritten marginalia, lower left:] Don't put this

ization of the territorial state. This new system has gradually been established as the main outcome of the successive decentralization reforms that have been aimed at 'modernizing' (what else?) France's territorial organization.

Regions, as regional governments, are the first element of the new system. Once a weak level of financial planning for the state in the 1960s, they became a weak level of government representing various interests in the 1970s under the pressure of Alsacian and Breton elites in particular. The decentralization reforms of the 1980s marked the coming of age of 22 regions as regional governments, elected for the first time in 1986. Despite weak budgets and limited powers, they slowly gained resources (through regular tax increases, though starting from a very low level) and political legitimacy.

France was late to urbanize. From the 1960s onwards, former regional capitals away from Paris have been enjoying continuous rapid growth. Boring provincial towns became booming European cities, in particular Lyon, Grenoble, Nice, Montpellier, Toulouse, Nantes, Rennes, or Strasbourg and later Bordeaux or Lille. Local governments in those cities benefited from the Gaullist modernization plans and from massive investments in infrastructure, research centres, hospitals, museums and universities, thus feeding their dynamic growth in the following decades. A generation of Socialist mayors gained power in 1977 and became ministers in the 1980s. They pioneered the modernization and growth of urban government together with the promotion of new forms of intercommunal cooperation.

The last element of the new territorial system was the rise of intercommunal government, a silent revolution which has long-term consequences for policy delivery (Borraz and Le Galès, 2005). Indeed in the 1970s, in order to overcome the fragmentation of 36,700 communes, weak ad hoc cooperative bodies were created to organize the delivery of services for groups of communes (water or waste disposal). France has 36,565 municipalities (Table 10.1), 97.6 per cent of which have a population of less than 10,000. Yet, only a little more than half of the total population lives in these municipalities while almost a third lives in cities with a population over 30,000.

Amalgamation has always been a politically sensitive subject in France and the central government has systematically failed in reducing the number of municipalities. Confronted with multiple and intertwining structures, central government attempted in 1992 to simplify and standardize forms of municipal cooperation with limited success. By contrast the 1999 Chevènement Act went for a voluntary approach, mixing direct constraints with strong financial incentives. Three new forms of intercommunal governments were created with a set of compulsory powers and the obligation to choose among a list of optional functions together with a common tax system. Nowadays, this silent revolution of the past seven years is more or less over, 90 per cent of the population is governed by intercommunal organizations delivering public policies and collecting taxes, however with an indirectly elected council, hence a weak legitimacy.

Those two systems of territorial politics, the communes/departments/Senate versus cities/intercommunal/regions are always in competition. Each level of local government has some powers but each local authority feels it has a legitimate right to deal with all the problems of their inhabitants on their territory. Decentralization Acts after decentralization Acts, the choice was made not to choose between those various levels and no hierarchy exists between them. The latest one, the Raffarin Act, is a brilliant illustration of this phenomenon: while the previous Socialist government had strengthened the regions and the intercommunal organizations, the new Act mostly decentralized important budgets and resources going to the *départements* and undermined budgets for the urban intercommunal governments. Overlapping powers and competition between authorities are the rule. After two decades, the coming of age of regions has proved increasingly relevant but with no hierarchical powers over other levels of local government, their strength remains limited.

The two fundamental features that characterize the ongoing decentralization process are those of competition between the different levels of local authorities and the restructuring of the state. As the latter has been addressed in the Bezès chapter, we will limit our analysis here to competition between local authorities.

In France, political competition between different groups of elected representatives and between political parties is the main factor behind both the rise of local and regional government and the territorialization of public policies. Strong political battles take place both in Parliament and between national associations of local government (Le Lidec, 2002). These groups are permanently engaged in a ceaseless struggle to develop transfers of power from the state and to prevent other levels of government from benefiting at their expense. This competition between groups of politicians from different levels of government is an important competitive dynamic over time, even within political parties. The Left tends to emphasize the role of cities, urban areas, and regions to a lesser extent, without arguing for the suppression of *départements* whose representatives still held strong positions within the Socialist Party. The Right tends to support *départements* and sometimes regions at the expense of cities. The political situation matters very much. At a time when a majority of regions and *départements* are controlled by the Left, a right-wing government faces less opposition from within its own party if it wants to put pressure on, or to introduce a financial squeeze of those levels of government. It is easy to claim that financial crisis is the consequence of the failure of local and regional governments to deal properly with public finance. The counter-argument has also been often used with a lot of success: local and regional authorities will blame the state for their own financial difficulties, especially if an opposing party is in power nationally.

In many countries, political decentralization has gone hand in hand with the 'decentralization of penury' and implementation of cuts in public expenditure. Central governments delegate more service delivery responsibilities to local government but do not allocate commensurate taxing powers or transfer adequate resources. Although these pressures exist in the French case, and may increase in the near future – see above – this has not been the dominant pattern so far. Increased policy responsibilities have been matched by increased resources for local and regional governments, either in terms of increased taxes or increased transfers from the state, or usually both (see evidence within this chapter). Local interests have been well defended in the centre. Local and regional politicians have demonstrated their capacity for mobilization, both as local politicians, as represented by local government associations, and also as national politicians, either as ministers or parliamentarians (*députés, sénateurs*). In terms of the remaining prestige and resources controlled by urban mayors, let us just mention that it has been common for former Prime Ministers to become mayors of Lyon or Bordeaux or to come back as mayor of Lille. Becoming mayor of a large city, or president of a region (see Jean-Pierre Raffarin, or François Fillon) remains a classic way to become Prime Minister. Most national politicians in France are mayors or chair a region, and most deputies and senators still hold a local mandate. Leading representatives of the interests of local and regional government are vocal and present in Parliament. They are often powerful former ministers, for instance finance ministers, hence with a very high degree of expertise and political leverage to defend the interests of local and regional governments.

In some cases, the state has tried to decentralize penury. But the various levels of French local government have been reluctant to cut expenditure. Rather, in most cases, from education to social services or transport, local and regional governments in France, when given a new function, tend to improve the quality of the service and the infrastructure and to raise taxes in order to finance the quality improvement. This was the key to understanding the virtuous circle of decentralization for local and regional authorities. When given new powers, local and regional authorities have done a relatively good job at improving services but they have also increased taxes (Le Lidec, 2007). The internal dynamics of decentralization (including emulation and rivalry between authorities) are therefore central to understanding why high-quality public services have been delivered in France. In many ways decentralization goes hand in hand with improvements in the quality of services, as well as a reduction of unequal access to services (health, education). On the other hand, improvements have been paid for by increasing costs and increasing taxes (Dupuy and Le Galès, 2006). The territorialization of public services tends to lead towards greater effectiveness, good value for money, but not cost containment. The competition between levels of subnational governments and between them and state services has contributed, however modestly, to the rise of public expenditure in France related to GDP. Issues of cost or increasing value for money have not been uppermost in the minds of local managers and mayors, above all concerned to run good services.

The French territorial political system is therefore made of effectively four levels of local and regional governments, each of them with its own taxation system and powers. Crucially, there is no hierarchy between these levels (Table 10.1).

Measuring the long-term impact of decentralization is best undertaken through the analysis of resources. Thirty years ago, high-profile administrators were not attracted to serve in the administration of the main regions, *départements* and cities. This is no longer the case. Recent studies (Bachelet, 2005) demonstrate that local public service has gained in strength and reputation; these days top local civil servants are not so different from state civil service administrators. Some of the latter have actually preferred to work for the main local authorities. Moreover, local and regional authorities are now able to mobilize more intellectual resources and expertise than the state, whereas 30 years ago the state territorial services more or less had the monopoly of policy expertise. Even more crucially, between 70 and 75 per cent of public investment is France is under the control of local and regional governments. This is a massive change when they used to control less than 30 per cent. By contrast, the state is often short of funds for many

Table 10.1   *Local and regional authorities in France*

Local and regional authorities in France comprise:

22 regions (with 4 more in overseas territories)
100 *départements*
2,500 intercommunal bodies
36,700 communes
500,000 elected members (all authorities)

Local and regional authorities in France account for:

1.8 million public sector employees (about 30% of the public sector workforce)
45% of public expenditure and 70% of public investment

projects and the departmental state services do not have the resources to match those of local elected officials. Following the old adage that 'he who pays the piper calls the tune', local leaders have become more critical and more dominant in public policies than ever before. By contrast, representatives of state central ministries who used to run the country are increasingly marginalized through lack of expertise and resources.

Contracts, partnerships and plans to coordinate public policies

France is therefore governed sometimes by the central government and its local and regional representatives, sometimes and increasingly so by local and regional authorities. The politics and policies of decentralization have therefore become crucial in the implementation of most public policies and the organization of public services in France.

However, the picture presented earlier suggests more diversity and asymmetry within the French polity, together with more pressure to reduce inequalities. The question of steering, controlling and directing has become a major political issue. Two rather contradictory trends can be identified in French territorial politics, each an attempt to provide the means to coordinate the myriad actors involved in French territorial governance and to implement complex public policies.

Coordination through contracts, plans and partnership

The use of contracts and partnerships to coordinate public policy started in the 1970s to encourage cooperation between the state and local authorities to implement public policies of minor importance. However, this somewhat marginal instrument of French public policy moved to the centre of the political scene during the 1980s. Contracts were seen as a means of combating public policy failures, compensating the failings of state centralization and fulfilling the expectation of the decentralization reforms (Gaudin, 2007). Contracts have proved popular beyond France. The rise of this policy instrument at the EU level or in neighbouring countries reflects the search for less hierarchical instruments in order to mobilize different actors and their resources, to define a more situated general interest and to increase collective capacity to implement policy in a more effective way (Lascoumes and Le Galès, 2007). The role of the state is to mobilize and steer collective resources and capacities from different actors. In the French context, where the legitimacy of local political leaders to articulate some form of situated general interest remains very strong, contracts and partnership were mostly used to coordinate central governments and local and regional authorities. Associations (the voluntary sectors) or private firms are only rarely or gradually signatories to those contracts.

It follows that the political role of local political leaders has changed over time. They increasingly play the role of intermediary between interests, levels of governments and public administrations. They set priorities, mobilize interests and attempt to give a direction to the government of their territories. Nay and Smith (2002) refer to the generalization of 'compromise government' and the role of local leaders as mediators. Gaudin (2007) coined the phrase 'technonotable' (combining the technocratic role within those contracts and the more traditional role of political notables) to characterize the role of local and regional political leaders in those contracts.

In particular, the use of contracts – both with other levels of government and with private actors – became a central policy instrument for cooperation (Marcou et al., 1997). Contracts take different forms. Frequently they are inspired directly by corporate law and have helped to introduce market mechanisms into public management. At the same time, the use of contracts can contradict efforts to achieve intergovernmental coordination of policies and programmes by the use of public rather than private means (Le Galés and Mawson, 1995). Similar tensions arise with partnership approaches. Because of the rules governing public accounts in particular, partnerships require the development of complex bureaucratic structures. These structures, however, represent an additional barrier to engaging local residents and small associations in such partnerships. Moreover, local governments are only keen on developing such partnerships when they do not conflict with the political interests and legitimacy of the local political elites (Loncle, 2000).

At the end of the 1990s, several additional laws were passed to organize local development and planning through compulsory urban strategies, projects and contracts. These laws were mainly aimed at fostering cooperation between local governments in both urban and rural areas. These cooperative efforts were designed to secure the development of economic development strategies, planning strategies and the management of services and utilities.

Additionally, new policies were also introduced, most notably in the fight against poverty and social exclusion. Such tools usually called for the allocation of resources through contracts negotiated and signed between local authorities and state officials, an approach applied in different contexts. Initially they were focused on the neighbourhood, then were extended to the city level, and more recently to the larger urban area. Their application was also extended to other policy domains – from urban renewal to development and physical planning, then to social and health policies, and more recently to area-wide strategies for transport or housing. The multiplication of such schemes, however, brought a new incoherence into the system. Each policy instrument is supposed to be inclusive, to embrace a transversal global approach and to promote some kind of partnership. But political rivalries between local governments and ministries produce different frontiers for each contract and each development strategy. While stronger urban intercommunal bodies or *départements* may be able to achieve some coherence and develop a mode of integrated governance for the whole area, extensive confusion is the norm.

At the local and regional level, preparing the next round of contract, strategic document, or partnership has become a full-time job. Thanks to the increase in specialized high-qualified staff employed in economic development or planning agencies, some of them have become brilliant at producing strategic documents and contracts which are always more or less the same. The accumulation of supposedly strategic, cross-cutting, global, partnership and contractual documents automatically makes each of them far less relevant than they are supposed to be. These contractual documents have usually to be coordinated with European policy documents, which create problems of transparency. Moreover, the French state usually does not keep its word (or its funding commitments), creating a high level of cynicism surrounding the merits of strategic documents.

However, those factors have not prevented an extraordinary inflation of contracts, plans and strategic documents. In the 1990s, following on from the now defunct state–regions plans (*contrat de plan État–région*), many ministries developed policies supposedly implemented via contracts with local authorities. City contracts (*contrat de ville*) set the pace, extending the partnership principle to the new urban policy dealing with neighbourhoods in crisis. Contracts for youth policy, sport, culture and social services followed and flourished. The practice was widely disseminated. As usual in the French case, contracts were not very precise and did not really have a beginning and an end. Rather they institutionalize(d) cooperation at a given moment, set priorities for joint public action by local actors and central ministries and mobilized extra resources. More negotiation was always going on in parallel ways, sometimes involving separate resources. Explicit negotiation brought new problems into the open and also promoted cross-organizational mobilization around specific public policies. But contracts were never more than another instrument in public policy development.

However, the rise of intercommunal bodies and of regions was accompanied in particular by the formulation of a new generation of strategic documents. Urban planning enjoyed a new phase of development (Pinson, 2004). A new family of plans has strengthened the institutional capacity of the intercommunal level, comprising city communities, urban communities or the more rural *pays* (zones much larger than individual communes designed for strategic planning). The intercommunal level gave birth to housing plans, environment plans, strategic plans, economic development plans and social service plans. Regions were also given by law the responsibility to develop regional planning plans (*schémas régionaux d'aménagement du territoire* – SRADT). As the *départements* could not get left behind, they also engaged in developing a round of strategic development plans that were implemented through contracts and partnerships.

French territorial politics is thus structured and organized by this new generation of acronyms, from the PLU (*plan local d'urbanisme,* local plans) to the PDU (*plan de déplacement urbain,* transport plans) to the 177 SCOT (*schéma de cohérence territoriale,* urban planning procedures), without omitting the 358 *chartes de pays* (another level of coordination for strategic planning) and the more than 120 urban agglomeration charters and the 22 regional plans (SRADT) alluded to above. Territorial politics and policies are becoming increasingly rationalized but not coherent. Political regulation remains central but few citizens are likely to understand the subtlety of the financial arrangements of these different plans, which always involve more than one public authority. Contractualization has greatly increased the bureaucratization of politics and policies and made more central the need for democratic participation mechanisms and schemes.

The counterpart to bureaucratization has been systematic innovation to reinforce the role of citizens and associations within the decision-making process at the intercommunal, and sometimes regional, levels, to identify collective priorities in strategic planning documents in particular (Bacqué et al., 2005). Citizen juries, expert hearings, consultation mechanisms, neighbourhood committees (an old scheme which has been revisited), access on the net to relevant expertise reports and data, systematic public enquiries for new investments: these experiments are now systematically developed in order to take into account existing interests and also to foster the direct participation of inhabitants.

The above developments indicate a more plural and more negotiated French democracy within which local and regional political leaders play a major role in structuring priorities, channelling resources and implementing policy. This world is also more mosaic-like, asymmetric and inflationary. It is not well understood and has not been very well evaluated.

The marginalization of the territorial state

The coming of age of local and regional government in terms of financial, strategic and human resources has marginalized the external services of central ministries which were one of the pillars of the traditional model of the French Republic. Once powerful *directions départementales* for the ministries of Agriculture, Infrastructure and Housing or Social Services have lost most of their resources, have transferred their personnel to local authorities or have lost the most qualified and dynamic staff. This profound crisis is reinforced by the restructuring of the central state underlined by Bezès in his chapter. The LOLF is a powerful mechanism of centralization which seriously limits the autonomy of external services of the state. The creation of executive agencies in the field of urban policy has also reduced territorial priorities because prefects are not part of the decision-making process of agencies. The old departmental apparatus of the state is therefore nowadays in retreat under the leadership of the once powerful prefect, whose legitimacy and leadership are increasingly challenged by local and regional political leaders. Tellingly in the French context, top civil servants from the *Grands Corps* have become reluctant to work for the Ministry of Infrastructure at the departmental level.

The state apparatus is now being reorganized at the regional level. Regional prefects have been given and have seized a more general coordinating role for the implementation of public policies in regions, and for the representation of the state interests in the regions. For once, a clear hierarchy between state services and between levels has been created which strengthens the regional level of organization of the state under the leadership of the regional prefects. The once all-powerful departmental prefecture is now hardly more than a departmental agency for the regional prefecture. Several tasks that departmental prefectures used to perform have been transferred to the regional level. The reorganization of budgets following the LOLF reform is leading towards a massive recentralization of budget steering and control at the regional level of the state (see Chapter 11 for a full discussion). This shift to the regionalization of the state also marks a changing role, one that is less interventionist on a day-to- day basis, yet more regulatory and strategic.

Is the party over? Hands-off policies, targets and evaluation

As is usual in the French context, decentralization issues did not come out among the main themes of the 2007 presidential campaign. Of course, most candidates sang the praises of virtuous local and regional authorities and underlined the need to reorganize the state. Candidate Ségolène Royal, who is also the president of the Poitou–Charentes region, promised to strengthen the role of regions while for once, the candidate Nicolas Sarkozy did not raise the question but emphasized, rather, the old role of the nation and the state. In the shadows, the national associations of communes, of intercommunal organizations, of departments, of regions were, once again, preparing for another round of competition between them to get more powers and resources. More surprisingly, the opening speech of the new Prime Minister Fillon in Parliament hardly mentioned local and regional authorities.

Business as usual? Possibly not. A series of reports have, for the first time, seriously criticized the territorial organization of the state, along with the mosaic-like organization and the spending patterns of local and regional authorities. Usually considered, by nature, as virtuous, democratic and relatively effective, local and regional authorities and, at a more general level, the decentralized organization of the Republic are now under fierce criticism for reasons of financial profligacy and a lack of political accountability. The pressures are mounting.

Targets, performance indicators and hands-off policy

In terms of central local relations, Epstein (2005) has revived the term 'government at a distance' (*gouvernement à distance*) to analyse the transformation of territorial policies. The emergence of new regulatory agencies has been spread over the last 10 years. Of course, some of them have a longer history but several dozen were recently created, reflecting the wider trend of 'agencification' of the state. Some of tasks performed by ministries and their external services have been passed to those agencies. The links between those agencies and local or regional interests are far more tenuous, and as mentioned earlier, the prefects are usually marginalized in this system. The search for effectiveness and/or efficiency led by some of the state elites (usually the Ministry of Finance) is a factor driving the creation of new agencies which bypass the usual systems of representation of local and regional interests. The case of the regional hospital agency (ARH), created in particular to reform the location of hospitals, has shown the effectiveness of those agencies in bypassing local interests or in imposing restructuring (see Chapter 13 for a full discussion). In this way, the very rich field of territorial politics has become slightly less relevant. Those agencies are often following their own logic of rationalization and standardization, which overlaps or disturbs existing forms of local and regional political 'regulation'. The old model of the interaction between the prefect and state services on the one hand and local and regional political leaders on the other has weakened in the face of agencies and national performance indicators.

Even in the field of territorial policies, and faced with the disappointing results of 'contracts', state elites have been pushing towards the creation of new agencies to run new programmes. The most well known of these is ANRU, the national agency for urban renovation (Agence Nationale de la Rénovation Urbaine). Created by minister J.L. Borloo in the Raffarin government, it is in charge of all the budgets for urban policy, dealing with neighbourhoods in crisis and in particular the massive programme of destruction/rebuilding within the largest social housing concentrations in France. ANRU organizes competitive bidding procedures and negotiates with city mayors, imposing its own priorities, indicators, measures of the problems, norms and standards. Similarly, the transformation of the old regional agency direction (DATAR) into the revamped DIACTE (Délégation Interministérielle à l'Aménagement et la Compétitivité des Territoires) underlines a different logic of policy instrumentation. Again, contracts tend to be replaced by competitive bidding for projects in order to set priorities. The competitive cluster (*pôles de compétitivité*) programme of the Villepin government stemmed from a similar logic. In theory, this programme represented a major innovation in the French context. Firms, universities and research centres were encouraged to develop coherent projects and to bid for money from central funds. The label of *pôle de compétitivité* would be given to successful teams of bidders, in recognition of their 'world class' potential and the territorial synergies they demonstrated between members of the consortia. The bidding process ought to have presupposed a degree of competition, with winners and losers. In the event, pressure from local and regional interests and the mobilization of local actors led to the selection of 71 *pôles de compétitivité*, encompassing almost all bidders.

The French state has sought to insulate itself from local and regional interests by creating more 'interregional agencies' to deal with major services such as road construction or defence. These interregional agencies are more centralized, piloted by the centre, and tend to use the divide and rule strategy (between regions) to impose their priorities. State central services are currently organized at the regional level but they are increasingly adopting a more regulatory role.

These three changes signal a shift of national priorities in territorial politics. More than two decades after the decentralization reforms, state elites are at last learning the rules of the new polity. They have created new policy instruments to pilot public policy implementation and sought new ways of more effective central steering. The French state is slowly assuming a more regulatory role, whereby it performs the lead role in structuring the rules of the game, but leaves more autonomy to actors to deliver the policies that it has designed.

Financial pressure

Last but not least, the decentralization debate is entering a phase where, for the first time in over three decades, local and regional authorities appear as non-virtuous and inflationary. The high level of public deficits and the debt (63 per cent of GDP) is stirring an important public debate. As reform proves very difficult due to powerful local and regional interests rooted in Parliament (with the most conservative interests in the Senate), one temptation is to rule through macro-financial indicators to impose cuts. This option, which has not yet been decided, is reputedly on the cards. If so, this policy change will have been prepared by a series of reports.

The Cour des Comptes, the French National Audit Office, opened fire with a report (1985) seriously criticizing the cost of decentralization, the rationale of some intercommunal organization and the lack of savings within the state. A parliamentary report (Maritino report) was then issued criticizing the latest developments of decentralization and the costs associated with it. The issue of cost became central as the question of the massive rise of the French public debt since the 1980s (from about 30 per cent to 63 per cent of the GDP) was somehow related to the cost of decentralization including rising taxes and ongoing investments. The Pebereau report on public finances and the competitiveness of the country (2005) (named after a former top civil servant who became the CEO of the largest French banking group BNP Paribas) noted the importance of the local public sector, and argued that local and regional authorities could not escape from the required cuts in public expenditure if France seriously wanted to do something about a debt which had risen to 63 per cent of GDP.

In a more subtle way, the Pierre Richard report (2006) – named after of the former French civil servant who was in charge of writing the Defferre decentralization law before launching and developing the European DEXIA financial group (the main banker for French local authorities) – also underlined the cost of decentralization, as well as the need to improve efficiency, and to create robust performance indicators. Last but not least, for the first time ever, opinion polls seemed to register some lack of trust in local authorities, and indicated signs of protest due to increasing local and regional taxes.

National associations of local and regional authorities are taking this threat very seriously and are engaged in experiments to identify criteria for performance, or to develop their expertise in order to contest the criteria which will be put forward by national ministries, in the Ministry of Finance in particular.

In parallel, as indicated by Bezès, the general review of public policy initiated by the Fillon government will probably lead to serious spending cuts. Decentralizing penury has been a key motive for decentralization reforms across Europe. Until now, France was surprisingly an exception due to the power of local and regional interests. In many ways, the collective capacity of local and regional interests is now well understood and taken into account by the Ministry of Finance. The ministry is working on new financial tools and modes of control (evaluation, audit) in order to limit the growth of the local and regional public sector. For the first time ever, the question of the performance of public policy implementation is also progressively being raised, a classic instrument to put pressure on local and regional authorities to improve efficiency.

Conclusion

In 1979, Mrs Thatcher, the new Conservative Prime Minister of the United Kingdom, hardly mentioned local authorities in her election campaign and her first speeches in Parliament. However, she went on to implement the most radical ever shake-up of local authorities in the UK. The point here is not primarily a comparative one. However, the temptation must be strong to review the financial framework of local and regional authorities in the name of controlling public spending and reducing the debt and deficit. Converging pressures from public opinion (protesting against local tax increases), state elites (determined to limit the debt), and business interests might well prove too powerful for local and regional elites to resist.

This would signal the end of a cycle of 25 years of uninterrupted growth and development of decentralization. But the impact of two decades of decentralization will not disappear overnight. Changes that have produced more coherent intercommunal authorities in urban areas will probably remain, for instance, as will the importance of the budgets, human resources and expertise that local and regional authorities can count upon. However, one suspects that a new cycle of territorial politics is about to start in France, one that is less negotiated, more competitive and forced to operate within a stricter financial framework.

Chapter 11

The Reform of the State: the French Bureaucracy in the Age of New Public Management

PHILIPPE BEZÈS

The reform of the state refers to at least two distinct, though linked, phenomena. With a narrow definition, the reform of the state identifies an ongoing process of modernization within the civil service, defined classically in terms of government departments, their field services, the system of professional corps and the processes of management reform therein. As part of this process, reform of the state denotes a set of distinct policy programmes introduced by governments from the late 1980s onwards. Attention is focused by and large on the elites in central government departments and their rivalries, on their interaction with politicians, on the reshaping of the administrative machinery, on the evolution of the rules and tools used for coordinating the machinery of state and controlling the outcomes of public policy. Reforming the state can also refer to efforts undertaken by French governments to modernize the delivery of public services in areas of traditional state involvement, such as education, taxation and the public industrial sector. This broader reform of the public sector brings into play powerful public sector unions with the capacity to cause major disruption. While of primordial importance, this dimension of collective action does not form part of this chapter, which focuses more narrowly upon top civil servants and (to a lesser degree) politicians. Chapters 5 and 14 provide more commentary on the mobilization of public sector unions and the broader exercise of state reform.

The French bureaucracy has often been considered as one of the most 'frozen' public administrations, even by comparison with other continental European (Germany) or Napoleonic states (Spain or Italy). In some recent studies, France is still portrayed as a laggard in terms of administrative reforms (Pollitt and Boukaert, 2004), in the main resistant to the influence of New Public Management ideas (Rouban, 2006). While many changes have occurred in various important sectors such as economic policy, Europeanization, defence or social programmes (Culpepper et al., 2006), the French administration has reputedly remained a resilient rock in rough seas. Some observations lend support to this statement. In the mid-1990s, pressures from above (through European integration), from below (following the decentralization policies of the early 1980s) and from within (via budgetary deficits, the underlying crisis of the civil service and technological changes), each challenged the French administration, but its structural rules remained apparently intact. Observers might legitimately draw the conclusion that nothing much has changed and that sociologist Michel Crozier's theory view of France as a 'stalled society' with a 'stalled state' (Crozier, 1963) is still the right framework to interpret the French process of administrative changes.

Following from Crozier's portrayal, the French administration has traditionally been characterized as a centralized and hierarchical system that embodied the power and legitimacy of the French state and the general interest of the nation as whole (Stevens, 1996). It has its origins in the Napoleonic model of administration. The organizational structure of the French administration is primarily constituted by the central ministries in Paris and their field services situated in the 22 regions and 96 *départements*. Some core features of this traditional model included: a hierarchical mode of operation whereby central ministries determine policy objectives that the field services are expected to implement (Jones, 2006); a tightly defined politico-administrative elite, symbolized in the figure of the *énarque,* part politician, part civil servant; a close interpenetration between politicians and civil servants (Bezès and Le Lidec, 2007) and the role of the corps as a basic organizing principle of the civil service. The latter is of particular interest in this chapter, so some preliminary description is required. Although the French civil service system is said to be a unified career system with a strong legal statute organizing the professional life of all the civil servants, it is also a very fragmented system whose management is widely organized by corps, i.e. institutionalized forms of grouping public agents in relation to their rank (assigned to the individual civil servant after the *examination* when s/he enters into the French civil service and that confers rights on him or her) (Rouban, 1998: 38). Such a system promotes strong professional, corporate loyalties within the state that lends itself to conservatism and constitutes an obstacle towards any move towards performance-related pay or targets.

The idea that nothing happened in the French bureaucracy in the 1980s and 1990s is wrong. We insist upon the importance of silent, low-profile and incremental institutional changes (notably the institutionalization of administrative reform policy in France through the creation of the DIRE/DGAFP) (Bezès, 2005, 2007; Le Galès, 2005). Ideas, policy instruments, goals and the scope of reform have been largely redesigned since the mid-1990s, to such an extent that the New Public

Management 'tool-kit' is now widely circulating in the French state and is the dominant inspiration in administrative reform policies. In the course of the last decade, there have been dramatic changes in the French administrative system. State reform is now firmly on the political agenda, with President Sarkozy advocating new radical solutions which are likely to strengthen the neo-managerialization of the French administrative system.

This chapter will offer a broad picture of the ongoing process of how the French bureaucracy has been put under pressure and how it has changed. The chapter first analyses the pressures for reform of the French administrative system and new ideas of reform since the 1990s. The next section examines the managerial path-breaking turn of administrative reform brought about by the adoption of a major reform of the French budget procedures on 1 August 2001. The last part of this chapter provides an overview of the administrative reforms undertaken during the first six months of the Sarkozy presidency. The focus of the analysis is mainly that of the top civil service and the machinery of government. Rather than merely limiting analysis to details of civil service structures that might be considered rather arcane, however, the chapter describes real shifts in the way that the machinery of state works that have an impact upon all levels of public administration and the public sector in France and that pose fundamental issues of convergence and resistance to change.

The French administrative system under pressure

The French administrative system was challenged in important respects in the course of the 1990s. It was called to justify itself in terms of efficiency and legitimacy and to define its core role. Relationships between state and non-state actors were modified. The traditional foundations of the French administration have been called into question by the distinct processes of financial reform, Europeanization and the territorial dimensions of state reform.

Firstly, the French government had to face a worsening financial situation and a degradation of public accounts throughout the period of 1990–2000. The deepening deficit of public administrations was matched by the state's worsening budgetary deficit, which increased from 18.6 billion euros in 1991 to 61.9 billion in 2003 (3.9 per cent of GDP), decreasing to 51 billion euros in 2005. From 1992 onwards, concerns linked to deteriorating public finances (deficits and debts) became particularly acute for two reasons. Firstly, public finances were a key part of the new quasi-legal context linked to the Maastricht Treaty of 7 February 1992 (and to the negotiations that preceded it), establishing the process that would lead to European monetary union.

The European Treaty, through article 104C of the Maastricht Treaty, imposed new budgetary policy norms: the famous convergence criteria, limiting budget deficits to 3 per cent of GDP and debt to 60 per cent of the same GDP. Secondly, the strong growth in deficits and debt was a key feature of the context created by the emergence of an economy of financial markets (Siné, 2006). Free capital flows mean that 'markets' have the capacity to sanction governments on the basis of indicators such as deficit and debt. Traditional means of exercising budgetary policy that were used in the 1980s and early 1990s (low-profile cutbacks, centralized budgetary regulation of ministries, spending freezes) have proved inadequate to face the new challenges. Governments have had to acknowledge the structural erosion of their room for manœuvre. An ever-increasing part of the state's public spending cannot be restricted because it has to be renewed from one year to the next; this growth is due notably to staff costs, interest charges on debt and operational expenditure.

In the course of the 1990s, senior civil servants in the Budget Directorate, the core bureaucratic unit concerned with public finances, started to consider other ways of reining in the expenditure of the spending ministries. They introduced experimental managerial tools such as 'aggregated heading' (pooling budget appropriations under a single, broad, aggregated heading), 'contracting' between ministries and the Budget Directorate and adopting new budgetary procedures in order to encourage managers in ministries to make choices to reduce staff and operating expenditure, to introduce more restrictive reporting tools and to improve budgetary information.

Over the same period, all ministries have faced a real crisis due to major and increasing pressures caused by the impact of decentralization. Local authorities have considerably strengthened their administrative capacities while the territorial field services of government departments have seen the number and the scope of their functions and tasks considerably reduced. Decentralization has also weakened the prefects' and the Interior Ministry's capacities for coordination and control over state territorial policies. Local authorities no longer maintain a quasi-exclusive relationship with the Interior Ministry, but they have also developed new relations with ministerial field officials against the prefect and have developed their own substantial bureaucracies. The powers of the prefects have been reduced and it has become politically delicate to exercise prefectoral authority over the local authorities (Le Lidec, 2005). The state's field services at the local level have lost influence, functions and financial resources, though they have survived alongside stronger local and regional authorities (see the discussion in Chapter 10).

Faced with the challenge of decentralization, there have been key changes within the territorial organization of the state. From 1992 (the law of 6 February 1992 on the Territorial Administration of the Republic), planning a reorganization of the territorial state (the ministerial 'field services' and the prefects) became a major concern in state reform programmes. The Interior Ministry, which had specifically taken the lead on this, argued in favour of administrative devolution by affirming that 'the central administration should fulfil, at the national level, the roles of design, pace-setting, orientation, evaluation and monitoring' while implementation tasks ought to be carried out by devolved state services. The 1992 reform sought to reserve the implementation of public policies to the prefect (given new powers of coordination and control), representing the central state, and the decentralized authorities in the localities and the regions. In practice, subnational coordination proved much more difficult than anticipated.

Thirdly, the French administrative system has also been affected by the European integration process. Although there is no official 'administrative European model' since civil service systems are not part of EU policies, European pressures have been increasingly influential in the French context through the judgements of the European Court of Justice concerning the free access of European citizens to positions with the French administration. Since the removal of barriers to the free movement of persons became a central part of the European integration process, the ECJ has condemned France several times for the closure of its civil service entrance examinations to European citizens. Put in a nutshell, the historical structuring of the French civil service – a career system based on a system of corps – has been challenged by ECJ rulings defending the openness of the public service labour market. From the late 1980s to the early 2000s (Le Bihan-Graf and Coudroy, 2005), this external threat forced the Civil Service Ministry to think about possible adaptations of the French rules in order to respect EU laws by introducing more flexibility in recruitment and by giving more attention to skills as criteria for choosing officials.

By the late 1990s there was an atmosphere of crisis in the French civil service. Top officials felt a growing sense of frustration due to dissatisfaction with career prospects, salaries and declining social status. This sense of a threat to professional duty became more acute in 2000 when the General Planning Commission made public the forecast that 45 per cent of state public agents were scheduled to retire by 2012. Reducing the numbers of civil servants required setting up a genuine human resource policy, which had proved difficult to implement in the past due to the fragmentation of corps and the major role played by civil service trade unions. In the early 2000s, the functioning of the French 'civil service' was facing unprecedented challenges.

The circulation of New Public Management ideas in the French state

By the 1990s, there was a widespread belief that the French administrative state was in crisis, its traditional organization unable to cope with pressures from above, below and within the state. There was a steady ideological conversion of many top civil servants to ideas of New Public Management (NPM). New ideas circulated in the successive state reform task forces that were set up from 1995 to 2005. The first 'state reform unit', created in 1995, then became the Interministerial Delegation on State Reform (DIRE – Direction Interministérielle de la Réforme de l'État) within the Civil Service Ministry (1998–2002). It was then reshaped (2002–5) into three agencies attached to the Prime Minister and respectively in charge of quality concerns and users, e-government and organizational and managerial change. Over 10 years, these reform committees gathered expertise from many top bureaucrats and became clear loci for the formation of real – if small – networks of senior civil servants socialized towards NPM ideas. They were supported by major consultancy firms that accelerated the diffusion of these new ideas. A systematic 'new' organizational form was thus elaborated within these task forces and widely diffused in public or confidential reports to the public and within the French higher civil service.

The various documents produced by these state reform task forces articulated certain dominant traits of NPM and of the reforms conducted abroad. These included first the separation of the strategic functions of decision-making and steering – as well as monitoring or evaluating public policies – from the functions, usually referred to as 'administrative', that involve responsibility for implementation. Second, the documents advocated strengthening the hierarchical role of the 'directors' (the top officials) in central government departments making them 'real bosses', responsible for their ministry's specific public policies. Third, attempts were undertaken to rationalize relations between central administrations and their devolved (field) services by negotiating contracts defining the objectives to be pursued by the services, the resources granted and the methods for measurement and systematic evaluation of results and providing an overall budget (including a staff budget) and more autonomy. These three core ideas largely imported and adapted to the French context reflected the dominant ideas about administrative reorganization that were circulating in international circles as NPM.

Over the same period, many higher civil servants from the *grands corps* were involved in shaping state reforms. After 1998, for instance, the Financial Inspectorate (Inspection Générale des Finances) was committed to promoting 'benchmarking studies' in key areas identified as ripe for reform, such as the tax system, the budgetary process and the performance management system (Lépine et al., 1999; Guillaume et al.,

2000). Members of the Court of Accounts (Cour des Comptes) also contributed to reform plans using NPM ideas while some top officials of the Council of State (Conseil d'État) also made proposals that significantly departed from the French civil service tradition (Conseil d'État, 2003). NPM solutions were advocated by networks of senior French civil servants interacting with non-national organizations and actors from the European institutions, in bodies like the OECD, or in consultancies. This advocacy coalition exercised a major influence and thus performed a key role in developing and disseminating prototypical solutions (frequently called 'best practices' and not belonging a priori to any particular state) within the French context.

In spite of the growing influence of new managerial ideas among top civil servants, by 2000, no significant administrative reform had occurred. This changed in the early 2000s with the unexpected voting of a radically new budgetary Act.

The managerial turn of administrative reform: reforming the bureaucracy through the budget

There is no doubt that the major change in the French administrative system – specifically in terms of the adoption of NPM methods and tools – has come from the 2001 reform of the French budgetary procedure. The 2001 budgetary reform contained within it the adoption of a number of internationally diffused instruments of performance management as well as a significant attempt to reinforce the role of the French Parliament in the procedure of budgeting. The reform was voted through the Organic Act on Budget Legislation (*Loi organique relative aux lois de finances*, or 'LOLF'), adopted on 1 August 2001 and implemented since January 2006. Let us first briefly describe the reform and its policy-making process before outlining its many cascading effects on French administrative reform design and confirm the change by stressing the parallel emergence of a new policy towards the top bureaucracy also based on NPM tools.

The unusual alliance between the Budget Ministry and deputies

Broadly speaking, LOLF involves a major change in the procedure and contents of the budget, moving away from line-item budgeting towards public policy and performance-sensitive frames. The reform institutes a programme budget based on 34 missions (supposedly corresponding to the French state's major public policies) broken down into a set of programmes (132) to which appropriations are allocated.

LOLF also aimed to restore the balance of power between government and Parliament by giving more stringent control over the budgetary process to MPs in the constitutional law on the Budget Act. Indeed, the new budgetary procedure has changed the way that Parliament votes on the budget. Rather than approve or reject ministerial budgets, deputies are now invited to vote by mission (regrouping a consistent set of programmes). The intention is to foster more awareness in the examination of budgets of issues, priority objectives and the results achieved by the spending ministries. This change of budgetary procedure has been accompanied by the setting up of a management by performance structure. Every year, programme managers and ministers have to make commitments to meet specific objectives and targets and achieve specific results through an Annual Performance Plan (APP) appended to the Budget Act. When the budget has been executed, spending ministries have to give MPs an Annual Performance Report (APR) appended to the Budget Review Act with explanations for the levels of performance they achieve according to the resources they have been allocated. Both plans contain the main goals relating to the policy with performance indicators, expected/achieved results and related tax expenditure.

The introduction of these 'global' programme-oriented budgets shapes a new form of accountability of spending departments to Parliament. Various formal powers have thus been given to MPs: greater access to rationalized information, stronger control powers due to greater investigative and hearing powers (for the finance committees of both assemblies) and extended powers of amendment (the possible reallocation of appropriations between the various programmes within a mission). LOLF introduced new managerial and performance tools that aimed at reinforcing the controlling powers of Parliament. The origins of the Act largely explain this orientation. The ideas of a Budget Act first emerged from a cross-party working group of deputies, created in 1998, who endeavoured to increase the financial power of Parliament over public expenditure. From 1998 to 2000, with the support of the President of the National Assembly, Laurent Fabius, Socialist deputy Didier Migaud (of the Finance Committee), and RPR Senator Lambert (chief of the Finance Committee), two working groups of members of Parliament were set up to study the possibility of reforming the traditional budgetary procedure (*ordonnance organique du 2 janvier 1959 relative aux lois de finances*) (Migaud, 1999). This cross-party work resulted in a reform proposal coming from both assemblies in July 2000. Deputies sought to obtain a greater role, with extended constitutional powers within the budgetary process and increased powers of control over the administration. In March 2000, Laurent Fabius became Minister of Finance and Budget and was forced to honour his promise. These actors played a crucial role in crafting new solutions, persuading right-wing deputies to work together with the Left and building coalitions. The common basis for agreement across Left and Right, National Assembly and Senate, was the belief that the previous 1959 Budget Act had withdrawn too much power from Parliament and was both opaque and inefficient in reducing French deficits. However, this first dimension was not the only one.

Perhaps more important, the new budgetary procedure has introduced managerial decentralization and autonomy, but accompanied tougher performance indicators and compulsion. Programmes and their sub-programmes (called operational budget programmes) have allowed the use of 'frame-budgeting'. Managers in spending ministries are supposed to receive their appropriations under a broad aggregated heading and are given delegated responsibility and (supposedly) a great deal of latitude in how they (re)allocate appropriations within this frame. This 'globalization' is supposed to offer much more flexible management because of its possibilities for reallocation of appropriations between sub-programmes or type of expenditure. The counterparts for more (supposed) flexibility for spending departments are a stronger accountability to Parliament but, above all, a new 'managerial chain of command' based on management by objectives and performance indicators connecting the Budget Directorate, the central administration, programme (in central administrations) and sub-programmes managers (in local units of the state). This new chain of command and accountability has been designed to save money and reduce staff. Personnel expenditure is indeed the only exception to the globalization principle: within a global heading, staff expenditure is the only appropriation that cannot be topped up with other appropriations. Payrolls (the amount and numbers of personnel) are capped. Whereas the 'external' dimension of the Budget Act was publicly endorsed, this 'internal' one, creating a new framework for inner managerial steering of the bureaucracy and reinforcing the control of the Budget Directorate over the spending ministries, is more a low-profile change due to its high political costs and the concern for avoiding social conflicts and blame.

This second dimension resulted from the low-profile negotiations between the Budget Ministry (the minister, his cabinet and the most reformist people within the Budget Directorate) and deputies from September 2000 to August 2001. The strategy of the administrative elite within the Budget Ministry was to benefit from the Budget Act to impose a new constraining framework that would allow the Budget Division to develop new ways of controlling spending ministries with management control, indicators and performance measurements. The Budget Division sought to keep the reform under its control and opposed any element which could challenge its powers. Indeed, from 2001 to 2006, the Budget Division and the Budget Reform Division (created in 2003) undertook immense efforts to transform the law ('externally' aimed at increasing Parliament's powers) into a set of managerial tools that would allow a new mode of managerial regulation inside the French administration. This has mostly been done through 'soft laws', that is to say through a series of budgetary decrees and circulars that did not have very high legal value (Herzog, 2006; Lascombe and Vandendriessche, 2006) but they do allow the Ministry of Finance to monitor the performance of ministerial departments against their objectives and targets. To put it differently, the measures aimed at changing the administrative system have been introduced on the periphery of the Budget Act. This is specifically the case of the operational budget programme which was not included in the Budget Act but has been entirely invented *ex post* by the experts of the Budget Reform Division as an instrument aimed at installing a managerial hierarchy within the French bureaucracy.

The cascading effects of the Budget Act

There is no doubt that this reform is a major one with many consequences. First, there has been a strengthening of the Ministry of Finance which had been put at the heart of the whole process of state reform. While the 1990s were characterized by an equilibrium between three ministries (Budget, Civil Service, Interior), the 2000s have been marked by the domination of the financial view of the budgetary actors. This has several consequences. In March 2003 a new Budgetary Reform Directorate was created within the ministry in charge of the reform process. In 2005, this directorate and the three agencies in charge of administrative reforms were transformed again into a General Directorate for Modernizing the State (DGME – Direction Générale de la Modernisation de l'État) with a staff of about 170 people and which has been put under the supervision of the Budget Ministry. The unit brings together senior civil servants with experts under contract and it systematically brings consultancy firms within its orbit. While the state reform portfolio was historically and symbolically 'owned' by the Civil Service Ministry (Bezès, 2001), it was given to the Budget Ministry in June 2005 under the Villepin government, marking a clear break with tradition. For the first time under the Fifth Republic, state reform is now fully controlled by the Budget Ministry. Within the reform process, many initiatives have been developed. LOLF has widened the competences of the Court of Accounts from financial and compliance auditing to some new investigations of performance issues. Seven waves of 'modernization audits' (127 audits all in all) were launched in 2006–7 on specific issues concerning the functioning of the state or public organizations. They were usually led by a team that included a member of the Financial Inspectorate and members from ministerial inspectorates. As observed in the UK (Hood et al., 1999), the managerial turn considerably helps controlling bodies to revalue their positions within ministries and to enrich their jobs.

The new budgetary and managerial framework is also bringing about other changes. By offering the (theoretical) possibility for managers in the field services of the state to make autonomous budgetary choices between appropriations, the reform paves the way for more devolution in personnel policies. LOLF contains within it the possibility that state field services might develop their own human resources management policies at local level. It offers the prospect of more differentiated career and pay structures, via a strengthening of autonomy and flexibility at the local level. However, a 'classic' tension has already been observed between the purported objectives of more responsibilities and autonomy for managers and the real strengthening of vertical control by the Budget Directorate through performance management techniques and the practical obstacles to managerial devolution introduced by the Act (Lambert and Migaud, 2006). Thus, central administrations within ministries, sometimes with the support of the Budget Directorate, limited the use and the effects of frame-budgeting by the managers of state field services in 2006, a finding similar to that observed in the UK (Hood et al., 1999).

LOLF has also had an impact upon the organization of the territorial state. From 1992 to 2004, several strategic plans were introduced which attempted to reorganize ministries in terms of their vertical chain of command, to enhance the autonomy of the state field services, while strengthening the coordinating role of the prefect, the state's representative in the *départements*. These reforms combined the desire to decentralize policy responsibility to the specialists in the field services, while improving the coordination of state services on the ground by boosting the coordinating role of the prefect. The prefects were notably given responsibility to schedule mergers between field services in their area, thus directly intervening in the territorial management of government departments. This process provoked resistance from the central bureaux and had floundered by the end of the 1990s. In a second wave of reforms, the French government recognized the need for a more pragmatic procedure by identifying 'focal areas', but without insisting on mergers. In 2004, an outline plan for reorganizing the territorial administration of the state was adopted. It created eight focal subject areas in the regions. These were: education and training; public sector management and economic development; transport; housing and planning; public health and social cohesion; the agricultural economy and the rural fabric; employment development and workforce integration and culture (Decree no. 2004-1053 of 5 October 2004 and Circular of

19 October 2004 on reform of the territorial administration of the state).

As LOLF was driven by the Budget Ministry, it produced reactions from other players. The Ministry of the Interior reacted to LOLF by issuing a new framework from the constitutional revision of 28 March 2003, which legally reinforced the powers of prefects by putting state field services under the regional prefects' authority. The objective here was to implement a 'nationwide territorial administrative framework' (three-year targets negotiated between the regional prefectures and the field services of the various ministries) and with more tools for the coordination and steering of local services (Decree no. 2004-1053 of 5 October 2004). This reinforcement of the prefect over the state field services mainly resulted from the strong pressures of local politicians who traditionally exert more influence on prefects than on the directors of the field services. This initiative was revealing of the ongoing competition between the Interior and the Finance ministries. There were obvious incompatibilities between the new budgetary and managerial rules and the still existing territorial state architecture. More than ever, conflicts between vertical lines (moved by the Budget Act, Budget Directorate and central administrations) and horizontal lines (defended by departmental prefects and local units of the state) are crucial matters in the French context.

The Budget Act was not the only managerial policy launched during the period 2002–7. Inspired by NPM doctrines, there was an attempt to design a real human resources policy for top officials. Since 2004, top civil service managers are required to develop new skills in fields such as negotiation, human resources management, accountability techniques and team management. Most fundamentally, the most characteristic feature of the French civil service – the system of administrative corps – is being scrutinized as part of a radical and global rethinking. From 2002 to 2007 there emerged the project of transforming the multiform corps into a more limited number of larger occupational definitions. The idea of creating job-based frames (such as in health, security, social, financial administration, culture, training and general management) was discussed and developed from 2002 to 2005 although it was not finally transformed into a piece of legislation as planned initially. More restrictively, there have been fusions of a significant number of corps. The *grands corps* have been quite reluctant to accept these ideas and their strong resistance, of course, was anticipated. However, they have also been the object of other managerial reforms. Following a report to Prime Minister Raffarin (Silicani, 2004), a reform of terms of payment for the general directorates of the ministries was launched in June 2004. This experiment introduced incentive payments for 44 general directorates of central administrations in six ministries (Finance, Home Office,

Defence, Public Work, Agriculture and Prime Minister's Services). Performance-related pay mechanisms have been set up, varying between 6 and 16 per cent of salary among ministries, a provision extended to all general directorates in 2006. In the French context, these notions of skills, occupations or performance pay within the higher civil service seem to respond to two distinct logics, already noted in other countries (Hood and Lodge, 2004). First, they are a response to dissatisfaction among lower-level top civil servants (*administrateurs civils* for instance) who criticize the lack of personnel management. Second, these notions offer senior bureaucrats 'the claim to have the same sorts of skills as private sector top executives, thereby underpinning claims for higher pay and professional recognition' (Hood and Lodge, 2004).

Managerial and budgetary reform under Sarkozy's 'disruptive' leadership

This mid-term survey of administrative reform policy raises a paradox. Before the 2007 presidential election, several reform processes had been introduced in the wake of the Budget Act. Throughout the period 1997–2007, the Ministry of Finance imposed its leadership in the domain of state reform. Interestingly, however, programmatic reforms were not explicitly endorsed by the executive. Prime Minister Jospin surprisingly did not make any use of the Budget Act in the 2002 presidential campaign, whereas the LOLF reform was among the most important reforms launched since the early Fifth Republic. The Raffarin government endorsed the Act 2 of French Decentralization in 2003–4, largely as a result of the influence and demands of local government leaders (Le Lidec, 2005, 2007). However, he remained very cautious before engaging in a structural reform of the rules of the French administration. As shown with the top civil service, changes were in the main introduced as experiments that were gradually extended. By contrast, more thoroughgoing reform proposals concerning the transformation of the corps system were prepared but remained finally undeveloped while the reform of the ENA was more limited than initially planned (Gally, 2007). To sum up, before 2007, many initiatives had been undertaken within the French bureaucracy but without real significant political commitment. This pattern has drastically changed since the presidential campaign and the first six months of the Sarkozy presidency. In a nutshell, the various stocks of previous reform proposals and the 'new' top bureaucrats socialized to NPM ideas have now found a political support in Sarkozy's new disruptive style of leadership.

Administrative reform, the political game and the presidential agenda

Compared to the presidential election of 2002, a striking feature of the 2007 presidential campaign was the important place given to the issues related to the civil service. Quite unusually, for instance, the TV debate of 4 May 2007 after the first election round between candidates Ségolène Royal and Nicolas Sarkozy tackled at length the issue of the number of public and state employees and the need to downsize staff. During the campaign, candidate Sarkozy for the UMP offered a twofold argument about the French administrative system. On one hand, he advocated a global financial plan dominated by economic and budgetary aims and searching for significant cuts in public expenditure. Strong emphasis was put on reducing deficits while also promising a real decrease of the tax burden (from 45.3 per cent of GDP to 41.5 per cent). Savings were to be found in significant reductions in the number of state employees and the endorsement of the Budget Directorate's objective of not replacing one retiring civil servant in two. On the other hand, candidate Sarkozy argued strongly in favour of a rise of the purchasing power of civil servants and asked for a smaller civil service but one with better wages and increased social status. By contrast, Royal for the Socialist Party developed a more defensive approach by reaffirming the French model. Denouncing Sarkozy's plans for downsizing, she vetoed the goal of staff reduction and made several proposals designed to increase public employment in the ministries of Justice, Education, Interior (police) and in hospitals. In return, she emphasized a more efficient management for public finances with cutbacks in the day-to-day functioning appropriations.

Once elected President in early May 2007, Sarkozy repeated his belief that the French administrative system needed reforming. He reaffirmed this belief in several important political speeches. Prime Minister François Fillon also made clear that the domain of state reform was one where the Prime Minister retained an influence (as officially suggested by the Constitution in articles 20 and 21). In many ways, compared to previous post-election periods (Bezès, 2001), the 2007 moment offered major opportunities for French leaders to endorse initiatives to reform the administration. The new leadership, the presidential executive in particular, was able to call for change in the 'old' art of government and public administration. In sharp contrast to previous occasions, when existing institutional arrangements in policies were resilient and defended by solid coalitions, the 'old' public administrators appeared vulnerable to change. The traditional administrative elites were now perceived as unable to deal with new problems.

As shown above (see Section 1) this diagnosis was shared by administrative reformers within the state, especially in the top bureaucracy.

Sarkozy's election facilitated an alliance between reformers from within the top civil service and the new political elite. The new political situation has induced a twofold effect. On one hand, it favours a significant reinforcement of the budgetary and managerial trends of reform by giving even more central powers to the Ministry of Finance. On the other hand, the new political configuration seems to offer more opportunities for exercising political leadership over the Finance Ministry and for disrupting existing relationships.

Continuing the budgetary and managerial trend

Following from the first of these perspectives, the early Sarkozy era can be analysed in terms of continuity with previous state reform initiatives of the early 2000s. The evidence from the first six months of the Sarkozy regime suggests an acceleration of the managerial trend. Already the allocation of the 'state reform' portfolio to the Budget Minister in the Villepin government and the creation of a General Directorate for State Modernization within the Budget Ministry in July 2005 were an early sign of the centrality of budgetary actors. The Fillon government has further strengthened budgetary dominance by creating an enlarged Ministry for Budgeting, Public Accounts and the Civil Service given to Eric Woerth, a graduate from the French business school HEC and a former manager in the consultancy firm Arthur Andersen. As a consequence, the objective of not replacing one retired public servant in two in order to reduce the overall number of staff has been politically endorsed by the Fillon government. For the 2008 budget, and after arbitration, the suppression of 22,802 posts of state civil servants globally met the 'one in two' target except for the Education, the Higher Education and the Justice ministries which were able to plead special presidential priority. On the other hand, the Defence (–6037), Finance (–2380) and Interior ministries sustained the most considerable losses.

In the same perspective, a General Public Policy Review was launched in July 2007 with explicit reference to the Canadian Program Review initiated by the Liberal Chretien government in 1995–96 (on this experience, see Armit and Bourgault, 1996) or the 'spending reviews' done in the UK since 2002. Systematizing and refocusing the 'modernization audits' developed in 2006–7 by targeting public policies, the French *Révision Générale des Politiques Publiques* (RGPP) claims to engage in 'rethinking the state' with direct ties to the fiscal imperatives of dealing with the debt and the deficit. In clear echoes of the contradictions that have been observed in countries that developed NPM reforms, ambivalence is at the heart of this initiative between reducing the size of government and implementing managerial-type reforms intended to strengthen the effectiveness of the bureaucracy.

This tension is reflected in the core questions of the analytical grid that will be used as a new tool to screen state expenditure. In this grid, ministries are asked not only about what they do, but also about what public needs they serve. They are questioned over whether their current objectives, instruments and ways of implementing and financing specific public policies should be maintained or whether and how goods could be delivered better and less expensively. Finally, ministries are challenged over whether other public or private actors would be better placed to deliver better and cheaper services. These audits of public policies will be held by several small 'teams' mixing members of ministerial and interministerial inspectorates with private consultants, the first time that resorting to private consultancy firms has been publicly endorsed.

As part of this process, 14 ministerial areas have been identified where issues concerning the modes of state production (organization, process, staff, costs) and welfare expenditure (*dépenses d'intervention*) will be subject to scrutiny. Thus, ministries will be asked to plan expenditure reductions but they will also be expected to redesign their own roles and to consider alternative service delivery strategies for their public policies. Six large welfare policies have also been specifically put under deep scrutiny through audits (employment, the development of firms, housing, family, health insurance and poverty programmes), along with four interministerial issues (human resource management, the organization of the territorial state, relationships between the state and local authorities and simplification of internal processes). The audit process will be managed by a committee both supervised by the general secretary of the Presidency and by the Prime Minister's cabinet director with the technical assistance of the General Directorate for State Modernization. A Council for Modernizing Public Policies, chaired by the President, has also been created: it will examine the various proposals and will make choices in May 2008.

It is, of course, far too early to evaluate the nature and effects of these ongoing audits. A first issue is the extent to which this review will favour ministerial cooperation or will be exclusively elaborated by small closed circles of top bureaucrats and consultants. A complementary one is whether the implementation of this review will rely on a positive partnership with ministries, or whether the review will simply be transformed into a budget-driven exercise. Without full ministerial cooperation, the policy review would be as limited as the previous similar (although less radical) initiatives (see for instance the ministerial strategies of reform, launched in 2002–5). A third question deals with the linkage between this policy review and the effects of the budgetary reform we considered above. Although the logic of LOLF is annual, it has been announced that audits will be accompanied by the introduction of a pluri-annual budgeting exercise

(2009–11). The coherence between the major initiatives is open to some question.

A degree of incoherence has also been noted between the objectives of reducing debt and deficit, the state's downsizing programmes, on the one hand, and the fiscal policy which was decided in July 2005 on the other. By offering a 15 billion euro 'fiscal package' through tax reductions to the most favoured households, the presidency and the Fillon government have reinforced the urgency of cutting down public expenditure but have also undermined the credibility of their views on the need for budgetary retrenchment.

Innovation and disruption

From the late 1990s to 2007, many radical reform proposals (the suppression of corps in the French civil service, the reform of ENA, drastic cutbacks in staff and expenditure or the structural reforms of ministries) were abandoned due to a lack of real political support and a window of political opportunity. Since May 2007, however, political circumstances have been more favourable for reform. Sarkozy's reformist agenda faces administrative institutions that are far weaker than in the past. Contrary to other periods in the 1980s and 1990s (Bezès, 2001), several institutional conditions seem to favour more radical administrative reform initiatives: the large majority in the National Assembly and the Senate, the strong subordination of the Prime Minister to the presidency and the ongoing dynamics of reinforcing the powers of Parliament (see Chapter 8). Third, the Civil Service Ministry has now been integrated into the Finance Ministry so that previous power struggles between Budget, Interior and Civil Service have now considerably weakened.

Political circumstances are favourable to change. There are two probable directions of future activity. One involves the increased politicization of the higher reaches of the civil service, and the prospect of creating an American-style spoils system; the other relates to terms and working conditions of public servants.

Sarkozy's presidency will likely introduce a significant increase in the politicization of the French top civil service. A tighter political control over top nominations will be combined with a radical next step in making the heads of central administrations more responsible for the successes and failures of public policies. This idea has been referred to by President Sarkozy and also by his director of cabinet, Emmanuèle Mignon (*Le Monde*, 7 September 2007). While changes in the heads of directorates in ministries have been increasingly used under the Fifth Republic (Bezes and Le Lidec, 2007: 126), the project would be to institutionalize a systematic and explicit 'spoils system' for the 120 heads of the most strategic central administrations. This move would strengthen political control and loyalty. Additional measures would reduce by two the number of heads of central directorates and significantly reduce the size of ministerial cabinets in order to clarify responsibilities and obtain a more partisan-driven politicization of top bureaucrats.

The second orientation focuses on the reform of the terms and conditions of civil service employment. It was made public in Sarkozy's speech of 19 September 2007 while visiting a regional school of administration (IRA). In his first major speech on state reform, the President announced the convening of a major conference on the values, missions and occupations of the future French civil service. Bringing together experts, civil service trade unions, ministries and representatives of the Ministry for Budgeting, Public Accounts and the Civil Service, this 'public debate' will take place from October 2007 to March 2008 but has already been framed by several 'radical' and 'liberal' objectives defended by President Sarkozy about public sector employment. The suppression of the corps and the development of a job-based civil service, strong emphasis on mobility within the administrative system and between the three civil services (state, local authorities, hospitals) and financial incentives to leave the civil service are not completely new ideas in the French context but for the first time these solutions have been publicly endorsed by the executive as a programme. More radical and 'new' has been the announcement that, for specific jobs in the French bureaucracy (to be defined), a new recruit would have the choice between acquiring the status of 'civil servant' (with its pre-fixed rights, obligations and rewards) and a private law contract negotiated by mutual agreement with possibly better wage conditions in exchange for the loss of a career-based appointment and a 'job for life'. Clearly influenced by the Italian reform of the civil service with the rules regarding the careers of public employees being defined by employment contracts, the Sarkozy programme could significantly change, if implemented, the foundations of the French administration.

Conclusion

Since the 1990s, there has been growing public criticism of the French administrative system. There have been moves to control expenditure and increase fiscal stringency. Reforms have been influenced by a new ideological conception of the state. Innovative managerial tools have been introduced through the 2001 Budget Act. Compared to the Anglo-Antipodean countries, however, the managerial rationalization has only just started. The traditional French administrative system has shown itself to be resilient and somewhat reluctant to change. The mix between new managerial imperatives, robust veto players and existing institutions makes the overall reform process multi-centred and cross-cutting in terms of issues and levels of negotiations. Strong trends have been institutionalized: these include decentralization, the leading role of the Budget division to conduct top-down managerial reforms and the ideological conversion of top civil servants to NPM ideas. Since May 2007, the Sarkozy presidency has brought about a new kind of leadership and clearer lines of politicization within the civil service. This might well have significant effects on the content and scope of administrative reform policy in the future. It is possible that more radical reforms lie just over the horizon, inspired by the prospect of budgetary retrenchment, and an overhaul of the traditional corps-based system. However, retrenchment policies and structural reforms will be limited in their impact if they do not tackle the real concerns of the largest clusters of the 'operational' French civil servants: the officials in central administrations, now implementing NPM reforms and endorsing their costs; the public agents in the local units of the state facing the strong dismantling effects of decentralization policies and the impoverishment of the territorial state. At this stage, the future direction of the French administrative system is uncertain. There is an obvious tension between ideas of New Public Management and new management tools, on the one hand, and the still resilient and structuring pattern of the more traditional bureaucracy (with its strong territorial state, its complicity with local authorities and its system of corps) on the other. Whether the liberal ethos of NPM transforms the state or is transformed by it will provide the key for understanding the future.

Chapter 12

Economic Policy

BEN CLIFT

Two key challenges facing the French economy are how to tackle two decades of high unemployment and how to face up to increased international competition, including from new players in the global political economy. In most countries, a (neo-)liberal approach is seen to provide the logical responses to such challenges. However, in France more than in many of its competitors, an alternative, neo-mercantilist policy tradition continues to exert influence. Thus French economic policy over the past 25 years has blended elements of liberalization with new kinds of neo-mercantilist intervention.

This chapter explores the challenges to French economic policy-making presented by international liberalization, asking what remains of the traditional *dirigiste* model in the twenty-first century. It summarizes the key developments under the latter Chirac presidency, analysing the evolution of macroeconomic policy, responses to delocalization, and strategic state interventionism. It then explores whether the Sarkozy presidency represents a departure in political economic terms from French economic policy-making over the last 25 years. It concludes that the new Sarkozy regime has embarked upon a novel recombination of liberalism and neo-mercantilism, with the centre of gravity of French economic policy shifted in a more neo-liberal direction.

A new millennium: a crisis for the French model?

At the core of the traditional *dirigiste* model is the assumption that the state should operate as an organizer and regulator of economic activity, a protector of the public sector, and as a strategic actor (Dyson, 1980: 95–7; Schmidt, 1996: 73–93). The 2000s have been a period of considerable introspection for French political economic actors, asking whether the French state should, or indeed could, continue to play these roles. Fear for the health of the French economic model combines with anxiety about its compatibility (or not) with the heavy tendencies of globalization and Europeanization.

191

Dirigisme presumes a *volontariste* (interventionist) economic policy approach, emphasizing the discretionary actions of policy-makers. In the post-war era, preferential trade policy, public procurement, price controls, strategic state aids, state-directed access to credit for key industries, and 'competitive devaluations' were integral parts of French economic policy-making. A broadly Keynesian set of fiscal and welfare state policies (Rosanvallon, 1989) combined with a panoply of instruments and institutions geared towards microeconomic interventionism.

What flowed from this model and these state traditions was a presumption on the part of administrative, economic and political elites, and the wider populace, that the French state could and should pursue economic interventionism. Policy-makers sought to deliver economic growth, full employment and, in accordance with Republican values of equality and social cohesion, limited redistribution of wealth. These elements of political economy and state ideology coalesced into a relatively cohesive vision. In rhetoric and in practice, there was a link between *dirigisme* and the *trente glorieuses*. The prevailing interpretation from the 1950s until the 1970s was of a successful, nimble state strategically pulling the levers of economic policy-making and steering France's dramatic economic recovery, generating strong economic growth and improving living standards for most.

The oil crises and world economic slowdown in the 1970s challenged this comfortable narrative. Many doubted whether the French model was ever as coherent as the picture painted by Zysman (1983) and Shonfield (1969), and how much 'glorious' growth was really due to indicative economic planning and strategic interventionism creating 'national champions' (see e.g. Hancké, 2001: 309–12; Guyomarch et al., 1998: 161–68; Levy, 2000: 321). The breakdown of Bretton Woods meant certain policy levers, such as competitive devaluation, were no longer available. The intractable problem of inflation began to hurt the French trade and payments situation. Unemployment began to rise, making France's industrial infrastructure look less healthy. The French state, meanwhile, was still intervening and spending, but seemed to be 'picking losers' more often than it was 'picking winners'.

This generated a climate of anxiety surrounding French capitalism, which has ebbed and flowed since the 1970s. In the 2000s, the political salience of French capitalism's viability *as a model*, has risen dramatically, addressed frequently in books, articles and media discussion programmes. France's oft-maligned international competitive position is often painted in an excessively poor light. It remains the world's fifth largest economy, and a leading nation in terms of inwards and outwards foreign direct investment. Its stock markets have welcomed international capital on a colossal scale in the last decade. The productivity of its labour force (per hour worked) is among the highest in the world, and France has many leading and extremely successful large enterprises. Nevertheless, the 'declinist' thesis has gained ground in French public debate (Baverez, 2003; Smith, 2004), and an increasing range of commentators see France as in irrevocable decline, in need of radical reform of its institutions and the political economic underpinnings of its policy approach.

There is increasing willingness to look abroad for inspiration from other (Nordic, or even Anglo-Saxon) models of capitalism. At the same time, attachment to aspects of the French model remains strong. French economic policy-makers seek to embrace globalization while preserving a Republican, inclusive, policy regime. This self-image papers over the cracks of France's social welfare institutions, which are patchy in their coverage and do not deliver on the Republican ideal of equality for significant sections of their citizenry (Palier, 2007). Nevertheless, the public's reluctance to move towards a more minimal welfare and workers' rights regime are powerful constraints on any economic reform programme. The social movement of 1995, the spring 2006 protest against de Villepin's flexibilizing labour market reform, the first employment contract (*contrat de première embauche* – CPE), and the autumn/winter 2007 protests against Sarkozy's planned pension retrenchment demonstrated this reluctance eloquently.

Unemployment and delocalization

Some nagging economic realities underlie 'declinist' perceptions of the French crisis. The inability of successive governments to tackle two decades of high unemployment threatens France's economic and social model. Jospin's Socialist government of 1997–2002 promised *volontariste* economic policies and enjoyed some notable successes with redistributive measures as well as welfare state reform, and apparent success in state-led responses to unemployment. However, the impression that too much political capital had been spent on the 35-hour work week, which in turn had not generated sufficient employment, began to gain ground with the world economic downturn in the early 2000s. This took the shine off the Jospin government's otherwise credible record as unemployment began to creep stubbornly, if slowly, back up. Unemployment did decline at the end of the second Chirac presidency, but even the lower end of the unemployment level in France, which has oscillated between 12 and 9 per cent for over two decades, was, in comparative terms, not something to boast about. In this context, the relatively generous welfare programmes and institutions predicated on social insurance assuming full employment were proving very costly (Palier, 2002). French public debt stood at 20 per cent of GDP in 1980. It grew to 30 per cent of GDP in 1990, then to around 55 per cent by 1997, before briefly levelling off. Public debt began to rise once more in the 2000s, reaching 66 per cent of GDP in 2005 (OFCE, 2006: 85–7).

Another source of anxiety in France is delocalization, or the off-shoring of production. Delocalization, the ability of increasingly mobile productive capital to reorganize global production chains, brings together a heady brew of touchstone issues in France: globalization, multinational corporations (especially foreign ones), unemployment, and the (lack of) power of the French state to regulate capitalism. Most often associated with distant production, notably in China, it also has European and 'neighbourhood' variants, with the increasing threat of delocalization to central and Eastern European member states of the EU, Turkey and the Maghreb.

Powerful political polemics on delocalization are common to all. On the radical Left (and Right), quite simply delocalizations represent those parts of global neo-liberal capitalism which France will not tolerate. A number of mainstream politicians promise the withdrawal of all state aid from any firm delocalizing while making a profit, and (less realistically) reregulation at the WTO level enforcing minimum social or environmental standards on producers and subcontractors. In recent years, the weighty Beffa (2005), Grignon (2004) and Roustan (2004) reports have all mapped out France's possible responses to deindustrialization and delocalization. These reports paint the picture with greater complexity than French political leaders. They note, for example, that French multinationals benefit from the outsourcing and cost-reducing opportunities of delocalization, and that resultant profits, even if made abroad, are for the most part repatriated. Furthermore, rising demand for French exports in the fast-growing, cheap-labour economies (and its positive impact on skilled employment in France) has to be factored in. The reports also point out the benefits of the new international division of labour for French consumers in terms of much cheaper commodities. This reduces the high cost of living, and has a knock-on effect on purchasing power, increasing domestic demand, which in turn *creates* jobs.

The 'real' impact of delocalization on employment has been calculated variously as between 40,000 and 500,000 jobs lost. Taking into account both negative and positive effects on French employment over 20 years, the OFCE estimates 'globally, the net loss of employment is in the region of 2.75 per cent of total employment' (OFCE, 2006: 107–8). Meanwhile, the overall number French jobs, from 1970 to 2002, *increased* by 18 per cent from 21 million to nearly 25 million, according to OECD data (Daudin and Levasseur, 2005: 137).

Industrial employment has dropped in France from 25 per cent (5.5 of 22 million) in 1978 to 14 per cent (3.7 of 24.9 million) in 2004 (OFCE, 2006: 106). Technological advances account for some of the reduced numbers. Nevertheless, there have been significant reductions in low-skilled French jobs in the textiles, leather, clothing and consumer electronics sectors most penetrated by international competition, where delocalization is a prevalent phenomenon (Daudin and Levasseur, 2005: 138). The 'post-industrialization' of the French economy has seen manufacturing employment decline 30 per cent from 5.4 million to 3.8 million between 1970 and 2002. By contrast, service sector employment grew 75 per cent during this period from 10.5 million to 18.4 million (Daudin and Levasseur, 2005: 137). Partly because of the pride in France's post-war industrial resurgence, there is disquiet about France losing its industrial base. Questions are raised about the desirability of a shift towards a service-based economy. Pay and conditions within many service sectors in Anglo-Saxon economies are well below desired minimum standards on the French labour market, raising questions about the compatibility of a service-based economy and the Republican *acquis sociaux* (or the French social model).

Yet the reconfiguration of the international division of labour presents opportunities, as well as costs, in terms of France's repositioning away from old labour-intensive, low value-added production roles towards more hi-tech, high-skilled, higher value-added areas of global production. France could potentially forge a higher skill growth path for the twenty-first century. This line of thinking chimes with the Lisbon Agenda, committing the EU to becoming the premier knowledge-based economy.

What is to be done? Neo-liberalism, neo-mercantilism and French economic policy

One policy response to France's economic problems, both perceived and real, builds on a long-established tradition of neo-mercantilism, drawing on the economic nationalist theories of political economy advanced by Friedrich List (see List, 1856; Helleiner, 2002; Crane, 1998; Levi-Faur, 1997). Assuming the primacy of nations (and their state institutions) over markets, its policy programme thus involves extensive state intervention and regulation of economic activity. Domestically, neo-mercantilism prioritizes strategic economic interventionism to promote industry. Internationally, the emphasis is on relative gains vis-à-vis competitors, possibly secured through protectionist trade policies.

List's 'National system of political economy' may seem anachronistic amidst the freer global markets and economic flows of the twenty-first century, yet it aligns with the powerful French tradition of *dirigisme* noted above. Economic nationalism rests upon national identity, taking account of specific national traditions, ideas and institutions. It is consonant with directing state intervention in economic activity presupposed by the Republican *étatiste* tradition (Hazareesingh, 1994: Chs 3 and 6; Dyson, 1980: 27–9). Listian emphasis on historical uniqueness is also easily reconciled with French 'exceptionalism', and the observation that France is difficult to categorize within comparative *varieties of capitalism* (see Schmidt, 2003; Hall and Soskice, 2001).

Neo-mercantilist political–economic ideas have long been a significant undercurrent of the French policy debate. In the post-war period, neo-mercantilist rhetoric and practice mobilized myriad policy levers to secure France's international competitiveness and 'national champions'. In the early 1980s, Mitterrand attempted a *dirigiste* dose of reflation and nationalization. The Mitterrand era began in 1981–83 with an ambitious countercyclical 'redistributive Keynesian' (Hall, 1986) demand boost combined with *dirigisme* in a wide range of industrial, economic and social policy areas. This did not have the desired effect, and quickly proved incompatible with a changing international political economic context, provoking successive financial crises and mounting external pressures.

In 1983, the Socialist government embarked upon a U-turn which reset the parameters of French economic policy-making, jettisoning significant parts (though not all) of the post-war *dirigiste* heritage. This episode demonstrated how global financial markets could powerfully constrain French governments. It was a salutary lesson of the need to rethink France's engagement with emergent globalization. One crucial evolution in French economic policy since 1983 has been the coexistence of *dirigiste* market-directing impulses with neo-liberal market-conforming initiatives, institutions and policies.

Thus, alongside traditional *dirigisme*, another policy response to France's economic problems has advocated a whole-hearted embrace of the neo-liberal political economic vision, inspired by Hayek and Friedman, which profoundly transformed the British political economy in the 1980s and 1990s. This view, favoured by some French economists and politicians and by the EU Commission, contends that if France is to swim rather than sink in the choppy waters of stiffer international competition and economic liberalization, it needs to plot a radically different (much more neo-liberal) course from that of the post-war era and indeed the last 25 years. The policy corollaries are liberalization, deregulation, further flexibilization of French labour markets, retrenchment of state spending, and the reduction of the French public sector. These are seen as necessary conditions of economic competitiveness. Sarkozy himself has not been deaf to their pleading. His economic programme underwent a transformation between 2004 (as interventionist Minister) and his 2007 presidential campaign, seduced as he was by neo-liberal and 'Anglo-Saxon' arguments.

In truth, these ideas and policies are not alien to the French political economy. Chirac's flirtation with neo-liberalism between 1986 and 1988 pushed further in the direction of market liberalization and privatization already undertaken by 'modernizing' Socialists after 1983. Financial markets were reconstructed and liberalized, and their role within French capitalism expanded. French state/market relations were becoming much more liberal in character. Neo-liberalizing elements have become part of French labour markets, capital markets and 'New Public Management'-oriented state reform processes since the 1980s (Cole, 2008: 46–72). Meanwhile, the European single market, built upon neo-liberal and decidedly non-*dirigiste* economic foundations, has had wide-ranging implications for French industrial and economic policy. *Dirigiste* industrial policy has become less viable, given weakening traditional policy instruments, advancing Europeanization, and a Commission policing 'unfair' competition with increasing vigour.

Yet it would be wrong to regard neo-mercantilism and neo-liberalism as incompatible. 'Economic nationalism' (or neo-mercantilism) can, under certain circumstances, refer to liberal economic policies and institutions, hence Helleiner's apparently anachronistic notion 'liberal economic nationalism' (2002: 308). Helleiner underlines the potentially diverse policy content of a neo-mercantilist strategy, which is in no way limited to protectionism. For example, in the nineteenth century, British economic nationalism was rooted in the liberal institutions of the gold standard and free trade (Helleiner, 2002: 320–2).

The 'competitive disinflation' strategy which was the fulcrum of macroeconomic policy after 1983, was neo-mercantilism par excellence, but also unambiguously neo-liberal. It engendered a paradigm shift of priorities in macroeconomic policy, relegating full employment to a distant future aspiration, and promoting tackling inflation to priority number one. Its rationale was to achieve lower inflation in France than in Germany, and hence (given pegged exchange rates) improve French competitiveness vis-à-vis its European trading partners (see Lordon, 1998; Blanchard and Muet, 1993). Similarly, the 'social VAT' reforms recently undertaken in Germany, and under serious consideration by Sarkozy, are both a neo-liberal tax-shifting strategy, and a neo-mercantilist economic strategy (reducing production costs, and hence the price of goods on international markets). It is neo-mercantilist in intent, yet liberal in character. Thus, the two are not mutually exclusive. Globalization, liberalization and Europeanization do not render neo-mercantilism 'irrelevant', but change its context, entailing a shift in the balance between *dirigisme* and liberalism in the pursuit of national economic interests.

The policy content of contemporary French neo-mercantilism is more market-oriented at present, despite rhetorical flourishes suggesting otherwise. Domestic liberalizing economic reforms, compounded by

Europeanization, globalization, and the internationalization of French capitalism, have partially undermined the coherence and distinctiveness of the French national system of political economy. Neo-mercantilist economic ideas still have a role to play in both discourse and policy in France. However, although being an ongoing underlying rationale for much economic policy-making in France, the changing nature of state–market relations (and the constraints of European economic governance) make certain formerly favoured neo-mercantilist policies and strategies decreasingly viable. Sarkozy's anachronistic presidential platform could be interpreted in this light as a bid to develop a new 'neo-liberal neo-mercantilist' French economic strategy for the twenty-first century. Before exploring this point further, we consider economic policy developments under the Chirac presidencies.

Macroeconomic policy

In terms of macroeconomic policy, the euro provides a particular fiscal and monetary policy context within which French governments tackle unemployment. Public spending and public debt are, in theory, hamstrung by the European Stability and Growth Pact (requiring public deficits below 3 per cent and public debt below 60 per cent of GDP). Despite these straightened circumstances, the fiscal policy approaches of the Raffarin and de Villepin centre-Right governments, like Jospin's Socialist government before them, were decidedly *volontariste*, with at times expansionary fiscal policy and sizeable tax cuts. Public spending decisions were made in the context of a pervasive assumption of the absence of harsh constraint, permitting the delaying of tough spending reduction decisions. By 2004, French public expenditure was running at 53.3 per cent of GDP, 5 per cent above the EU average, and approaching Swedish levels (56.7 per cent) (OFCE, 2006: 35).

Expansionary economic policies pursued by first Left then Right governments created deficits in breach of the Stability and Growth Pact. The conflict of interest between domestic political economic priorities and European obligations came to a head in 2003 (less dramatically than 1983) as the European Commission sought to punish French pact-breaking profligacy. Meanwhile, French budget plans continued to flout the pact's fiscal requirements. France thus remained an 'unrepentant sinner' (Mathieu and Sterdyniak, 2003: 154, 159; Creel et al., 2002). After a protracted crisis, a revised pact emerged in early 2005, involving much greater interpretive flexibility, taking more account of specific national conditions, economic circumstances and the economic cycle. Sanctions became a much more remote possibility, and the degree of deficit constraint was reduced. The political context of a Franco-German axis on deficit forgiveness facilitated revision of the pact to align more closely with French *dirigiste* preferences (Clift, 2006).

Success in changing the fiscal policy architecture contrasts, however, with the monetary policy situation. For years French politicians of Left and Right have argued that the German-inspired European Central Bank needed to be subjected to a 'political counterweight' to bring concern about jobs and growth to bear alongside its myopic focus on price stability (low inflation) (Dyson and Featherstone, 1999: 172–245; Clift, 2006; Howarth, 2001, 2002). Unaccommodating (tight) monetary policy had a deleterious impact on French employment, and with a rising euro undermined the competitive position of many French firms (Martin, 2004; Ross, 2004). In this constrained monetary policy context, tackling employment in France often focuses on micro-economic, rather than macroeconomic, policy change.

Industrial policy

Neo-mercantilism informs French industrial policy proposals. The Grignon report (2004) recommended 'European neo-Colbertism', rearticulating French *dirigiste* industrial policy at the European level to meet the challenges of deindustrialization and delocalization. European-wide investment in research and development focused on strategic sectors would foster 'European champions'. The scale was changed, but the neo-mercantilism underpinning the strategy was, to French ears, familiar. This was a much more state-centric and public-power-driven vision of the route to the knowledge-based economy than that identified by the EU as a whole at the 2000 Lisbon Summit. There is little sign of the EU generally, and the European Commission in particular, warming to this approach.

Perhaps for this reason, carving out a new industrial policy focused on the national level. Surprisingly, as large French firms became inter-nationalized through cross-border mergers and acquisitions strategies, neo-mercantilist 'economic patriotism' discourse remained influential. French governmental interventionism still tries to emulate the 'strategic state' model set out in the Roustan report (2004). The promotion, by public, private and para-public measures, of innovation, risk-taking and research and development are central to France's attempted inter-national economic repositioning. There is a particular *dirigiste* French twist to how this can be achieved, predicated upon greater reliance upon public sector investment and state aids to orchestrate the emergence of an innovative, knowledge-based economic infrastructure in France. The French state still wants to 'pick winners'.

The de Villepin government acted on the Beffa report, founding a new national research agency aiming at industrial innovation. It set up new competitive clusters (*pôles de compétitivité*) (now numbering 71), bringing together universities and industry in the search for new hi-tech opportunities, although the French state was only able to dedicate a modest 200 million euros to promoting them in 2006 (OFCE, 2006: 109). The emphasis on the role of universities within the new 'competitiveness poles' indicates the crucial nexus of education policy and economic restructuring in the 'knowledge-based' economy, which the French state has been slow to grasp.

A range of measures have been advocated, including retraining assistance for lower-skilled workers and less stringent restrictions on targeted state aids seeking to expand research and development in innovative, hi-tech, potential growth sectors. These longer-term strategic efforts coexist with short-termist 'sticking plaster' aids to prop up sectors particularly exposed to delocalization (on the rationale that it is cheaper keeping them going than paying unemployment benefits if all the jobs migrate). More generally, ever since 1993, specific employment policy measures have been pursued, targeting lower-skilled workers (i.e. the principal losers from delocalization). The Jospin government's *prime pour l'emploi* boosted the after-tax take-home pay of lower-skilled workers. Meanwhile, on the macroeconomic policy front, depreciation of the euro (of which there is no immediate prospect) is seen as a necessary condition for renewed competitiveness of many French firms. All these measures are either fairly weak palliatives, or long-term measures which can only hope to be effective over many years. As such, the relative impotence of the French state in tackling delocalization ensures its enduring political salience, as politicians and media alike continue to draw dire conclusions from each episode.

Restructuring French capitalism and 'economic patriotism'

One area where neo-mercantilist political economic thought has infused the political debate in France is in the economic restructuring of large French firms. Although the term 'national champions' is today less commonplace, the idea remains pertinent. Its contemporary iteration is 'economic patriotism' in the new global economy, seeking to protect France's economic and corporate patrimony. There is some disjuncture between the rhetoric and the reality of economic patriotism. As noted above, the degree of state autonomy, influence and discretion assumed by 'economic patriotic' policy elites is not always commensurate with the internationalizing and liberalizing reforms that, ironically, the same elite introduced over the last 20–25 years.

Economic patriotism used to be pursued by the French state, through the 'hard cores' of France's 'protected capitalism' (Schmidt, 1996) exploiting its extensive range of holdings in large French firms, as well as a much wider set of informal links to elites throughout France's 'financial network economy' (Morin, 1998, 2000). The French state induced the emergence of a set of interlinked relationships in major French firms cemented by cross-shareholdings and interlocking board memberships. The hard cores began to unravel in the 1990s amid the privatizations, mergers and acquisitions, and the internationalization of French capitalism. In certain cases, the French state sought to retain traces of the prior 'protected capital' era. Thus, in the negotiating of some privatizations, the French government was careful to secure 'golden share' holdings to fend off potential takeovers. This means of protecting its 'national champions' eventually attracted the European Commission's disapproving attention, forcing the French state to sell off its 'golden share' in Elf-Aquitaine in 2002. However, while *some* golden shares have gone, others remain, including in five of France's largest firms, notably in strategic industries such as defence (Thalès).

The financial nexus of France's political economy changed as more large French firms relinquished cross-shareholdings, and retained only holdings seen as essential to their core business. This heralded a shift from the old protective logic, towards Anglo-Saxon shareholder value norms (Morin, 1998, 2000: 37–41; Goyer, 2001, 2003; O'Sullivan, 2003). These changes in the behaviour and capital structure of many large French listed companies undermined further elements of the traditional French *dirigiste* policy approach. Not all large French firms have been transformed to the same degree, and one important differentiation is between those companies with close ties to the French state, and those without. The former still comprise more than half of the CAC 40 (France's top 40 firms), including Total, Suez and Vivendi. The elitist networks of the *grandes écoles* which historically provided the social cement of the French model also endure. Significantly, there is a much higher prevalence of *énarques* among the CEOs of those state-linked firms (more than half compared to less than a quarter). This suggests an enduring (although less significant) orchestrating role for the French state within France's 'financial network economy'.

There are also new kinds of interventionism. Given increasing interconnectedness of global capital markets, France has seen dramatic rises in transborder mergers and acquisitions, French companies listing overseas, French portfolio investment in foreign stock markets, and foreign ownership of stocks listed on the Paris Bourse. This has enmeshed French firms in a set of global financial markets and networks. The protective barriers behind which French capitalism restructured in the 1980s have become much more porous today, with major implications for the French political economy's point of insertion into, and articulation with, its international context. In this climate, a central focus of economic patriotism is protecting France's leading global firms from foreign 'raiders'. Hence the apparently technical issue of corporate takeover regulation has acquired considerable political salience. A range of opaque defensive mechanisms impede the development of a market for corporate control in France, and policy-makers have carved out scope for *volontariste* interventionism in relation to 'strategic' sectors. Laws in 1996 and 2003 specified that French state approval was required for takeover or investment in 'strategic sectors' such as national defence, public health and – somewhat dubiously – casinos(!).

Hostile takeovers are also the subject of often intemperate press coverage and political discussion. French state actors have in recent years re-engaged dramatically in the public debate that surrounded such takeovers, as when rumours spread of a possible hostile takeover of Danone by Pepsi in July 2005. The Interior and Finance ministers vociferously opposed the move. Sarkozy said that the government 'could not remain inactive when faced with a hostile takeover bid' for Danone. The public authorities had to 'do their utmost' and deploy all their 'powers of persuasion' to block the move (*Le Monde*, 22 July 2005). Notably, they sought the French state's investment arm, the Caisse des Dépôts et Consignations (CDC) to deploy its considerable holdings, and exploit a clause within Danone's statutes which could prevent Pepsi taking control unless it could muster more than 66 per cent of the shares. The French state's open hostility to the planned bid probably scuppered the takeover, which never materialized.

Prime Minister de Villepin and Finance Minister Thierry Breton ramped up the 'economic patriotism' from 2005 onwards, with more interventions to help large French firms arm themselves against hostile takeovers. The Breton Law of July 2005 created a further obstacle to certain hostile takeovers (designed to protect Renault), requiring bidders to also bid for overseas subsidiaries of a target parent company. In December 2005 the government introduced legislation protecting firms in 11 identified 'strategic' industries from hostile takeover. In addition to which, the very substantial financial assets of the CDC were to be deployed strategically, investing to preserve the national interest by buying up stakes in large 'strategic' French firms. Although reduced since privatization, the French state's shareholder role in numerous large French firms endures.

The de Villepin government also transposed the EU Takeover Directive. While the intended direction of this reform was liberal, facilitating takeovers, its legislative passage coincided with the French government's vocal opposition to Indian steel magnate Mittal's (ultimately successful) hostile takeover bid of Arcelor in January 2006. This ramped up the political salience of takeover regulation, provoking an economic patriotist response. The de Villepin government opted out of some liberalizing features of the EU Takeover Directive, and used the opportunity to introduce US-style 'poison pill' takeover defences into French law for the first time. Transposition of the supposedly liberal-oriented EU Directive into French law paradoxically *expanded* the range of anti-takeover defences available to target boards in France. Far from dismantling institutional and structural impediments to takeovers, in fact new forms of protection were introduced (European Commission, 2007: 6, 10–11).

As the successful hostile takeover of Arcelor demonstrated, the government has limited powers, and its more arm's-length *dirigisme* cannot always protect French industrial patrimony as it would like. The French state still has the resources and policy levers to influence outcomes in some 'strategic' sectors, and in firms with large public contracts. In these cases, the rhetorical flourishes of economic patriotism carry more weight than in the increasingly internationalized parts of France's economy (with foreign ownership of substantial stakes in many of France's largest firms). Nevertheless, with a fairly extensive legislative and regulatory arsenal, economic patriotic French governments have resisted takeovers, exemplifying enduring selective state intervention in a more liberalized, internationalized French economy. Hostile foreign takeovers will probably remain comparatively rare occurrences in France.

Economic policy under Sarkozy's presidency

Sarkozy's economic platform is a complex blend of liberal solutions to relaunch economic dynamism (accepting a neo-liberal analysis of the labour market and tax causes of delocalization), but also 'economic patriotism' and industrial interventionism. Recalling earlier ambitions to reinvent *dirigisme* on a European scale, Sarkozy is also a proponent of EU-level, neo-mercantilist trade and industrial policies, what he calls a 'real' European industrial policy.

The neo-mercantilist rationale behind his proposed shifts is a focus on France's 'productive powers' and the ability to create wealth. Sarkozy's early reformism focused on the university sector, seen as a crucial means to improve the international competitiveness of the French economy. This recalls List's emphasis on 'mental capital' and the essential role of skill, initiative and knowledge. Sarkozy is alive to quality concerns about French education and its ability to forge the 'mental capital' of the nation's youth. In higher education, Sarkozy's autonomy-increasing university reforms are part of a competitiveness agenda. The relative weakness of French higher education in global league tables, and the relative unattractiveness of French universities as destinations for international postgraduates, are often highlighted as evidence that the tools to equip France with the requisite knowledge and skills base in the new global economy are in need of some sharpening.

From the firm side of the crucial university/business nexus Sarkozy has expanded the number of 'competitiveness poles', and also expanded the research tax credit (*crédit impôt recherche* – CIR), increasing from 10 to 30 per cent the state reimbursement of a firm's expenses on research. Yet on the university side, the Fillon government faces staunch resistance to reform from entrenched vested interests, as well as problems of historic underfunding. This taps into a wider debate about the relative merits of internationalization, and the role of the French university sector within the French and the global economy.

The state continues to play a selective role in orchestrating the restructuring of French capitalism. Early in his presidency, Sarkozy 'relaunched' French industrial policy, mapping out a *volontariste* approach for a selectively activist state. He neglects potential inconsistencies with free market-oriented EU and WTO rules, but even within these confines Sarkozy has identified scope for a more muscular industrial policy. While Economics and Finance Minister, Sarkozy had intervened to 'save' Aventis from the proposed takeover by Swiss company Novartis, engineering the fusion of Aventis with a French firm, Sanofi. In September 2007, his *dirigisme* took on concrete form. 'The state needs a strategy within globalization', was Sarkozy's explanation in announcing the merger of Suez and GDF (*Le Monde*, 5 September 2007). He had earlier opposed this marriage (because it began as de Villepin's idea to prevent a hostile takeover from the Italian energy giant Enel), but has now embraced the creation of a major European gas and electricity player. There are more plans for state-orchestrated restructuring of France's nuclear energy firms with Areva (global no. 1) contemplating *rapprochement* with Bouygues and Alstom (which Sarkozy also 'saved' in 2004). The French state is playing a key role in reorganizing the French (and European) energy sector (*Le Monde*, 5 September 2007), employing a familiar 'financial network economy' approach. The Suez–GDF merger meant Suez had to sell off Suez Environnement, and Sarkozy's Élysée office arranged the sale to ensure that the 'hard core' fell into safe hands (Suez Environmental is now shored up by a hard-core alliance of Groupe Bruxelles Lambert, Crédit Agricole, Areva, Caisse des Dépôts and CNP) (*Le Monde*, 6 September 2007). Sarkozy's new *dirigisme*, or 'neo-liberal mercantilism', is not straightforwardly statist, but illustrates an ongoing rebalancing act between state and market within the French political economy. Previously Sarkozy had pledged to keep GDF from privatization, but this deal sees GDF substantially privatized (with the state as key shareholder – still holding 34 per cent).

Nor is Sarkozy's neo-mercantilism confined to large French firms. He is committed to introducing a French 'small businesses Act', on the US model, giving preferential treatment to French small businesses in securing public contracts (*Le Monde*, 30 August 2007). This could again flout EU and WTO unfair competition restrictions, yet Sarkozy's economic patriotism has pretensions to reorient EU and global trade regulation to permit more *dirigisme*. His industrial policy speech emphasized the need for a more aggressive EU trade policy vis-à-vis global competitors. This dovetails with Sarkozy's campaign promises to revitalize 'community preference' as an instrument of neo-mercantilist EU trade policy. He has also harangued both US and Chinese policy-makers about unfair competition from their undervalued currencies. Within Europe, Sarkozy promises to seek reform of the European Central Bank, adding employment and growth to its statutory focus on inflation. Yet this kind of reorientation is unlikely, given the antipathy of many European partners (notably Germany) to such moves.

Sarkozy also threatens a reinvention of *dirigisme* at the EU level. As the simplified EU Treaty was agreed on 23 June 2007, Sarkozy flexed his neo-mercantilist muscles and succeeded in getting the reference to 'free and fair competition' removed from the mini treaty (although the objective of the internal market remains intact). The aim was to facilitate the emergence of national and European champions, and to have the Commission help, not hinder, the process. This is a long-standing complaint of the French political elite, who regard the Commission as excessively Anglo-Saxon, or 'ultra-liberal' in industrial policy. However, despite the symbolism (notably given the rift it generated with the UK government), it will change little in European market regulation, or Commission operating norms, as enshrined in the existing treaties.

The anti-delocalization and employment creation agendas overlap in Sarkozy's strategy for labour market reform. A more flexible labour market (and simplified labour code) are needed to aid the employment situation and dissuade mobile capital from delocalization (see Chapter 13 for fuller discussion). Sarkozy has also made very public his desire to facilitate firing (calling for 'amicable separation' between employees and firms) within the 'modernization' of the employment contract. The inspiration is Danish. This is 'flexicurity' French style, making it easier for firms to fire, and a better resourced 'one-stop shop' to aid the unemployed to re-enter the labour market. There is also a lifelong learning element, focusing on transferability of training, and entitlement to training, in what Sarkozy hopes will become a more fluid labour market.

Taxation policy under Sarkozy accepts the hyperglobal (neo-liberal) capital flight argument, 'if we tax labour too much, it delocalizes, if we tax capital too much, it delocalizes' (cited in *Le Monde*, 13 August

2007). Summer 2007 saw Sarkozy's 'fiscal shock' delivering on his election tax reduction pledges. Spuriously justified in terms of positive employment effects of a mooted resultant boost in demand, in reality these measures disproportionately benefit the affluent (Heyer et al., 2007: 6). The total cost of the 'fiscal shock', reducing taxes on over-time earnings, capping personal taxation at 50 per cent of revenues, diminishing the inheritance tax, and allowing partial deductibility of interest payments on home mortgages, is calculated at 11.6 billion euros for the whole year. Its impact on employment will be limited, or even negative, favouring working 'insiders' over the unemployed 'out-siders' (Heyer et al., 2007: 4). While the positive macroeconomic effects are dubious (Heyer et al., 2007: 1, 6), its political significance is considerable. Firstly, reducing tax and social security contributions on overtime signals a rupture with the Jospin government's 35-hour work week. Secondly, reducing taxes on inheritance, wealth and high-earners panders to an aspiring, successful 'France of early risers', as Sarkozy puts it.

The public finance impact of the 'fiscal shock' (estimated in *Le Monde*, 31 July 2007 to cost 30 billion euros by 2012) demonstrates continuity with established *dirigiste* practice of governments of both Left and Right overstepping Stability and Growth Pact debt and deficit targets in order to fund interventionist economic policies (see Clift, 2006). Signalling ongoing unrepentant sinning on the public finances, Budget Minister Eric Woerth explicitly recognized the need for a 'pause' in deficit and debt reduction soon after Sarkozy's victory (*Le Monde*, 5 June 2007). The new President subsequently went to a euro-group meeting to explain to European partners why France would renege on the agreed timetable for restoring the public finances, delaying the elimination of the public deficit from 2010 to 2012.

Yet to meet these now longer-term public finance obligations, more (and more difficult) reforms are required. On the expenditures side, top priorities include 'structural' reforms of pensions, health insurance and civil service staffing levels (and, more broadly, the French public administration). These will be politically sensitive, and pension reform has already sparked off a wave of strikes. On the revenues side, the 'fiscal shock' is but the first phase of tax reform. Further costly reforms include the planned 'ambitious' reform of business taxes (most notably the *taxe professionnelle*) reducing industry labour costs, justified by Sarkozy as 'a real remedy against delocalization' (*Le Figaro*, 23 June 2007). Thereafter, Sarkozy promised a radical review of taxation and social charges (and their impact on firms) in France. Also on the horizon is the neo-mercantilist 'social VAT', shifting the tax burden from producers (through employers' social security contributions and taxes) to consumers, with the aim of improving French competitiveness by reducing production and labour costs.

Sarkozy promises structural reforms creating a French state which 'consumes less and invests more'. His neo-liberal state reform agenda pledged to reduce the size of the state, claiming only one in two retiring civil servants would be replaced. For all the tough talk, this goal was not met in the 2008 budget (see Chapter 11 for fuller discussion). It is being phased in slowly, adding even more to France's galloping public deficit. Extensive consultations are scheduled with public sector 'social partners' in 2007/8 to discuss the public service mission and values, professional development and mobility within the civil service, and salaries. The outcome of these discussions, and also the evolution of UK-style performance-related public financing reforms first introduced in LOLF, will be crucial to whether Sarkozy has more success than previous governments, many of whom tried and failed to reshape the French state and modernize the French public sector.

Conclusion

The dramatic liberalization and internationalization of the French economy since 1983 has changed the parameters of French economic policy, moving broadly in a more liberal and less *dirigiste* direction than during the *trente glorieuses*. The *volontariste* impulse has been exaggerated under Sarkozy, and neo-mercantilist economic patriotism has been a prominent feature of the early Sarkozy presidency, but Sarkozy's advocacy of neo-mercantilism is often broadly neo-liberal in orientation. The increasing prevalence of the market limits the scope for potential state interventionism.

The claimed objective of economic patriotism within French economic policy is to tackle France's ongoing unemployment problem. However, it is not clear the state *can* solve the unemployment problem – because its economic policy levers do not to seem to have sufficient purchase over France's economic infrastructure. For example, much attention is paid to the 'activation'-oriented welfare and labour market policies in Denmark and Sweden, with many arguing such a direction of travel could hold the key to France's employment problems (see Chapter 13 for fuller discussion). However, even if a French government wanted to introduce such policies, the French state is hamstrung because the social partners, rather than the state, run the French unemployment insurance regime. Meanwhile, in attempting to tackle delocalization, 'neo-Colbertist' economic nationalist interventionism runs up against European Commission competition regulations. Furthermore, as the Arcelor case proves, even the best efforts of the French state to protect French firms cannot always prevail over powerful financial and industrial resources.

French economic policy discourse is today a paradoxical amalgam which is at once liberalizing in some areas and staunchly statist and *dirigiste* in others. Certainly in rhetorical terms, *dirigisme* is not dead. That said, in terms of policy practice, the record is doubtless more liberalizing than the rhetorical recourse to *dirigisme* would care to concede. The presupposition in favour of *dirigiste* interventionism has come under increasing threat in the last 25 years from structural changes in global financial markets, from the EU, and from the ideological ascendancy of neo-liberalism. Sarkozy can be seen as trying to develop a neo-liberal mercantilism for the twenty-first century, but its coherence is questionable, and his reformist zeal may be blunted by social partners, political obstacles and economic difficulties.

Chapter 13

Between State and Market: Crisis and Transformation in French Industrial Relations

CHRIS HOWELL

The image of France as a blocked society, unable to reform itself, prone to social conflict that regularly spills into the streets, and divided between militant, ideologically divided interest groups that resist change as they jealously guard their privileges, is perhaps nowhere more prevalent than in the sphere of industrial relations. For 40 years, since at least the strikes and demonstrations that paralysed the nation in May and June 1968, class relations in France have appeared especially conflictual, and every government, regardless of their political stripe, has attempted some form of industrial relations reform project designed to introduce the European norm of regularized collective bargaining in France. On the surface, it is easy to believe that little has changed, that the stalemate continues, and that efforts to reform the French social model inevitably founder on the shoals of industrial and social conflict. It is not only abroad that French social immobilism is widely excoriated: indeed, it was a central theme of the successful presidential campaign of Nicolas Sarkozy in 2007. Envious glances are increasingly cast at other European countries, with particular interest directed towards the system of 'flexicurity' in Denmark. Certainly, there is evidence from recent years to support this view, and the high-profile battle over government efforts to introduce more flexible work contracts for young people in 2006, a battle that the government lost, seemed to confirm France's standing as a society incapable of necessary reform.

Beneath the surface, however, French industrial relations are in the process of being transformed. A dense network of mostly non-union institutions representing workers has been implanted inside French firms, the scope and scale of social dialogue or collective bargaining inside the firm have expanded, and, despite the popular image of the French labour market as incorrigibly rigid, flexibility and individualization – in work time, work organization and payment systems – have become widespread. To be sure, the ultimate trajectory of French industrial relations is not yet clear, the reform efforts have often been

209

incoherent or contradictory, and change has bred resistance. This is in large part because of a fundamental obstacle. Any stable system of firm-level collective bargaining requires that employers have a partner on the labour side that is both representative of workers, and has sufficient independence and capacity that it can bargain effectively. Such an actor does not exist in France. The labour movement continues its 30-year decline and is undergoing a profound crisis of representation. In the absence of a strong labour counterweight, unilateral action on the part of employers to reshape the firm, generates insecurity and inequality. The result has been a hesitant, halting process of reform in which the French state remains a central actor, simultaneously encouraging the social partners to take more responsibility for managing change, and putting limits on how that change can take place.

Background

Post-war France has anchored one end of a comparative spectrum of industrial relations, characterized by weak, divided trade unions, limited collective bargaining, and a strong, interventionist state. French industrial relations were marked by four main features during the *trente glorieuses* years of post-war economic growth. First, by any conventional standards, French trade unions have been extremely weak. Trade union density (which is notoriously difficult to measure in France) declined after 1945 to a low of around 17 per cent in the early 1960s. It then recovered in the wake of the strike wave of 1968 to reach a peak of almost 25 per cent in 1974 before beginning a long, slow decline that lasted until around 1990, and left France with a trade union density of less than 10 per cent (and this heavily concentrated in the public sector), the lowest in the industrialized world. French unions are also divided. Immediately after the Second World War, several unions, notably FO, split from the communist-allied CGT; then, in the early 1960s, the catholic trade union confederation divided into a larger socialist union, the CFDT, and a catholic rump, the CFTC. The result has been five officially recognized union confederations and a number of smaller autonomous unions. French law bestows representative status on these five confederations, based upon factors such as independence, support and patriotic behaviour (in other words, non-collaboration) during the Second World War. This status was last assigned more than 40 years ago – in a quite different union landscape – and it permits only these union confederations to sign national agreements and to stand in the first round of professional elections. These union confederations have historically been bitterly divided along ideological and confessional lines, have competed for members, and have only rarely been able to work together.

The second distinctive feature of post-war French industrial relations has been the limited development of collective bargaining, particularly inside the firm. The cornerstone of French labour law since 1950 has been a strict hierarchy, giving priority to legislation over collective agreements, and higher-level collective agreements over lower ones. Legislation and national agreements set patterns and minimum wages and conditions. Bargains reached at the firm level have not been allowed to derogate (undercut) legislation and national agreements, thereby preventing employers from using firm bargaining to achieve flexibility, and effectively removing any incentive from reaching such agreements. The result has been that for most of the post-war period, firm-level bargaining has been all but non-existent outside the public sector and a few large firms with well-implanted unions.

The third, much-remarked upon, feature of post-war French industrial relations has been high levels of industrial conflict. The absence of firm-level institutions for managing conflict, combined with politicized trade unionism and the social costs of rapid economic growth, produced large numbers of strikes, and, given the prominent role of the French state in industrial relations, strikes frequently became directed at the state. Industrial conflict took the form of strike waves, especially in 1968, 1988–89 and 1995. While adept at exploiting strikes, trade unions have rarely been the instigators of strike waves – they have been described as 'skilled surfboard riders' – serving more as interlocutors with the state and employers in the process of settling strikes.

The final distinctive element of French industrial relations has been the central role played by the state, especially after 1968 when it became a political imperative to avoid a future explosion of social protest. There has been a consistent effort from every government since 1970 to try to construct autonomous industrial relations institutions inside the firm which could take the weight of regulating the social relations and the labour market. These efforts largely failed, at least until the end of the 1980s. As a fallback, state authorities resorted to direct regulation of the labour market: an aggressive use of the minimum wage; imposition of agreements reached in a single industry or region on all the firms in the country (the so-called 'extension' procedure); limitations on the ability to hire and fire; and partial decommodification of the labour market through generous unemployment benefits. The French state came, in effect, to substitute for a weak labour movement. For example, thanks to the extension procedure, collective agreements cover 92 per cent of French employees, even though unions represent less than 10 per cent of the workforce. The result has been a relatively rigid labour market, without a great deal of flexibility for firms, but a rigidity that derives from the role of the state rather than trade unions.

Changing social actors

In recent years, France's social partners have become more willing to bargain over critical issues, rather than turning to the state for solutions. However, this evolution has been contested on both the labour and employer side. Three important changes stand out.

First, the CGT finally broke with the Communist Party in the early 1990s, ending its long-term institutional ties and ending its isolation from other unions at both the international and national level; it joined the Confederation of European Unions in 1999. Its general secretary since 1999, Bernard Thibault, has pursued a more pragmatic strategy, showing himself willing to seek compromise with other French unions and to more frequently sign collective agreements. The national agreement on professional training in 2003 was the first significant interconfederal agreement the CGT had signed since 1971. Nonetheless, for all the reforms introduced by Thibault and his predecessor at the head of the CGT, he was only able to stabilize the organization's membership (which had lost two-thirds of its membership between 1977 and 1991). Its structure is highly decentralized, with only limited autonomy or resources at the confederal level, making it extremely difficult to implement new strategies for growth. An internal dispute over whether the union would publicly oppose the EU Constitutional Treaty in 2005 demonstrated the limits on the ability of the centre to lead. In the past, the ideology of communism had provided the glue which permitted a unified direction; that is now gone. The wider problem for the CGT is that it is caught between the reformism of the CFDT and the radicalism of the autonomous unions.

The second development has been the emergence of the CFDT as the privileged partner of employers and conservative governments. When François Chérèque was elected general secretary in 2002, the CFDT had reason to congratulate itself on the success of its strategy since the end of the 1980s, and to believe that it was best placed to bring about the modernization and normalization of French trade unionism. In contrast to every other major union, it had seen strong membership growth through the 1990s to become the largest union, particularly in the private sector, though these gains were not matched in professional elections. The CFDT had also come to replace other unions on the boards of jointly managed social programmes. These were seen by the union as the benefits of a strategy that has been labelled 'hyper-reformism' (Pernot, 2005). It involved an acceptance of the constraints imposed on bargaining by employers and the state, and an emphasis upon negotiation as an end in itself.

The CFDT has also been much more willing to support the reform of the welfare state than other unions, an approach which culminated in the CFDT breaking ranks with other unions in 2003 to endorse the pension reform of the Raffarin government, thereby averting a crisis like that of 1995, the last time public sector pension reform was attempted. For the CFDT, the result was massive internal dissent which manifested itself in the disaffiliation of several prominent federations, losses in professional elections, and a decline in membership of roughly 10 per cent between 2002 and 2005. Unlike the CGT, the CFDT is highly centralized and it has tended to respond to internal dissent with intolerance, suspensions and expulsions. The growth of autonomous unions (see below) has been fuelled by refugees from the CFDT. By 2005, the CGT was once again the largest union, and the CFDT was facing up to its membership losses with a new recruitment campaign based upon a corps of dedicated recruiters. In the highly competitive world of French trade unionism, there are limits to the reformist strategy pursued by the CFDT.

The third development is the resurgence of autonomous unions (those not affiliated with the five officially designated representative unions). These unions are overwhelmingly in the public sector, and have a strong occupational identity. Their recent growth has been driven by schisms within the CFDT and competition among public sector union federations. After 1988, a number of CFDT federations, particularly in mail, telecommunications and rail, left the CFDT in frustration at its unwillingness to resist government-led public sector reforms more aggressively. These took the name SUD (Solidaires, Unitaires, et Démocratiques), and along with some more long-standing autonomous unions, formed a loose confederation in 2004 entitled Solidaires, encompassing 36 unions and claiming 80,000 members. Meanwhile another pole of autonomous unions, the UNSA (Union Nationale des Syndicats Autonomes) has also emerged and shown some success at professional elections. The Solidaires unions, in particular, represent a militant, oppositional force within the labour movement, quick to strike and unwilling to sign collective agreements. The autonomous unions have proved durable and been able to make gains in profession elections, though they have been able to grow only by taking existing members from other unions, not new recruitment. Nevertheless, autonomous unions are a newly important actor in French industrial relations, and indicate the continued fissures and disagreement on the labour side about how to confront public sector restructuring.

The main employers' organization became radicalized and politicized in the course of the 1980s and 1990s, particularly in response to two Socialist reform initiatives: the Auroux laws, expanding workplace consultation and participation, and the 35-hour work week. The result was the creation in 1997 of a new organization, MEDEF (Mouvement des Entreprises de France), with a much stronger neo-liberal prescription for France's economic ills, and a greater combativeness when it came to its relationship with both the state and the unions. There was a discursive element to MEDEF's project, as its first president, Ernst Antoine Sellière, tried to replace the traditional word 'patron' with that of 'entrepreneur' to symbolize the dynamism and market orientation of employers. Along with a new name and a new ethos, MEDEF also had a new method. After two years of largely fruitless harrying of the Socialist government of Lionel Jospin over the 35-hour week reforms, in 1999 MEDEF launched what it called a social refoundation (*refondation sociale*) and invited the trade unions to join it. At its core, the new social foundation was an appeal for the state to stay out of regulating the labour market and instead to leave the social partners free to negotiate reforms as they saw fit. It would involve derogation writ large, with firms granted greater flexibility than legislation currently allowed as long as change was negotiated.

This strategy was predicated upon at least one major trade union being willing to support a call for greater autonomy of industrial relations and the labour market from the state, despite the attendant risk that autonomy in the context of weak labour organizations would translate into a flexibility that benefited employers more than workers. Thus the CFDT's strategic shift towards 'hyper-reformism' enabled this new employer strategy, and ensured that the CFDT would be the MEDEF's privileged interlocutor. The culmination of the *refondation sociale* came with a joint employer–union statement in 2001, signed by all the unions except the CGT. The statement emphasized the need to privilege collective bargaining over legislation, to create greater space for decentralized bargaining, and to encourage the greater legitimacy of collective agreements by ensuring that the signatories were genuinely representative. This declaration created the political space for legislation in 2004 that rewrote French industrial relations (see next section). It should also be noted that MEDEF was anxious to re-emphasize social dialogue, not just at the firm level but also at the national level where it wanted to reform many of the social programmes jointly managed with the unions. The period after 2000 saw a number of national, interconfederal agreements including ones dealing with unemployment insurance, workplace health, supplementary pensions, professional training and gender equality at work.

However, when the Right won control of the National Assembly in 2002, it became clear that the new social foundation was more a strategy designed for a period when the Left controlled the legislature – hence the demand for less state intervention – than one appropriate to a friendly government. MEDEF took an unusually high-profile role in the run-up to the 2002 elections, launching a nine-point manifesto designed to set the terms of debate for the various right-wing candidates for President. The manifesto included the call for a new legal and constitutional framework for social dialogue along the lines of the *refondation sociale.* MEDEF looked to the new conservative government to legislate in a number of areas, refusing to negotiate an easing of the 35-hour week on the grounds that it was the government's responsibility to legislate in that area. After initially warm relations between the government and the employers' organization (Jean-Pierre Raffarin was the first Prime Minister to address a MEDEF conference), the employers became increasingly impatient with the slow pace of change and cautious approach of the government. The employers' organization has continued to urge reforms that are quite radical in the context of French industrial relations – including weaker employment protection, less consultation on layoffs, and also ending the union monopoly in professional elections – and it tacitly supported Sarkozy in the run-up to the 2007 presidential elections. Laurence Parisot's election as the new president of MEDEF in 2005 inaugurated a somewhat quieter approach, though a neo-liberal diagnosis and prescription for French labour market ills remains dominant within the organization, as evidenced by her quip that, just as many things in life are insecure, such as love and health, so work should also be a little more insecure.

Public policy and the state

The role of the state has been central to French industrial relations since at least 1968, and has included extensive direct regulation of the labour market, in effect substituting for weak unions, and creating or conferring legitimacy upon interest organizations. The legacy of the last 40 years has been that the primary obstacle to labour market flexibility has been the state itself, rather than collective agreements and workplace trade unionism. As the capacity of the French economy to create new employment worsened in the 1980s and 1990s, and the unemployment rate remained stubbornly high by international standards, employment policy came to drive industrial relations policy, giving an urgency to reform projects; in short, the decentralization of French industrial relations came to be seen as a prerequisite for workplace flexibility and thus for tackling unemployment.

While the focus of this chapter is the conservative government of 2002–7, it is important to recognize just how bipartisan public policy has been with respect to industrial relations in the period since the Socialist Party underwent its 'conversion' to the market in the mid-1980s. There have been different emphases, to be sure, but the main outlines of policy have remained constant. Both Left and Right have accepted EMU as a commitment device limiting the ability of national governments to use the demand side to create jobs, and both have followed a strategy of 'social anesthesia' (Levy, 1999), using the welfare system to cushion workers from the consequences of economic restructuring. Both have focused upon the supply side of the labour market, seeking ways to reduce the cost to employers of unskilled labour. Socialist governments tended to offer greater protection to workers in return for accepting flexibility, to demand that flexibility be negotiated and to subsidize employers for hiring, while governments of the Right have been more willing to contemplate easing employment protection. But even on the Right, the language of social cohesion, and social dialogue as the privileged mechanism of change, has trumped neo-liberalism, at least until the 2007 presidential elections. Across the political spectrum, the dilemma was the same: how to increase labour market and workplace flexibility to create employment in the absence of a labour partner strong enough to protect workers.

The Socialists have introduced two important reforms. The first, in the early 1980s, was the Auroux law (*loi Auroux*), which rewrote a third of the labour code and, in many ways, set the agenda for reform efforts – by both the Left and the Right – ever since. The goals of the Auroux law were to encourage the development of collective bargaining, strengthen unions and give workers more of a voice in their daily work life. The focus of these reforms was the firm, where unions and collective bargaining remained poorly implanted. While French unions continued their decline despite these reforms, the Auroux reforms opened the first breach in the hierarchy of law and collective bargaining, creating limited opportunities for firm-level agreements to derogate from legislation and thereby giving employers seeking flexibility an interest in the further spread of firm-level bargaining.

The second important Socialist initiative were the Aubry laws (*lois Aubry*), which introduced the 35-hour work week, and the legacy of that reform continued to influence government action and industrial relations after the victory of the Right in the 2002 elections. Despite being hugely controversial – so much so that debate over the impact of these laws continued in the 2007 presidential elections – a balanced assessment suggests that they were not a serious burden for employers, and that any increase in labour costs was offset by improved flexibility and work organization (Hayden, 2006). Furthermore, the manner in which work reduction was introduced encouraged both firm-level bargaining and the strengthening of new forms of worker representation; it became increasingly the case that the negotiation inside the firm required by Aubry was conducted by non-union representatives (whether elected delegates or mandated employees) or simply consisted of employer proposals ratified by the workforce in a referendum.

The industrial relations policy of the Raffarin and de Villepin governments went through four phases over the five years of their existence and policy evolved largely in response to external events. The initial phase of industrial relations policy was cautious as Raffarin and his Minister of Employment, François Fillon, tried to avoid inflaming the trade unions ahead of the December 2002 elections to the industrial tribunals and in anticipation of difficult negotiations over pensions reform in 2003. During the first year of the new government, the focus of policy was upon easing existing Socialist legislation. The 35-hours legislation was not repealed but its application to small firms was suspended and greater flexibility was introduced by increasing recourse to overtime, enabling employers to offer increased pay in lieu of more days off in small firms, and exempting managerial staff from some parts of the legislation. The absence of a frontal attack on the 35-hour week spoke to its popularity, but by 2007, so many exemptions and alternatives to reduced time had been created that employers had a great deal of flexibility in how to implement it. In addition, several clauses of a 2002 Socialist law which offered greater protection to workers in the event of layoffs were suspended and the unions and employers were urged to negotiate an alternative. Negotiations failed and the government was forced to legislate in 2004.

The second phase of industrial relations policy was concentrated in 2003–4 and focused upon the reform of France's welfare system. Reforming welfare programmes in France involves industrial relations policy both because several of the largest programmes are funded by employer and employee contributions and jointly managed by the social partners so that reform requires bargaining, and because changing public sector pensions schemes risked industrial upheaval, as a previous conservative government had discovered in 1995. It was pensions reform that was the cornerstone of the Raffarin government's efforts in this area, and it succeeded in May 2003 in large part because of divisions within the labour movement and the willingness of the CFDT to approve the proposed legislation. Up to that point, trade unions had shown impressive unity and a mounting capacity to launch massive national demonstrations. However, after the CFDT signed off on the legislation, strikes and demonstrations petered out. Reform of the sickness insurance system also required government action in order to restore budgetary balance (see Chapter 14 for further discussion). Legislation achieving this passed in the summer of 2004 over the objections of the CGT and CGT-FO, both of which argued that the burden of reform fell overwhelmingly on patients, through increased contributions and payments, while employers and health-care professionals were largely spared. Reforming the unemployment insurance system took place in late 2002 as a result of agreement between employers and three of the five representative unions: the CGT and CGT-FO again opposed the reform while the CFDT again signed the accord. The core of the reform involved strict new eligibility rules and a reduction in the amount of time unemployment benefit could be claimed.

Relative success in the politically and socially explosive sphere of welfare reform emboldened the government to embark on a reform of collective bargaining, something that has the most potential to change the French industrial relations system in the long term. The Fillon law, passed in April 2004, incorporated two important sets of changes, both of which followed from the joint statement signed by employers and all the union confederations except the CGT in July 2001. One set of changes permitted wider recourse to derogatory collective agreements, while the other attempted to incorporate the so-called 'majority principle' into bargaining. The logic of the linkage was simply that there should be some assurance that derogatory agreements would be signed by organizations or institutions that were genuinely representative of workers. To put it crudely, the employer demand for greater flexibility should be balanced by a trade union demand that labour signatories represent a majority of the relevant group of workers.

The first part of the changes did involve a significant modification of the traditional bargaining hierarchy, permitting derogation in firm-level agreements unless explicitly denied in collective agreements or legislation. In firms without a union delegate, firm-specific bodies such as the works council could be authorized to sign agreements, and in the absence of any elected employee representative, a union-mandated worker could sign an agreement and the workforce then ratify it. The second part of the reforms, however, was implemented in much weaker fashion. MEDEF never fully supported the majority principle, for the obvious reason that it limited the ability of employers to sign agreements with weak, non-representative unions, and successfully lobbied to undermine the majority principle in the final version of the legislation. Minority unions retained significant power because, at sectoral and interprofessional levels, majority and minority were defined in terms of the number of officially recognized trade union organizations, regardless of the relative size of those unions. The result of the Fillon law, therefore, was to both enhance the autonomy of the firm from the wider industrial relations system, and encourage the shift in worker representation from trade unions to non-union, firm-specific institutions, while doing little to counterbalance this shift with a strong assertion of the need for majority representation where unions existed.

However, almost as soon as the ink was dry on the Fillon law, the government began to shift focus, lose confidence in its capacity to bring about fundamental change through social dialogue, and tack away from the mild neo-liberalism of the Raffarin and Fillon period. The shift followed losses in the 2004 regional elections, the French 'no' to the EU Constitutional Treaty, and the eruption in flames of the suburbs (*banlieues*) in late 2005. President Chirac rediscovered the language he had used in his 1995 presidential bid, and spoke of healing the 'social fracture', Fillon was replaced in April 2004 with Jean-Louis

Borloo, who took over an expanded portfolio of employment, labour and social cohesion, and Raffarin was replaced by Dominique de Villepin in 2005.

This period ushered in an almost exclusive emphasis within industrial relations upon the introduction of new kinds of work contracts which either subsidized employers for hiring, or made it easier to fire recently hired workers, or both. It rested upon the assumption that the fastest way to reduce unemployment, especially for young people and the long-term unemployed, was to make it easier and cheaper for employers to hire and fire new workers. Thus labour market deregulation became a priority. The result was the introduction of a dizzying array of work contracts, each targeting a particular group. The main innovation of Borloo's initial plan was a two-year contract which offered 26 hours of work and 9 hours of training in return for 75 per cent of the minimum wage. This was followed in 2005 with a new employment contract (*contrat nouvelle embauche* – CNE) targeted at new hires in small firms. Employers could unilaterally fire a worker hired on a CNE without cause, and without the usual separation costs, during the first two years of the contract. This in turn led in 2006 to the proposal for a first employment contract (*contrat première embauche* – CPE), targeted at those aged under 26 in any size firm, and promising employers the same ability to fire without cause and without cost.

Thus after a cautious start, and the implementation of long-term reforms of the industrial relations system and social programmes linked to employment, the conservative government found itself seeking a quick fix to the problem of unemployment in the form of piecemeal deregulation of the labour market. The result, as we shall see below, was the crisis over the CPE in the spring of 2006 and the eventual humiliation of the government.

Industrial conflict and social mobilization

France has traditionally been known for high levels of industrial conflict and social mobilization, as strikes have rapidly spread and become politicized. In a society without extensive, well-defined institutions for managing labour grievances inside the firm, or for representing labour interests in national politics, it should come as little surprise that the inherent micro-conflictuality of capitalist society escapes the bounds of the firm and escalates into full-blown social and political crisis. Nonetheless, the scale and nature of industrial conflict have changed in recent years. The number of days lost to strikes steadily declined from its historic highs at the end of the 1960s and through the middle of the 1970s. Between 1975 and 1985, an average of 2300 days were lost in strikes a year. That fell to an average of a little more than 600 in the next decade, and to less than 400 a year in the most recent decade (http://www.travail-solidarite.gouv.fr/etudes-recherche-statistiques/ statistiques/relations-professionnelles/conflits-collectifs/les-conflits-collectifs-du-travail-2300.html). Each decade has seen lower strike levels than the last and, from once being a high-strike country, France is now down to the EU strike average and below the OECD strike average.

Conflict has not disappeared, however; it has changed form. Conflict is less likely to take the form of strikes, but more likely to involve 'soft' conflict: other forms of collective action (petitions, demonstrations, a refusal to work overtime), or individual legal action as recourse to the industrial tribunals has increased. This is clear both at the workplace level and at the national level where public and trade union opposition to government policy – for example pensions reform or the new youth contracts – has manifested itself in more rallies and days of action than in traditional strikes. Strikes themselves are more difficult to sustain for a range of reasons that are common to most industrialized countries, and France is not alone in seeing a decline in levels of industrial conflict. To more general factors, one can add the strategic shift within the CFDT away from strike action (which is important given that the CFDT is the largest union in the private sector), the fact that governments have learned since the strike wave of 1995 to avoid antagonizing workers in the transportation industries, where unions have retained the ability to strike effectively, and the emergence of firm-level industrial relations institutions able to channel grievances and integrate workers into the firm.

The largest industrial mobilization of the recent period concerned the proposals for specialized youth contracts, the CPE, made by the de Villepin government early in 2006. The argument made by the government and its supporters for these contracts was that they targeted a group with a stubbornly high unemployment level, reduced the risk to employers of hiring young people as new workers (because they could be easily fired), and provided a 'trampoline' into permanent employment. Opponents charged that this kind of specialized contract created relatively few new jobs, instead encouraging employers to replace existing secure jobs with insecure ones, that employers would recycle workers with young people through two-year contracts without ever offering permanent employment, and that the real obstacle facing young people in the labour market was a lack of adequate and appropriate training, not the cost to employers of hiring. Furthermore, while the CPE might help young people without qualifications to find a job, for those with diplomas who could have expected permanent employment, the CPE opened the possibility that they would now find themselves in insecure jobs, worse off than before.

Regardless of the merits of the CPE, it was incompetently implemented. In marked contrast to the government's preparation for pensions reform in 2003, in 2006 the government did not consult the
social partners ahead of time, and it attempted to push through the legislation under article 49.3 of the Constitution, without amendment and
with limited debate. The absence of consultation was particularly
damning because the Fillon law had included a 'solemn promise' on
the part of the government not to legislate on industrial relations issues
without first allowing the social partners to reach agreement. In this
case, the unions, including the CFDT, presented a united front in
opposition to the CPE, and even MEDEF was dubious. Students and
unions made common cause, and a series of national days of action
began in early February 2006 and escalated throughout February and
March. It is worth noting that the protests did not take the form of
strikes; they were, in a sense, a middle-class version of the more violent
protests on the part of alienated young people only a few months
earlier. In a humiliating reversal, Chirac promulgated the legislation
but immediately declared it inoperable pending revision. The CPE was
officially dead on 13 April when the National Assembly stripped the
key elements of the youth contracts from the bill.

It is possible to interpret the fate of the CPE as evidence of social
stalemate and the inability of French society to change, but this would
be to overinterpret this episode, and to ignore the countervailing evidence. The recent past has seen a great deal of change in French industrial relations, and an important liberalization of the labour market.
The cumulative effect of reforms over the five years of the conservative
government is more important than the fate of one relatively minor
proposal. The failure of the CPE reflects more the incompetence of the
de Villepin government, panicked by the intractability of youth unemployment, than the persistence of labour power and a blocked society
in France.

The future of French industrial relations

The last two decades have seen a quiet transformation of French industrial relations, belying the image of stalemate and perpetual class conflict. This transformation has been driven by public policy, strategic
shifts on the part of the main class organizations, and changing industrial structure, as smaller, family-owned firms embodying authoritarian
and Taylorist labour practices have given way to modern corporations
employing sophisticated human resource management. What has developed is an increasingly firm-centric industrial relations system
marked by firm-level collective bargaining and institutions of labour
representation inside the firm, and the spreading of flexible, even

individualized, forms of pay and work organization. This section briefly surveys these developments before concluding with the likely impact on French industrial relations of the new government of President Sarkozy and Prime Minister Fillon.

Historically, industry-level bargaining has been the most important locus of collective bargaining in France. After declining in the second half of the 1990s, the number of such agreements has risen steadily since 1999 to the point where more than 95 per cent of firms employing 11 or more workers are now covered by an industry agreement. More significant has been the rise in the number of firm-level agreements since the early 1980s. They rose in two main periods: first, after the Auroux laws with the opportunity to reach derogatory agreements on work time in the mid-1980s; second, as a result of the Aubry laws at the end of the 1990s. In 1983, approximately 2 million French workers were covered by firm-level agreements; by 2002, that had doubled. However, firm-level bargaining is far more sensitive to public policy than industry bargaining. Its rise and fall closely track legislation requiring, or encouraging, firm-level bargaining. Firm-level bargaining peaked in 2002 as a result of work time bargaining, but fell by more than half the next year when the Aubry laws had run their course. Unsurprisingly, firm-level bargaining is much more prevalent in large firms than small ones.

Who is signing these agreements, since, as noted above, unions continue to lose members, and there has been only a modest increase in the coverage of union delegates? The answer is that French firms have seen a widespread increase in non-union forms of worker representation. These include works councils, employee delegates, a new form of delegate that fulfils the duties of both works council and employee delegate in small firms, and the innovation of mandated workers. By 2004–5, fully 77 per cent of firms employing 20 or more workers had some form of elected or mandated employee representative, with that figure rising to 93 per cent in firms employing 50 or more workers (Jacod, 2007). Thus workplace representation has become ubiquitous in France, and as it has, so the different roles of each institution have become blurred. In 2005, only half of firm-level collective agreements were signed by a union delegate; the remainder were signed by a works council, an employee delegate or merely ratified by employees by way of referendum. The blurring of roles matters because non-union forms of employee representation are likely to be weaker and less independent of management than unions; they are more likely to function as communication channels than as a form of countervailing power.

The last 20 years have also seen a remarkable increase in flexibility in work organization and the labour market. This has been apparent across a wide range of areas: the diffusion of individualized payment arrangements; the spread of total quality programmes of various types;

dramatic increases in contractual flexibility that have led to an expansion in the number of workers on part-time, temporary or fixed-term contracts; and, of course, the opportunities for reorganizing work made possible by flexible work time. The proportion of employees working part-time increased from 8 per cent in 1980 to 18 per cent in 2003, and those on fixed-term contracts increased almost 2 percentage points to 11.1 per cent between 1996 and 2003 (IRES, 2005). Firms took advantage of the wide range of options for how to introduce reduced work time under the 35-hour legislation in order to experiment with different kinds of shift work, and scheduling that corresponded better to demand. By creating a greater financial disincentive to use overtime, the 35-hour week legislation forced employers to contemplate a more fundamental reorganization of work. In all these areas, state intervention has underwritten change, either by creating the institutional preconditions for negotiating flexibility or by providing strong incentives for firms to introduce flexibility. The common theme to all these developments has been state-led modernization of industrial relations practices.

The emphatic electoral victory of Sarkozy in 2007 on an explicit manifesto of rupture in the labour market and industrial relations (in marked contrast to the promise of social stability and continuity in Chirac's successful campaign of 1995), his choice of Fillon (the Employment Minister from 2002 to 2004) as Prime Minister, and the speed with which he moved in this area (proposing legislation and setting deadlines for action by unions and employers during the summer and early autumn of 2007), all suggest that reform of industrial relations is indeed a major priority of the new government and that France may be about to experience accelerated change. The schedule set out by Sarkozy anticipated that the bulk of the industrial relations reforms would be completed by the end of 2007. Sarkozy's initial method has been to give the social partners a deadline by which to negotiate change on a set of specific issues, with bargaining to take place through the summer and autumn 2007, under the threat of quick legislation if they fail to agree. He has promised, in keeping with the solemn promise in the *loi Fillon*, that he will make negotiation the primary means for bringing about industrial relations change, with legislation reserved for the failure of bargaining or to generalize agreements. Of course, the knowledge that legislation from a conservative government is waiting the wings, puts pressure on the unions to be flexible in their bargaining stance.

Progress on Sarkozy's industrial relations reform agenda was slowed by a wave of public sector strikes in November 2007, of which the most important were in the transport sector where the government was attempting to finally harmonize pension regimes across the private and public sectors. By the time the strikes were called off, after nine days of chaos on the railroads and Metro, the outlines of an agreement had become visible: the government would get a common number of years required for a full pension and indexation of pensions to prices rather than wages in return for a series of financial sweeteners that would boost the value of those pensions.

There are four main planks to the reform package proposed by Sarkozy. The first is to put in place some minimum guarantee of public transportation during strikes, something given new urgency by the November strikes. Legislation was passed in August 2007 that created a requirement that each public transport entity negotiate a plan to provide a minimum service in the event of a strike. If employers and unions fail to agree on such a plan, legislation will impose minimum service, with the legislation to take effect at the beginning of 2008. This part of the legislation is not particularly contentious; it permits the social partners to decide upon the details of a plan, and the RATP had already negotiated a minimum service plan prior to the 2007 election. However, the legislation goes further in several respects, including a requirement that two days' notice be given of strikes, and that a secret ballot be held one week into a strike to see if there remains majority support to continue the strike. Both potentially infringe the constitutional right of French workers to strike, but the secret ballot requirement would also be an important innovation in French industrial relations. The goal is to prevent a single picket line or a small minority of workers closing down a transportation network, but there is no precedent for strike ballots in French law, and the unions argue that a *collective* vote undercuts what is an *individual* right to strike.

The second plank involves exempting supplementary hours above the 35-hour limit from taxation and social charges. This did not require negotiation and was passed in an emergency package of legislation, the Work, Employment and Spending Power Act (*Loi en faveur du travail, de l'emploi et du pouvoir d'achat* – TEPA), in August 2007. This further undercuts the 35-hours legislation as the financial benefits of working longer now greatly limit its use. It is hard to see how this legislation will help employment when both workers and employers have such strong incentives to work longer hours rather than hire more workers. This legislation also exempts students from taxation for employment, and offers a series of measures designed to lower the cost to workers and employers of working. Furthermore, the government has floated the idea of ending the legal regulation of work time altogether by allowing each firm to decide upon its working time, as long as the result is the product of negotiation. In other words, firm-level working time agreements could derogate from both legislation and industry agreements. It is hard to see how this would be consistent with international conventions and EU legislation.

The remaining two planks of the Sarkozy reform project have been the most controversial and difficult to negotiate. The social partners were given until December 2007 to negotiate the 'modernization' of the labour market, with the goal being a new 'unique' work contract that would replace the existing distinction between permanent employment contracts (or those without a fixed duration) and limited duration employment contract; in other words, between secure and insecure employment, and between labour market 'insiders' and 'outsiders'. Sarkozy has repeatedly emphasized the need to protect people rather than jobs, and to suggest that a quid pro quo for more insecure employment might be more generous unemployment benefits. The idea behind a single employment contract would be to phase in employment security with seniority, so that legal protections against firing are weaker for new and recent hires. Employers and trade unions began talks on a new work contract in September 2007, with MEDEF emphasizing the need for a trial period for all new hires during which a worker could be fired with few costs, and then the option in all contracts for what the employers coyly term 'a friendly separation' (*séparation à l'amiable*). Agreement was finally reached in January 2008, with only the CGT refusing to sign the accord. It provided for a trial period during which new employees could be easily fired, a new form of fixed-term contract, and the option for mutually agreed employment termination. All in all, the final agreement closely mirrored the goals of the employer organizations, with few sweeteners for the unions. The government has promised to translate the agreement into law early in 2008.

The final reform plank involves the thorny issue of trade union representativeness/representation: how to measure the strength and influence of unions so as to ensure that only truly representative unions benefit from the official status of being able to negotiate national agreements and compete in the first round of professional elections, and that the labour signatories of agreements represent a majority of workers concerned. Just prior to the 2007 elections, the previous government endorsed an approach that would place overwhelming weight in determining influence on the vote in professional elections. This will be a difficult issue on which to reach agreement both because it raises the possibility of the autonomous unions entering the select group of representative unions (which, given the militancy of the SUD unions, is hardly in the interests of the government), and because it would be hard to avoid opening up the question of the representativeness of the MEDEF on the employer side. It is worth noting that Sarkozy has not made this issue a priority, and negotiations did not begin on the subject until late January 2008, and even then, employers insisted that only labour representation be on the table.

All in all, the early months of the Sarkozy presidency suggest that the reform of industrial relations is a priority and that the new government believes it has the political capital to demand reform from the social partners. Whether this determination will outlast the anticipated opposition from trade unions, which have already organized national protests against the minimum service legislation, remains unclear.

Chapter 14

Welfare Policies and Politics

PATRICK HASSENTEUFEL

Welfare policies in France have evolved very considerably in the course of the past 20 years. The French welfare state created in the post-war period was mainly of the Bismarckian variety. This welfare model is one whereby welfare rights are dependent upon employer and employee contributions, where the social partners (the employers' and workers' unions) jointly manage social insurance funds and where the state is kept at a distance. In the past two decades, this traditional model has been accompanied by a move to universal benefits, by the recognition of the need to provide minimum social standards to protect the very weakest in society and towards financing from general taxation.

One of the leading experts, Palier (2005), identifies a 'double dualization' of the French welfare state. Social security reforms tend to reinforce the separation of the two 'worlds of welfare' within the French social protection system. In the world of social insurance (mainly old age and unemployment insurance), professional solidarity is central and benefits are still acquired through work. As we will see in this chapter, however, employees are being asked to pay higher levels of contribution than before to obtain benefits. Palier's second world of welfare is one of national solidarity. It entails health care, family benefits and policies aimed at fighting social exclusion. Here, the benefits can be either universal or means tested, but they are financed out of taxation and the state plays a more important role than before. The backdrop to this chapter is that of a 'second dualization', which separates the French population into two different groups. A group of 'insiders' is made up of people who are still able to rely on social insurance (complemented by private schemes) to provide their (still generous) social protection. A smaller but significant part of the population (10–15 per cent) has to rely on targeted minimum benefits. Shrinking social insurance also means a bigger reliance on private insurance for the rest of the population (especially in health care and in pensions).

This chapter will demonstrate that the state plays a stronger, yet different role than before. It has assumed more power within the system because it needs to contain the cost of welfare, either by reducing social insurance benefits, or by replacing contributory benefits by less generous targeted benefits. At the same time, government intervention has been focused on restructuring social benefits so that they entice people back into the labour market.

In the shadow of the Juppé Plan

Defending welfare rights and national solidarity has been a cornerstone of French political discourse at least since the creation of the social security system in 1945. Any attempts to rein in France's generous system of welfare and health provision have produced strong reactions, making the management of the welfare sector especially difficult for French governments. The backdrop to our discussion was the failure of the Juppé Plan announced six months after Jacques Chirac's first presidential election and finally adopted in 1996.

The Juppé reforms attempted to introduce a budgeting logic in social protection, setting out precise spending limits for health care in particular. Since the constitutional amendment of 1996, Parliament has had the obligation to vote the total amount of the social security budget. Therefore every year, Parliament passes a social security law which determines the total resources and expenditure for social protection. That Parliament should have the right to determine expenditure ceilings remains vigorously contested in France, by the medical profession and by consumers alike. The 1996 constitutional amendment in theory sets a national ceiling for health expenditure (*objectif national de dépenses d'assurance maladie*). The logic is mainly a financial one: the amount of social security expenditure has to be adapted to the economic and financial situation in the context of the adoption of a single European currency and of a high deficit for social security, incompatible with the Maastricht criteria. The social protests of November and December 1995 that brought France to a standstill were rooted in popular protest against an attack on a cherished social model. There was a world of difference between the political discourse of the candidate Jacques Chirac, strongly highlighting the absolute necessity to reduce the gap between the haves and the have-nots and the Juppé Plan that set in motion tighter control over welfare expenditure. The lack of political tact was not lost on the French protesters, insofar as the reforms were announced to coincide with the fiftieth anniversary of the French social security system.

In addition to imposing limits on health expenditure, the Juppé measures attempted to reform the civil servant pension system and the generous special pension regimes, reserved in general for groups of public sector workers such as employees of the state rail company, SNCF, or the electricity provider EDF. Juppé proposed to increase the number of years that civil servants and groups of workers in the special pension regimes had to contribute before being able to retire on a full pension (in the private sector 50 per cent of final salary). The public transport workers responded with fury, blocking for almost one month all the railway and subway traffic and bringing the country grinding to a halt. There had been no prior negotiation of this pension reform, an authoritarian method that sparked a high level of popular protest that eventually led to the withdrawal of the public sector pension reform. In the health sector the enforcement mechanisms for the respect of budgets also triggered the opposition of the medical profession. Doctors led a successful legal battle against the proposed financial penalties for overspending, which were finally abandoned (Hassenteufel, 2003). As a consequence of this sustained mobilization, governments backtracked on enforcing the national ceiling for health insurance expenditures. In one year only – 1997 – were the targets met, but never again thereafter. The social security budgets were ineffective because of the failure of an enforcement mechanism and the withdrawal of penalties for non-compliance.

At a political level, the right-wing government lost the parliamentary election in 1997. The 1996 social security reform is usually considered as a main factor for this defeat, explaining losses in the popular electorate and in the traditional electoral clientele of right-wing parties like doctors. The political cost of social security reform, especially for retrenchment of pensions, also explains why the Socialist Jospin government (1997–2002) shied away from any pension reform between 1997 and 2002 (Palier, 2004). This painful experience of social security reforms during the first presidential term of Jacques Chirac suggests not only why welfare issues were absent from the electoral campaign in 2002, but also why the pressure for new reforms was so great after the election because of the growing financial difficulties of the pension and health insurance systems.

The first period of the second presidential mandate of Jacques Chirac (2002–5: corresponding to the Raffarin government) was dominated by two reforms: the pension reform in 2003 and the health insurance reform in 2004. But, as we will see in the first part of the chapter, the Raffarin government was unable to resolve the underlying financial problems of the French welfare state. Though financial issues still dominate the social security reform agenda in the aftermath of Nicolas Sarkozy's election, welfare reform policies undertaken since 2002 have not been framed solely in terms of finance. There has also been a growing politicization of welfare issues, with an emphasis on the responsibilities of welfare recipients, symbolized by the creation of a 'minimum activity income' (*revenu minimum d'activité*) in 2003. Finally, social protection policies have had to react to unforeseen crises, as in the case of the new plan for the dependent elderly after the heatwave of summer 2003 led to the deaths of some 15,000 senior citizens, or the new rights for housing after the installation of a camp for homeless people near the canal Saint-Martin in Paris at the end of 2006.

Pension and health reforms

During the 2002–7 period, two main reforms were introduced, both with limited effects.

The 2003 pension reform

Nine months after his re-election, Jacques Chirac announced a new pension reform, one aimed at bringing public sector pensions into line with those of the private sector that had previously been reformed in 1993. The government decided that public sector employees, like their private sector counterparts, would have to contribute for 40 years in order to qualify for a full pension. The 2003 reform also aimed at extending progressively the length of contributions in order to qualify for a full pension. Under the 2003 reform, the period of contributions would be increased for everybody (public and private sector) to 41 years in 2008 and 42 years in 2020. It was also decided that the indexing of public pensions would be based on the evolution of prices (rather than on wages, as was then the case for civil servants). A new system of incentives for people to retire as late as possible was also created: a bonus (*surcote*) is given if people retire after the legal age (60 years) and a sanction (*décote*) in case of retirement before this age and in case of missing years of contributions. Finally, the reforms introduced tax incentives to help the development of saving for pensions. Two systems of voluntary saving were introduced, one individual (PERP: *plan d'épargne retraite populaire*), which can be proposed to individuals by any bank or private insurer, and one collective (PERCO: *plan d'épargne retraite*), to be organized within the firm or the peak organization by the social partners. In the two cases, the government was explicit that people should try to compensate by their own saving for the inevitable decline in compulsory pay-as-you-go pensions (Palier, 2004).

The final draft of the reform proposal adopted by the government at the end of May 2003 was the result of an agreement with two trade unions (CFDT and CGC) and the tacit agreement of a third (CFTC): 'Unlike Juppé, Raffarin did not prepare his reform in secret but spent months consulting with the social partners' (Natali and Rhodes, 2004: 17). From February to May several meetings with the social partners were organized by the government. The announcement of the measures provoked a round of strikes and demonstrations, with more than 1 million civil servants demonstrating throughout the country on 13 May 2003. The then Social Affairs Minister François Fillon announced a number of concessions to the trade unions. The pension guarantee for low-paid workers was raised from 75 to 85 per cent of the minimum wage (SMIC), at a time when the average rate of replacement in France was 74 per cent. Workers who have worked more than 40 years before 60, and who began to work in their mid-teens, could retire at 58. Civil service pensions would still be calculated on the basis of the salary of the last six months of employment (instead of the last three years, as the government proposed initially). Employers' old age pension contributions were increased and the unions' management role was consolidated.

This trade-off made the support of the moderate trade unions possible but, at the same time, it became clear that the reform was insufficient in itself to rescue the French pension system, because it would only cover one-third of the future deficit. The government was forced to announce an increase of 0.2 per cent in the social contributions after 2006 in order to finance the provisions to allow retirement before 60, as well as an increase of the contribution period for a full pension to 41 years between 2008 and 2012, and a new negotiation of the pension reform in 2008. It counted on the expected decline of unemployment in order to finance the deficit of the pension systems. But this decline, only starting in 2005, was far from sufficient. Worse, the provision that those who had started to work between 14 and 16 years could retire on a full pension at 58 led to a strong increase of the number who retired (over 4 per cent). The consequence was that the deficit actually grew.

The financial shortcomings of the 2003 reform explained why the reform of pensions was again an issue on the political agenda during the 2007 presidential campaign. The need for a new reform was stressed in the fourth report of the advisory committee on pensions (Comité d'Orientation des Retraites), published in January 2007 (COR, 2007). It underlined the financial needs of the pension system. It recommended extending the length of contributions, making it more attractive for employees to continue working after 55 years: at 37.8 per cent, France's activity rate for people between 55 and 64 years in 2005 is much lower than the average rate in the European Union (42.5 per cent). The report also called for the reform of the 'special regimes' prevailing in some professions (especially railways, underground, electricity and gas employees of public companies) which were not affected by the 2003 reform. The reform of those regimes, which failed in 1995, has been one of the core demands of Nicolas Sarkozy, seen as a test of his capacity for reform. At the beginning of October 2007, the government announced that the 'special regimes' would be brought into line with the other main public and private sector schemes, whereby employees have to contribute for 40 years in order to get a full pension. This announcement was met with a predictable strike in the transport sector. After nine days of a debilitating transport strike, government and trade unions began negotiating in earnest on the concessions that might accompany the reform of the special regimes: wage increases, an increase in the level of pensions or the creation of a top-up pension system were all floated. The key lesson, however, was that Sarkozy appeared to have succeeded where Juppé failed. Though the strikes of November 2007 were evidence that President Sarkozy would not have an easy ride, the principle that some reform of the special regimes was needed was accepted by the main trade union federations.

The 2004 health insurance reform and beyond

By the 2000s, health insurance issues had moved right up the political agenda, driven by a combination of professional demands, governmental attempts at financial control and consumer resistance to the increased costs of health care. At the beginning of 2002 general practitioners began protests in favour of higher fees, with the GPs demanding an increase of fees to 20 euros per visit. The demonstrations and strikes of French GPs offered Jacques Chirac's Gaullist party (RPR, then transformed into UMP) the opportunity to overcome the divorce with the medical profession that had been a lasting legacy of the 1996 Juppé Plan. President Chirac supported the doctors' claim, but these were resisted by the left-wing government of Lionel Jospin. In consequence the first decision of the new government, headed by Jean-Pierre Raffarin, after Chirac's re-election, was to accede to GPs' demands. This political decision was made at a time when the deficit of the health insurance system was again growing because of the worsening of the economic situation and the failed implementation of the Juppé reform. As we have already mentioned, the target of the national ceiling for health insurance expenditures was temporarily reached in 1997, but never again in the years after. Health caps were ineffective because of the lack of any enforcement mechanism (Hassenteufel, 2003). Since 1997 health expenditure has continued growing, always outpacing budgets, but no penalties have been levied on doctors.

The deteriorating finances of the health branch of the social security system (which posted a 10.6 billion euros deficit in 2003) eventually produced a new law on health insurance in spring 2004, finally voted by the Parliament in August 2004. This reform marked a clear change in cost containment policies, favouring professionals over consumers. The logic of capping health budgets was de facto withdrawn, the law making no mention of penalties on doctors if the expenditure objectives are overshot. But patients were called upon to increase their own financial contribution to their health care costs. The law introduced a 1 euro increase in the hospital flat rate, the contribution patients make to their hospital costs. Moreover, a number of expensive drugs were no longer to be reimbursed. Visits to the doctor would cost 30 per cent more, approved charges on drugs were increased by 40 per cent and there was even an increase of 20 per cent for hospital costs (though acute care remains almost fully covered). This trend was followed in 2005 with the introduction of a payment of 18 euros for important medical acts (*actes lourds*) and a further increase in the hospital flat rate. During the electoral campaign Nicolas Sarkozy announced his intention to introduce prescription charges (*franchises médicales*), a measure included in the 2008 social security finance law. Prescription charges now concern drugs (50 cents per box), a contribution to ambulance costs (2 euros) and various paramedical acts (50 cents). The new law introduces a limit of 50 euros a year per insured person, though those people on the basic income (CMU) as well as children under 18 years and pregnant women are exempted.

The 2004 law on health insurance attempted to tackle the problem of rising costs, duplication and inefficiency. All insured French people now have to register with one doctor, the registered physician (*médecin traitant*). This doctor may be a GP or a specialist in any setting (a hospital, a health care centre or an independent practice). Patients who do not register with a doctor, or see another doctor without referral (except for paediatricians, ophthalmologists and gynaecologists), will have to pay extra user charges. Failure to stay with the registered physician is penalized by a lower rate of reimbursement from the social security system (reduced from 70 to 60 per cent in 2004 and to 50 per cent in 2007). Moreover, specialists may charge extra fees.

This new policy attempted to avoid direct conflict between GPs and specialists. First, it allowed specialists to take on the role of the registered physician. Moreover, it satisfied a long-standing demand of specialists who are able to charge additional fees. Since the philosophy of the reform is rather demand-oriented, the government saw a way to reconcile the demand of specialists with incentives directed towards patients (Polton, 2005). The 2004 reform was accepted by the main doctors' trade union, which was not very surprising, since this law gives specialists the right to set higher fees when patients go directly to them, without being referred by a GP. The main effort is being asked of patients, in the form of raising charges for medical visits, as well as the rate of the social contribution (CSG) that finances a proportion of health care costs. The reform also created an electronic personal medical record (*dossier medical personnel* – DMP) in order to facilitate the control of patient consultations. It will include all visits, procedures, medical or surgical treatments, drugs and medical devices prescribed. All professionals dealing with the patient will be able to access this record and complete it. Patients without a DMP will have to pay extra charges.

But the implementation of the 2004 law has faced a lot of difficulties, in part due to the power of the medical professionals, in part because of the complexities of the proposed reforms. The health professionals have proved remarkably effective at defending their positions. The doctors' unions were able to pressure the government to obtain financial compensation in highly specialized areas that they argued would be damaged by the reform. This led, in March 2006, to an amendment of the agreement between doctors and the sickness fund (one of the pillars of the French social security system). The sickness fund now agreed to compensate the future financial loss of specialists in six specialist areas where activity had declined significantly: rehabilitative care, dermatology, endocrinology, rheumatology, otolaryngology and internal medicine. In these specialist areas, the prices for certain procedures were increased. Moreover, the GPs' fees were again raised in 2006, a few months before the presidential election.

Health care reforms have been highly complex. The scheme introducing the registered physician is misunderstood and complicated. Both health professionals and patients have difficulty in understanding how much is reimbursed (or not) and under which circumstances (Bras, 2006). There is also a perverse incentive built into the system, since specialists are better paid if they treat patients who have not been referred to them by GPs. Richer citizens can go direct to the specialist, whereas poorer people must go first to the GP. It has been argued that this will create inequity in access to care (Polton and Mousquès, 2004b). And finally, the sickness fund's IT system is not yet fully capable of tracking patients within the system. An estimated 5 per cent of reimbursed treatments are eventually classified as 'out of pathway' because of errors in filling out the forms (Dourgnon, 2006). And the implementation of the electronic personal medical record, initially planned for July 2007, has been postponed because of technical and legal problems. Because of these limits, the financial effects were clearly below the government's expectations, which had promised the return to equilibrium in 2007.

In spite of efforts at reform, the deficit of the health insurance scheme remains stubbornly high. The Fillon government has attempted to address this deficit, notably in the debate on the finance law for social security for 2008. Insofar as doctors are concerned, the government proposes to give the sickness fund the possibility of contracting with individual doctors and paying them a flat rate in return for specified obligations and objectives. On the other hand, early evidence from the Fillon government once again demonstrated the power of resistance of the medical profession. Seeking to ensure that access to medical services is spread evenly across the country, the Fillon government at first proposed a system of penalties and incentives to encourage new doctors to set up their practices in isolated rural areas. The stick was the proposition that the sickness fund would refuse to integrate new doctors into the health insurance system if they set up in areas where there was already an adequate supply (the Mediterranean coast, notably). This measure was withdrawn after a one-month strike of doctors in October 2007, confirming the unwillingness of the government to enter into a conflict with the medical profession.

The Fillon government has also expressed its concern with the overall productivity of the health care system and has proposed extending and simplifying an activity-based payment system for hospitals (*tarification à l'activité* – T2A). This new payment system was first introduced both for public and private hospitals in the finance law for social security for 2004. Previously, public and private hospitals were paid under two different schemes. The public and most private not-for-profit hospitals had global budgets based on their historical costs, while private for-profit hospitals had an itemized billing system with different components. Since January 2004, part of the revenues of all public sector acute care hospitals have been financed through an activity-based scheme (T2A) whereby a payment is made for each patient treated in acute care. The activity-based element of the payment increases gradually each year. Private hospitals have been paid entirely using the new system since 1 March 2005. The extension of this activity-based payment system (T2A), proposed by the Fillon government, runs the risk of creating inflationary pressures, as public hospitals multiply treatments to increase their revenues.

Thus, like its predecessors, in health policy the Fillon government is caught between a medical profession determined to defend its interests, a growing need to rein in public expenditure in the health sector and an attempt to craft a regulatory health care state to ensure greater state oversight of health policy (a theme developed in the final section). Rather like its predecessors also, the Fillon government has attempted to ensure a new policy mix in issues relating to work, employment and obtaining welfare benefits.

Anti-poverty politics: a liberal or symbolic turn?

Like in other Bismarckian systems, the change of the work–welfare interface has become a major issue in France. The new reform agenda can be captured by the notion of proactive incentive building (*activation* in French). It is based on the idea that the welfare state should intervene more proactively in the (re)integration of those without work into available jobs. Proactive incentive building (henceforth 'activation') initiatives attempt to move unemployed individuals off social benefits – which come to be seen as 'passive' policies, fostering dependency and acting as an unwelcome brake on labour market adjustment – and into more productive activities (Clegg, 2007).

Towards a workfare state?

In France the trend towards 'activation' had started already in 2000. In that year, the social partners signed an agreement reforming unemployment social insurance, which created a new individualized contract for every job seeker (*plan d'aide et de retour à l'emploi* – PARE). The PARE was based on the idea that unemployment insurance benefits should not only compensate for the loss of income, but also encourage people to find a new job through linking benefits and training. The originality of the PARE was that it was signed by the social partners, the employers and the trade unions, rather than imposed by the government. Its fate was sealed, however, once the Right won back power in 2002 and preferred direct legislation rather than ratifying a scheme initiated by the social partners.

With the return of the Right in 2002, there was a renewed emphasis on linking social benefits, training and the provision of other increased incentives to make work attractive. During the 2002–7 government a number of new measures were introduced to encourage people on minimum social benefits to go back to work. These measures were symbolized by the creation of a minimum activity income (*revenu minimum d'activité* – RMA) in December 2003. Under the RMA, the employer receives a direct grant from the government in order to enhance the income of those having received the RMI, a basic income support, for two years. The idea was to incentivize employment for employers and for the poorest in society. But, lacking an element of compulsion, one year after the creation of the RMA only 1600 people had benefited from it, a paltry figure compared to the 1.2 million people who receive the RMI (Palier, 2005: 341).

The Villepin government of 2005–7 introduced a new family of employment contracts, including contracts for the future (*contrats d'avenir*) for the long-term unemployed and those on minimum social benefits. Granted by the state, they concern part-time jobs, paid at the level of the minimum wage, and are combined with compulsory vocational training time. This orientation is being pursued by the new government, invigorated by the 'rehabilitation of work' theme that was a central issue in Sarkozy's presidential campaign, symbolized in the expression 'work more to earn more'. This belief that work should pay explains not only the progressive withdrawal of the 35-hour work week, started in 2003, but also the introduction of yet another new type of minimum income, the active solidarity income (*revenu de solidarité active* – RSA), financed half by the state and half by the *départements*. The RSA was experimented from November 2007 in 17 *départements* and is planned to be generalized from 2009. The purpose of this measure is to encourage those on minimal benefits to work by giving them an extra income so that in all cases they earn more by working than by remaining on the dole (this has not necessarily been the case up to now, especially for part-time workers).

The trend towards 'activation' is also obvious in childcare and policies for care of the elderly (Morel, 2007). A new benefit was introduced in 2004: the *prestation d'accueil du jeune enfant* (PAJE), which brings together and replaces various schemes and child benefits. It comprises a birth allowance and a means-tested benefit paid until the child turns three. Parents also receive a 'free choice supplement' which takes the form of either a paid leave from work until the child turns three or help covering the cost of a private nanny or registered childminder. This 'supplement' varies according to parents' income. Though strongly reminiscent of the previous schemes, the novelty here is that this new scheme includes special measures to encourage mothers on leave to work part-time and to re-enter the labour force.

Concerning elderly people, a new personalized autonomy allowance (*allocation personnelle d'autonomie* – APA, created by the Jospin government) was implemented in 2002 to help remedy some of the main problems identified with the dependency allowance (*prestation sociale dépendence* – PSD) created in 1996. Dependency criteria have been extended, which has considerably increased the number of people eligible for this benefit. The benefit is no longer means-tested but the amount is reduced progressively for beneficiaries whose resources are above a certain ceiling (€949/month in 2002). As with the PSD, the benefit can be used to remunerate an unemployed relative who provides care. This new measure has proven very successful and the number of recipients increased rapidly, leading to higher than expected costs. This prompted the new right-wing government to introduce new reforms in 2003 to reduce the cost of the benefit, most dramatically by lowering to €623 the income ceiling below which one is entitled to full benefits.

By providing a cash benefit to the dependent elderly, the idea is to give dependent persons the means to decide on the type of care they want – i.e. to promote free choice – but also to develop low-skilled, low-paid, personal service jobs by transforming the dependent elderly into private employers. This has proved quite a successful employment strategy: between 1994 and 2004, the number of people employed in personal service jobs (home-help, cleaning, childcare) almost doubled, from 639,000 up to 1.26 million. However, these consist mainly of short part-time jobs and as the great majority of workers have little or no qualifications, wages are consequently quite low.

Thus, whether for young children or for the elderly, care policy reforms in France have increasingly sought to boost employment – albeit low-skilled and low-paid employment – by providing cash benefits to families to become private employers. Such a strategy was further reinforced by the introduction in 2005 of a universal service cheque to enable people to hire the help they need, and thus to create employment (Morel, 2007).

The politicization of welfare policies since 2002 is not only due to the efforts to make the social security system more 'work friendly' but also to otherwise unrelated events which forced the government to react.

Reactive symbolic welfare policies

As well as implementing more or less planned reforms, governments have been forced to react to unforeseen events, such as the heatwave during the summer of 2003 which caused the death of more than 15,000 (mostly old) people, and the establishment of a camp of homeless people in the centre of Paris (on the banks of the canal Saint-Martin) during the Christmas period in 2006. Making policy on the hoof has had a number of unintended consequences.

During the 2003 heatwave, the Raffarin government was accused of a delayed reaction, and had subsequently to prove that it was genuinely concerned with the problems of elderly people. Put under pressure, the government proposed in November 2003 the Ageing and Solidarity Plan. This had two main provisions. The first aimed to keep the elderly in their own homes, as well as reinforcing the provision of care in institutions (by improving the health care supply in nursing homes, and creating new places in health units). The second dimension concerned handicapped people. A law voted in June 2004 declared that the elderly and the handicapped should be assisted by creating an extra day of work 'for solidarity'. This extra day of work would allow €2 billion to be raised, with €800 million designated for nursing homes, €800 million for the handicapped and €400 million to support the elderly in their own homes. The law also created a 'national solidarity fund for autonomy' (CNSA). This new institution has three missions: financing 'support services' for the dependent elderly and handicapped; ensuring the equal treatment for all people across the French territory; providing information and analysis concerning the service needs of dependent people. A second law, in February 2005, defined new rights for the handicapped. However, the way these reforms have been financed created a lot of controversy (Debrand and Or, 2005). First, because salaried employees are the only group to subsidize the CNSA. Second, the transformation of a religious holiday (*Pentecôte*) into a working day created opposition from not only the trade unions but also the clergy. The government reacted to criticisms by giving employers the freedom to decide which extra day they would work. The plan was not even supported by local authorities, which stood to benefit in some respects.

The other burning issue was that of housing and the homeless. When homeless people began pitching their tents alongside the Saint-Martin canal in late 2006, the state reacted much more rapidly. In his New Year speech for 2007, President Chirac announced the creation of a new right to housing for everybody. And two months later the law establishing this new right (*loi sur le droit au logement opposable*) was passed. The guarantee of access to a 'decent and independent' home will concern six categories of people (especially homeless persons or people living in apartments unfit for habitation) from December 2008, and for all persons having a right to social housing from 2012.

In those two cases the government has tried to show its social concern by making rather fast and visible decisions. But the difficulties or the delay in their concrete implementation indicate that their main purpose was symbolic, the symbolic dimension being also rather important for activation as the case of the RMA shows.

From Bismarck to Beveridge? The strengthening of the state

How far has the state been increasing its influence over the French social security system, one historically managed by the social partners? This core structural question will now be addressed in the final section of this chapter. This central question can be answered by analysing the institutional and financial evolution of the French welfare state.

Towards a regulatory health care state? The institutional aspects of health reforms

From an institutional point of view the most important reform was the introduction of the voting of a finance law for social security in 1996. For the first time in France, Parliament took part in the debate on the social security budget, which previously was seen as not being part of the state budget. This strengthening of the state is most obvious in relation to the health insurance system (Hassenteufel and Palier, 2005, 2007). The 1996 reform gave new institutional tools to the state in order to increase its control over the health insurance system. In the hospital sector the new regional state agencies (*agences régionales d'hospitalisation*, ARH) have taken on those powers previously held by the sickness fund. Moreover, the scope of collective bargaining between the sickness funds and the doctors' organizations has been reduced, and the state is allowed to supplant the social partners when the latter are not able to reach an agreement. The 1996 reform also obliged the Parliament to vote every year a national ceiling for health expenditures (ONDAM), as we have already discussed. With this reform the government can more easily adopt yearly cost-containment measures, since this budgetary vote is now a constitutional obligation (the Parliament in France being strongly controlled by the government). The use of the new parliamentary competence helps the government to control the social policy agenda. Instead of having always to legitimize its intervention in a field originally belonging to labour and employers, with the institutionalization of a parliamentary vote the government is now able regularly to plan adaptation measures, especially cost-containment ones.

The 2004 health insurance law furthered this trend by creating a national union of sickness funds (UNCAM) directed by a senior civil servant, nominated by the government. This 'general director' has the power to nominate the directors of local sickness funds and heads negotiations with the different medical professions. This role had previously been performed by a representative of the social partners. Indeed, the law has replaced the previous administrative board of the social partners by advisory boards on which both users and Parliament have representatives. There is clearly a shift of power from the board to the general director (Polton and Mousquès, 2004a). The 2004 reform also created the High Authority on Health (Haute Autorité de Santé, HAS), built on the basis of the former National Agency for Accreditation and Evaluation in Health Care (ANAES), with an extended role. This independent authority assesses the medical efficacy of procedures, drugs and devices, elaborates and disseminates practice guidelines, conducts medical audits of independent professionals and accredits hospitals. While most of these missions are not new, the emphasis now is on the important influence that this agency will have, through its advice, on the package of care eligible for reimbursement, and on the improvement of the evaluation of effectiveness and efficiency of health care.

The development of the regional hospital agencies (ARHs) lies at the heart of this new regulatory health care state. The ARHs were set up in 1996, given powers of accreditation and merger of public hospitals and vested with specific budget resources to finance an ongoing restructuring programme of hospitals. Their powers to control both public and private hospitals were strengthened in 2003. The ARHs have the power to grant, withdraw or suspend authorizations for public hospitals and health care professionals to practise. Moreover, under the new generation of regional health plans, the ARHs have to set quantified objectives determining the location of services and costly equipment as well as a framework of activity including length of stays, number of visits and surgical procedures. The ARHs conclude multi-year contracts with hospitals, defining objectives and means, so that hospitals will only get funding if they achieve the agreed objectives. According to figures from the Ministry of Health there have been several hundred regroupings (mostly small facilities) or mergers of activities in the past five years (Or, 2007).

This evolution can be analysed in terms of the growth of a regulatory health care state. The regulatory health care state is not based on the extension of the public sphere but rather on the reduction of the autonomy of the non-state actors that traditionally played a central role in health care policies. Tighter control is henceforth exercised by independent agencies whose mission is to enforce clinical standards and budgetary efficiency (Hassenteufel, 2007). Thus, in the domain of health the affirmation of a regulatory state is based more on the loss of autonomy for sickness funds and hospitals than for doctors. The French situation illustrates a paradox of reform: the strengthening of the state vis-à-vis the sickness funds has gone hand in hand with the increased managerial autonomy of hospitals, while doctors, because of their capacity of resistance to evaluation and control, have largely maintained their professional and financial autonomy. These institutional evolutions have been strengthened by the financial evolution of the welfare state that we will now consider.

The debate on financing: more taxes, less social contributions?

In France, until 1996, 80 per cent of social protection was financed through employment-related contributions, corresponding to the Bismarckian welfare state logic. But, since the late 1980s, governments have adopted contribution exemptions for employers in order to encourage job creation. These measures are usually targeted at some particularly disadvantaged groups, such as the long-term and young unemployed, or at small companies, which are considered to be the most affected by the relatively high cost of unskilled labour. In order to generalize this movement of lowering labour costs by reducing the level of social contributions paid by employers, governments have progressively resorted to direct taxation (Palier, 2005). A new tax was created in December 1990: the general social contribution (*contribution sociale généralisée* – CSG). Unlike insurance contributions, the CSG is levied on all types of personal incomes. When it was introduced, the CSG appeared to play a marginal role in the system and was levied at 1.1 per cent of all incomes. In 1996, the Juppé Plan set it at 3.4 per cent of all income and it has been rising steadily ever since.

These two trends were clearly followed between 2002 and 2007. Employers were exempted from a number of new contributions. On the other hand, the 2004 Health Insurance Law increased the rate of the CSG again, especially for welfare benefits. As a consequence social contributions now represent only two-thirds of the financing of social protection. During his campaign Nicolas Sarkozy suggested an increase of VAT in order to be able to lower the employers' contributions. This proposal, inspired by the German example of a 'social VAT' (*TVA sociale*) is very controversial because it would probably transfer a part of the responsibility for financing the social security system from companies to consumers. Raised inadvertently just before the second round of the June parliamentary election, the measure was postponed once it became clear that it would not be popular.

There has been a core shift in financing social protection over the past 20 years. There is a strong belief in France that the joint management of employers and employees is only acceptable if schemes are financed through employment-related contributions. Social partners have less legitimacy to participate in the decision-making and the management of social security provision financed through general taxation. As the social partners play a less important role, the state has sought to assume more responsibility. The shift towards general taxation has been accompanied by pressure for a transfer of control from the social partners to the state, a process that is likely to continue.

Conclusion: the limits of reforms

This institutional strengthening of the state does not mean a clear increase of the capacity to reform the French welfare state. The pension reform of 2003 was half-baked, based on a trade-off with the moderate trade unions. The current conflict on the special regimes for public sector employees is therefore a key test of the power of the state. The same analysis can be made for the health insurance reform of 2004, which was unable to reduce the deficit and which made important concessions to the medical profession. Even the orientation towards a workfare state is more symbolic than effective. Last but not least, how to finance welfare remains one of the most important issues for the future of the French welfare state. Whether or not the Fillon government will rise to the challenge of long-term finance, for example by introducing a 'social VAT' system along German lines, is still an open question. If the state has gained institutional power in the social security system, it is still highly dependent upon other actors for the acceptance and implementation of reforms and constrained by the high welfare expectations of French citizens.

Chapter 15

France and the World, from Chirac to Sarkozy

SOPHIE MEUNIER

In its relations with the rest of the world, France has long oscillated between two policy goals, sometimes clashing, sometimes complementary: on one hand, the pursuit and defence of France's national interests, as defined by geographical, economic and historical constraints; on the other, the promotion of its values, believed to have a universal quality. In the pure Gaullist tradition, President Jacques Chirac pursued a foreign policy that will be remembered for France's insistence on independence and multilateralism. Under his leadership, France tried to project a confident image that it still had a special, useful role in the world – that of reminding other countries of the dangers of unilateralism and the importance of allegiance to collective security – in spite of the shared national anxiety about its lack of purpose and lack of relevance in contemporary international affairs. As he took over the French presidency, Nicolas Sarkozy attempted to modernize, redirect and re-energize French foreign policy. The main Gaullist tenet of maintaining the rank of France on the international scene still features prominently on Sarkozy's agenda, but this will be achieved by closer ties to the United States (US), a reinvigorated transatlantic alliance, and stronger language towards recalcitrant countries, in addition to the usual assets of a privileged position at the United Nations (UN) and the possession of nuclear power. How much room to manoeuvre does President Sarkozy possess in transforming French foreign policy? This chapter explores the legacy of Chirac in foreign policy and the constraints that this legacy, as well as economy and geography, impose on Sarkozy as he devises a foreign policy to respond to the challenges faced by France in the twenty-first century.

The foreign policy legacy of Jacques Chirac

Jacques Chirac wanted his second term (2002–7) to be remembered in history for his foreign policy. Like most presidents of the Fifth

Republic, he tried to stay above the melee of domestic politics, leaving his successive prime ministers the ungrateful task of dealing with social and economic reforms, while concentrating instead on imprinting his French mark on the world. By showing that France still mattered in world affairs, he hoped to overcome the sense of national *malaise* and anxiety so pervasive in the domestic context. True to his Gaullist heritage, he helped fashion a foreign policy designed to keep a meaningful, independent role for France and projecting French ideas and values in a multipolar world. His own understanding of the world had been very much shaped by two old prisms – the Cold War and France's colonial ties – through which he analysed the events that unfolded during his tenure. We do not need much hindsight to pinpoint exactly what Chirac's foreign policy legacy will be in history. It is made up of two famous 'No's: the French 'No' to the US on Iraq in 2003, thanks to Chirac's support, and the French 'No' to the European Constitution in 2005, in spite of Chirac's personal support. The rest of France's involvement in the world during this period pales in comparison to these two defining events.

France and the US: the Iraq fallout

Throughout its history, the United States has been allied with France, but this bilateral relationship has not always been easy. The 2003 French–American confrontation over Iraq, however, was unanimously described as the deepest rift between France and the US since de Gaulle withdrew France from NATO's integrated structure in 1966. The dire predictions about the irreparable damage done to the bilateral relationship and, more generally, to the transatlantic alliance never materialized. Even during the height of the name-calling in the two camps, France and the US continued to cooperate deeply on the most pressing issues, above all counter-terrorism. The boycotts of French products in the US and of American products in France did not impact the overall economic relationship in any significant way. But this well-publicized rift came to define French foreign policy during the last five years of Chirac's tenure.

Chirac's second term started under favourable auspices for the United States. After the tragedy of September 11, with which the French deeply empathized, France stood by American foreign policy. In the weeks following the terrorist attacks, France joined the US in 'Operation Enduring Freedom' in Afghanistan, where it is also participating in the International Security Assistance Force under NATO (France still had a contingent of 1000 troops in Afghanistan in 2007).

Historians are now debating when and why relations between France and the US turned sour over the proposed intervention in Iraq. The deeper roots of antagonism between France and the US were, in addition to centuries of cultural prejudices, worries about the US role in propagating laissez-faire, neo-liberal globalization and about its unilateralism vis-à-vis the rest of the world, as illustrated for instance in climate change, the International Criminal Court and trade disputes. The more immediate roots of the dispute were laid down in late 2002. In the autumn of 2002, France was very instrumental in mediating a compromise resolution at the United Nations (Resolution 1441) to reinstate weapons inspection in Iraq. Yet relations between France and the US started to deteriorate the following month, when the Bush administration argued that Iraq was impeding the inspections and concealing weapons of mass destruction (WMD), and was therefore in breach of Resolution 1441. For the US, further decisive action was needed to obtain compliance by the Iraqis, including the use of military force. The French government disagreed with this interpretation and wanted to give the inspections more time, since the inspectors had no evidence that WMDs were being concealed.

French–American relations took a nasty turn at the end of January 2003. At a public meeting on Martin Luther King Day, Secretary of State Colin Powell felt that he had been ambushed and double-crossed by the French when he learned there that France would not authorize a second UN resolution. French policy-makers also felt double-crossed when they realized that the Bush administration had already made up its mind about invading Iraq, no matter what their efforts in brokering a compromise solution. In February 2003, the US circulated a draft UN resolution that would justify military action against Iraq, with the ultimate objectives of regime change and the establishment of democracy in Iraq, to serve as a model for the whole Middle East. The French government disagreed loudly with these objectives, in addition to disagreeing that Iraq was actually impeding the inspections and concealing weapons. As a permanent member of the UN Security Council, France threatened to use a veto if the US-proposed resolution were submitted to a vote. The French government also actively tried to convince the other members of the Security Council not to support this new resolution, thereby becoming the number one enemy among America's allies.

As a result of French opposition, and opposition from other countries spearheaded by France, the Bush administration decided to go to war in Iraq in March 2003 without the legitimacy of a new UN resolution. The sour relations between the US and France continued even in the face of the initial, apparent success of the operation, beyond the American overthrow of the Hussein government in April 2003. Chirac and his Foreign Minister, Dominique de Villepin, continued to be very vocal in their criticisms of the American invasion, denouncing it as an occupation and predicting that the situation would soon deteriorate. They argued that only 'a true provisional government whose legitimacy will be underpinned by the UN and will benefit from the support of the countries of the region' could avoid chaos in the long run. As a result, France repeatedly refused to send forces to Iraq as part of the US-led multinational force, since it did not want to condone the American invasion and occupation of Iraq.

The Iraq conflict is often presented as a poster child of French anti-Americanism in action – with French leaders, bowing to their public opinion enraged by the media, having acted more out of genuine subversion than legitimate dissent. But was anti-Americanism the primary driver of French policy during that period? Most likely, the anti-war position of France was motivated primarily by a very different understanding of the threats facing the world, by a rational assessment of its interests in the post-Cold War, post 9/11 geopolitical environment, as well as by a distrust of unconstrained unilateralism.

France had long disagreed with the US over the threat posed by Saddam Hussein and over what to do about it, seeing him as dangerous above all for his own people, but not for the moment for the rest of the world, thanks to the international pressure exerted by multilateral sanctions and inspections. Moreover, France had expressed strong reservations and concerns over the new American doctrine of pre-emption, according to which the US should pre-empt an attack by striking first when suspecting future harm, if not supported by the UN. It is not that France had totally ruled out the use of force in principle; rather, force should only be a last recourse and its legitimacy could only come from the UN. Finally, for French foreign policy, the sole legitimate objective in Iraq was to destroy any existing WMD, which would be done through inspections and, if they failed, through the use of force mandated by the UN – the objective was not regime change or a remodelling of the map of the Middle East. The consistent strands of this policy reflect more distrust of American unilateralist temptations than bias and hatred directed to sabotage US policy.

French foreign policy was also shaped by the specificities of French history and experiences. French intelligence was convinced that the Iraqi regime and Al Qaeda had had no significant contact. Moreover, the recent lessons learned by France in fighting Islamic terrorism, after a wave of attacks in the mid-1980s and mid-1990s, suggested that the war proposed by the United States was not the right approach. Most importantly, many French analyses of the Iraq situation, including those of President Chirac, were informed by their own experiences in Algeria during the war of independence against France from 1954 to 1962, which served as the main prism through which they understood what might happen in Iraq and predicted more frustration, anger and bitterness in the Arab and Muslim world.

Yet if not the cause of the Franco-American crisis over Iraq, anti-Americanism was instead a by-product of the crisis, as was French-bashing in the US. In the aftermath of 9/11, French public opinion had initially given the benefit of the doubt to the US foreign policy strategy. But the deeper the rift between the French and American positions, the stronger the anti-American prejudices that appeared in the French media – and the stronger the stereotypical French-bashing that surged in the US. The French even gave mixed signals about whether they really wanted America to succeed in Iraq, so much so that in April 2003 French Prime Minister Jean-Pierre Raffarin had to remind public opinion that 'the Americans are not the enemies. Our camp is the camp of democracy.' The same was true about anti-French prejudices in the US. In May 2003, the French ambassador in the US, Jean-David Levitte, formally delivered a letter to administration officials and members of Congress, complaining about and detailing a series of false stories that had appeared in the US media over the past nine months, undiplomatically referred to as part of an 'ugly campaign to destroy the image of France' by anonymous administration officials. The extreme public name-calling on both sides of the Atlantic lingered for several months, if not years, even after diplomacy had resumed its normal course.

France and Europe: the referendum fallout

The second defining foreign policy legacy of Chirac was his decision to hold a referendum on the European Constitution in May 2005. The failed 2005 referendum is dealt with elsewhere in this volume in terms of its electoral sociology and domestic political significance, in Chapters 1, 4 and 16 notably. Our remarks here broadly concern the foreign policy dimension and consequences of the failed referendum. One can debate the extent to which Europe is still considered foreign policy for France. After all, for most matters relating to the internal market and economic activity more broadly, from the regulation of food safety to antitrust policy, Europe has been internalized in France as a source of domestic policies. But Europe is also an object, and an essential component, of French foreign policy. The electorate's rejection of the European Constitution was a major blow to the standing of France in Europe and in the world, perpetuating the very feeling of loss of relevance of France in the European project (and the world, more generally), which the naysayers had been trying to combat.

For several decades after the founding of the European Community in 1957, France had been one of the main engines of European integration and its co-leadership with Germany had gone, for the most part, unchallenged. Its influence within Europe, however, was seriously weakened over the years by the successive enlargements which have shifted Europe's geographical and cultural centre and diluted French power. France was no longer the heart and soul of a European Union of 27 members. The negative results of the referendum further diminished the influence of France by sidelining it and destroying its ability to lead the EU. The Plan B promised by many of the French opponents of the Constitution did not materialize, nor did the informal establishment of a core group of countries (presumably led by France) which would have been able to integrate further in some areas, at a more rapid pace. The Lisbon 'mini-treaty' agreed to in October 2007 certainly does not represent this elusive Plan B.

Another negative side effect of the French 'No' is that it thwarted, at least temporarily, French efforts to engineer real changes to European foreign and security policy, such as strengthening its military capabilities or integrating it further among the member states. The draft EU Constitution proposed the creation of a post of EU minister of foreign affairs, the granting of an external legal personality to the EU so as to be able to conclude treaties on its own behalf, and the progressive framing of a common defence. If passed, this would have strengthened the potential impact of France in the world, if one believes that the voice of European countries is heard louder throughout the world when Europe is united. The Constitution would also have enabled France, through Europe, to counterbalance American power and stand up more forcefully to the US when needed. Chirac insisted on these arguments during the campaign in favour of the referendum in May 2005, but they proved insufficient to carry the day. As a result of the negative vote on the referendum, France was sidelined in Europe and almost silent in the world for the remainder of Chirac's second term.

France and the world

The firm French stance against an invasion of Iraq not legitimated by the UN in 2003 put France back temporarily on the map of major foreign policy players, even though *ex post* interpretations of the role France really played diverge. For the Bush administration, France went much further than a simple disagreement between friends. Instead, the active French campaign to prevent the US from obtaining the blessing of the UN was a betrayal and certainly contributed to the quagmire in which the US then found itself in Iraq. By contrast, for many in France, the 2003 episode represents the apex of French foreign policy, if not diplomacy, in the past decade. The run-up to the war in Iraq indeed crystallized all the defining elements of French foreign policy, for better or for worse: UN legitimacy, multipolarity and independence from, not subservience to, the United States. And history, at least for now, seems to show that the French were indeed right when they argued that the threat posed by Saddam Hussein was not imminent, that democracy-building in Iraq would be a lengthy and bloody process, and that such a perilous intervention would trigger more anti-Western sentiment in the Muslim world.

Yet, what is puzzling about this episode is that France did not derive more benefit or more clout in the world from this act of bravura and prescience. The image of France in the world was at its highest level of popularity in the two years following the US-led invasion of Iraq. But French foreign policy was not able to capitalize on the stance it took in 2003, especially in the Middle East when one could have expected France to have gained stature and momentum as an 'honest broker' thanks to its holding out against the US. Nor did French foreign policy seem to be following a coherent strategy or be guided by a particular vision. It had been mostly oppositional and opportunistic, with France presenting no elaborated alternative, aside from abstention, to the American policy on Iraq. French foreign policy lacked conceptual thinking, and no grand vision was articulated by any of the successive foreign ministers – Dominique de Villepin (2002–4), Michel Barnier (2004–5), Philippe Douste-Blazy (2005–7). For the remaining four years of Chirac's presidency, French foreign policy vis-à-vis the rest of the world was anaemic, low-key and uneventful, with the exception of the disastrous referendum on the European Constitution.

The only time when France found itself at the forefront of world affairs again was in 2005 and 2006 in Lebanon. After the assassination of former Prime Minister Rafik Hariri and the subsequent protests over Syria's involvement in the country, France teamed up with the US to demand an immediate and total withdrawal of all Syrian troops and intelligence agents from Lebanon and to apply successful pressure for Syria to comply. French diplomacy was implicated in this affair probably more out of Chirac's personal, long-time friendship with Hariri and France's traditional historical ties with French-speaking Lebanon, rather than out of immediate national interest or promotion of values. France was involved again in the Lebanese crisis in the summer of 2006, during the war between Israel and Hezbollah. French diplomacy succeeded in pushing Resolution 1701 through the UN, demanding the full cessation of hostilities, the disarmament of Hezbollah and the withdrawal of all Israeli forces from Lebanon, as well as the deployment of UN forces in the south. However, the high profile taken by French foreign policy was tarnished when France subsequently displayed reluctance and wavering in deploying troops and taking the command of the United Nations Interim Force in Lebanon (UNIFIL). After some hesitation, the French finally took lead of the peacekeeping operations in Lebanon and had 1700 troops stationed there in 2007.

Apart from Lebanon, France was neither heavily involved, nor particularly creative, in the Middle East during that period. Instead, the bulk of French foreign policy focused on France's traditional sphere of influence in Francophone Africa. France took part in a military intervention in the Ivory Coast, as part of a UN mission, which included helping in the evacuation of foreign residents and protecting civilians from warring factions. It now has a contingent of 3500 soldiers in the Ivory Coast. France also sent 1000 soldiers as part of a EU peacekeeping force in Congo and currently has soldiers deployed in Chad, Djibouti, Senegal and Gabon.

With the US mired in Iraq and partially discredited as an interlocutor in the Muslim world, France tried to broker the growing Iranian nuclear crisis. Along with Britain and Germany, France led negotiations with Iran over its nuclear programme on behalf of the EU. The 'EU-3' agreed to recognize Iran's nuclear rights in exchange for a commitment by Iran to cooperate with the International Atomic Energy Agency. Chirac, who did not believe that economic sanctions are effective, had a particular stake in seeing a successful resolution of the international crisis triggered by the Iranian nuclear build-up, since it could prove that France was still a major world player and French diplomacy could succeed where others had failed.

Towards Europe, French foreign policy was two-pronged. On one hand, Chirac wanted to push for further integration of European security and defence capabilities, in the hope that France, a medium-sized power, would see its voice and ambitions better heard and its force multiplied throughout the world – provided that Europe could be fashioned by France. On the other hand, France slowly started its reintegration into NATO and participated, as part of NATO, in providing peacekeeping troops in Kosovo and Bosnia–Herzegovina.

As for the rest of the world, outside France's traditional sphere of influence, especially in Asia, French foreign policy was neither much involved, nor very coherent. The most notable action was the 2004 decision of France, alongside Germany, to try to end the 16-year-old embargo on arms sales to China – much to the dismay of the US. France argued that the embargo, which had been imposed after the Tiananmen events, was obsolete in light of China's changes since 1989 and its growing inclusion in the international community, from the World Trade Organization to the Olympics. Instead, the embargo should be lifted, but accompanied by a 'code of conduct' and demands for China to ratify the UN International Covenant on Civil and Political Rights. This move was interpreted in Washington as a confrontational, anti-American action, because of the potential for China to use European arms in a fight against the US over Taiwan and the meddling of Europe in a part of the world where it has no stakes – a clear balancing move initiated by France to curb the American hyperpower. The French position on the Chinese arms embargo may have been more about commercial greed than grand geopolitical ambitions, however. China, the world's most dynamic economy, had adroitly put pressure on France and Germany, dangling the carrot of more Airbus and high-speed train purchases, in addition to submarines, helicopters and other avionics technology, should the embargo be lifted. Moreover, several European countries (including France) have said that the EU move on the arms embargo to China was not designed as a confrontation against the US, since China's main suppliers of high-technology weapons then were two friends of the United States – Russia and Israel. After China's decision to pass an 'anti-secession law' against Taiwan in March 2005, the EU put off plans to lift the arms embargo indefinitely, but for France the idea is not a moot point.

New leadership, new foreign policy?

With the changing of the guard in 2007, after the election of Nicolas Sarkozy, a new team and new generation acceded to power in France, without the foreign policy baggage of the Chirac administration. It was accompanied by a radical change in tone, if not in policy, with a more optimistic view about the possibilities of French influence on the international stage. And indeed, the first few months of the Sarkozy presidency were marked by a whirlwind of foreign policy activity, trying to mend fences and repair partnerships in Europe and in the US, as well as new positions on Darfur, Russia and, more controversially, Iran. But can Sarkozy really change the direction of French foreign policy in the near future? Does he genuinely have the opportunity to set the counter back to zero and conduct a foreign policy breaking with those of his predecessors? For as much as Sarkozy has been portrayed as innovative and activist, French foreign policy operates within a set of constraints – historical, geographical, economic and domestic – that limit the options available.

Foreign policy and the 2007 presidential election

Foreign policy has long been a non-issue in France, at least not an electoral issue, given the broad consensus that has prevailed since the days of de Gaulle. On the Right as on the Left, everyone seemed in agreement that French foreign policy should promote France's independence and universal values. It is as if there were a firewall between domestic policies, very contentious, and foreign policies, very consensual. Not surprisingly, foreign policy was not a central topic of debate in the 2007 presidential campaign either. Gaullist policy, and Chirac's policies more specifically, were not questioned. Did the Gaullist approach serve France best? How did France benefit from it? Did it enhance French influence in the world? What comes next? No one asked these questions with any resonance.

The absence of foreign policy debate in 2007 can, additionally, be explained, by two facts. First, none of the main candidates (Bayrou, Royal and Sarkozy) had much foreign policy experience, hence they had more to lose than to gain in engaging these issues. Indeed, foreign policy appeared to be a slippery slope, an easy way to make gaffes, as was demonstrated several times by Ségolène Royal in particular, for instance when she praised the expediency of the Chinese justice system. Therefore the candidates tried to avoid this as much as possible during the campaign. The second reason for the absence of foreign policy from the debate is that, unlike in the United States, the war in Iraq was not perceived as an immediate, pressing issue. With no apparent stake in the conflict, the French population is very detached from the Iraq War, with not even a debate or an interest about the possible role of France in the future of this country. Indeed, in a CSA exit poll taken during the first round of the election, only 9 per cent of the thousands of respondents said foreign policy was a factor in their choice for president. By contrast, 44 per cent said proposals for job creation played a role.

An activist French foreign policy

If foreign policy played a low-key role in the Sarkozy platform, it has been anything but low-key since Sarkozy came to power. His acceptance speech was replete with references to what France would do abroad in the months to come: reach out to Europe, reassert France as a friend of the US, fight global warming, build a Mediterranean Union, free the Bulgarian nurses jailed in Libya and Ingrid Betancourt held hostage in Colombia, and so forth. And indeed what is most striking in the first few months of the Sarkozy presidency is how activist French foreign policy has been – some say 'hyperactive' – especially compared to the torpor in which it had apparently lain since the height of France's omnipresence on the world stage in the spring of 2003. Sarkozy's inauguration was immediately followed, on the same day, by his first trip abroad, to Germany. Since then, French foreign policy has constantly been in the headlines, providing one diplomatic coup after another and giving to the French and to the world the impression that with enough effort and energy France can do anything.

The first action was the relaunching of the constitutional process in Europe, or rather the end of the paralysis and French isolation brought by the French rejection of the EU Constitution in 2005. Sarkozy personally spearheaded the negotiation of a 'mini-treaty' in June 2007 (agreed to by the 27 member states in October 2007 in Lisbon), which gives new functions to European foreign policy, extends majority voting to 40 new areas, and grants the EU legal personality. With this move, France appeared to have re-established its central role in European affairs. This pro-European activism has been counterbalanced, however, as Sarkozy has simultaneously criticized the independence of the European Central Bank, revealed deep protectionist streaks and combated the inclusion of references to free and undistorted competition in the EU treaty, all of which might eventually create tensions between France and Germany and France and the UK.

The next diplomatic coup of Sarkozy was the July 2007 liberation of the Bulgarian nurses jailed in Libya for allegedly having deliberately infected Libyan children with HIV in 1998. This is another example of a very activist policy – one where France's interests do not seem directly at stake, but which contributes to raising the profile of France as a diplomatic actor. This initiative earned France, and Sarkozy, triumphal headlines – if only briefly. Very quickly, criticisms emerged. First, Sarkozy's intervention ruffled a lot of feathers among France's European partners. The release of the nurses had been steadily negotiated by European diplomats for a long time, and they did not appreciate that Sarkozy, thanks to his last-minute effort, was the only one taking credit and reaping the public benefits from the liberation. Another criticism was the lack of transparency surrounding the whole operation, and in particular the blurry role played by Sarkozy's then wife, Cecilia, in the process. This irritated a lot of people, including in French diplomatic circles. But the biggest cost of this diplomatic coup may be what it really took France to obtain the release of the nurses – which came out in public sooner than Sarkozy seemed to have anticipated and intended: Gadaffi's son revealed that Libya would benefit from a military agreement with France to manufacture arms and purchase several 100 million euros worth of French anti-tank missiles. It was also later revealed that France may have sold a nuclear reactor to Libya as part of the deal. As for Gaddafi, he was invited to a high-profile, five-day visit to Paris in December 2007, crowning his rehabilitation in the West.

The next diplomatic coup came a few weeks later, when Sarkozy spent two weeks of summer vacation in the United States – unheard of for a French president – and used this opportunity to meet with President Bush and his family in Kennebunkport. This seemed to ease the rapprochement between France and the US much faster and in an easier way, at least for public opinion, than if the rapprochement had been initiated and conducted by traditional diplomatic channels alone.

No sooner was Sarkozy back in France than he gave his first major foreign policy speech, at the end of August 2007. The highlight of the speech was France's new hard-line position on the Iranian nuclear crisis. Sarkozy declared that 'a nuclear-armed Iran is for me unacceptable' and raised the spectre of bombing Iran (without saying that France would do it) if all else failed. In a serious policy inflexion from the Chirac era, Sarkozy also suggested that France may be ready to envision economic sanctions, alongside the US and the UK, but outside of the UN framework, in order to stop Iran from enriching uranium.

Adding fuel to the fire, in September, French Foreign Minister Bernard Kouchner declared that the world should prepare for possible war against Iran. Kouchner's remarks were echoed the next day by Prime Minister François Fillon, who called for hard negotiations to force Iran to abandon key nuclear activities. Even though Kouchner was later forced to backtrack and Sarkozy disavowed his mention of war, arguing that France is committed to using diplomacy to resolve the nuclear crisis with Iran, this whole episode signalled that France, once again, was back at the forefront of world affairs.

Sarkozy's foreign policy ubiquity has continued ever since. Over the following months, Sarkozy multiplied official state visits to foreign countries, including Morocco, China and Algeria. These visits were opportunities for commercial as well as for traditional diplomacy, once again showing off the image of a dynamic and re-energized France. Sarkozy also visited the United States, where he delivered an address to Congress and was treated to an official visit to Mount Vernon to celebrate the anniversary of Lafayette, a symbol of Franco-American friendship.

Contingencies and constraints

Will this activist policy be able to continue and what shape will it take? How far can the Sarkozy team go in departing from the path traced by 50 years of Gaullist foreign policy? The shape of French foreign policy will be determined in part by the following three conditions: whether the particular historical juncture persists; how the power play between the President and his Foreign Minister plays out; and whether the domestic and international constraints remain the same.

The activism of French foreign policy under the Sarkozy presidency has been made possible by a particular historical juncture. On the one hand, President Bush has been seriously weakened, both domestically and internationally, and he is on the way out. The world sees him as a 'lame duck president'. With the US less strong and less credible, it is an opportune time for European (and therefore French) diplomacy to step up. On the other hand, President Sarkozy is on the way in, with both his domestic opposition and the international community giving him the benefit of the doubt and a long honeymoon period. But this favourable historical juncture can change as Sarkozy stops being perceived as successful at home, where his initially sky-high approval ratings have plummeted, and once the US elects a new President in November 2008.

The shape of French foreign policy will also depend on the political power play inside French foreign policy circles. Traditionally under the Fifth Republic, foreign policy has been the reserved domain (*domaine réservé*) of the President. The President appointed a Prime Minister to take care of domestic affairs, and he took care of foreign policy himself, with a docile Foreign Minister. Not under President Sarkozy, where the division of powers has become blurry with respect to foreign policy. It is not that Sarkozy went the other way, being a hands-on President on domestic affairs while leaving the care of the external relations of France to a competent diplomat. Rather, the division of labour between the President and his Foreign Minister and the division of the President's time between domestic and foreign affairs are open questions under the Sarkozy presidency. Sarkozy may turn out to be an activist President both in domestic affairs and in foreign affairs.

Sarkozy appointed Bernard Kouchner as Foreign Minister, in a shrewd political move that stunned everyone, most of all Kouchner's fellow Socialists. A world-famous human rights activist, Kouchner is the founder of Doctors without Borders and an outspoken proponent of the right to interfere in the domestic affairs of countries that violate the rights of their citizens. Therefore, he supported the American intervention in Iraq in 2003, albeit only for humanitarian reasons (not WMD). If Kouchner were to truly direct French foreign policy in the years to come, one could expect more humanitarian intervention to promote international solidarity and justice and less Gaullist efforts to maintain French independence. For now Kouchner has kept a low profile and has not dissented on even the thorniest issues, such as the visit of Gaddafi to Paris in December 2007. However, how the potential power struggle between the Foreign Minister and the Élysée will play out will determine partly the direction of French foreign policy.

Finally, the shape of French foreign policy will also depend on how domestic and international constraints exert themselves. On the domestic front, both public opinion and budgetary constraints have the potential to affect foreign policy. In the first months of the Sarkozy presidency, activism in foreign policy paid off at home. According to a poll taken in August 2007, for the first time in years a majority of French people think that the international role of France is getting stronger. But the French may start to question Sarkozy's activist foreign policy when they discover that there are indeed costs to a strong French presence in the world. The ambitious economic and social reform agenda of President Sarkozy may lead to disgruntlement and demonstrations in France, with the effect of reinvigorating anti-globalization positions and limiting the budget available for foreign policy ventures. Economic strains at home and declining presidential popularity may also reduce the goodwill granted to Sarkozy's initial pro-American alignments.

International constraints are also an vital determinant of the room for manoeuvre given to Sarkozy in foreign policy. Some of these constraints will, predictably, challenge French foreign policy. For example, the entry of Turkey into the EU, which Sarkozy openly opposes, will be the topic of negotiations in Europe in the next few years. Sarkozy would prefer for Turkey to form a partnership with the EU, along the lines of his proposed Mediterranean Union – a bloc of moderate Muslim states along the Mediterranean whose main interlocutor would be Europe. It is unclear, however, whether either Turkey or France's European partners support this alternative.

Other looming challenges in Europe include the question of the status of Kosovo; the evolution of the Russian regime; and the future of NATO. Indeed, as part of his Atlanticist agenda, Sarkozy envisions a complete return of France to the integrated military structure of NATO if two conditions are met: a parallel advance in an independent European defence capability, and a profound institutional renovation of NATO that would enable France to have a greater voice and a leading role in NATO's command structures. This vision is controversial both among France's partners and at home. Indeed, some analysts and policy-makers in France are openly questioning how rejoining NATO's military command would be beneficial to French political and strategic interests.

Iraq is a constraint on French foreign policy, whether the French population likes it or not. For many years, the French argued with the US that 'you broke it, you own it'. But the collapse of order in Iraq affects a much broader number of actors than those involved in the current conflict, and French interests and national security are indeed at stake in the Iraq conflict. French foreign policy will therefore be more involved in trying to mastermind a solution in Iraq, not out of sheer alignment with the US, but in order to protect its own interests.

Another predictable challenge is the inevitable occurrence of terrorism directed against Western nations, including France. More generally, French foreign policy is deeply concerned with the proliferation of nuclear weapons and WMD, in particular in the case of Iran, on which France has taken a firm stance and leadership role. Other threats and challenges may seem less salient and more remote, but they can be identified: global warming; uncontrolled globalization; the rise in economic and political power of China.

Within a few months of the election of Nicolas Sarkozy, French foreign policy has already undergone a radical transformation, both in tone and in actions. France has been omnipresent on the world stage, from Libya to Iran, from state visits to China and Algeria, from pushing for a UN force in Darfur to advocating a 'planetary New Deal'. The same method seems at play in foreign policy as in domestic policy: French foreign policy has been a frenzy of proposals, a ubiquitous involvement of France, a constant whirlwind. The style of French foreign policy certainly has changed as the President changed: while

Chirac was cautious and grandiloquent, Sarkozy is aggressive and opportunistic. The instruments of foreign policy may be different too: oppositional and reactive for Chirac, constructive and proactive for Sarkozy. But deep down, the objectives of French foreign policy are still the same. The main goal is to get France to be taken seriously again and to enable it to project its power and values throughout the world, like in de Gaulle's time. Sarkozy declared to the *New York Times* in September 2007, 'if France doesn't take the lead, who will?' Like so many presidents before him, Sarkozy believes that France is in a unique position to steer world affairs, that French values are universal and therefore ultimately destined to radiate throughout the world.

Chapter 16

France and the European Union under the Chirac Presidency

HUSSEIN KASSIM

Despite the opportunities and advantages that it affords, membership of the European Union confronts national governments with permanent and often severely testing challenges (Kassim, 2005). Politically, they are challenged to find ways to reconcile their participation in a system of shared decision-making and collective governance, where their fate and destiny are bound up with other states (Smith, 2006), with the myth of national independence. In policy, they champion national preferences for adoption by the EU or seek to block decisions that are likely to impose costs domestically, of a political or economic nature, but are committed to accepting the Union's decisional outputs whether or not they accord with existing policy orientations or require the abandonment of traditional policy instruments, goals or paradigms. Organizationally, they are called upon to put in place systems and procedures to ensure that national interests are defined domestically and presented and defended in Brussels, while also complying with their obligations in regard to the implementation of EU policy within their territories.

Most member governments experience a degree of difficulty, but in France's case commentators agree that the country's relations with the EU have become especially problematic (see, for example, Menon, 1996; Grossman, 2007; Schmidt, 2007). Indeed, a narrative of 'malaise' (Grossman, 2007) has emerged which commands wide consensus among scholars working in the field. According to this viewpoint, France's relationship with the EU is now fraught with difficulty. In political terms, France's influence over the direction of European integration and over policy choices has been eroded, while at the same time the constraints that the Union imposes on France have become all too apparent. Under these conditions, successive governments have found it increasingly difficult to construct a legitimating discourse that communicates the benefits of EU membership (Schmidt 1997a, b, 2007).

This chapter examines France's relationship with Europe during the Chirac presidency in historical context. It looks at France's EU policy, considers the impact of Union action on France, and discusses change and continuity in the way in which France formulates its European policy, and aims to qualify the central tenets of the 'malaise' thesis. It makes three arguments. The first is that the EU's impact on France has been more complex than is often thought and is certainly more intricate than typically presented in French political debate. Second, despite changes at the EU level, on the one hand, and domestic factors, such as inconsistencies in the content and tone of Chirac's European policy, and the increased salience of 'Europe' as a political issue, France has continued to exert an important influence at the EU level. Third, there is evidence of learning in respect of EU policy-making, as the reform of the machinery for coordinating EU policy in France testifies.

The discussion is organized into two parts. The first considers Chirac's inheritance. It looks at the conditions that had allowed France to play a leading role in European integration for much of the post-war period and how they came to be eroded in the late 1980s and early 1990s. It considers the threats to France's influence at the EU level, the political and policy challenges posed by the Union to France, and the tensions that had emerged prior to Chirac's victory in the presidential elections of 1995. The second examines Chirac's approach to the EU during Chirac's *septennat* (1995–2002) and *quinquennat* (2002–7). The focus on an individual statesman is especially important in France due to the personal authority exercised by the French President in EU policy-making (see Menon, 2000; Lequesne, 1993; Guyomarch, 2001). While by no means untrammelled, especially under cohabitation, the autonomy the President enjoys is arguably unique among the EU-27. A short overview of how the President dealt with EU matters with France's partners in the Union and at home is followed by an assessment of France's continued influence over EU policy-making and policy, and a discussion of how France has responded to the political and policy challenges outlined above.

Chirac's inheritance

France's relationship with 'Europe' had been generally unproblematic for more than three decades following the launch of the Schuman Plan in 1950. The chapter will employ inverted commas throughout to acknowledge that, though 'Europe' is used in political debate to refer to the European Communities or the European Union, Europe is not in fact coterminous with either organization. Throughout that period, largely as a consequence of its senior role within the privileged partnership it enjoyed with Germany, France had been able to shape 'Europe' according to French preferences and therefore to ensure the compatibility of Community requirements with national policy. During this era, European integration was not a salient domestic political issue. However, this began to change in the late 1980s and early 1990s for three reasons: first, France's influence over the direction of integration was challenged by structural changes at EU level; second, the constraints imposed by Union action and policies became increasingly visible and domestically politicized with the consequence that 'the cultivated ambiguity [used by French politicians] to reconcile the rhetoric of integration with intergovernmental decision making and the staunch defence of national priorities and objectives' (Menon, 1996: 238) began to fail; and third, 'Europe' and France's position within it became politicized during the ratification debate that followed the Maastricht Intergovernmental Conferences.

French influence under threat

For much of the post-war period, France like other member states used regional integration as a means to pursue its national interests, as well as to achieve goals that could not be realized individually. In contrast to its partners, however, France was able to shape the development of the Communities to serve its ambitions. From the European Coal and Steel Community to the Treaty of European Union, France adopted a strategy of the *fuite en avant* (Menon, 1996), proposing new forms of cooperation or treaty reform to resolve existing or emerging national problems. Thus, for example, the European Coal and Steel Community, which originated in the French-inspired Schuman Plan, enabled France to achieve its main security objective – namely, to manage and contain Germany – by bringing the governance of these two key strategic industries within a transnational framework. While the European Atomic Community (Euratom) had promised to strengthen the bonds of the Six by enabling them to develop nuclear expertise independently of the US and the Soviet bloc, the common market at the heart of the European Economic Community provided a means to assist France's economic recovery and to modernize its economy.

In policy terms, France was able to influence 'high politics'. De Gaulle's ambition to use Europe as a multiplier of French power and to develop a bloc that would match US power was shared by his successors. Georges Pompidou championed European political cooperation in the late 1960s, and François Mitterrand the Common Foreign and Security Policy at Maastricht. In economic policy, France supported cooperation to stabilize its currency. France was an advocate of the first initiative to bring about Economic Monetary Union, set out in the 1970 Werner report. Giscard d'Estaing in pursuit of a strong franc played a key part in establishing the Economic Monetary System in the

1970s and the ERM in 1979. Édouard Balladur, Finance Minister from 1986 to 1988, began a discussion that would lead ultimately to EMU, and Mitterrand's interventions with respect to its design and schedule at Maastricht were decisive. In other areas too, France was able to ensure that Community objectives were aligned with its national preferences. It has, for example, been the main beneficiary of the Common Agricultural Policy (CAP). Less well known, but no less successful, was France's ability in other areas, such as development policy (Dimier, 2003, 2004), to transfer its policies from Paris to Brussels.

No less important was France's success in ensuring that the EEC's institutional structures suited its preferences for a 'strong Community with weak institutions' (Menon, 1996). France has attempted consistently to concentrate decision-making authority in Community bodies representing member governments, while limiting the powers of its supranational institutions. Hence, its wish for the Commission services to be composed of officials seconded from the member states rather than a career civil service and for de Gaulle's clashes with Hallstein, the first Commission President, who wanted to establish 'une grande administration' that would rival national administrations. Its desire for integration to be led by national governments can be seen in de Gaulle's conception of the Community as a Europe of Nations ('Europe des patries') and the model he proposed as part of the Fouchet Plans. It was also evident in Pompidou's preference for summitry, Giscard's support for the institutionalization of the European Council, and Mitterrand's commitment to the 'Maastricht temple', which brought foreign policy and home affairs within the scope of European cooperation, but preserved intergovernmental decision-making in the second and third pillars. The opposition of successive French Presidents to strengthening the European Parliament was similarly motivated by a desire to keep decision-making authority in the hands of member governments.

A further indication of French influence was its ability to impose its will even when its conception of the Community did not coincide with those of its partners. The 'empty chair' crisis of 1965, when French representatives boycotted meetings of the Council to protest against Commission proposals that would have given the Community some financial autonomy and introduced qualified majority in the Council, is one example; de Gaulle's vetoes of Britain's applications to join the Community in 1961 and 1967 are a second.

France's ability to shape the trajectory, scope and form of integration resulted, partly, from its size and status as a larger member state. However, its relationship with Germany, struck in the early 1950s and formalized by the Élysée Treaty in 1963, was pivotal. The Franco-German axis played a decisive role at key stages in the development of the Communities. Although integration was of critical importance to the Bonn Republic, Germany could not take the initiative for reasons relating to its recent history. France was therefore able to assume a leading role.

The foundations of France's privileged status and its influence over integration, however, began to be eroded in the late 1980s and early 1990s. The first challenge came with German unification, which fundamentally rebalanced the Franco-German axis, although had the UK not been such an 'awkward partner' after its accession in 1973, it is possible that France's pre-eminence might have been challenged a lot earlier. If Germany was historically the subordinate partner, the end of the Cold War marked the end of the post-war settlement that had kept Germany divided and allowed it to recover full sovereign status. Once France had accepted the inevitability of unification, the prospect of which had initially caused considerable unease in Paris, it lent its support to political union as a continuation of its aim to contain its eastern neighbour. At the same time, Germany was keen to demonstrate its continued commitment to Western Europe through the further deepening of integration. The Kohl–Mitterrand initiative that led to the second IGC on political union concealed, however, a fundamental shift of power within the alliance, with Germany no longer prepared to act as paymaster of the Community or to shrink from defending its political interests. The tilt of the relationship in favour of Germany was further strengthened, moreover, by the growth of Germany's sphere of influence in central and Eastern Europe, as countries that were formerly in the Warsaw Pact became independent and turned towards the West.

Enlargement was a second factor. The accession of states in 1995 that were previously members of EFTA expanded Union membership from 12 to 15 and increased the number of small member states. The result was not only to dilute the influence of any single member state – a function not only of more numbers, but also of accompanying changes in the weighting of individual votes – but to bring into the Union countries that shared few ideological or cultural affinities with France. The Nordic states, in particular, brought a very different economic outlook and administrative approach to the Union.

Although France's power during what the dominant view presents as a golden age of French influence has undoubtedly been exaggerated, the impact of German unification and the 1995 enlargement was significant. Along with these structural factors, Jacques Delors's departure from Brussels after heading three Commissions (1985–89, 1990–93, 1993–95) left France without a key channel of influence in Brussels. Shaping integration in ways that suited its purposes and preferences became considerably more difficult for France.

Europeanization: the impact of EU action on French policy

Although some authors have argued that Europeanization, which refers to how the EU affects domestic processes, embraces not only cases where the Union initiates action, as an independent agent, but also instances where national actors invoke the EU as a real or imagined constraint in order to bring about domestic change (Radaelli, 2004; Cole and Drake, 2000), France's experience in the 1980s and 1990s demonstrates that bringing together essentially different phenonema within the same concept diminishes its explanatory power. The argument here is that at least four processes, involving a series of direct and indirect factors, were at work in relation to France's relationship with 'Europe' that led to domestic problems.

The first concerns the consequences of Mitterrand's decision in March 1983, his famous choice for Europe, to stay in the EMS and finally abandon the policies of 'Keynesianism in one country' that France's first Socialist government since the mid-1930s had pursued since its election in 1981. This key milestone cannot in itself be considered an instance of Europeanization, since it was essentially a domestic political choice, not forced upon France by Brussels, but the decision to remain within the EMS and to pursue a *franc fort* policy has serious implications. The growth of unemployment was an immediate consequence. This confronted the government with a series of hard choices, not only because mass employment was new in France, but because the Bismarckian system of social insurance, predicated on the assumption of full employment, was unable to cope and acted as a tax on jobs, since revenue was raised through contributions partly paid by employers, not through direct taxation.

Moreover, as Cameron (1996) has argued, the EMS privileged stronger currencies, such as the Deutschmark, while imposing costs on weaker currencies, including the franc. In addition, the mark was the anchor currency within the ERM, 'so that the monetary policy adopted by the Bundesbank became in effect the monetary policy of all ERM members' (Cameron, 1996: 339–40). However, the Bundesbank's function was to set interest rates to ensure the well-being of Germany, not of other economies. Although French governments, particularly of the Right, expressed reservations about German leadership, their aim was to reform the system not to replace it. Thus, as Prime Minister in 1986–88, Chirac had allowed the franc to fall through the ERM floor, considering that the French currency's low valuation was the result of the overvaluation of the Deutschmark. His Finance Minister, Édouard Balladur, meanwhile, attempted to strengthen the EMS in order to reduce the mark's influence. After his efforts led to the Basle–

Nyborg Agreements, signed in September 1987, he called for further changes, 'especially in terms of the obligations of participating member states to defend currencies under attack and called for larger credit facilities to support such interventions' (Cameron, 1996: 340). In an initiative claimed by some to have begun the process that led to EMU, Balladur called for the creation of a common currency that would be managed by a single central bank (Cameron, 1996: 340).

France's support for EMU was motivated, in Mitterrand's words, as the only way to gain 'the right to participate in the discussion, to have a say' (*Le Monde*, 14 April 1992, cited by Menon, 1996: 233). Mitterrand personally played a key role in the process surrounding the negotiation of EMU. First, he secured an agreement from the German Chancellor, Helmut Kohl, that the IGC on EMU at Maastricht would begin in December 1990, so that the second stage could coincide with the creation of the single market. Second, at Maastricht he succeeded in securing agreement on 1 January 1999 as the start date for the third stage, should a majority of member states not have satisfied the convergence criteria by the end of 1996.

The second factor reshaping France's relationship with 'Europe' was the Single European Act. Until the mid-1980s, action on the part of the Communities had not required politically significant domestic adjustment in France. Nowhere was this more important than in industrial policy. State interventionism, a long-standing tradition in France, had been extended after 1945 in order to reconstruct and to modernize the French economy. Although the EEC Treaty's central aim had been to establish a common market based on liberal principles, French policy had remained relatively unchanged after 1958. Notably, 'national champions', publicly owned companies in strategic sectors that had been granted monopoly rights by the state, as well as other forms of protection, had prospered. The provisions of the Rome Treaty relating to state aid and public monopolies, which were far-reaching in terms of the powers that they entrusted to the Community and also to the Commission, remained a dead letter, while the Community lacked an instrument for controlling mergers. More broadly, as Élie Cohen (1992) made clear, the French formula of state credit control, an inflationary social compromise, and *grands projets* was not threatened by Brussels until the 1980s.

However, this changed with the adoption and implementation of the 1992 project. Mitterrand had been a strong advocate of the single internal market, believing like other European leaders that a concerted effort to remove national barriers would allow European (and French) businesses to benefit from continent-wide economies of scale and restore the continent's competitiveness against the United States and Japan as well as the economies of the South East Asia. Indeed, Mitterrand played an instrumental role in putting in place the preconditions for the single internal market and in bringing it about. However, the effects of the single market programme were difficult and far-reaching for France, effectively removing the state's ability to control the movement of goods, services, capital and people across its borders through a series of targeted measures and the introduction of general principles, such as mutual recognition. Moreover, an invigorated Commission mobilized competencies it had been previously reluctant to use, including the formidable array of competition powers entrusted to it by the treaty, with the aim of liberalizing sectors, such as air transport, telecommunications and energy, that had historically been protected in France. In particular, it began actively to implement the provisions of the treaty relating to state aid. The adoption of the merger regulation in preparation for the single market provided the Commission with a further instrument that enabled it to control the use of one of France's favoured industrial policy instruments.

Although the single internal market project was challenging for most member states, its impact on France was especially dramatic. Socialist governments in the early 1980s had begun to implement reforms that aimed to effect a withdrawal of the state from some areas of activity, but French industrial policy was still characterized by interventionism and support for national champions. In a series of high-profile cases, the Commission investigated the granting of state aid to Renault, Bull and Air France, while in the de Havilland case it prohibited the planned merger with ATR. It had become clear that the traditional instruments employed by the French state to sponsor and support French companies could only be used subject to the approval of Brussels. Although the active application of Community competition rules was the most obvious manifestation of the new constraints on French governments, other tools used by Paris to protect producers were also ruled out of court. Voluntary export agreements, such as those that had enabled France to limit the import of Japanese cars in the 1980s, were terminated before the single market deadline of 1 January 1993. In short, the single European market deprived French governments of the tools that they had historically used to manage the French economy and forced traditional policy goals, if not the traditional model of French industrial policy, to be abandoned.

A third problem concerned the communicative discourse used by French political leaders to support European integration. Until the early 1990s, rhetoric that presented 'Europe' as a vehicle for French ambitions and the interests of the two as the same seemed plausible. However, this discourse lost credibility as the constraints imposed by the EU became increasingly visible, and it became ever more apparent that the Union was not an intergovernmental system. Nor was the discourse used by political leaders, such as Laurent Fabius, who had presented the Community as a shield against globalization, any more convincing, as the stream of reforms in relation to the labour market and social security was linked in the public mind with the demands imposed by EMU. Moreover, few politicians of the political main-stream openly advocated the benefits of the market as a pro-European argument.

A final challenge related to the pressure on France deriving from the expansion of EU competencies and the intensification of EU activity. While the Élysée, following the *domaine reservé* principle in the field of foreign affairs, took the lead in policy-making, particularly in rela-tion to constitutional reform and high politics, the machinery for coordinating policy day to day, the Sécretariat Général du Comité Interministeriel (SGCI) was located at the Hotel Matignon under the authority of the Prime Minister (see Lequesne, 1993). Before the SEA, both the division of labour between President and Prime Minister, and the operation of the SGCI as a strong central coordinating body, ensuring interdepartmental agreement on EU dossiers, were unprob-lematic. However, with the growing volume of EU business and the importance of EU issues within each ministry's remit, the boundary between presidential and governmental spheres of action became increasingly blurred, while individual departments, particularly the main ministries, sought to ensure that their preferred policy prevailed and resisted compromise with other parties (Menon, 2000; Guyo-march, 2001). France's ambition to speak with one voice became more difficult to realize.

Maastricht and French national identity

The ratification of the Treaty of European Union marked a major milestone in terms of popular attitudes towards 'Europe' in France, as developed in detail by Nicolas Sauger in Chapter 4 (see also Cameron, 1996: 345–63; Flynn, 1995). Although France was by no means the only state to experience a Maastricht effect, marked by the end of 'integration by stealth' and the beginning of close public scrutiny of developments at the EU level, the debate over the treaty's ratification was particularly significant as 'Europe' became a do-mestic political issue for the first time. Crucially, the issue came to be framed in terms of the threat posed to French identity. The con-straints and adjustments imposed by Brussels in economic, industrial and social policy challenged traditional beliefs about the French state, its independence and its ability to protect and to safeguard its citizens.

Despite the fact that France had achieved its main goals, Mitterrand's decision to hold a referendum to ratify the treaty occa-sioned a fierce and at times bitter debate about France and European integration. With opponents of the treaty on the Left, most notably

Jean-Pierre Chevènement, who split from the PS, and on the Right – Gaullists, such as Philippe Séguin and liberals, such as Alain Madelin – explicitly linking the constraints imposed by ERM membership and low growth and high unemployment, public opinion grew increasingly hostile. Although the referendum vote went in favour of the yes campaign, the result was extremely narrow, with only 51.04 per cent endorsing the treaty. Importantly, however, 'Europe' became a party-political issue, cutting across parties, as well as leading to the formation of Eurosceptic parties, such as de Villiers Mouvement pour la France, and a salient political issue among the population more broadly.

In short, France's relationship with the EU was increasingly troubled by the mid-1990s. Paris was perceived to have lost influence at the EU level, and 'Europe' had become politically contentious at home.

Chirac in office, 1995–2007

The situation that Chirac inherited in 1995 was far from auspicious. Within the Union, France's influence appeared to have diminished, while 'Europe' had become a contentious domestic issue. Although the result of the referendum on the ratification of the Constitutional Treaty (see Chapter 4, this volume) will inevitably be seen as the defining moment of the Chirac presidency, it should not be allowed to obscure other important developments. The picture that emerges from an analysis of the full 12 years is far more complex. Though there were clear domestic failings in *politics*, there were important successes at the EU level and in domestic *policy*. These suggest, moreover, that the thesis of French decline has been exaggerated. In fact, France has remained an influential player in the EU.

The Chirac presidency: France at EU level

Chirac engaged positively with the Union, despite the Euroscepticism he had evidenced earlier in his political career (see Parsons, 2003: 17), notably in his famous 1978 diatribe, and even if at times he took less care to disguise his sometimes narrow pursuit of French interests. There was an important continuity between Chirac's approach to integration and that of his predecessors, particularly with regard to the preference for a 'Europe' led by the member states and for a 'Europe' that was powerful on the international stage. Indeed, the rapprochement with NATO that he announced soon after his election victory seemed to make the development of a European security and defence identity a serious possibility. Chirac's EU-level policy is best considered in two phases: before and after the Convention on the Future of Europe.

Chirac 1995–2001

Although in this period France scored a number of successes in regard to the protection of French interests and the advance of its intergovernmentalist and foreign policy agenda, its approach to the 1996–97 Intergovernmental Conference (IGC) was somewhat muted, while the French Council presidency in the second semester of 2000, which ended with the adoption of the Nice Treaty, was not warmly regarded. Indeed, the negotiations of the latter were widely agreed to have been among the most acrimonious ever and the actions of the French President himself were the object of much criticism.

France approached the 1996–97 IGC, the aim of which was to negotiate the institutional reforms necessary to prepare for enlargement, with uncharacteristic hesitation. President and government were initially reticent about the course the EU should take, provoking the observation that for the first time, 'France is proposing nothing ('la France ne propose pas') (see Menon, 1996: 243). When French spokesmen did voice an opinion, they repeated their traditional emphasis on the need to retain national autonomy, with Foreign Minister, Hervé de Charette, declaring that the 'approach of the founding fathers is no longer appropriate' (*Les Echos*, 10 July 1995). Although France expressed its willingness to accept that QMV would have to be extended in an enlarged Union, it made clear that its acceptance would be based on a reweighting of votes tied to the size of national populations and financial contributions to the Union's budget, thus privileging large states.

With respect to the Common Foreign and Security Policy (CFSP), the only policy area that French political leaders addressed in any detail, the emphasis was again on national autonomy with an insistence on intergovernmental decision-making and the importance of unanimity. Reflecting traditional ideas that Europe should have a strong international role, France called for the creation of a single office to represent the Union – a 'Monsieur PESC' (Mr CFSP). It also showed acceptance of the idea that there should be a move towards a common European defence, proposing a clear linkage between the West European Union and the EU. This came as a surprise to many governments, given that, having announced in December 1995 France's formal return to some part of the NATO structure – a move that followed a NATO agreement in 1994 that European governments should be allowed to launch military operations without US commitment – Chirac had subsequently insisted that a French officer be appointed to NATO's southern command. This was too high a price for Washington.

Although EU member states failed to agree on institutional reforms, the Amsterdam Treaty did create a High Representative for EU Foreign Affairs and committed the Union to a closer relationship with the West

European Union – both objectives that France had sought. Moreover, France successfully pursued its foreign policy agenda in the wake of Amsterdam, signing a bilateral agreement with the UK at Saint-Malo, that was to mark a major milestone in the development of the EU's military capacity. Following further discussions at meetings of heads of state and government at Cologne, Helsinki and Nice, the Union developed an operational force for the first time.

A further IGC was convened for 2000 in a second attempt to negotiate institutional reforms in advance of enlargement. Although agreement was reached on Council decision-making (the so-called 'triple majority') and the reweighting of votes, few delegations emerged happy from negotiations that were among the most bitter in the Union's history. The French presidency attracted considerable criticism for its management of the discussions, particularly in the endgame. However, France, which had insisted on voting parity with Germany for largely symbolic reasons, despite its argument that votes should be distributed among member states in proportion to population size, secured this objective, resisting pressure to accept a simpler double majority system. It also succeeded in preserving unanimity in a number of areas that it believed should remain the preserve of national governments. With regard to foreign policy, it was agreed at the European Council that the EU capability should be operational by 2003 and that permanent bodies – a political and security committee (COPS), a military committee and a common HQ – would be created within the Council.

Despite the fact that he had done so in a way that had sometimes alienated France's European partners, Chirac succeeded in advancing and securing French aims at both IGCs. Moreover, French successes were not limited to institutional reform and the CFSP. Over the same period, the EU had adopted a Charter of Fundamental Rights, which had been a project championed by France. France was also one of the main advocates of the inclusion of a commitment to employment in the Amsterdam Treaty. With respect to the Lisbon Process, which was intended to bring about economic reform to make Europe the most competitive knowledge-based world economy by 2010, France managed to ensure that there was a commitment to the preservation of the European social model – a move that it hoped would reduce pressure on it to undertake further social policy reform. It adopted similar tactics at Nice, where a European social agenda was adopted that set out strategies relating to employment, social exclusion and discrimination.

Chirac 2002–7

This second Chirac presidency was dominated by the Convention on the Future of Europe and its aftermath, where France took a more relaxed, and arguably more *communautaire*, approach than it had done at Nice or Amsterdam (see Jabko, 2004). Interestingly, Chirac began during the course of his *quinquennat* to express his vision of the EU as a 'federation of nation states'. Previously taboo, Chirac's use of the f-word represents an updating of de Gaulle's favoured conception of the Community as a 'Europe des patries'. However, the period 2002–7 was also notable for France's contravention of the Growth and Stability Pact, as well as its success in postponing reform of the CAP, its opposition to the Bolkestein Directive and its blocking of the Doha Round.

Also important during this period was the revival of the Franco-German alliance, which had fallen into abeyance during Chirac's first term as President. Chirac had not shared the instinctive pro-Europeanism of Helmut Kohl, while Schröder had not initially shown the same enthusiasm for the Franco-German alliance as his predecessors. The first German Chancellor to have been born after the war, Schröder believed that the time had come for Germany to assert itself as a fully sovereign power and had a closer ideological affinity to Blair than Chirac. However, while the early interaction between the British Prime Minister and the German Chancellor did not develop into a more lasting relationship, senior officials in Paris and Berlin grew increasingly alarmed at the drift in relations between their two countries and decided that efforts were necessary to bring the two sides together. A summit was held towards the end of 2001, which was followed by further informal meetings in 2002. Although there were disagreements on some policy issues, including the CAP, it was decided at a meeting in Schwerin in July to relaunch the partnership (Pedersen, 2003). The relationship between Chirac and Schröder was further cemented when they found themselves on the same side in their opposition to the Iraq War.

The impact of the revitalization of the Franco-German relationship was felt within the convention from the beginning of 2003, though their cooperation in the autumn of 2002 had led to a breakthrough on the CAP and on defence cooperation (see below). Prior to that date, France had welcomed the convention as a new, more inclusive and democratic, method of treaty reform. At the Convention on the Future of Europe, which opened in February 2002, it took a far more conciliatory approach than it had done at Nice (Jabko, 2004) and defined three main goals – a constitution for Europe; a Permanent President of the European Council; and a powerful Europe – the latter two reflecting long-standing French preferences. However, partly due to the elections, the French government was slow to set out detailed proposals.

On the fortieth anniversary of the Élysée Treaty in January 2003, both France and Germany made positive statements about the importance of their partnership. This was followed by a joint proposal to the convention on the institutions of the EU, which involved a compromise on the part of both countries. The call for a dual presidency reflected France's desire for a permanent presidency of the European Council, and Germany's wish for the Commission president to be elected by the European Parliament. Importantly, Jabko (2004) argues that France's renewed commitment to its alliance with Germany, combined with the pressures that derived from the convention setting requiring deliberation rather than hard bargaining, involved a dilution of its preferences. The most telling example was France's preparedness to accept the proposal of the convention's president, Valéry Giscard d'Estaing, for a double majority, which entailed giving up its historical claim to voting parity with Germany. Although the paper on institutions was the most important, other joint initiatives concerned defence and security, judicial cooperation, tax harmonization and Turkish accession.

France was active in the IGC that followed the convention, calling for the draft constitutional treaty not to be amended. As Jabko (2004) points out, Chirac, unlike Blair (or, more likely, Brown), had no red lines that it considered needed protection. However, selling the treaty at home proved problematic and ultimately ended in failure when French voters rejected the proposed Constitution in a referendum on 29 May 2005 (see Chapter 4 in this volume; see also Hainsworth, 2006). As a consequence the French President effectively became a lame duck as a player in the EU, with France's partners waiting anxiously for the outcome of the 2007 presidential elections in order to make an assessment as to whether the treaty project could be revived.

The revitalization of the Franco-German alliance undoubtedly strengthened French influence. It helped, for example, that both countries ran up excessive budget deficits in contravention of the Growth and Stability Pact, which had been introduced at Germany's initiative in the run-up to the third stage of EMU in order to impose fiscal discipline on governments to prevent the development of inflationary pressures. That neither country was sanctioned despite the Commission's opening of the excessive deficit procedure, contrary to the experience of both Portugal (2002) and Greece (2005), demonstrates the ability of the larger member states to withstand naming and shaming, and to carry the Council, which decides on punitive measures.

It was also as a consequence of a deal between Chirac and Schröder that France succeeded in postponing the reform of the CAP. In October 2002, in advance of a European Council meeting, Chirac and Schröder agreed to retain CAP spending at existing levels until 2013, much to the consternation of the UK. Only three years previously at the Berlin European Council, Chirac had opposed Germany's proposal to move to a system of 'co-financing' jointly by the EU and national governments.

A further French success concerning the Bolkestein Directive, however, was in fact achieved without the help of Germany. The

Commission had sought in its original proposal to address one of the major gaps in the single European market by liberalizing services across the Union, thus removing barriers in a sector accounting for 70 per cent of Europe's GDP. Although France, with a strong services sector, stood to benefit from the directive, fears were raised – not least by the French Eurosceptic, Philippe de Villiers, who introduced the figure of the 'Polish plumber' into the domestic debate – about the effects of competition in its domestic market. France was the most vocal opponent of the measure and following Chirac's insistence in March 2005 that it should be radically revised, the Commission amended and significantly diluted its original proposal. It was further weakened after debates in the European Parliament and Council negotiations.

Though the referendum defeat would eventually prove his downfall, Chirac's record at EU level shows that France had not lost its influence in choices concerning either Union institutions or key areas of policy. Although French power may have become more conditional in the sense that the Franco-German alliance could not always be relied upon, France nevertheless demonstrated continued ability to shape decision-making.

The Chirac presidency: Europe and the domestic arena

In the domestic arena, a more complicated picture emerges. In policy, France showed that it was able to influence the EU's impact at least in certain areas. Politics, however, proved more problematic.

Shaping the domestic impact of EU policy

Like its partners, France is obliged to implement EU policy and to introduce changes that may not be compatible with existing national policy orientations and instruments. Though the trend in EU policy across a range of sectors has been away from France's preferred position, France has shown that it is able to shape the domestic impact of EU policy at least in some areas.

The spread of regulation and the creation of regulatory agencies are typically presented as evidence of the triumph of Anglo-Saxon liberalism over the French statist model. However, France has demonstrated an ability to adopt regulatory mechanisms, while adapting them to suit its policy preferences. In his survey of network industries (telecommunications, energy, water, postal services and the media) in France and Britain, Thatcher (2007) has shown that the regulatory model has been adopted by France, apparently representing a 'sharp change' from existing policy. However, he finds that French policy-makers have proved adept at adopting the model to suit their purposes and have used it to 'keep alive' an 'activist industrial policy' that the single market had threatened to eliminate (2007: 1028). In particular, while liberalizing domestic markets, regulators have sought to ensure that the domestic market remains profitable, allowing large (French-owned) suppliers, such as EDF and France Télécom, time to adjust to new circumstances. Not only, in contrast to Britain, have governments continued to involve themselves in pricing decisions of state-owned suppliers, but they have continued to use traditional methods, such as encouraging mergers or sponsoring particular international alliances (Thatcher, 2007: 1036).

France's continued ability to support national champions is exemplified in energy, where it has successfully managed to circumvent efforts on the part of the Commission to liberalize. In electricity, for example, national monopolies have survived, despite the fact that they have been targeted by Brussels for over a decade. Moreover, although it may have been believed that the creation of the Commission for the Regulation of Energy following a law adopted in 2000 would presage liberalization, in fact the same technocratic elite dominate the regulator as before, suggesting continued complicity between regulator and regulated (Bauby and Varone, 2007). France has also shown considerable ingenuity in developing mechanisms that are designed to combat the perceived excesses of Anglo-Saxon liberalism, which Brussels is spreading. The case of the 'poison pill', considered by Ben Clift in Chapter 12, is instructive in this regard.

Furthermore, France appears to have exploited the opportunities provided by what Dimitrakopoulos (2001) calls 'post-decisional politics'. Its implementation record has traditionally been poor, placing France firmly among the laggards. In some areas, implementation has been especially problematic. This is true of certain sectors, such as environmental policy, where France has been either a 'partial implementer' (Lavoux, 1992) or has used instruments that make coherent implementation difficult. Buller (2004) suggests that there are several reasons for this: that the French system, which is centralized and vertically administered, finds it difficult to manage traversal issues (Buller, 2004: 81); that EU environmental policy 'emphasizes scientific and normative criteria' (Buller, 2004: 84), whereas the traditional conceptualization of the environment in France is territorial and humanist; that there is a tension in France between the technocratic and bureaucratic approach (see Lascoumes, 1994) to environmental protection and ecologists; and that, while in some cases such as the bathing water directive and environmental impact assessments France has exported its preferences at the EU level, in others, such as the use of soft policy, there has been an uncomfortable clash of styles.

'Europe' as a domestic political issue

France has encountered much more difficulty in managing the domestic political fall-out from Europe. Although the cleavages that appeared with Maastricht appear to have become less salient, some authors have suggested that a new fault line has emerged, separating those who have benefited from EU action and those who have been disadvantaged by the spread of the market. Moreover, although it may be the case that differences over 'Europe' are not effectively expressed through competition between political parties, it is clearly a divisive issue. The problem largely derives from the association made between EU action and the demands of membership, on the one hand, and rising unemployment and the reform of social and labour market policy, on the other. It is compounded by the failure of mainstream political parties to explain the weaknesses of the French welfare system and labour market, to celebrate French market or globalization successes (see Meunier, 2004), such as Airbus, and their tendency to portray the EU only as a constraint.

As the above discussion has shown, the association was made before Chirac became President, but it has been strengthened by the policies he has advocated and those implemented by the governments over which he has presided. In his electoral campaign, Chirac pledged both to heal France's 'social fracture' and to meet the convergence criteria. His appointment of Alain Juppé as Prime Minister and the reform programme announced by the latter's administration made clear that the second of these commitments took priority. Though Juppé's radical welfare reform proposals were regarded by many observers as well-crafted and appropriate (see, for example, Ross, 2004: 92), they provoked widespread opposition and indeed strike action. The government became extremely unpopular and many of the measures were abandoned, with the result that key reforms went unimplemented. When Chirac dissolved the National Assembly in June 2007, the Right lost the elections.

A five-year period of cohabitation ensued with a 'Plural Left' coalition in government, headed by Lionel Jospin. Jospin had campaigned on a programme of reforming the Growth and Stability Pact and creating an 'economic government' to superintend the ECB. However, he achieved little headway in his pursuit of either objective at the Amsterdam European Council. Forced to govern subject to constraints that he had criticized, Jospin appeared determined to demonstrate that space existed for domestic policy change (Ross, 2004: 93). As well as the introduction of the 35-hour week, he adopted a programme intended to encourage the employment of young people.

Following Chirac's victory in the 2002 presidential elections, France returned to the Gaullist model of President–Prime Minister relations with the appointment of Jean-Pierre Raffarin. The government in its three years in office faced a number of EU-related issues. The flouting of the Stability Pact, discussed above, was a serious problem, even though it resulted in a suspension of the rules in France's favour. However, Drake suggests that the Prime Minister's explanation that: 'Mon devoir c'est l'emploi et non pas d'aller rendre des équations compatables et de faire des problèmes de mathématiques pour que tel ou tel bureau, dans tel ou tels pays, soit satisfait' (2005a: 303) lived longer in the memory than the event itself. A second issue concerned the French engineering giant, Alstom. When the company was threatened by bankruptcy, the French state offered a rescue package that included the purchase of a 21 per cent stakeholding. As an issue of state aid, the transaction was subject to control by the European Commission. As has become customary in such cases, the French government rejected the 'liberal' label, but demonstrated its preparedness to negotiate terms with Brussels (Howarth, 2004).

Raffarin was also Prime Minister during the convention, though his role was limited. He 'resigned' (in effect he was forced out by the President) two days after the referendum and was replaced by Dominique de Villepin. One of de Villepin's most important actions, though probably one of the least visible, was to implement the first major overhaul of the SGCI since its creation in 1948. The reform originated in the belief that lack of information and an exclusionary approach to EU policy-making were sources of ignorance about, and hostility to, the Union. Its aim was to involve Parliament, subnational authorities and interest groups more closely in the development of France's European policy. The SGCI was rechristened the General Secretariat for European Affairs (Secrétariat Général des Affaires Européennes – SGAE), entrusted with new functions, including the organization of a monthly interministerial meeting on Europe chaired by the Prime Minister, where the main policy guidelines would be agreed and reported to the press immediately thereafter. In addition, whereas historically the SGCI had been responsible to both the Prime Minister and the Finance Minister, the SGAE would report only to the Hotel Matignon (see Lanceron, 2007).

Conclusion

This chapter has argued that, though 'Europe' has undoubtedly become a difficult domestic issue, the malaise thesis that has become the dominant perspective on France's relationship with, and place in, the EU exaggerates the extent of France's decline. Examination of the Chirac presidency has shown that France is not only capable of exerting an influence on the direction of EU policy in institutional and high politics, as well as in day-to-day policy matters, but that it has retained a degree of freedom of action at the domestic level. Although it may have been compelled to import unfamiliar policy practices, it has been able to use these mechanisms to pursue traditional policy objectives.

Although it is too early to judge whether and, if so, how French policy will change under Nicholas Sarkozy, there is evidence of some broad continuity in key French positions such as 'economic governance' and criticisms of the ECB, combined with a new willingness to make concessions in order to end the crisis brought about by the French 2005 rejection of the draft constitutional treaty. Consistent with the style of the new President in other domains, Sarkozy's activism since his election in May 2007 has been at least as important as the substance of his proposed remedies for Europe's ills. In a short space of time, Sarkozy had personally negotiated a new 'mini-treaty' for European integration with some of the same provisions (mostly relating to institutions) of the rejected constitution. Other initiatives included a renewed push for a Mediterranean Union, a much tougher position towards the prospects of Turkish membership of the EU, and calls for more protection of European goods and industries. In short, Sarkozy has engaged a more energetic defence than his predecessor of what are perceived to be core French interests, while at the same time engaging positively with France's European partners, thereby ending a period of French isolation. Sarkozy's visit to Berlin on the same day as his investiture as President sent a powerful message that France was back at the table and that the Franco-German relationship would be a key element of France's European policy.

Guide to Further Reading

Chapter 1   From Chirac to Sarkozy: a New France?

There are several good general books in English about France, of which Knapp and Wright (2005) and Cole et al. (2005) are two recent examples. The most complete recent overview of the evolution of French policy-making since 1981 is Culpepper et al. (2006.), a very detailed and policy-centred book that is a good companion to *Developments in French Politics 4*. Cole (2008) and Levy (1999) provide distinctive individual accounts.

Chapter 2   The 2007 French Elections and Beyond

On the 2007 elections themselves, the best material available at the time of writing (December 2007) is the wealth of studies produced by the CEVIPOF team and available on http//www.cevipof.msh-paris.fr/bpf/analyses/analys0.htm. A series of articles on related aspects of the 2007 elections appeared in the *Revue française de science politique* 57 (3–4), 2007. On the 2002 elections, a very full treatment is Lewis-Beck (2003). The French cartographical tradition in electoral studies is present in two recent 'Atlases': Salmon (2001) covers the whole range of elections since 1848, while Perrineau (2007a) includes, with electoral maps, a more general introduction to French voting behaviour under the Fifth Republic. Finally, on voting and voting behaviour Andersen and Evans (2003) is a classic piece. Cautrès and Mayer (2004) provide a thorough treatment in French of trends up to and including 2002.

Chapter 3   Political Parties and the Party System

The two main works in English on the French party system are Evans (2003) and Knapp (2004a). Both include chapters on individual parties as well as on the system as a whole; both are affected, to some degree, by having been largely written in the wake of the 2002 elections. Haegel (2007a) has a similar format, but the chapters on individual parties are less general and more focused on specific aspects. This work also looks forward to 2007 more than back to 2002. Grunberg and Haegel (2007) put forward a provocative, but well-argued, thesis of

277

'bipolarization' which is reinforced rather than undermined by the elections held a month after its publication.

Chapter 4   Attitudes towards Europe in France

Perrineau (2005) is a useful study of the relationship between the party system and the European issue. The 2005 referendum is given its fullest treatment in Tiberj and Brouard (2006) and also Sauger et al. (2007). Hainsworth (2006) also provides a good accessible account in English. Evans (2007) investigates the European dimension in French public opinion and Drake (2005c) provides a very useful account of France's sometimes troubled relationship with the European Union.

Chapter 5   Social Movements and Protest Politics

There are not many books on social movements and protest politics in France available in English. For a historical perspective, Tilly (1986) remains the single best reference. Kriesi's book (1995) is perhaps the best comparative study of French social movements in the 1980s, even though its reliance on *Le Monde* to assess protest events has been criticized. Hayes (2002) examines environmentalist mobilizations at the local level. In French, Fillieule (1997) presents a rigorous analysis of protests and the police based on police archives rather than newspaper data. Béroud et al. (1998) provide an interesting study of the 1995 strikes. Siméant (1998) discusses the mobilization for the *sans-papiers*. Finally, Crettiez and Sommier (2002) offer a very useful and comprehensive survey of most contemporary social movements in France.

Chapter 6   Gender and Multiculturalism: the Politics of Difference at a Crossroads

For more information on the evolution of gender and politics issues across a wide range of issues under the Fifth Republic, see Jenson and Sineau (1995) and Mazur (1995, 2005). On parity and feminism, Scott (2005a) and Upinard (2007a) are core references. On immigration and anti-discrimination policies, Geddes and Guiraudon (2004) and Guiraudon (2005) are of central importance, as is Favell (1998). On citizenship, Brubaker (1992) remains a classic reference, and Duchesne (2005) makes an insightful contribution. Sabbagh (2004) and Hargreaves (2004) are good on affirmative action and anti-discrimination policy. Finally, the issue of slavery is dealt with by Vergès (2006).

Chapter 7   The Return to a Strong Presidency

Leading analyses of the concept and practice of semi-presidentialism in comparative perspective include Duverger (1986), Elgie (1999), Lijphart (1997) and Skach (2005). On the functioning of the executive under the French Fifth Republic, refer to Bell (2002), Elgie (1993), Hayward and Wright (2002) and Massot (1986). For a first-hand account of the 1958 constitutional projects drafted by Debré, under the direction of de Gaulle, see Debré (1975). With respect to the co-evolution of the executive and the party system since 1958, see Converse and Pierce (1986) and Suleiman (1986).

Chapter 8   Parliament and Political Representation

On Parliament, a good starting place is the special issue of *Pouvoirs* on 'Le parlement' (no. 91, 1999). Camby and Servent (2004) is up to date and concise. Magnette (2004) provides a good comparative overview of the renewal of legislatures in Europe. In English, Knapp (2005) provides a useful account and P. Smith (2006) is definitive on the French Senate.

Chapter 9   Checks, Balances and the New Rules of the Political Game

On the Constitutional Council, the classic studies are those of Stone (1992), Favoreu and Philip (2005) and Avril and Gicquel (2005), while Stone (2000) provides a useful comparative study. On party finance, Pujas and Rhodes (1999) provide a good comparative account. Lascoumes (1999) is an excellent study of corruption, of which Mény (1992) also provides a classic study. Knapp (1991) provides a classic account on the *cumul des mandats*, a theme revisited by A. Francois (2006) and others in a special issue of *French Politics*.

Chapter 10   Territorial Politics in France: le Calme avant la Tempête?

Loughlin (2007) provides a good pedagogic account of sub-national government and territorial politics in France. Cole (2006) and Pasquier (2004) offer detailed accounts of the French regions from a comparative European perspective. Pasquier et al. (2007) combine conceptual sophistication with some good empirical accounts of new forms of territorial governance in France. Smith et al. (2007) provide an innovative study of territoriality and globalization via the wine industry in Bordeaux. Pinson (2008) focuses on processes of planning, while Epstein (2006) identifies new processes of central steering and performance management in the governance of French localities. On the recent turn in decentralization policies, see Le Lidec (2007).

Chapter 11   The Reform of the State: the French Bureaucracy in the Age of New Public Management

Administrative reform policies and the effects of New Public Management have been widely studied in the field of public administration. Among many scholars and for overviews and comparative perspectives, books by Pollitt and Boukaert (2004), Hood and Lodge (2004), Dreyfus and Eymeri (2006) or Page and Wright (2007) are suggestive. On the Budget Act and its aftermaths, see Arthuis (2006), Lambert and Migaud (2006) and Arkwright (2007). Other aspects of the French administration have been studied. On the National Administration School (ENA) as an institution, see Eymeri (2001), and on the effects of reform on ministerial field services, see Cole and Jones (2005). Changes in the French top civil service are explored by Bezès and Le Lidec (2007). The politicization of the civil service is explored by Rouban (2006). Budgetary policy before the Budget Act is examined by Siné (2006).

Chapter 12   Economic Policy

On the classic post-war French model, see Shonfield (1969) and Zysman (1983). On key changes in the 1980s and 1990s, see Clift (2004), Levy (1999), Schmidt (1996) and Hall (1986). On economic policy under the Socialists in the 1990s and early 2000s see Clift (2003). On European economic constraints and French economic policy, see Howarth (2001) and Dyson and Featherstone (1999).

Chapter 13   Between State and Market: Crisis and Transformation in French Industrial Relations

A good overview of French industrial relations since industrialization is Jefferys (2003), while Howell (1992) concentrates on government reform efforts after 1968. For a good account that emphasizes the politics of French trade unionism, see Ross (1982). The best account of more recent developments in French industrial relations is Lallement (2006). Ross (2006) examines the strikes and protests over youth work contracts. Finally, there is a wealth of government statistical analyses and reports on industrial relations at http://www.travail-solidarite. gouv.fr/espaces/travail/771.html

Chapter 14   Welfare Policies and Politics

Though there is an abundant literature on welfare reform in France, certain references stand out. Palier (2004, 2005) are key references on various aspects of France's welfare state. Clegg (2007), Hassenteufel and Palier (2007) and Natali and Rhodes (2004) provide a comparative perspective of unemployment insurance, health care and pension reforms respectively. Wilsford (1993) provides a rare account in English of the French medical profession. Smith (2004) paints a bleak portrait of the future of French welfare.

Chapter 15   France and the World, from Chirac to Sarkozy

Good general, historical accounts of French foreign policy are those of Gordon (1995), Keiger (2001), (2005) and Cogan (2003). Gregory (2000) and Menon (2001) focus more specifically on issues of defence. On the conflict between France and the US over Iraq, Cantaloube and Vernet (2004) and Gordon and Shapiro (2004) provide good accounts. On France and Europe, the key reference is Parsons (2003).

Chapter 16   France and the European Union under the Chirac Presidency

There is an abundant literature on France and Europe. Lequesne (1993), Menon (1996) and Drake (2005c) provide insightful accounts of various aspects of France's relationship with the European Union. Parsons (2003) is a key reference. Ladrech (1994), then Cole and Drake (2000) explored France and Europeanization, a theme dealt with systematically in Meunier (2004) and Grossman (2007), who coordinated a special issue of the *Journal of European Public Policy* dedicated to France's relationship with the European Union.

Bibliography

Alexander, M. S. (ed.) (1999) *French History since Napoleon*. London: Arnold.

Ancelovici, M. (2002) 'Organizing against Globalization: the Case of ATTAC in France'. *Politics and Society* 30 (3): 427–43.

Anders, H. (2006) 'France's 35-Hour Week: Attack on Business? Win–Win Reform? Or Betrayal of Disadvantaged Workers?' *Politics and Society* 34 (4): 503–42.

Andersen, R. and Evans, J. (2003) 'Values, Cleavages and Party Choice in France, 1988–1995'. *French Politics* 1 (1): 83–114.

Ansell, C. and Di Palma, G. (eds) (2004) *Restructuring Territoriality*. Cambridge: Cambridge University Press.

Arkwright, E. (2007) *Economie politique de la LOLF*. Paris: Documentation française.

Armit, A. and Bourgault, J. (1996) *Hard Choices. Assessing Program Review*. Toronto: Institute of Public Administration of Canada.

Arthuis, J. (2006) 'La première discussion budgétaire «en mode LOLF». Un véritable pouvoir d'arbitrage exercé par le Parlement'. Report no. 312 (2005–2006), 12 April 2006, Paris, Senate.

Assemblée Nationale (2005) *Rapport sur l'évolution de la fiscalité locale*. Document no. 2436, July.

Auby, J.B. (2006) *La Décentralisation et le droit*. Paris: LGDJ.

Avril, P. (1965) 'Le vote bloqué'. *Revue de droit public et de la science politique* 3: 399–457.

Avril P. and Gicquel, J. (2005) *Le Conseil constitutionnel*. Paris: Montchrestien.

Bachelet, F. (2005) 'Les hauts fonctionnaires intercommunaux'. *Les Annales de la recherche urbaine* 99:119–25.

Bachelet, F., Menerault, P. and Paris, D. (eds) (2006) *Action publique et projet métropolitain*. Paris: L'Harmattan.

Bacqué, M.H., Rey, H. and Sintomer, Y. (eds) (2005) *Gestion de proximité et démocratie participative*. Paris: La Découverte.

Balme, R. and Woll, C. (2005) 'France: between Integration and National Sovereignty'. In Bulmer, S. and Lequesne, C. (eds) *The Member States of the European Union*. Oxford: Oxford University Press.

Balme, R., Faure, A. and Mabileau, A. (1999) *Politiques locales et transformations de l'action publique locale en Europe*. Paris: Presses de Sciences Po.

Baraize, F. and Négrier, E. (eds) (2001) *L'invention politique de l'agglomération*. Paris: L'Harmattan.

Barthélemy, M. (2000) *Associations: Un nouvel âge de la participation?* Paris, Presses de Sciences Po.

Bartolini, S. and Mair, P. (1990) *Identity, Competition and Electoral Availability: the Stabilisation of European Electorates, 1885–1985*. Cambridge: Cambridge University Press.

Bauby, P. and Varone, F. (2007) 'Europeanization of the French Electricity Policy: Four Paradoxes'. *Journal of European Public Policy* 14 (7): 1048–60.

Baverez, N. (2003) *La France qui tombe*. Paris: Perrin.

Beffa, J.-L. (2005) *Pour une nouvelle politique industrielle*. Paris: Documentation française.

Bell, D. (2002) *Presidential Power in the Fifth French Republic*. Oxford: Berg.

Belot, C. and Cautrès, B. (2004) 'L'Europe, invisible mais omniprésente ?' In Cautrès, B. and Mayer, N. (eds) *Le nouveau désordre électoral*. Paris: Presses de Sciences Po, pp. 119–41.

Ben Mabrouk, T. (2006) *Le pouvoir d'agglomération en France, logique d'émergence et modes de fonctionnement*. Paris: L'Harmattan.

Benoit, O. (2003) 'Les chambres régionales des comptes face aux élus locaux: les effets inattendus d'une institution'. *Revue française de science politique* 53 (4): 535–58.

Berger, S. (1974) *The French Political System*. New York: Random House.

Beriss, D. (2004) 'Culture-as-Race or Culture-as-Culture: Caribbean Ethnicity and the Ambiguity of Cultural Identity in French Society'. In Chapman, H. and Frader, L. L. (eds) *Race in France, Interdisciplinary Perspectives on the Politics of Difference*. New York: Berghahn Books.

Béroud, S., Mouriaux, R. and Vakaloulis, M. (1998) *Le mouvement social en France: Essai de sociologie politique*. Paris: La Dispute.

Bezès, P. (2001) 'Defensive versus Offensive Approaches to Administrative Reform in France (1988–1997): the Leadership Dilemmas of French Prime Ministers'. *Governance* 14 (1): 99–132.

Bezès, P. (2005) 'Le modèle de "l'Etat-Stratège": genèse d'une forme organisationnelle dans l'administration française'. *Sociologie du travail* 4: 431–50.

Bezès, P. (2007) 'The Hidden Politics of Administrative Reform: Cutting French Civil Service Wages with a Low-Profile Instrument'. *Governance* 20 (1): 23–56.

Bezès, P. and Le Lidec, P. (2007) 'French Top Civil Servants within Changing Configurations. From Monopolisation to Challenged Places and Roles?' In Page, E. and Wright, V. (eds) *From the Active to the Enabling State. The Changing Roles of Top Officials in European Nations*. Basingstoke: Palgrave Macmillan.

Birnbaum, P. and Badie, B. (1982) *Sociologie de l'État*. Paris: Grasset.

Blais, A. (2006) 'The Causes and Consequences of the *Cumul des Mandats*'. *French Politics* 4 (3): 266–8.

Blanchard, O-J. and Muet, P-A. (1993) 'Competitiveness through Disinflation: an Assessment of French Macro-Economic Strategy'. *Economic Policy* 16: 12–50.

Bleich, E. (2003) *Race Politics in Britain and France: Ideas and Policymaking since the 1960s*. Cambridge: Cambridge University Press.

Blondiaux, L. (ed.) (1999) *La Démocratie locale: représentation, participation et espace public*. Paris: PUF.

Bogdanor, V. (1984) *What is Proportional Representation? A Guide to the Issues*. Oxford: Martin Robertson.

Borraz, O. (2000) 'Le gouvernement municipal en France. Un modèle d'intégration en recomposition'. *Pôle Sud* 13: 1–26.

Borraz, O. and Le Galès, P. (2005) 'Local Government in France: Intercommunal Revolution and New Forms of Governance'. In Denters, B. and Rose, L. (eds) *Comparing Local Governance: Trends and Developments* Basingstoke: Palgrave Macmillan.

Boy, D. and Chiche, J. (2007) 'L'image des candidats dans la décision électorale'. *Revue française de science politique* 57 (3–4): 329–42.

Bras, P-L. (2006) 'Le médecin traitant: raisons et déraison d'une politique publique'. *Droit Social* 1: 59–72.

Bréchon, P. (2007) 'Logiques d'inscription, logiques d'abstention'. *Revue politique et parlementaire* 1044: 58–67.

Bréchon, P., Cautrès, B. and Denni, B. (1995) 'L'évolution des attitudes à l'égard de l'Europe'. In Perrineau, P. and Ysmal, C. (eds) *Le vote des douze: les élections européennes de juin 1994*. Paris: Presses de Sciences Po.

Brouard, S. and Tiberj, V. (2006). 'Déclin, modèle français et mondialisation'. *Baromètre Politique Français (2006–2007)*. Paris: CEVIPOF–Ministère de l'Intérieur, pp. 1–16.

Brubaker, R. (1992) *Citizenship and Nationhood in France and Germany*. Cambridge: Harvard University Press.

Buller, H. (2004) 'France: Getting between the Vertical'. In Jordan, A. and Liefferink, D. (eds) *Environmental Policy in Europe. The Europeanization of National Environmental Policy*. London: Routledge.

Caillosse, J., Le Galès, P. and Loncle, P. (1997) 'Les sociétés d'économie mixte locales en France. Outils de quelle action publique urbaine? In CNRS (collectif) *L'Action publique urbaine et les contrats*. Paris: Descartes.

Camby, J.-P. and Servent, P. (2004) *Le travail parlementaire sous la Cinquième Republique*. Paris: Montchrestien.

Cameron, D.R. (1996) 'National Interest, the Dilemmas of European Integration, and Malaise'. In Keeler, J. and Schain, M. (eds) *Chirac's Challenge. Liberalization, Europeanization and Malaise in France*. New York: St Martin's Press.

Campbell, J. and Pedersen, O. (2007) 'The Varieties of Capitalism and Hybrid Success: Denmark in the Global Economy'. *Comparative Political Studies* 40 (3): 307–22.

Cantaloube, T. and Vernet, H. (2004) *Chirac contre Bush: l'autre guerre*. Paris: Lattès.

Caporaso, J., Green Cowles, M. and Risse, T. (eds) (2001) *Transforming Europe*. Ithaca: Cornell University Press.

Cautrès, B. and Mayer, N. (eds) (2004) *Le Nouvel desordre électoral*. Paris: Presses de Sciences Po.

CEVIPOF (1995) *Post Electoral Survey*, Paris: CEVIPOF. Available at: http://cdsp. sciences-po.fr/enquetes.php?idTheme=idTheme=1&idRubrique=enquetes FR&lang=FR.

CEVIPOF (2002) *Panel Electoral Français*, Paris: CEVIPOF. Available at: http:// cdsp.sciences-po.fr/enquetes.php?idTheme=idTheme=1&idRubrique=enquetes FR&lang=FR.

CEVIPOF-Ministère de l'Intérieur (2007) *Baromètre Politique Français: Résultats d'ensemble, 4e vague* Paris, CEVIPOF (http://www.cevipof.msh-paris.fr/bpf/ barometre/vague4/001/R15581BPF41_%20Ensemble.pdf).

Chagnollaud, D. and Quermonne, J.-L. (1996) *Le gouvernement de la France sous la Vᵉ République*. Paris: Fayard.

Charlot, J. (1967) *L'U.N.R.* Paris: Armand Colin.

Charlot, J. (1995) *Pourquoi Jacques Chirac?* Paris: Éditions de Fallois.

Chevallier, J. (1995) 'Les autorités administratives indépendantes et la régulation des marchés'. *Justices* 1: 81–90.

Christin, T. and Hug, S. (2002) 'Referendums and Citizen Support for European Integration'. *Comparative Political Studies* 35: 586–617.

Clegg, D. (2007) 'Continental Drift: on Unemployment Policy Change in Bismarckian Welfare States'. *Social Policy and Administration* forthcoming.

Clift, B. (2003) *French Socialism in a Global Era: the Political Economy of the New Social Democracy in France*. London: Continuum.

Clift, B. (2004) 'The French Model of Capitalism: *Still* Exceptional?' In Perraton, J. and Clift, B. (eds) *Where Are National Capitalisms Now?* Basingstoke: Palgrave Macmillan.

Clift, B. (2006) 'The New Political Economy of Dirigisme: French Macroeconomic Policy, Unrepentant Sinning, and the Stability and Growth Pact'. *British Journal of Politics and International Relations* 8 (3): 388–409.

Cogan, C. (2003) *French Negotiating Behaviour. Dealing with La Grande Nation*. Washington, DC: United States Institute of Peace Press.

Cohen, E. (1992) *Le Colbertisme high tech. Economie des Télécom et du Grand Projet*. Paris: Hachette.

Cohen, E. (1996) *La Tentation hexagonale*. Paris: Fayard.

Cohen, E. (1998) 'A *Dirigiste* End to *Dirigisme?*' In Maclean, M. (ed.) *The Mitterrand Years: Legacy and Evaluation*. Basingstoke: Macmillan.

Cohen-Tanugi, L. (1992) *Le droit sans l'État: sur la démocratie en France et en Amérique*. Paris: PUF.

Cole, A. (1993) 'The Presidential Party and the Fifth Republic'. *West European Politics* 16 (2): 86–103.

Cole, A. (2006) *Beyond Devolution and Decentralisation. Building Regional Capacity in Wales and Brittany*. Manchester: Manchester University Press.

Cole, A. (2008) *Governing and Governance in France*. Cambridge: Cambridge University Press.

Cole, A. and Drake, H. (2000) 'The Europeanization of the French Polity: Continuity, Change and Adaptation'. *Journal of European Public Policy* 7 (1): 26–43.

Cole, A. and John, P. (2001) *Local Governance in England and France*. London: Routledge.

Cole, A. and Jones, G. (2005) 'Reshaping the State: Administrative Reform and New Public Management in France'. *Governance* 18 (4): 567–88.

Cole, A., Le Galès, P. and Levy, J. (2005) *Developments in French Politics 3*. Basingstoke: Palgrave Macmillan.

Colton, T. J. and Skach, C. (2005) 'The Russian Predicament'. *Journal of Democracy* 16 (3): 113–26.

Comité d'Orientation des Retraites (COR) (2007) *Retraites: questions et orientations pour 2008*, 4th report. Paris.

Commissariat Général du Plan (2000) *Fonctions Publiques: enjeux et stratégie pour le renouvellement*. Paris: Documentation française.

Conant, L. (2006) 'Individuals, Courts, and the Development of European Social Rights'. *Comparative Political Studies* 39 (1): 76–100.

Conseil d'État (2003) *Rapport Public 2003: Perspectives pour la fonction publique*. Paris: Documentation française.

Converse, P. E. and Pierce, R. (1986) *Political Representation in France*. Cambridge: Harvard University Press.

Cour des Comptes (2003a) *La déconcentration des administrations et la réforme de l'État*. Paris: Cour des Comptes.

Cour des Comptes (2003b) *Rapport Public: la déconcentration des administrations et la réforme de l'État*. Paris: les éditions des journaux officiels.

Coutard, O. (2001) *Le bricolage organisationnel: crise des cadres hiérarchiques et innovations dans la gestion des entreprises et des territoires*. Paris: Elsevier.

Crane, G. (1998) 'Economic Nationalism: Bringing the Nation back in'. *Millennium* 27 (1): 55–75.

Creel, J., Dupont, G., Le Cacheax, J., Sterdyniak, H. and Timbeau, X. (2002) 'Budget 2003: Le pécheur non repenti'. *La Lettre de l'OFCE* 224: 1–4.

Crettiez, X. and Sommier, I. (eds) (2002) *La France rebelle*. Paris: Michallon.

Crozier, M. (1963) *Le phénomène bureaucratique*. Paris: Le Seuil.

Crozier, M. (1987) *État moderne, État modeste*. Paris: Grasset.

CSA-CISCO (2007) *Les élections législatives: explication du vote et perspectives politiques, juin 2007* (http://csa-fr.com/dataset/data2007/opi20070610-les-elections-legislatives-explication-du-vote-et-perspectives-politiques.pdf).

Culpepper, P. (2006) 'Capitalism, Coordination and Economic Change: the French Political Economy since 1985'. In Culpepper, P., Hall, P. and Palier, B. (eds) *Changing France. The Politics that Markets Make*. Basingstoke: Palgrave Macmillan.

Culpepper, P., Hall, P. and Palier, B. (eds) (2006) *Changing France. The Politics that Markets Make*. Basingstoke: Palgrave Macmillan.

Daudin, G. and Levasseur, S. (2005) 'Delocalisations et concurrence des pays emergents: mesurer l'effet sur l'emploi en France'. *Revue de l'OFCE* July: 131–60.

Davezies, L. (2001) 'Revenu et territoires'. In *Aménagement du Territoire, Rapport du Conseil d'Analyse Économique*. Paris: Documentation française.

Debrand, T. and Or, Z. (2005) 'Solidarity Fund for Financing Dependency'. *Health Policy Monitor* (available at http://www.hpm.org/survey/fr/a6/5).

Debré, J-L. (1975) *La Constitution de la Vᵉ Republique*. Paris: PUF.

Dehousse, R. (1998) *The European Court of Justice. The Politics of Judicial Integration*. Basingstoke: Palgrave Macmillan.

Della Porta, D. (2005) 'The Social Bases of the Global Justice Movement: Some Theoretical Reflections and Empirical Evidence from the First European Social Forum'. Programme Paper No. 21, Civil Society and Social Movements, United Nations Research Institute for Social Development (UNRISD).

Dély, R. (1999) *Histoire secrète du Front national*. Paris: Grasset.

Desjardin, X. (2006) *Intercommunalité et décentralisation, les recompositions territoriales sous le regard des chercheurs*. Rapport PUCA/Université Lumière Lyon 2.

De Vreese, C. H. (2005) 'Why European Citizens will Reject the EU Constitution'. *Center for European Studies*, Harvard University, working paper 116.

Dewoghélaëre, J., Magni Berton, R. and Navarro, J. (2006) 'The *Cumul des Mandats* in Contemporary French Politics: an Empirical Study of the XIIe Législature of the Assemblée Nationale'. *French Politics* 4 (3): 312–32.

Dimier, V. (2003) 'Institutionnalisation et bureaucratisation dans la Commission européenne: le cas de la DG DEV'. *Politique Européenne* 11: 35–44.

Dimier, V. (2004) *Le gouvernement des colonies: regards croisés franco-britanniques*. Brussels: Editions de l'Université de Bruxelles.

Dimitrakopoulos, P.G. (2001) 'The Transposition of EU Law: Post-Decisional Politics and Institutional Economy. *European Law Journal* 7 (4): 442–58.

Direction Générale des Collectivités Locales (2005) *Les collectivités locales en chiffres 2004–2005*. Paris: Ministère de l'Intérieur.

Douillet, A. C. (2003) 'Les élus ruraux face à la territorialisation de l'action publique'. *Revue française de science politique* 53 (4): 583–606.

Dourgnon, P. (2006) 'Preferred Doctor Reform'. *Health Policy Monitor*, available at http://www.hpm.org/survey/fr/a8/2

Drake, H. (2005a) 'Jacques Chirac's Balancing Acts: the French Right and Europe'. *South European Society and Politics* 10 (2): 297–313.

Drake, H. (2005b) 'Perspectives on French Relations with the European Union: an Introduction'. In Drake, H. (ed.) *French Relations with the European Union*. London: Routledge.

Drake, H. (ed.) (2005c) *French Relations with the European Union*. London: Routledge.

Dreyfus, F. and Eymeri, J.-M. (eds) (2006) *Sociologie politique de l'administration*. Paris: Economica.

Duchesne, S. (2005) 'Identities, Nationalism, Citizenship and Republican Ideology'. In Cole, A., Le Galès, P. and Levy, L. (eds) *Developments in French Politics 3*. Basingstoke: Palgrave Macmillan.

Duchesne, S. and Frognier, A.-P. (2002) 'Sur les dynamiques sociologiques et politiques de l'identification à l'Europe'. *Revue française de science politique* 52 (4): 355–73.

Dudouet, F.-X., Mercier, D. and Vion, A. (2006) 'Politiques internationales de normalisation: quelques jalons pour la recherche empirique'. *Revue française de science politique* 56 (3): 367–92.

Duhamel, O. (1999) *Droit constitutionnel. Le pouvoir politique en France*. Paris: Seuil.

Duhamel, O. (2007) '2007: une présidentielle très nouvelle'. In *SOFRES: L'État de l'opinion 2007*. Paris: Éditions du Seuil.

Dupoirier, E. (2007) 'L'électorat présidentiel de Ségolène Royal. Premiers éléments d'analyse'. *Revue française de science politique* 57 (3–4): 475–87.

Dupuy, C. and Le Galès, P. (2006) 'The Impact of Regional Governments'. In Greer, S. (ed.) *Territory, Democracy and Justice. Regionalism and Federalism in Western Democracies*. Basingstoke: Palgrave Macmillan, pp. 101–26.

Dupuy, F. and Thoenig, J.-C. (1985) *L'administration en miettes*. Paris: Fayard.

Duran, P. and Thoenig, J.-C. (1996) 'L'État et la gestion publique territoriale'. *Revue française de science politique* 4: 580–622.

Duverger, M. (1951) *Les Partis politiques*. Paris: Armand Colin.

Duverger, M. (1986) *Les régimes semi-présidentiels*. Paris: PUF.

Dyson, K. (1980) *The State Tradition in Western Europe*. Oxford: Martin Robertson.

Dyson, K. and Featherstone, K. (1999) *The Road to Maastricht: Negotiating Economic and Monetary Union*. Oxford: Oxford University Press.

Eichenberg, R. C. (1998) 'Measurement Matters: Cumulation in the Study of Citizen Support for European Integration'. Paper presented at the American Political Science Association Conference, Washington, DC.

Elgie, R. (1993) *The Role of the Prime Minister in France, 1981–1991*. London: Palgrave Macmillan.

Elgie, R. (ed.) (1999) *Semi-Presidentialism in Europe*. Oxford: Oxford University Press.

Emmanuel, W. (2007) *Nicolas Sarkozy, La Fringale du Pouvoir*. Paris: Flammarion.

Endo, K. (1999) *The Presidency of the European Commission under Jacques Delors*. Basingstoke: Palgrave Macmillan.

Epstein, R. (2005) 'Gouverner à distance, quand l'État se retire des territoires'. *Esprit* 11: 96–111.

Estebe, P. and Le Galès, P. (2003) 'La métropole parisienne, à la recherche du pilote?' *Revue française d'administration publique* 107: 345–56.

European Commission (2007) 'Commission Staff Working Document: Report on the Implementation of the Directive on Takeover Bids' (http://ec.europa. eu/internal_market/company/docs/takeoverbids/2007-02-report_en.pdf).

Evans, J. (2003) 'Introduction'. In Evans, J. (ed.) *The French Party System*. Manchester: Manchester University Press.

Evans, J. (2007) 'The European Dimension in the French Public Opinion'. *Journal of European Public Policy* 14: 1098–116.

Eymeri, J.-M. (2001) *La fabrique des enarques*. Paris: Economica.

Falkner, G., Treib, O., Hartlapp, M. and Leiber, S. (2005) *Complying with Europe: EU Harmonization and Soft Law in the Member States*. Cambridge: Cambridge University Press.

Faure, A. (1994) 'Les élus locaux à l'épreuve de la décentralisation. De nouveaux chantiers pour la médiation politique locale'. *Revue française de science politique* 44 (3): 462–79.

Faure, A. (1997) 'Les apprentissages du métier d'élu local: la tribu, le système et les arènes'. *Pôle sud* 7: 72–9.

Faure, A. and Douillet, C. (eds) (2005) *L'action publique et la question territoriale*. Grenoble: Presses Universitaires de Grenoble.

Favell, A. (1998) *Philosophies of Integration. Immigration and the Idea of Citizenship in France and Britain*. Basingstoke: Palgrave Macmillan.

Favell, A. (2005) 'Europe's Identity Problem'. *West European Politics* 28: 1109–16.

Favier, P. and Martin-Roland, M. (1990) *La décennie Mitterrand. 1. Les ruptures (1981–1984)*. Paris: Seuil.

Favier, P. and Martin-Roland, M. (1996) *La décennie Mitterrand. 4. Les déchirements*. Paris: Seuil.

Favoreu, L. (1988) *La politique saisie par le droit: alternances, cohabitation et Conseil constitutionnel*. Paris: Economica.

Favoreu, L. (2007) *Droit constitutionnel*. Paris: Dalloz.

Favoreu, L. and Philip, L. (2005) *Le Conseil constitutionnel*. Paris: PUF.

Featherstone, K. and Radaelli, C. (eds) (2003) *The Politics of Europeanization*. Oxford: Oxford University Press.

Fillieule, O. (1997) *La stratégie de la rue*. Paris: Presses de Sciences Po.

Fitoussi, J.-P. (1995) *Le débat interdit: Monnaie, Europe, Pauvreté*. Paris: Arléa.

Flynn, G. (1995) *Remaking the Hexagon. The New France in the New Europe*. Boulder: Westview Press.

Foucault, M. (2006) 'How Useful is the *Cumul des Mandats* for Being Reelected? Empirical Evidence from the 1997 French Legislative Elections'. *French Politics* 4 (3): 292–311.

Fourquet, J. (2007) 'L'échec de Jean-Marie Le Pen à la présidentielle de 2007: les causes d'une hémorragie'. *Panel Électoral Français 2007, Enquête post élection présidentielle 2007*. Paris: CEVIPOF (http://www.cevipof.msh-paris.fr/bpf/analyses/Fourquet_Le%20pen2007.pdf).

François, A. (2006) 'Testing the "Baobab Tree" Hypothesis: the *Cumul des Mandats* as a Way of Obtaining More Political Resources and Limiting Electoral Competition'. *French Politics* 4 (3): 269–91.

Francois, B. (2006) *Le régime politique de la Ve République*. Paris: La Découverte.

Franklin, M. N. (2002) 'Learning from the Danish Case'. *European Journal of Political Research* 41 (6): 751–7.

Franklin, M. N. and Van Der Eijck, C. (2004) 'Potential for Contestation on European Matters at National Elections in Europe'. In Marks, G. and Steenbergen, M. (eds) *European Integration and Political Conflict*. Cambridge: Cambridge University Press.

Franklin, M. N., Mclaren, L. M. and Marsh, M. (1994) 'Uncorking the Bottle: Popular Opposition to European Unification in the Wake of Maastricht'. *Journal of Common Market Studies* 32 (4): 455–72.

Frémontier, J. (1990) *Les cadets de la droite*. Paris: Éditions du Seuil.

Gabel, M. (1998) *Interests and Integration: Market Liberalization, Public Opinion, and European Union*. Ann Arbor: University of Michigan Press.

Gaffney, J. (ed.) (1996) *Political Parties and the European Union*. London: Routledge.

Gally, N. (2007) 'Démanteler l'Ena? Une sociologie de la réforme d'une institution (2002–2004)'. Unpublished dissertation, Paris: Sciences-Po.

Garry, J., Marsh, M. and Sinnott, R. (2005) '"Second-Order" versus "Issue-voting" Effects in EU Referendums: Evidence from the Irish Nice Treaty Referendums'. *European Union Politics* 6 (2): 201–21.

Gaspard, F., Servan-Schreiber, C. and LeGall, A. (1992) *Au pouvoir citoyennes! Égalité, liberté, parité*. Paris: Seuil.

Gaudin, J.-P. (2007) *Gouverner par contrat*. Paris: Presses de Sciences Po.

Geddes, A. and Guiraudon, V. (2004) 'Britain, France and EU Anti-Discrimination Policy: the Emergence of an EU Policy Paradigm'. *West European Politics* 27(2): 334–53.

Gilbert, G. (1999) 'L'autonomie financière des collectivités locales est-elle en question?' *Les 2ème entretiens de la Caisse des Dépôts et Consignations*. La Tour d'Aigues: Éditions de l'Aube.

Gilbert, G. and Thoenig, J.-C. (1999) 'Les cofinancements publics – des pratiques aux rationalités'. *Revue d'économie financière* 1: 7–40.

Gobille, B. and Aysen, U. (2005) 'Cosmopolites et enracinés'. In Agrikoliansky, E. and Sommier, I. (eds) *Radiographie du mouvement altermondialiste: Forum social européen 2003*. Paris: La Dispute.

Gordon, P. (1995) *France, Germany and the Western Alliance*. Boulder: Westview Press.

Gordon, P. and Meunier, S. (2001) *The French Challenge: Adapting to Globalisation*. Washington: Brookings Institution Press.

Gordon, P. and Shapiro, J. (2004) *Allies at War: America, Europe, and the Crisis over Iraq*. McGraw-Hill.

Goyer, M. (2001) 'Corporate Governance and the Innovation System in France: 1985–2000'. *Industry and Innovation* 8(2): 135–58.

Goyer, M. (2003) 'Corporate Governance, Employees, and the Focus on Core Competencies in France and Germany'. In Milhaupt, C. (ed.)

Global Markets, Domestic Institutions. New York: Columbia University Press.

Gregory, S. (2000) *French Defence Policy into the Twenty-First Century*. Basingstoke: Palgrave Macmillan.

Gremion, P. (1976) *Le pouvoir périphérique: bureaucrates et notables dans le système politique français*. Paris: Le Seuil.

Grignon, F. (2004) *Sénat rapport d'information fait au nom de la commission des Affaires économiques et du Plan par le groupe de travail sur la delocalisation des industries de main d'œuvre*. Paris: Documentation française.

Grossman, E. (2007) 'Introduction: France and the EU: from Opportunity to Constraint'. *Journal of European Public Policy* 14 (7): 983–91.

Grossman, E. and Sauger, N. (2007) 'Political Institutions under Stress? Assessing the Impact of European Integration on French Political Institutions'. *Journal of European Public Policy* 14 (7): 1117–34.

Grunberg, G. and Haegel, F. (2007) *La France vers le bipartisme? La présidentialisation du PS et de l'UMP*. Paris: Presses de Sciences Po.

Grunberg, G. and Schweisguth, E. (1997) 'Vers une tripartition de l'espace politique'. In Boy, D. and Mayer, N. (eds) *L'électeur a ses raisons*. Paris: Presses de Sciences Po.

Grunberg, G., Perrineau, P. and Ysmal, C. (eds) (2002) *Europe at the Polls*. New York and Basingstoke: Palgrave Macmillan.

Gueranger, D. (2004) 'L'impensé de la réforme intercommunale, la mise en place administrative des communautés d'agglomération'. *Revue française d'administration publique* 111: 461–72.

Guillaume, H., Dureau, G. and Silvent, F. (2000) *Mission d'analyse comparative des systèmes de gestion de la performance et de leur articulation sur le budget de l'État*. Paris: Inspection Général des Finances.

Guiraudon, V. (2000) 'European Integration and Migration Policy. Vertical Policy-Making as Venue Shopping'. *Journal of Common Market Studies* 38 (2): 251–71.

Guiraudon, V. (2005) 'Immigration Politics and Policies'. In Cole, A., Le Galès, P. and Levy, J. (eds) *Developments in French Politics 3*. Basingstoke: Palgrave Macmillan.

Guyomarch, A. (2001) 'The Europeanization of Policy Making'. In Guyomarch, A., Machin, H., Hall, P. and Hayward, J. (eds) *Developments in French Politics 2*. Basingstoke: Palgrave Macmillan.

Guyomarch, A., Machin, H. and Ritchie, E. (1998). *France in the European Union*. Basingstoke: Palgrave Macmillan.

Haegel, F. (2004) 'The Transformation of the French Right: Institutional Imperatives and Organisational Changes'. *French Politics* 2 (2): 185–202.

Haegel, F. (ed.) (2007a) *Partis politiques et système partisan en France*. Paris: Presses de Sciences Po.

Haegel, F. (2007b) 'Le pluralisme à l'UMP: structuration idéologique et compétition interne'. In Haegel, F. (ed.) *Partis politiques et système partisan en France*. Paris: Presses de Sciences Po.

Hainsworth, P. (2006) 'Frances Says No: the 29 May 2005 Referendum on the European Constitution'. *Parliamentary Affairs* 59 (1): 98–117.

Hall, P. (1986) *Governing the Economy*. Cambridge: Polity.

Hall, P. (1990) 'The State and the Market'. In Hall, P., Hayward, J. and Machin, H. (eds) *Developments in French Politics*. Basingstoke: Macmillan.

Hall, P. (2006) 'Introduction: the Politics of Social Change in France'. In Culpepper, P., Hall, P. and Palier, B. (eds) *Changing France. The Politics that Markets Make*. Basingstoke: Palgrave Macmillan.

Hall, P. and Soskice, D. (2001) 'An Introduction to Varieties of Capitalism'. In Hall, P. and Soskice, D. (eds) *Varieties of Capitalism*. Oxford: Oxford University Press.

Hancké, B. (2001) 'Revisiting the French Model: Coordination and Restructuring in French Industry'. In Soskice, D. and Hall, P. (eds) *Varieties of Capitalism*. Oxford: Oxford University Press.

Hanley, D. (1999) 'Compromise, Party Management and Fair Shares: the Case of the French UDF'. *Party Politics* 5 (2): 171–89.

Hanley, D. (2002) *Party, Society, Government: Republican Democracy in France*. Oxford: Berghahn.

Hargreaves, A. (2004) 'Half-Measures: Anti-Discrimination Policy in France'. In Chapman, H. and Frader, L. (eds) *Race in France, Interdisciplinary Perspectives on the Politics of Difference*. New York: Berghahn Books.

Hassenteufel, P. (2003) 'Le premier septennat du plan Juppé: un non-changement décisif'. In De Kervasdoué, J. (ed.) *Carnet de santé de la France 2003*. Paris: Dunod.

Hassenteufel, P. (2007) 'New Policy Elites and the Growth of the Regulatory Health Care State in Europe'. ECPR Joint Sessions, Helsinki.

Hassenteufel, P. and Palier, B. (2005) 'Les trompe-l'œil de la "gouvernance" de l'assurance maladie. Contrastes franco-allemands'. *Revue française d'administration publique* 113: 13–28.

Hassenteufel, P. and Palier, B. (2007) 'Towards Neo-Bismarckian Health Care States? Comparing Health Insurance Reforms in Bismarckian Countries'. *Social Policy and Administration*, forthcoming.

Hayden, A. (2006) 'France's 35-hour Week: Attack on Business? Win–Win Reform? or Betrayal of Disadvantaged Workers?' *Politics and Society* 34(4): 503–42.

Hayes, G. (2002) *Environmental Protest and the State in France*. Basingstoke: Palgrave Macmillan.

Hayward, J. and Wright, V. (2002) *Governing from the Centre: Core Executive Coordination in France*. Oxford: Oxford University Press.

Hazareesingh, S. (1994) *Political Traditions in Modern France*. Oxford: Oxford University Press.

Heidenheimer, A. (1978) *Political Corruption*. New Brunswick: Transaction.

Heilbroner, R. (1992) *The Worldly Philosophers*. New York: Touchstone.

Helleiner, E. (2002) 'Economic Nationalism as a Challenge to Economic Liberalism? Lessons from the 19th Century'. *International Studies Quarterly* 46 (3): 307–29.

Herzog, R. (2006) 'Quelques aspects de la loi organique relative aux lois de finances dans ses rapports avec le système administratif'. *Actualités Juridiques-Droit Administratif (AJDA)*, 13 March: 531–8.

Heyer, E., Plane, M. and Timbeau, X. (2007) 'Le "Choc" fiscal tiendra-t-il ses promesses?' *Lettre de l'OFCE* 288: 1–8.

Hoffman-Martinot, V. (1999) 'Les grandes villes françaises: une démocratie en souffrance'. In Gabriel, O.W. and Hoffmann-Martinot, V. (eds) *Démocraties urbaines. L'état de la démocratie dans les grandes villes de 12 pays industrialisés*. Paris: L'Harmattan.

Hood, C. and Lodge, M. (2004) 'Competency, Bureaucracy and the Orthodoxies of Public Management Reform: a Comparative Analysis'. *Governance* 17 (3): 313–33.

Hood, C., Scott, C., James, O., Jones, G. and Travers, T. (1999) *Regulation inside Government. Waste-Watchers, Quality Police and Sleaze-Busters*. Oxford: Oxford University Press.

Hooghe, L. and Marks, G. (2001) *Multilevel Governance and European Integration*. Lanham: Rowman & Littlefield.

Howarth, D. (2001) *The French Road to European Monetary Union*. Basingstoke: Palgrave Macmillan.

Howarth, D. (2002) 'The French State in the Euro Zone'. In Dyson, K. (ed.) *European States and the Euro-Zone*. Oxford: Oxford University Press.

Howarth, D. (2004) 'Rhetorical Divergence, Real Convergence? The Economic Policy Debate in the 2002 French Presidential and Legislative Elections'. In Gaffney, J. (ed.) *The French Presidential and Legislative Elections of 2002*. Aldershot: Ashgate, pp. 200–21.

Howell, C. (1992) *Regulating Labor: the State and Industrial Relations Reform in Postwar France*. Princeton: Princeton University Press.

Hug, S. (2002) *Voices of Europe: Citizens, Referendums, and European Integration*. Lanham: Rowman & Littlefield.

Hug, S. and Schulz, T. (2005) 'Using Mass Survey Data to Infer Political Positions'. *European Union Politics* 6 (3): 339–52.

Imig, D. and Tarrow, S. (eds) (2001) *Contentious Europeans: Protest and Politics in an Emerging Polity*. Lanham: Rowman & Littlefield.

Inglehart, R. (1997) *Modernization and Post-Modernization: Cultural, Economic and Political Change in 43 Societies*. Princeton: Princeton University Press.

IPSOS (2007) '1er tour présidentielle 2007' (http://www.ipsos.fr/CanalIpsos/poll8427.asp).

IRES (2005) *Les mutations de l'emploi en France*. Paris: La Découverte.

Jabko, N. (2004) 'The Importance of Being Nice: a Institutionalist Analysis of French Preferences on the Future of Europe'. *Comparative European Politics* 2 (3): 282–301.

Jacod, O. (2007) 'Les institutions représentatives du personnel'. *Première synthèses informations* 5, 1.

Jaffré, J. (2006a) 'La défiance politique, enjeu crucial de 2007'. Baromètre politique français (2006–2007) Paris, CEVIPOF/Ministère de l'Intérieur, 2nd wave, autumn (http://www.cevipof.msh-paris.fr/bpf/barometre/vague2/v2-synthese/BPF-V2_Jaffre_DefiancePol.pdf).

Jaffré, J. (2006b) 'Le paradoxe Le Pen'. Baromètre politique français (2006–2007) CEVIPOF/Ministère de l'Intérieur, 3rd wave, winter 2006 (http://www.cevipof.msh-paris.fr/bpf/barometre/vague3/v3-synthese/JJ-rapport_BPF_V3.pdf).

Jan, P. (1999) *La saisine du Conseil constitutionnel*. Paris: LGDJ.

Jefferys, S. (2003) *Liberté, Égalité and Fraternité at Work: Changing French Employment Relations and Management*. Basingstoke: Palgrave Macmillan.

Jelen, B. (2005) '"Leur histoire est notre histoire". Immigrant Culture in France between Visibility and Invisibility'. *French Politics, Culture and Society* 23(2): 101–25.

Jenson, J. and Sineau, M. (1995) *Mitterrand et les françaises: un rendez-vous manqué*. Paris: Presses de Sciences Po.

Jessop, R. (1995) 'The Regulation Approach, Governance and Post-Fordism: Alternative Perspectives on Economic and Political Change'. *Economy and Society* 24: 307–33.

Jones, G. (2006) 'Why Public Sector Reform does not Transform: a Processual Explanation of the 1989–1997 French Experience'. *International Journal of Public Sector Management* 19: 79–94.

Kassim, H. (1997) 'French Autonomy and the European Union'. *Modern and Contemporary France* 5 (2): 167–80.

Kassim, H. (2005) 'The Europeanization of Member State Institutions'. In Bulmer, S. and Lequesne, C. (eds) *The Member States of the European Union*. Oxford: Oxford University Press.

Keating, M. (1998) *The New Regionalism in Western Europe*. Aldershot: Edward Elgar.

Keiger, J. (2001) *France and the World since 1870*. Oxford: Oxford University Press.

Keiger, J. (2005) 'Foreign and Defence Policy'. In Cole, A., Le Galès, P. and Levy, J. (eds), *Development in French Politics 3*. Basingstoke: Palgrave Macmillan.

Knapp A. (1991) 'The Cumul des Mandats, Local Power and Political Parties'. *West European Politics* 14 (1): 18–40.

Knapp, A. (2004a) *Parties and the Party System in France: a Disconnected Democracy?* Basingstoke: Palgrave Macmillan.

Knapp, A. (2004b) 'Ephemeral Victories? France's Governing Parties, the Ecologists, and the Far Right'. In Mair, P., Müller, W. and Plasser, F. (eds) *Political Parties and Electoral Change*. London: Sage.

Knapp, A. (2005) 'Prometheus (Re-)Bound? The Fifth Republic and Checks on Executive Power'. In Cole, A., Le Galès, P. and Levy, J. *Developments in French Politics 3*. Basingstoke: Palgrave Macmillan.

Knapp, A. and Wright, V. (2005) *The Government and Politics of France*. London: Routledge.

Kriesi, H. (1995) *New Social Movements in Western Europe: a Comparative Analysis*. Minneapolis: University of Minnesota Press.

Kriesi, H. (2006) 'Globalization and the Transformation of the National Political Space. Six European Countries Compared'. *Cahier de recherche PACTE*. Grenoble.

Kriesi, H. (2007) 'The Role of European Integration in National Election Campaigns'. *European Union Politics* 8 (1): 83–108.

Ladrech, R. 1994. 'Europeanization of Domestic Politics and Institutions: the Case of France'. *Journal of Common Market Studies* 32 (1): 69–88.

Lallement, M. (2006) 'New Patterns of Industrial Relations and Political Action since the 1980s'. In Culpepper, P., Hall, P. and Palier, B. (eds) *Changing France: the Politics that Markets Make*. Basingstoke: Palgrave Macmillan.

Lambert, A. and Migaud, D. (2006) *La mise en œuvre de la loi organique relative aux lois de finances. A l'épreuve de la pratique, insuffler une nouvelle dynamique à la réforme*. Report to the French Government, October.

Lanceron, V. (2007) *Du SGCI au SGAE. Évolution d'une administration de coordination au coeur de la politique européenne de la France.* Paris: L'Harmattan.

Lascombe, M. and Vandendriessche, X. (2006) 'Le droit dérivé de la LOLF'. *Actualités Juridiques-Droit Administratif (AJDA),* 13 March: 538–44.

Lascoumes, P. (1994) *L'Eco-Pouvoir: environnement et politiques.* Paris: La découverte.

Lascoumes, P. (1997) *Elites irrégulières: essai sur la délinquance d'affaires.* Paris: Gallimard.

Lascoumes, P. (1999) *Corruptions.* Paris: Presses de Sciences Po.

Lascoumes, P. and Le Bourhis, J.P. (1998) 'Le bien commun comme construit territorial: identités d'action et procédures'. *Politix* 42: 37–66.

Lascoumes, P. and Le Galès, P. (2007) 'Understanding Public Policy through its Instruments: from the Nature of Instruments to the Sociology of Public Policy Instrumentation'. *Governance* 20 (1): 1–23.

Lavoux, T. (ed.) (1992) *L'Application de la législation communautaire environnement en France.* Paris: Institut pour une Politique Européene de l'Environnement.

Le Bihan-Graf, C. and Coudroy, C. (2005) 'S'appuyer sur le droit communautaire pour donner sa pleine mesure au modèle de fonction publique de carrière'. *Les Cahiers de la fonction publique* 2: 4–8.

Le Galès, P. (2005) 'Reshaping the State? Administrative and Decentralization Reforms'. In Cole, A., Le Galès, P. and Levy, J. D. (eds) *Developments in French Politics 3.* Basingstoke: Palgrave Macmillan.

Le Galès, P. and Mawson, J. (1995) 'Contracts versus Competitive Bidding: Rationalizing Urban Policy Programmes in England and France'. *Journal of European Public Policy* 2 (2): 205–41.

Le Lidec, P. (2002) *La République et ses maires, 1907–1997: 90 ans d'histoire de l'AMF.* Paris: Fouchier.

Le Lidec, P. (2005) 'La relance de la décentralisation en France. De la rhétorique managériale aux réalités politiques'. *Politiques et management public* 23 (3): 101–25.

Le Lidec, P. (2007) 'Le jeu du compromis: l'État et les collectivités territoriales dans le décentralisation en France'. *Revue française d'administration publique* 121–22: 111–30.

Lépinard, E. (2007a) *L'égalité introuvable. La parité, les feministes et la République.* Paris: Presses de Sciences Po.

Lépinard, E. (2007b) 'The Contentious Subject of Feminism: Defining *women* in France from the Second Wave to Parity'. *Signs* 32 (2): 375–404.

Lépine, J.-L., Gouiffès, P.-F. and Carmona, J. (1999) *Mission d'analyse comparative des administrations fiscales.* Paris: Inspection Général des Finances.

Lequesne, C. (1993) *Paris-Bruxelles. Comment se fait la politique européenne de la France.* Paris: Presses de la Fondation Nationale des Sciences Politiques.

Le Saout, R. (2000) 'L'intercommunalité, un pouvoir inachevé?' *Revue française de science politique* 3: 439–61.

Le Saout, R. and Madore, F. (eds) (2004) *Les effets de l'intercommunalité.* Rennes: Presses Universitaires de Rennes.

Levi-Faur, D. (1997) 'Economic Nationalism: from Friedrich List to Robert Reich'. *Review of International Studies* 23: 359–70.

Levy, J. D. (1999) *Tocqueville's Revenge: State, Society, and Economy in Contemporary France.* Cambridge: Harvard University Press.

Levy, J. D. (2000) 'France: Directing Adjustment?' In Scharpf, F. and Schmidt, V. (eds) *Welfare and Work in the Open Economy*, Vol. 2. Oxford: Oxford University.

Levy, J., Cole, A. and Le Galès, P. (2005) 'The Shifting Politics of the Fifth Republic'. In Cole, A., Le Galès, P. and Levy, J. (eds) *Developments in French Politics 3*. New York: Palgrave Macmillan.

Lewis-Beck, M. (ed.) (2003) *The French Voter before and after the 2002 Elections*. Basingstoke: Palgrave Macmillan.

Lijphart, A. (1997) 'Trichotomy or Dichotomy'. *European Journal of Political Research* 33 (1): 125–38.

Lijphart, A. (1999) *Patterns of Democracy*. New Haven and London: Yale University Press.

Lindberg, L. N. and Scheingold, S. A. (1970) *Europe's Would-Be Polity: Patterns of Change in the European Community*. Englewood Cliffs: Prentice-Hall.

Lipset, S. M. and Rokkan, S. (1967) *Party Systems and Voter Alignments*. New York: Free Press.

List, F. (1856) *The National System of Political Economy*. Philadelphia: J. B. Lippincott & Co.

Loncle, P. (2000) 'Partenariat et exclusion sociale en France: expériences et ambiguïtés'. *Pôle sud* 12: 47–62.

Lordon, F. (1998) 'The Logic and Limits of *Désinflation Competitive*'. *Oxford Review of Economic Policy* 14 (1): 96–113.

Lordon, F. (2001) 'The Logic and Limits of *Désinflation Compétitive*'. In Glyn, A. (ed.) *Social Democracy in Neoliberal Times*. Oxford: Oxford University Press.

Lorrain, D. (2000a) 'The Construction of Urban Service Models'. In Bagnasco, A. and Le Galès, P. (eds) *Cities in Contemporary Europe*. Cambridge: Cambridge University Press.

Lorrain, D. (2000b) 'Gouverner les villes. Questions pour un agenda de recherche'. *Pôle sud* 13: 27–40.

Lorrain, D. (2001) 'L'économie paradoxales des réseaux techniques urbains'. In Henry, C. and Quinet, E. (eds) *Concurrence et services publics, actes des conférences Jules Dupuit*. Paris: L'Harmattan.

Loughlin, J. (2007) *Subnational Goverment: the French Experience*. Basingstoke: Palgrave Macmillan.

Magnette, P, Costa, O. and Kerrouche, E. (2004) *Vers un renouveau du parlementarisme en Europe*. Brussels: Presses de l'Université de Bruxelles.

Mair, P. (2000) 'The Limited Impact of Europe on National Party Systems'. *West European Politics* 23 (4): 27–51.

Mandraud, I. (2002) 'Les socialistes réunis à Montreuil pour tirer le bilan des doléances des militants'. *Le Monde* 15 December.

Marcou, G., Rangeon, F. and Thiebault, J. L. (eds) (1997) *La coopération contractuelle et le gouvernement des villes*. Paris: L'Harmattan.

Marks, G. and Steenbergen, M. (1999) *Expert Survey on National Parties and the European Union*. Chapel Hill: Center for European Studies, University of North Carolina.

Marteau, S. and Tournier, P. (2006) *Black, blanc, beur...: La guerre civile aura-t-elle vraiment lieu?* Paris: Albin Michel.

Martin, A. (2004) 'The EMU Macroeconomic Policy Regime and the European Social Model'. In Martin, A. and Ross, G. (eds) *Euros and Europeans: Monetary*

Integration and the European Model of Society. Cambridge: Cambridge University Press, pp. 20–50.

Martin, A. and Ross, G. (2004) 'Introduction: EMU and the European Social Model'. In Martin, A. and Ross, G. (eds) *Euros and Europeans. Monetary Integration and the European Model of Society*. Cambridge: Cambridge University Press.

Massot, J. (1986) *La présidence de la République en France*. Paris: Documentation Française.

Mathieu, C. and Sterdyniak, H. (2003) 'Réformer le Pacte de Stabilité: l'état du débat'. *Revue de l'OFCE* 84: 145–79.

Mayer, N. (2007) 'Comment Nicolas Sarkozy a rétréci l'électorat Le Pen'. *Revue française de science politique* 57 (3–4): 429–46.

Mazur, A. (1995) *Gender Bias and the State. Symbolic Reform at Work in Fifth Republic France*. Pittsburgh: University of Pittsburgh Press.

Mazur, A. (2005) 'Gendering the Fifth Republic: New Beginnings or the Legacy of the Past?' In Cole, A., Le Galès, P. and Levy, J. D. (eds) *Developments in French Politics 3*. New York: Palgrave Macmillan.

Megie, A. (2005) 'Coopération intergouvernementale et processus d'Européanisation: la construction des espaces européens de la justice et de l'enseignement supérieur'. In Palier, B. and Sorel, Y. (eds) *L'Europe en action*. Paris: L'Harmattan, pp. 87–143.

Menon, A. (1996) 'France and the IGC of 1996'. *Journal of European Public Policy* 3 (2): 231–52.

Menon, A. (2000) 'France'. In Kassim, H., Peters, B. G. and Wright, V. (eds) *The National Coordination of EU Policy: the Domestic Level*. Oxford: Oxford University Press.

Menon, A. (2001) 'The French Administration in Brussels'. In Kassim, H, Menon, A., Peters, B. G. and Wright, V. (eds) *The National Coordination of EU Policy: the European Level*. Oxford: Oxford University Press.

Mény, Y. (1974) *Centralisation et décentralisation dans le débat politique français (1945–1969)*. Paris: LGDJ.

Mény, Y. (1992) *La corruption de la République*. Paris: Fayard.

Meunier, S. (2004) 'Globalization and Europeanization: a Challenge to French Politics'. *French Politics* 2 (2): 125–50.

Migaud, D. (1999) *Rapport du groupe de travail sur l'efficacité de la dépense publique et le contrôle parlementaire*. Paris: Assemblée Nationale.

Monks, R. and Minow, N. (2004) *Corporate Governance*. Oxford: Blackwell.

Moravcsik, A. (1999) 'A New Statecraft? Supranational Entrepreneurs and International Cooperation'. *International Organization* 53: 267–306.

Morel, N. (2007) 'From Subsidiarity to "Free Choice": Child- and Elderly-Care Policy Reforms in France, Germany, Belgium and the Netherlands'. *Social Policy and Administration*, forthcoming.

Morin, F. (1998) *Le modèle française de détention et de gestion du capital: analyse, prospective et comparaisons internationales*. Paris: Editions de Bercy.

Morin, F. (2000) 'A Transformation in the French Model of Shareholding and Management'. *Economy and Society* 29 (1): 36–53.

Mouchard, D. (2002) 'Les "sans-emploi"'. In Crettiez, X. and Sommier, I. (eds) *La France rebelle*. Paris: Michallon.

Muxel, A. (2007) 'La mobilisation électorale. L'envers de 2002 et le sursaut généralisé'. *Revue française de science politique* 57(3–4): 315–28.

Natali, D. and Rhodes, M. (2004) 'Trade-offs and Veto Players: Reforming Pensions in France and Italy'. *French Politics* 2(1): 1–23.

Nay, O. (2001) 'Négocier le partenariat: jeux et conflits dans la mise en oeuvre de la politique communautaire européenne'. *Revue française de science politique* 51 (3): 459–80.

Nay, O. and Smith, A. (eds) (2002) *Le gouvernement du compromis*. Paris: Economica.

Négrier, E. (2003) 'A French Urban Powershift?: the Political Construction of Metropolization'. *French Politics* 1 (2): 175–98.

Négrier, E. (2005) *La question métropolitaine: les politiques à l'épreuve du changement d'échelle territoriale*. Grenoble: Presses Universitaires de Grenoble.

Niedermayer, O. and Sinnott, R. (eds) (1994) *Public Opinion and International Governance*. Oxford: Oxford University Press.

Niedermayer, O. and Westle, B. (1994) 'A Typology of Orientations'. In Niedermayer, O. and Sinnott, R. (eds) *Public Opinion and International Governance*. Oxford: Oxford University Press.

OFCE (2006) *L'économie française 2007*. Paris: La découverte.

Or, Z. (2007) 'Hospital 2007'. *Health Policy Monitor*. Available at: http://www.hpm.org/survey/fr/a9/1

O'Sullivan, M. (2003) 'The Political Economy of Comparative Corporate Governance'. *Review of International Political Economy* 10 (1): 23–72.

Padioleau, J.G. (1991) 'L'action publique urbaine moderniste'. *Politiques et management public* 9(3): 133–43.

Page, E. and Wright, V. (eds) (2007) *From the Active to the Enabling State. The Changing Roles of Top Officials in European Nations*. Basingstoke: Palgrave Macmillan.

Palier, B. (1998) 'La référence au territoire dans les nouvelles politiques sociales'. *Politique et management public* 16(3): 15–31.

Palier, B. (2000) '*Does Europe Matter*? Européanisation des politiques sociales des pays de l'Union européenne'. *Politique européenne* 2: 7–28.

Palier, B. (2002) *Gouverner la sécurité sociale*. Paris: PUF.

Palier, B. (2003) *La réforme des retraites*. Paris: PUF.

Palier, B. (2004) *La reforme des retraites*, 2nd edn. Paris: PUF.

Palier, B. (2005) *Gouverner la sécurité sociale*. Paris: PUF.

Palier, B. (2006) 'The Long Good Bye to Bismarck? Changes in the French Welfare State'. In Culpepper, P., Hall, P. and Palier, B. (eds) *Changing France. The Politics that Markets Make*. Basingstoke: Palgrave Macmillan.

Palier, B. (2007) 'A Long Goodbye to Bismarck?' Seminar at the CEVIPOF, Sciences-Po, Paris: March.

Parodi, J.-L. (1991) 'Le nouvel espace politique français'. In Mèny, Y. (ed.) *Idéologies, partis politiques, et groupes sociaux*. Paris: Fondation Nationale des Sciences Politiques.

Parodi, J.-L. (2002) 'L'énigme de la cohabitation, ou les effets pervers d'une présélection annoncée'. *Revue française de science politique* 52 (5–6): 485–504.

Parsons, C. (2002) 'Showing Ideas as Causes: the Origins of the European Union'. *International Organization* 56: 47–84.

Parsons, C. (2003*) A Certain Idea of Europe*. Ithaca: Cornell University Press.

Pasquier, R. (2004) *La capacité politique des régions*. Rennes: Presses Universitaires de Rennes.

Pasquier, R., Simoulin, V. and Weisbein, J. (eds) (2007) *La gouvernance territoriale*. Paris: LGDJ.

Pébereau, M. (2006) *Rompre avec la facilité de la dette publique: pour des finances publiques au service de notre croissance économique et de notre cohésion sociale*. Paris: Documentation française.

Péchu, C. (2002) 'Les 'sans-logis''. In Crettiez, X. and Sommier, I. (eds) *La France rebelle*. Paris: Michallon.

Pedersen, T. (2003) 'Recent Trends in the Franco-German Relationship'. *Journal of Common Market Studies 41 Annual Review*, 13–25.

Pelizzo, R. (2004) 'From Principle to Practice: Constitutional Principles and the Transformation of Party Finance in Germany and Italy'. *Comparative European Politics* 2 (2): 123–41.

Pernot, J.-M. (2005) *Syndicats: Lendemains de Crise?* Paris: Gallimard.

Perrineau, P. (1993) 'Le Front National: la force solitaire'. In Habert, P., Perrineau, P. and Ysmal, C. (eds) *Le Vote sanction: les élections législatives des 21 et 28 mars 1993*. Paris: Presses de Sciences Po.

Perrineau, P. (ed.) (2003) *Le désenchantement démocratique*. La Tour d'Aigues: Editions de l'Aube.

Perrineau, P. (ed.) (2005) *Le vote européen, 2004–2005: de l'élargissement au référendum français*. Paris: Presses de Sciences Po.

Perrineau, P. (ed.) (2007a) *Atlas Électoral: Qui vote quoi, où, comment?* Paris: Presses de Sciences Po.

Perrineau, P. (2007b) 'Analyse de l'élection présidentielle. Enquête post élection présidentielle 2007'. *Panel Électoral Français 2007*. Paris: CEVIPOF (http://www.cevipof.msh-paris.fr/bpf/analyses/Perrineau_Analyse Presidentielle2007.pdf).

Perrineau, P. (2007c) 'L'image de Nicolas Sarkozy'. In *SOFRES, L'état de l'opinion 2007*. Paris: Éditions du Seuil, pp. 75–94.

Pierson, P. (1996) 'The Path to European Integration: a Historical Institutionalist Analysis'. *Comparative Political Studies* 29 (2): 123–63.

Pinson, G. (2004) 'Le projet comme instrument d'action publique urbaine'. In Lascoumes, P. and Le Galès, P. (eds) *Gouverner par les instruments*. Paris: Presses de Sciences Po.

Pinson, G. (2008) *Gouverner par la planification urbaine*. Paris: Presses de Sciences Po.

Pollitt, C. and Boukaert, G. (2004) *Public Management Reform. A Comparative Analysis*. Oxford: Oxford University Press.

Polton, D. (2005) 'Sickness Funds Reform: 2005 Physician Agreement'. *Health Policy Monitor* (available at http://www.hpm.org/survey/fr/a5/3).

Polton, D. and Mousquès, J. (2004a) 'Sickness Funds Reform: New Governance'. *Health Policy Monitor* (available at http://www.hpm.org/survey/fr/a4/3).

Polton, D. and Mousquès, J. (2004b) 'Improvement of the Coordination in Health Care'. *Health Policy Monitor* (available at http://www.hpm.org/survey/fr/a4/2).

Pujas, V. and Rhodes, M. (1999) 'Party Finance and Political Scandal in Italy, Spain and France'. *West European Politics* 22 (3): 41–63.

Quermonne, J.-L. (1991) *Le gouvernement de la France sous la Ve République*. Paris: Dalloz.

Radaelli, C. M. 'Europeanisation: Solution or Problem?' *European Integration online Papers* (EIoP), vol. 8 (http//eiop.or.at/eiop/texte/2004-016a.htm (checcked 16 March 2008).

Reif, K. and Schmitt, H. (1980) 'Nine Second Order National Elections: a Conceptual Framework for the Analysis of European Elections Results'. *European Journal of Political Research* 8 (1): 3–44.

Revillard, A. (2006) 'Work/Family Policy in France: from State Familialism to State Feminism?' *International Journal of Law, Policy and the Family* 20(2): 133–50.

Richer, L. (2003) 'La contractualisation comme technique de gestion des affaires publiques'. *Actualité Juridique, Droit Administratif (AJDA)* 19: 973–75.

Rivière, E. (2007) 'Aujourd'hui pire qu'hier et meilleur que demain. Le pâle moral des Français'. In *SOFRES, L'état de l'opinion 2007*. Paris: Seuil, pp. 95–111.

Robert, R. (2007) *La possibilité d'un centre: stratégies de campagne de François Bayrou*. Paris: Michalon.

Rosanvallon, P. (1989) 'The Development of Keynesianism in France'. In Hall, P. (ed.) *The Political Power of Economic Ideas: Keynesianism across Nations*. Princeton: Princeton University Press.

Rosenau, J. and Czempiel, E.-O. (eds) (1992) *Governance without Government. Order and Change in World Politics*. Cambridge: Cambridge University Press.

Ross, G. (1982) *Workers and Communists in France*. Berkeley: University of California Press.

Ross, G. (2004) 'Monetary Integration and the French Model'. In Martin, A. and Ross, G. (eds) *Euros and Europeans. Monetary Integration and the European Model of Society*. Cambridge: Cambridge University Press.

Ross, G. (2006) 'Myths and Realities in the 2006 "Events"'. *French Politics, Culture and Society* 24 (3): 81–8.

Rouban, L. (1998) *The French Civil Service*. Paris: La Documentation française.

Rouban, L. (2006) 'Réformer l'État: politique de l'emploi public et modèle social'. *La Revue administrative* 354: 638–48.

Roustan, M. (2004) *Assemblée nationale. Rapport d'information fait au nom de la délégation à l'aménagement et au développement durable au territoire sur la désindustrialisation du territoire*. Paris: Documentation française.

Rozenberg, O. (2007) 'Résister à l'Europe au nom du national, de la souveraineté, du local ou de l'antilibéralisme. Les conditions d'activation de quatre idéologies critiques de la construction européenne en France'. In Lacroix, J. and Coman, R. (eds) *Résister à l'Europe: figures des oppositions au modèle européen*. Brussels: Editions de l'Université de Bruxelles.

Sabbagh, D. (2004) 'Affirmative Action at Sciences-Po'. In Chapman, H. and Frader, L. (eds.) *Race in France, Interdisciplinary Perspectives on the Politics of Difference*. New York: Berghahn Books.

Salmon, F. (2001) *Atlas Électoral de la France, 1848–2001*. Paris: Éditions du Seuil.

Sapir, A. (2006) 'Globalisation and the Reform of European Social Models'. *Journal of Common Market Studies* 44 (2): 369–90.

Sarkozy, N. (2001) *Libre*. Paris: XO Éditions.

Sarkozy, N. (2006) *Témoignage*. Paris: XO Éditions.

Sauger, N. (2005) 'Sur la mutation contemporaine des structures de la compétition partisane en France: les partis de droite face à l'intégration européenne'. *Politique européenne* 16: 103–26.

Sauger, N. (2007) 'Le vote Bayrou. L'échec d'un succès'. *Revue française de science politique* 57 (3–4): 447–58.

Sauger, N., Brouard, S. and Grossman, E. (2007) *Les Français contre l'Europe? Les sens du référendum du 29 mai 2005.* Paris: Presses de Sciences Po.

Scharpf, F. (1999) *Governing in Europe: Effective and Democratic?* Oxford: Oxford University Press.

Schmidt, V. (1996) *From State to Market? The Transformation of French Business and Government.* Cambridge: Cambridge University Press.

Schmidt, V. (1997a) 'Economic Policy, Political Discourse, and Democracy in France'. *French Politics and Society* 16 (4): 1–16.

Schmidt, V. (1997b) 'Discourse and (Dis)integration in Europe: the Case of France, Germany, and Great Britain'. *Daedalus* 20: 167–97.

Schmidt, V. (2003) 'French Capitalism Transformed, yet still a Third Variety of Capitalism'. *Economy and Society* 32 (4): 526–54.

Schmidt, V. A. (2007) 'Trapped by their Ideas: French Elites, Discourses of European Integration and Globalization'. *Journal of European Public Policy* 14 (7): 992–1009.

Schweisguth, E. (2007) 'Droite et gauche: la France en transition', in Perrineau, P. (ed.), *Atlas Électoral: Qui vote quoi, où, comment?* Paris, Presses de Sciences Po.

Scott, J.W. (1997) '"La querelle des femmes" in the Late Twentieth Century'. *New Left Review* 226: 3–19.

Scott, J.W. (2005a) *Parité: Sexual Equality and the Crisis of French Universalism.* Chicago: University of Chicago Press.

Scott, J.W. (2005b) 'Symptomatic Politics. The Banning of Islamic Headscarves in French Public Schools', *French Politics, Culture and Society* 23 (3): 106–27.

Setbon, M. (1993) *Pouvoirs contre sida: de la transfusion sanguine au dépistage: décisions et pratiques en France, Grande-Bretagne et Suède.* Paris: Seuil.

Shonfield, A. (1969) *Modern Capitalism: the Changing Balance of Public and Private Power.* Oxford: Oxford University Press.

Silicani, J.-L. (2004) *La rémunération au mérite des directeurs d'administration centrale: mobiliser les directeurs pour conduire le changement.* Rapport au Premier Ministre. Paris: Documentation française.

Siméant, J. (1998) *La Cause des sans-papiers.* Paris: Presses de Sciences Po.

Simon, P. and Stavo-Bebauge, J. (2004) 'Les politiques anti-discrimination et les statistiques: paramètres d'une incohérence'. *Sociétés contemporaines* 53: 57–84.

Siné, A. (2006) *L'ordre budgétaire. L'économie politique des dépenses de l'État.* Paris: Economica.

Sirinelli, J.-F. (2007) *Les vingt décisives, 1965–1985: le passé proche de notre avenir.* Paris: Seuil.

Skach, C. (2005) *Borrowing Constitutional Designs: Constitutional Law in Weimar Germany and the French Fifth Republic.* Princeton: Princeton University Press.

Smith, A. (2006) 'The Government of the European Union and a Changing France'. In Culpepper, P., Hall, P. and Palier, B. (eds) *Changing France. The Politics that Markets Make.* Basingstoke: Palgrave Macmillan.

Smith, A., De Maillard, J. and Costa, O. (2007) *Vin et politique, Bordeaux, la France, La mondialisation.* Paris: Presses de Sciences Po.

Smith, P. (2006) *The French Senate.* Basingstoke: Palgrave Macmillan.

Smith, T. (2004) *France in Crisis.* Cambridge: Cambridge University Press.

Sommier, I. and Combes, H. (2007) 'The Global Justice Movement in France'. In Della Porta, D. (ed.) *The Global Justice Movement: Cross-National and Transnational Perspectives*. Boulder: Paradigm Publishers.

Sorbets, C. and Smith, A. (2003*) Le leadership politique et le territoire: les cadres d'analyse en débat*. Rennes: Presses Universitaires de Rennes.

Stevens, A. (1996) *The Government and Politics of France*. Basingstoke: Macmillan.

Stone, A. (1992) *The Birth of Judicial Politics in France: the Constitutional Council in Comparative Perspective*. Oxford: Oxford University Press.

Stone, A. (2000) *Governing with Judges. Constitutional Politics in Europe*. Oxford: Oxford University Press.

Stone, A. and Thatcher, M. (eds) (2003) *The Politics of Delegation*. London: Frank Cass.

Stone, A., Sandholz, W. and Fligstein, N. (eds) (2001) *The Institutionalization of Europe*. Oxford: Oxford University Press.

Strudel, S. 2007. 'Nicolas Sarkozy: Rupture tranquille ou syncrétisme tourmenté?' *Revue française de science politique* 57 (3–4): 459–74.

Strudel, S. and Le Hay, V. (2007) 'Nicolas Sarkozy: Analyse socio-démographique et politique des votes'. *Panel Électoral Français 2007, Enquête post élection présidentielle 2007*. Paris: CEVIPOF (http://www.cevipof.msh-paris.fr/PEF/2007/V1/rapports/NicolasSarkozy_RuptureOuSyncretisme_SS-VLH.pdf).

Suleiman, E. (1986) 'Toward the Disciplining of Parties and Legislators: the French Parliamentarian in the Fifth Republic'. In Suleiman, E. N. (ed.) *Parliaments and Parliamentarians in Democratic Politics*. New York: Holmes & Meier.

Suleiman, E. N. (1994) 'Presidentialism and Political Stability in France'. In Linz, J. and Valenzuela A. (eds) *The Failure of Presidential Democracy: Comparative Perspectives*. Baltimore: Johns Hopkins University Press.

Svensson, P. (2002) 'Five Danish Referendums on the European Community and European Union: a Critical Assessment of the Franklin Thesis'. *European Journal of Political Research* 41 (6): 733–50.

Taggart, P. (1998) 'A Touchstone of Dissent: Euroscepticism in Contemporary Western European Party Systems'. *European Journal of Political Research* 33 (3): 363–88.

Tarrow, S. (1996) 'States and Opportunities: the Political Structuring of Social Movements'. In McAdam, D., McCarthy, J. D. and Zald, M. N. (eds) *Comparative Perspectives on Social Movements: Political Opportunities, Mobilizing Structures, and Cultural Framings*. New York: Cambridge University Press.

Tarrow, S. (2005) *The New Transnational Activism*. New York: Cambridge University Press.

Thatcher, M. (1996) 'High Technology'. In Kassim, H. and Menon, A. (eds) *The European Union and National Industrial Policy*. London: Routledge.

Thatcher, M. (1999) *The Politics of Telecommunications. National Institutions, Convergence, and Change in Britain and France*. Oxford: Oxford University Press.

Thatcher, M. (2007) 'Regulatory Agencies, the State and Markets: a Franco-British Companion'. *Journal of European Public Policy* 14 (7): 1028–47.

Tiberj, V. and Brouard, S. (2006) 'The French Referendum: the Not So Simple Act of Saying Nay'. *PS: Political Science and Politics* 39 (2): 261–8.

Tilly, C. (1986) *The Contentious French: Four Centuries of Popular Struggle.* Cambridge: Harvard University Press.

Tops, P. (ed.) *Urban–Regional Cooperation in the European Union: Practices and Prospects.* London: Frank Cass.

Vergès, F. (2006) *La Mémoire enchaînée – Questions sur l'Esclavage.* Paris: Albin Michel.

Vion, A. (2002) 'Le gouvernement urbain saisi par l'internationalisation'. In Fontaine, J. and Hassenteufel, P. (eds) *To Change or not to Change. L'analyse des politiques publiques à l'épreuve du terrain.* Rennes: Presses Universitaires de Rennes.

Warin, P. (2004) 'La gestion de proximité à l'épreuve des politiques publiques en France'. In Booth, P. and Jouve, B. (eds) *La concertation dans les politiques urbaines au Canada, en France et en Grande-Bretagne.* Montréal: Presses de l'Université du Québec.

Webb, P. (2002) 'Conclusion'. In Webb, P., Farrell, D. and Holliday, I. (eds) *Political Parties in Advanced Industrial Democracies.* Oxford: Oxford University Press.

Weiler, J. (1999) *The Constitution of Europe. Do the New Clothes Have an Emperor? and Other Essays on European Integration.* Cambridge: Cambridge University Press.

Wilsford, D. (1993) 'The State and the Medical Profession in France'. In Hafferty, F. and McKinlay, J. (eds) *The Changing Medical Profession: an International Perspective.* New York: Oxford University Press.

Winock, M. (1995) *La fièvre hexagonale: les grandes crises politiques de 1871 à 1968.* Paris: Seuil.

Winock, M. (2003) *La France politique: XIXe–XXe siècle.* Paris: Seuil.

Woll, C. (2006) 'Lobbying in the European Union: From *Sui Generis* to a Comparative Perspective'. *Journal of European Public Policy* 13 (3): 456–69.

Zeldin, T. (1979) *France, 1848–1945: Ambition, Love and Politics.* Oxford: Oxford University Press.

Zysman, J. (1983) *Government, Markets, Growth: Financial Systems and the Politics of Industrial Change.* Ithaca: Cornell University Press.

Index